The Beginning of the End

"I'm gonna tell you what I know, and I'm gonna tell you how I know it," Alphonse D'Arco (acting boss of the Lucchese Family of la Cosa Nostra) began quietly, the prelude to a remarkable disquisition that was to continue, in one form or another, to the present day. In just the first few weeks of his debriefing, his photographic memory and apparently limitless power of recall filled nine hundred single-spaced pages of FBI reports. It amounted to an astonishingly detailed catalog of the Lucchese Family's criminal transgressions, along with a great deal about the rest of the American Mafia. Exhaustive double-checking failed to turn up even a minor error in the stream of names, dates, and places. D'Arco subsequently testified as the government's star witness in seven major trials of top Mafia leaders, including four high-ranking ~~~~~~~~~~ own Mafia family.

GANGBUSTERS

THE DESTRUCTION OF AMERICA'S
LAST GREAT MAFIA DYNASTY

ERNEST VOLKMAN

AVON BOOKS

An Imprint of HarperCollinsPublishers

AVON BOOKS
An Imprint of HarperCollins*Publishers*
10 East 53rd Street
New York, New York 10022-5299

Copyright © 1998 by Ernest Volkman
Published by arrangement with Faber and Faber, Inc.
Library of Congress Catalog Card Number: 98-11553
ISBN: 0-380-73235-1
www.avonbooks.com

The Faber and Faber edition contains the following Library of
Congress Cataloging in Publication Data:

Volkman, Ernest.
  Gangbusters: the destruction of America's last great mafia
dynasty/Ernest Volkman.
    p.   cm.
1. Lucchese family—History.   2. Mafia-New York (State)—History.
3. Organized crime—New York (State)—History.   I. Title.
HV6452.N7V65   1998   98-11553
364.1'06'09747—dc21   CIP

First Avon Books Printing: September 1999

Avon Trademark Reg. U.S. Pat. Off. and in Other Countries, Marca
Registrada, Hecho en U.S.A.
HarperCollins® is a trademark of HarperCollins Publishers Inc.

Printed in the U.S.A.

OPM 12 11 10 9 8 7 6 5 4 3

For the Toad

Tecum vivere amem, tecum obeam libens

Crime brings its own fatality with it.
WILKIE COLLINS

Contents

	Glossary	xi
INTRODUCTION	The Gallows and the Fool	1
ONE	Our Father Who Art in Heaven	8
TWO	"The Kiss of Death Wants to Talk to You"	38
THREE	Pontifex Maximus	68
FOUR	"We'd Go for Your Eyeballs"	101
FIVE	The Sun Luck Mafia	133
SIX	The Jaguar That Talked	168
SEVEN	"Call Me Gas Pipe and Die"	200
EIGHT	"How Come There's a Bomb on My Front Seat?"	234
NINE	Night of the Locust	264
TEN	The Big Heat	294
	Requiem	326

Glossary

Organized crime, like many other fields of human endeavor, has its own jargon impenetrable to the uninitiated. Because a number of examples of this jargon recur in conversations recounted in this book, here are some of the Mafia's more commonly used words and terms, some of them unique to the New York branch of la Cosa Nostra:

BABANIA: Heroin. Also called "junk," or "shit," or "H."

BANANA RACE: Fixed horse race.

BARRACUDA: Ugly woman.

BIT: Prison sentence. A short sentence is called a "banker's bit."

BOOK: List of outstanding loan shark debts.

BOOKS: Mafia membership list. Books are "opened" (promising apprentice gangsters are proposed for membership) or "closed" (such enlistments are suspended temporarily, usually due to concerns over FBI or police infiltration).

BOOST: Shoplift. Professional shoplifters are known as "boosters."

BORGATA: Criminal gang.

BOSS: Chief executive of a Mafia family. Rarely, "godfather."

BULL: Police detective.

CAN: Prison. See also "joint."

CAPO: Abbreviated form of *caporegime*, Mafia mid-level executive in charge of a "crew" (which see). See also "skipper."

CHASE: Banish a made member from the Mafia for violations of organizational rules.

CHOP SHOP: Mafia-controlled junkyard or auto repair facility used for the exclusive purpose of stripping stolen cars for expensive parts to be sold in the underground market.

COMMISSION: Governing body for the American Mafia, consisting of the heads of the twenty-four Mafia organizations in the United States.

CONTRACT: Organization-sanctioned order for murder, usually assigned to a specific member or team. A contract may be declared "open," meaning that any Mafia member is authorized to carry it out.

CREW: Subdivision of a Mafia family, usually ten to thirty made members, under the direction of a capo.

DELI: Mafia-controlled union delegate.

DOWN THERE: Florida.

DROP A DIME: Inform to law enforcement.

DRY CLEAN: Take evasive measures to elude law enforcement surveillance.

FLIP: Agree to become a prosecution witness.

FRIEND OF OURS: Required phrase used when introducing one made member of the Mafia to another made member. In the event the person being introduced is not a made member, the phrase "friend of mine" is used, signaling that caution is warranted in any conversation relating to Mafia business.

G: FBI agent. Also called "feebie."

GIRLFRIEND: Corrupt law enforcement source.

GYPSY WIRE: Illegal wiretap.

HAM AND CHEESE SANDWICH: Payoff.

HEAT: Uniformed police.

HIT: Organization-sanctioned murder. Also called "piece of work."

JOINT: Federal prison.

MADE: Formally inducted into the Mafia. Also called "straightened out," or "get a button," or "mobbed up."

MEET: Formal convocation of senior Mafia leaders.

MOB: Mafia. Also called "the Outfit" (Chicago) or "the Office" (New England). Rarely, la Cosa Nostra.

MOUSE: Girlfriend.

MULDOON: Stolen or forged credit card.

OFFICE: Bookmaking operation.

PARAKEET: Attractive woman.

PASS: Organization-decreed exemption from death penalty.

RAISE: Promote to caporegime or higher rank.

RAT: Informant. Also known as "stool," or "stoolie," or "snitch." The act of informing is called "rat out."

SHORT EYES: Pedophile.

SHYLOCK: Loan shark. Commonly abbreviated to "shy," also used as verb.

SITDOWN: Formal meeting to resolve intrafamily disputes.

SKIPPER: Caporegime, also known as "crew chief" or "captain."

SLAP AROUND: Beat severely.

SOLDIER: Lowest-ranking Mafia member. Also known as a "button."

SWAG: Stolen goods.

TAKE THE WEIGHT: Accept prison sentence without complaint.

TOPAZ: Cheap man's hairpiece. Also called "toupe."

UNDERBOSS: Second in command of a Mafia family.

VIGORISH: Interest on loan shark debt. Commonly abbreviated to "vig."

WHACK OUT: Kill. Also called "clip," or "put to sleep."

WISEGUY: Made Mafia member. Also called "good fellow."

ZIP: Sicilian.

The Gallows and the Fool

Strange as it may seem, men . . . of certain grades of
intellect and temperament deliberately devote themselves to lives of crime.

JAMES MCCABE, JR.,
New York by Sunlight and Gaslight, 1882

On a bitterly cold day during the early winter of 1991, Alphonse D'Arco, acting boss of the Lucchese Family of la
Cosa Nostra, sat in a windowless cinderblock room at the federal prison in lower Manhattan and regarded an expectant audience of FBI agents and federal prosecutors. Then, with the
calm air of an Italian delicatessen owner discussing his favorite recipe for lasagna, he uttered the words that were to finally
destroy the criminal organization to which he had dedicated
more than fifty years of his adult life.

"I'm gonna tell you what I know, and I'm gonna tell you
how I know it," D'Arco began quietly, the prelude to a remarkable disquisition that was to continue, in one form or
another, to the present day. In just the first few weeks of his
debriefing, his photographic memory and apparently limitless
power of recall filled nine hundred single-spaced pages of FBI
reports. It amounted to an astonishingly detailed catalog of the
Lucchese Family's criminal transgressions, along with a great
deal about the rest of the American Mafia. Exhaustive double-

1

checking failed to turn up even a minor error in the stream of names, dates, and places. D'Arco subsequently testified as the government's star witness in seven major trials of top Mafia leaders (all have resulted in convictions), including four high-ranking members of his own Mafia family.

The extraordinary act of betrayal by D'Arco, the highest-ranking mafioso ever to turn federal witness, was the final death blow to the most successful gang of organized criminals in history. The Lucchese Family was the crown jewel of la Cosa Nostra, and its collapse also brought down the rest of the American Mafia. A once formidable criminal enterprise is now broken beyond repair—its senior ranks decimated, the lower ranks thinned to a collection of untalented street hoods, its grip on certain industries loosened or removed altogether.

How all this came about represents a watershed in the history of organized crime, for the Lucchese organization reigned un-challenged at the apex of organized crime for more than six decades, seemingly invulnerable to prosecution. It was the one criminal organization that most directly affected the lives of ordinary Americans. The Lucchese Family's influence in the Garment Center in New York, the garbage collection industry on the East Coast, and the air freight operations at major air-ports exacted a hidden "Mafia tax" on every garment bought in the United States, much of the country's garbage, and every item that moved in and out of this country via air freight.

All the more remarkable considering that the Lucchese Family at its height numbered no more than 110 made mem-bers, working in partnership with another hundred or so "as-sociates," meaning business partners who for one reason or another were not fully inducted members of the Mafia (in most cases because they lacked the essential prerequisite for mem-bership, Italian blood). Although one of the smallest organized crime entities in terms of numbers, the Lucchese Family was ranked as the most lucrative, aggressive, and well-organized in the United States. Its influence was centered in New York City and extended eastward to Long Island, northward into Westchester County, south into the rich bedroom suburbs of Bergen County in New Jersey, and further south, into Atlantic City and Florida.

Thanks to the criminal genius of its progenitor and the acumen of his chief executives, the Lucchese organization was not only unsurpassed in its ability to dominate organized crime and earn billions of dollars, but also was noted for the impenetrable security screen built around itself. Gaetano Lucchese, the crime family's founder, endlessly counselled his henchmen that organized crime flourishes in as little sunlight as possible, away from the glare of publicity that tends to attract too much official interest. For many years, the organization he created balked all attempts to infiltrate its ranks, and there were no witnesses to testify to what was going on in its inner councils. Unlike such flamboyant Cosa Nostra infamies as John Gotti, no Lucchese senior executive ever made the mistake of touring Manhattan nightclubs in $2,000 custom-tailored Armani suits and a $140,000 customized Mercedes, daring his law enforcement adversaries to put him in prison.

Out of the limelight, the Lucchese organization for many years managed to remain free of the notoriety that would at some point afflict the other entities of the American Mafia. For most of its existence, the organization was virtually unknown to the outside world, barely mentioned, if at all, in newspaper accounts. The air of mystery and virtual anonymity suited the organization perfectly, all the better for its business to flourish. Not until its decline did the family come under a spotlight, most notably the movie *Goodfellas*, which focused on one of the family's crews.

This is not to say that the men of the Lucchese Family lived as reclusive paupers. They were in fact quite wealthy, but carried out elaborate attempts to keep low profiles and concealed their wealth and power behind carefully constructed façades. Their organization, which earned up to $300 million annually, had no headquarters, kept no books, and maintained no bank accounts. The men of the family's middle management were all millionaires by the time they were thirty years old, and even the street hoods enjoyed six-figure incomes from a criminal enterprise that produced profit like no other similar enterprise, before or since.

Like the rest of the American Mafia, the Lucchese organization represents something of a perverse American success story:

illiterate and poor Italian immigrants create a criminal enterprise that becomes, in the immortal phrase of Meyer Lansky, "bigger than U.S. Steel." In this twist on the Horatio Alger legend, a small, dark segment of society is spawned, and, like a virulent cancer, ultimately spreads to infect the body in which it has come to life. It was these deep roots in the American mainstream that made the task of removing it so difficult. A no-quarter underground war lasting more than twenty years was needed to achieve final victory, the capstone represented by Alphonse D'Arco's defection.

On one side of the war were men like Tommy Three Fingers, Christy Ticks, and Tony Ducks, criminal millionaires with fifth-grade educations whose "dese-dem-dose" crudeness concealed a sophisticated grasp of the criminal arts honed by years in the world of the streets. Their enemies, a varied coterie of FBI agents, police detectives, and prosecutors—the men known as "gangbusters," after the old radio serial—had superior educations but lacked the Mafia's mastery of the street jungles. For a long time, the gangbusters were further hobbled by bureaucratic inertia, high-level political corruption, and interagency rivalry. Eventually, these obstacles were overcome and they mastered the battleground of dark alleys.

But above all, they had to defeat an enduring legend.

No one is quite certain how the word *Mafia* originated. The weight of scholarly opinion believes that it is a derivative of the word *mafiusu* in Sicilian dialect, roughly meaning "beautiful" or "excellent." Mafia, meaning "place of refuge," probably originated during the eleventh century, when the Saracens ruled the island of Sicily; the word is very similar to an Arabic expression. When the Normans evicted the Saracens from the island, they imposed feudalism, forcing small landholders into serfdom. Many landholders revolted, hiding out in the hills to conduct guerrilla war against the occupiers. The insurgents, known as *mafiosi* for their custom of hiding out in caves, became heroes to the people of Sicily, and the legend of the Mafia was born.

The birth of the Mafia coincided with a long drumroll of misfortune in Sicilian history. Tragically, the 10,000-square-mile island's geostrategic position in the Mediterranean made it a perfect stepping-stone for expanding empires reaching out from all points on the compass. For nearly 2,500 years, the island was simply another bargaining chip in papal, feudal, and dynastic politics, its people oppressed by the whims of a succession of non-Sicilian rulers.

The long domination by successive waves of invaders produced a nation of Sicilians who were suspicious, diffident, and supremely antagonistic to any government. That antagonism extended to any kind of law enforcement, historically a tool of repression in Sicily, and to education, another weapon wielded by outsiders to destroy the unique Sicilian language and culture. Sicilians soon came to despise anything foreign, concluding that all the institutions imposed on them from the outside were threats. Sicilians developed their own system of underground government that sought to settle disputes without recourse to the hated foreigners, summed up in the Sicilian peasant saying, "The gallows is for the poor man, the law courts for the fool."

The insurgent mafiosi, the most widely respected men on the island, eventually dominated this underground world. In the process, *Mafia* acquired a broader meaning, the very quintessence of southern Italian culture: a "man of honor" who would protect fellow Sicilians against corrupt governments. Above all, he would protect the family; Sicily was a nation of families because Sicilians had learned that in a time of oppression, the family was the only certain guarantor of survival.

It was probably inevitable that the union of the underground world of Sicily and crime would occur at some point, for no more perfect conditions can be imagined for crime to flourish: a population openly contemptuous of all government (including law enforcement), an underground government and economy, and a group of outlaws elevated to the status of popular heroes.

In the late nineteenth century, a criminal genius named Calogero Vizzini accomplished that union, in the process creating the template for what would become modern organized crime. Vizzini took control of the Mafia and diverted it into a form of crime that had never been seen before. He called it *pizzu*, Sicilian dialect meaning "beak of a small bird," shorthand for *fari vagnari a pizzu* (wetting the beak). Simply, the

Mafia was to get a slice of everything, in return for its protection of the people of Sicily. In this Faustian bargain, Vizzini developed a vast clockwork of tribute, even extending to beggars in Sicilian cities. The beggars were rounded up and informed that henceforth they could only beg in Mafia-sanctioned territories. Further, each would be assigned a specific line of patter to encourage donations, so that there would be no overlapping sob stories. The idea was to maximize donations, which in turn increased the slice Vizzini took from the daily take. As the beggars learned the hard way, it was a bad mistake to attempt any shortchanging of the cut due the "men of respect."

So did every other business in Sicily, and Vizzini came to preside over a vast empire of criminal tribute. A number of innovations he introduced made it virtually invulnerable to attack from without. From the clannish Sicilian family system, he borrowed the tight bonds of family for his organization chart, then created a Pax Mafia: the organization would be invisible, would not conduct violent crime against Sicilians, would not involve "civilians" (anyone unaffiliated with the Mafia) in any intramafia disputes, would not peddle narcotics, would ensure that the streets were kept free of violent criminals, would serve as the court of last resort for local disputes, and, above all, would guarantee that no Sicilian would ever be endangered by an outsider.

The rise of Benito Mussolini, who vowed to destroy the Italian Mafia, drove Vizzini's mafiosi even more deeply underground; others fled to the United States. In the land of opportunity, they planted the seed of an American Mafia among the great waves of southern Italian immigrants. In time, they would merge some of the strengths of Vizzini's organization—cohesion, organization, *omerta* (silence), ruthlessness—with some of the strengths of American culture, including corporate methods of efficiency, pragmatism, and adaptability to changing social conditions, to create a uniquely American Mafia. That Mafia established two guiding organizational principles that would make it a powerful, nearly unassailable entity for the next sixty years:

- The organization is always supreme and is something more than the sum of its parts. All effort is aimed at ensuring the survival of the organization.
- There is no such thing as the indispensable man; people are only the parts for the larger machine.

The new American Mafia sprung up in every Italian immigrant community in the country, but its early center of gravity—and one that would remain—was New York City. One reason was that the bulk of Italian immigrants to the New World settled there. Another, eventually more important, reason was basic economics: that's where the money was. America's richest city was Mafia heaven: vast piles of money on the move, a thriving underground cash economy, endemic official corruption, large immigrant populations distrustful of the government, and a rampant spirit of capitalism.

It required only men of criminal talent to devise ways to steal at least some of all that wealth. Such talented men would arise and flourish, most of them in the hotbed of a noisy, dirty immigrant neighborhood of New York City known as East Harlem.

ONE

Our Father Who Art in Heaven

When you're on the street, it's like going to college. You learn something every day. The only thing is you don't get a diploma. Graduation is staying alive.

VINCENT TERESA

The morning had dawned suffocatingly hot in the summer heat wave that July of 1917, so Maria Lucchese sat by the open window, hoping to catch a stray breeze as she waited for her husband Giussepe to leave for work. When she was certain he had left, she rushed into the kitchen, poured the tomato sauce into several glass jars, and wrapped them in two towels. Carrying the jars with the care she once used for her son when he was an infant, she walked down the three flights of stairs from her tenement apartment and stepped onto East 104th Street.

Like the roar from an open blast furnace, the heat, smell, and noise of East Harlem enveloped her as she hurried up the street. The pushcart peddlers were already busy, loudly hawking their wares under striped umbrellas to protect their investments from the sun: vegetables, lemons, matches, paper bags, clothes, and baskets of pinwheels of cerise and green paper with scarlet tissue-paper roses in the hearts (handmade by local women trying to earn a few extra pennies at a time when most men in the neighborhood earned about $15 a

8

week). The pushcart peddlers struggled to make themselves heard over the rest of East Harlem's din—the wandering fish man proclaiming the freshness of his buckets of white fish wrapped in briny seaweed; the boys noisily playing stickball in the street; the loud rumble of the Second Avenue elevated subway line; the old men arguing over the arcane rules of the *bocce* game in the gutter; the "pretzel lady" hawking her basket of wares hung on sticks; the old organ grinder pumping out traditional tunes on his wheezy box as his pet monkey rattled pennies in a tin cup; the blind flutist piping an exquisite version of the music from *Il Trovatore;* the fortune teller swearing she could predict anyone's future by randomly selecting one of the dozens of white mice in a box.

Maria Lucchese nodded politely to some of the neighborhood women gathered on the front stoops busily engaged in the daily chore of exchanging gossip in rapid-fire Sicilian dialect about betrothals, funerals, births, and neighborhood scandals. Some gently rocked baby carriages; others suckled infants. Like her, they were dressed in the traditional Sicilian woman's garb: ankle-length black dress, black stockings, black shoes, their heads covered with three-cornered black shawls or lace scarves tied over their hair. Even on a hot summer day, it was unthinkable for any decent Sicilian woman to be seen in public wearing anything less.

Mrs. Lucchese hoped that none of her neighbors would know why she was hurrying up the street with a package wrapped in towels, but of course everybody knew. They knew because the neighborhood's intelligence service—the women who spent hours every day keeping a sharp watch on the streets from their open windows, arms resting atop pillows planted on the sills—saw all, knew all. So it was known that Mrs. Lucchese's only son, Gaetano, had been thrown out of the house a year before by his father when even beatings with a strap failed to keep the sixteen-year-old boy in school and deter him from a life of petty theft. According to the whispers around the neighborhood, Gaetano had joined a borgata (gang of boys), a group of delinquents who pilfered from pushcarts, burglarized stores, and sometimes did much worse. This gossip was repeated sympathetically, for no one in a community of close-knit families could fail to understand the anguish the religiously devout Maria Lucchese and her hardworking husband must be undergoing—their son a criminal, bringing shame on the family name. No wonder Giussepe Lucchese had decreed that his son no longer existed; his name was never to be mentioned again in the Lucchese household, and his wife was never to have any contact with him.

But as any mother in East Harlem knew, such an edict was impossible for a woman like Maria Lucchese to obey. Twice each week, after her husband had left for work, she would pack up her best tomato sauce, the magic elixir Sicilian mothers were convinced defeated all known diseases, and walk ten blocks north to a tenement on East 114th Street. There, in a shabby second-floor walkup apartment where her son had taken up residence with several other teenage boys who had also been thrown out of their homes, she would hand over the jars of sauce to her Gaetano, hoping it would keep him alive for another few days. More importantly, she would see her boy, touch and hug him gently.

Clutching her precious sauce, Mrs. Lucchese walked north along Third Avenue, crossing streets already pulsing with the summer heat. Other women were busy with their early-morning shopping, bargaining for the daily wares among the smells and noise of pushcarts, stalls, and stores. They picked among the tin tubs in front of the fish market filled with squid, a staple of the Sicilian diet, trays of minnows, piles of shrimp, boxes of squiggling live crabs, vats of sea snails. All the while, the store owner constantly shouted the exquisiteness of his fish and unbelievably low prices. The women ignored him, preferring to argue about the size of the steaks being cleaved from a huge horse mackerel by a man who insisted he was cutting only the largest pieces for the local customers, each of whom, he vowed, always got the choicest cuts.

At 106th Street, Maria Lucchese encountered the vista of bakeries, food stores and outdoor stands, an almost overwhelming smell of olive oil, prosciutto, anchovies, fennel, plum tomatoes, dried mushrooms, pine nuts, aniseed, capers, garlic, mint oregano, long loaves of Italian bread, spicy sausages, garlands of peppers, bunches of grapes hanging on strings, hard cheeses shaped like gourds, tubs of black olives. Even in a poor Italian immigrant community like East Harlem, there was no cutting back on the Italian zest for food.

However, the next block, 107th Street, was a different world. Here, there were no food stores or pushcarts; it was a street of taverns, pool halls, and whorehouses. People who lived on other streets called it "the cesspool," where the local pimps, strongarm thugs, stickup men, burglars, and thieves lived and worked. According to local gossip, dope dealers operated there, packaging opium they smuggled from China for delivery to "nigger Harlem" to the west and south to the Bohemians of Greenwich Village. The street also was dotted with what were called "political clubs," private clubs where men who seemed to have no jobs congregated. On summer days, they sat in wooden chairs in front of the clubs, even in the heat dressed in expensive suits and hats. Or they hung around inside, playing nonstop Sicilian card games like *briscola* and *trisette*. Maria Lucchese quickened her step, for these were the men of *la Mafia,* the men of mystery whom the people of East Harlem discussed only in guarded whispers. This was not a street where any decent citizen should linger.

At 108th Street, she made the sign of the cross as she passed the large stable. A place of evil, as the neighborhood gossip had it, the place where many men mysteriously disappeared. It was owned by Cirro Terranova, a notorious mafioso whose more prominent reputation was as "the artichoke king" for his monopoly of that essential vegetable in the Italian diet. Terranova reputedly settled disputes by luring those who made the mistake of arguing with him into the stable, killing them, then burying their remains under the dirt floor. (The local rumors turned out to be true: some years later, when the stable was razed to make way for an office building, twenty-eight skeletons were found buried under the floor.)

Finally, Maria Lucchese reached 114th Street, a block near the upper end of "Italian Harlem," an area of about a square mile that stretched from 104th to 120th streets between Fifth Avenue and the East River. Once a rustic valley between the Harlem River and the bluffs of Morningside Heights and Washington Heights, Harlem had been transformed almost overnight by a crash building program to erect enough tenement houses for the vast waves of immigrant workers. From 1900 to 1910, more than two million Italians had emigrated to the United States, most of them from the impoverished land of southern Italy and Sicily they called *mezzogiorno* (land of midday). Lured by tales of streets paved with gold, they poured through Ellis Island, most of them settling in a lower Manhattan neighborhood that became known as Little Italy. However, the clannish and insular Sicilians, preferring to live among their own kind, gradually moved north into the enclave of East Harlem, where they displaced poor Irish then moving onto the next upward rung in the immigration ladder. Almost to a man, the Sicilians planned on making their fortunes in the New World and then returning to Sicily to live out a comfortable retirement. But there were no streets paved with gold; predominantly illiterate and unskilled (with the exception of a few artisans), the Sicilians worked as day laborers for New York City's vast construction boom (Giussepe Lucchese earned $1.50 for a ten-hour day hauling cement on construction sites), trying to live on a bare subsistence wage that wedded them permanently to their neighborhood. It was a world that recreated Sicily in concrete, a world where language and customs remained intact, and where people who had never traveled beyond the sound of the church bells in their Sicilian villages could now survive in a very strange new environment. They were shocked by their first experiences of snow and slush and astonished that people actually burned wood—a rare commodity in barren and dusty Sicily—to keep warm. And they were endlessly puzzled by the strange American culture: why the Italian lottery was considered illegal gambling, yet Americans were allowed to gamble in the stock market; why the ancient Italian practice of making homemade wine was considered a violation of the law while distilleries and breweries were allowed to produce liquor by the millions of gallons; and why banks would not lend money to hardworking Italian shop owners because they allegedly had no collateral, yet would lend millions to rich Americans merely on the strength of their signatures.

Mrs. Lucchese entered one of the tenements that lined 114th Street. It was like all the other tenement buildings of East Harlem, a square concrete box of six stories, containing a number of railroad flats—four rooms behind each other in a straight line, with one bathroom per floor to serve all the families living on that floor. Though modest, each tenement building had an elaborate concrete stoop constructed by skilled Italian artisans; their unerring skill produced minor works of art that exist to this day. Other artisans, also working by hand without blueprints or plans, created exquisite ornamental ironwork for the stoops and fire escapes. (Developers added these grace notes to their cheap buildings because the artisans were paid only a few dollars a day for such artistry; similarly, the city graced its new subway stations with walls of hand-laid tile and the names of stops in elaborate mosaic tiles because the master Italian tileworkers, all immigrants, labored for low wages.)

She climbed to the second floor and knocked on the door of an apartment. The door was opened by Gaetano Lucchese, who even at seventeen years old was about the same height as his diminutive mother. Just over five feet tall, he weighed somewhere around a hundred pounds, a real runt of the litter. He greeted his mother with the standard Sicilian kiss on both cheeks, although it was clear he was not especially delighted with the timing of her visit. His nineteen-year-old friend and roommate Salvatore Lucania (leader of the borgata) stood nearby, smirking; Gaetano later would have to endure teasing from him and his friends about his mother bringing sauce to her "bambino."

Maria Lucchese glanced around the apartment with dismay. Even more dismal than her own, it featured an old sink, several rickety beds, a small table, and a gas-operated hot plate that required a dime deposited in the gas meter to work. Nails had been driven into the wall for hanging clothes. Even for the bargain price of three dollars a week, it wasn't much. Paint was peeling off the walls and chunks of the plaster ceiling were missing. The place was a hotbox in the July heat wave; in the winter, the wind howled through cracked windows.

Lucania greeted Maria Lucchese politely, a greeting she returned with icy civility. She did not like Lucania, the boy she was convinced had led her Gaetano down the wrong path. Lucania even *looked* evil, she often told her son; with those hooded eyes and the swarthy face badly scarred by a childhood bout with smallpox, he reminded her of Dracula. He was already notorious in the city's Italian communities as a criminal, with an arrest at the age of ten for shoplifting, another arrest at eleven for running a pennies-a-day protection racket that "protected" smaller schoolchildren against bullies, and a short spell in jail four years later when he was caught transporting narcotics. Even his efforts to spare his family the shame of his early notoriety by changing his name to Luciano and leaving his home in Little Italy to resettle in East Harlem failed to impress Mrs. Lucchese. Why, she often demanded of Gaetano, did he insist on spending his time with bums like Luciano, who was a criminal certain to drag Gaetano down with him? It was not a subject the son wanted to discuss. Nor did he want to argue with his mother about some of the other teenage boys he hung around with, troubled boys who were already acquiring police records, such as hoarse-voiced Francisco Castiglia, later to change his name to Frank Costello because it sounded "more Irish"; violent Albert Anastasio, later amended to Anastasia to spare his family the shame of his criminal career; a hulking teenage thug named Vito Genovese; the strikingly handsome Giuseppe Doto, who insisted on being called "Joe Adonis"; and two of Luciano's friends from the world of Jewish crime on the Lower East Side, Maier Suchowljansky (later Meyer Lansky), and Benjamin Siegel, called "Bugsy" because of his unpredictable eruptions of violent temper.

Maria Lucchese had no success in trying to pull Gaetano away from these dregs of America's immigrant class, nor could she convince him that there were plenty of ways for boys to *earn* money. For example, there were boys making good money serving as *shabbas goys,* as the Jews called them, Italian boys who would go into the Jewish neighborhoods on Saturdays and light the stoves in Orthodox Jewish homes, where such an act was forbidden for the devout on the Jewish sabbath. Grateful Orthodox Jews paid handsomely for this service.

But Gaetano simply shrugged at his mother's lectures, at some point brandishing his crippled left hand, missing two fingers after being mangled in a machine shop accident two years before during the only legitimate job he would ever hold. In his mind, that was proof enough of the folly of working for a living. Finally, his mother would leave, having succeeded in convincing him to put her tomato sauce on everything he would eat during the next few days, but having failed to divert him from a path she was convinced would lead to ruin. She trudged home, later to tell her husband a lie about visiting a neighbor. After dinner, she would join her neighbors in the community's social hall, the front stoops. In the cool of the evening, away from the hot apartment, she would tell lies about how her Gaetano was somewhere working hard, "learning a trade." The neighbors politely did not remind her who Gaetano really was, a street punk certain to wind up in jail one of these days. Maria Lucchese would sit on the stoop, staring north toward 114th Street, hoping that Gaetano would somehow see the error of his ways.

Gaetano Lucchese never came home. He was busy with his friends on 114th Street, hustling for dollars, stealing wallets from drunks, breaking through roofs to burglarize stores, and filching from pushcarts. Gaetano had his own dream of the future, a time when, as a powerful gangster, he would live in a big mansion, drive a big black touring car like the ones he had seen outside the Mafia clubs on 107th Street, have servants to cater to every whim, and keep a huge bankroll of hundred-dollar bills in his pocket to buy anything he wanted. His friends had similar dreams, and although none of them realized it at the time, they had taken the first step in what would become a very dark chapter in the history of their adopted country.

They were about to create the modern American Mafia.

To be sure, there already was a Mafia in the New World. In East Harlem, it was run by Ignazio Saietta, a psychopath known as "Lupo the Wolf," and his brother-in-law and fellow killer, Giuseppe Morello, known as "The Clutching Hand." Two other Mafia gangs existed in New York City: one in Manhattan's Little Italy, the other in Brooklyn's smaller Italian community. Actually, none of these gangs used the word *Mafia,* considered an Old World term; the gangs instead called themselves "Chairs." The three gangs hated each other, and shooting wars were frequent. But the Italian criminals were careful to keep to their own neighborhoods, under the prevailing criminal code which decreed that ethnic gangs prey strictly on their own people. Thus, Irish gangs like the Gophers and the Marginals were confined to the Irish neighborhoods on the West Side of Manhattan and the Hell's Kitchen area along the Hudson River waterfront, while the Jewish gangs restricted their operations to the Jewish enclaves on the Lower East Side. (One of the rare interethnic gang wars took place on the Brooklyn waterfront at the turn of the century, when Irish and Italian gangs battled for control, a war ultimately won by the Italians.)

The Italian mafiosi, predominantly Sicilian, who arrived in America at first were somewhat disoriented, for they had been removed from the centuries-old context in which they had long operated. Beginning in 1903, they hit upon the idea of raising cash by shaking down local merchants, an idea borrowed from an infamous Spanish band of terrorists who used the symbol of a black hand, meant to terrorize potential victims. Italian shopkeepers soon began receiving threatening letters, signed with a distinctive image of a black hand, demanding "protection money" to be paid on a regular weekly basis as immunity from assaults (to be carried out by the mafiosi themselves in event of nonpayment.) The term *black hand* used to describe these extortionists was coined by the editor of *Il Progresso Italo-Americano* to avoid using the term "Mafia," which he felt brought shame on the Italian immigrants. By the end of World War 1, the Mafia's black hand operations ended, largely because new restrictions on immigration had begun to dry up the pool of potential victims, and because the federal government had enacted new mail fraud statutes that made extortion by mail a serious felony.

That left the Mafia without a new source of income, and at that moment a member of the East Harlem Mafia decided upon a radical solution. But in the process, Giussepe (Joe the Boss) Masseria quite unwittingly was to ignite a revolution in crime.

Squat and fat, Masseria had all the social graces of a warthog. He regarded the world with a pair of small, slitted eyes that reminded everybody who knew him of a pig. There were further reminders: crude and illiterate, Masseria's waking hours were dominated by an appetite that defied belief. For lunch, he liked to devour three huge platters of spaghetti, a feat that attracted few luncheon partners, for Masseria like to talk while eating, spraying pieces of pasta and sauce in all directions.

A confirmed Mafia thug, Masseria concluded that the three separate Mafia gangs in New York had no hope of rising beyond their lowly status on the fringes of ethnic crime unless they were united under one powerful leader—Giussepe Masseria. To that end, he christened himself "Joe the Boss" and proceeded to shoot anyone who opposed him. Many did, and a nasty war got underway. Among its first victims were Lupo the Wolf and the Clutching Hand.

Masseria began to get the upper hand, largely because among his allies was Giacamo (Tom) Reina, who ran the cesspool on 107th Street. Reina was a not-too-bright mafioso, but he had the wisdom to recruit a gang of promising young street punks as apprentices, notable among them Salvatore Luciano and Gaetano Lucchese. Impressed with the success of Luciano's gang—which Luciano had simply named the "107th Street Gang" because he could not think of a more interesting appellation—Reina set them to work as shooters in Masseria's attempt to unify the New York Mafia under his command. Most often, their orders for a hit arrived after Masseria would scream at an underling, *"Livarsi na petra di la scarpa!"* (Take the stone from my shoe). By 1922, when Masseria's war reached its climax, the 107th Street Gang had already been involved in thirty murders. In that year, Masseria became a Mafia legend by somehow surviving an assassination attempt by three rival gunmen, who chased him through city streets while pumping twelve shots at him from a distance of less than three feet. Police found Masseria with his aching feet in a tub of hot water, still wearing his straw hat that had been shredded by near-misses. "I no understand why anybody try to kill me," he said in an expression of wide-eyed innocence.

In addition to a talent for killing, Lucchese had demonstrated the first hint of future criminal greatness by establishing a window cleaning service, which consisted of a group of young street punks he recruited, some mops and pails, and a supply of bricks. Lucchese visited businesses all over East Harlem, offering his window cleaning service. Those refusing would have their windows mysteriously shattered that night; a follow-up visit by Lucchese the next morning explaining how his service would guarantee that such misfortunes would not occur again was usually sufficient to gain new customers. Soon, Lucchese monopolized the window cleaning business in East Harlem, a stranglehold that was reinforced when he made sure that the new customers not only got the best cleaning, but also received a guarantee that no vandal would dare heave a rock through any "Lucchese window."

An impressed Masseria, heeding a suggestion by Reina, made Luciano his aide de camp, with Lucchese as Luciano's chief assistant and general utility man. Both shrewd young criminals proved invaluable, for Masseria did not have the vaguest idea of how to run a criminal organization (for one thing, Luciano did all the counting because his boss literally could not add two and two). There was a great deal of work for Luciano to do, for the government of the United States had just handed organized crime a golden opportunity.

In 1920, the Eighteenth Amendment to the U.S. Constitution was approved, making illegal the manufacture and sale of alcoholic beverages. But it did not prohibit *possession* of alcohol, an important distinction that criminal minds like Luciano and Lucchese immediately grasped as the route to the kind of profits the criminal world could only dream about. As they understood, people still wanted to drink, so a simple economic equation presented itself: produce enough liquor to fill that demand and rake in the profits.

However, Masseria's plan to capitalize on Prohibition was typically small-minded. He set up a network of small neighborhood stills in apartments all over East Harlem, crude "alky cookers" that kept fires burning under stills to skim distillate. The average home still could produce up to 350 gallons of crude alcohol a week, earning the owners anywhere from 50 to 75 cents a gallon profit. In a poor immigrant neighborhood, that kind of profit was very welcome. Soon, the stench of fermenting mash permeated every block.

But homemade booze varied in quality, usually from abysmal to toxic. Some drinkers went blind from imbibing the stuff; many others got so sick they swore off alcohol forever. "If you can light a wick in it, it's ready," the home brewers liked to say—not a very good testimonial to the quality of their product. True, desperate drinkers were buying the stuff (there were 32,000 speakeasies in New York City alone), but only because they couldn't get anything else. Masseria, awash in money for the first time in his career, was not disposed to upgrade quality and thereby raise production costs that would eat into his profits.

Luciano argued that this policy was shortsighted; even desperate drinkers at some point would become tired of drinking the rotgut and begin to demand the real stuff. So the organization somehow had to get its hand on genuine imported booze or, alternately, improve the domestic product enough that it would be hard to tell the difference. The argument fell on deaf ears.

Luciano's insight came from one of his closest henchmen, Meyer Lansky. Any fool, Lansky pointed out, could cobble together colored water, raw alcohol and a splash of real scotch for flavor to produce an ersatz liquor that a real drinker would realize was only a shadow of the real thing. Perfectly suitable for Skid Row bums and sleazy speakeasies, but that kind of rotgut would not attract repeat customers. More important, the real money in illegal liquor was in the upscale crowd, the kind of people willing to pay *anything* to get the real stuff. As Lansky summarized it, "If you have a lot of what people want and can't get, then you can supply the demand and shovel in the dough." It became known as "Lansky's Law," and came to serve as the economic foundation of all modern organized crime.

But the problem, as Luciano understood, was that in order to get the real stuff, vast smuggling operations would have to be set up—arrangements to buy genuine liquor in Great Britain and Canada, large ships to carry the merchandise to the three-mile limit, a flotilla of fast boats to move it to shore, fleets of trucks to move the liquor to warehouses, security details to protect the shipments, a distribution network to move the liquor to sales outlets, and, finally, a financial organization to keep track of it all and collect the profits. What was needed, in other words, was organized crime.

As things turned out, Luciano had the talent at hand, among his 107th Street Gang, to staff the new organization necessary for a whole new approach to the distribution and sale of an illegal substance. While Lansky organized the financial network, Lucchese organized the transportation system and Frank Costello, another Luciano confederate, set up a vast system of payoffs to keep police (and some corrupted Coast Guardsmen) away from shipments. Lansky's Law proved even more successful than Lansky dared hope—Scottish distilleries that were charging $17 for a twelve-bottle case of scotch in the years before Prohibition began to divert most of their production to the illegal American market. However, the Scots couldn't resist a little gouging; they raised their price to $26 a case, an increase they solemnly described to their American customers as "revenge for Yorktown."

Luciano's organization happily paid the increase, not bothering to tell the overseas producers that they were selling those genuine bottles of scotch for $30 a bottle, with high-grade, 12-year-old scotch fetching up to $175 a bottle. As a delighted Lansky reported to Luciano, each shipment of three thousand cases from overseas returned at least $1 million in net profit—at a time when the Ford Motor Company, in a move that other industries claimed would destroy the American economy, began paying its workers the unbelievable sum of $15 for an eight-hour working day.

By the mid-1920s, organized crime was making millions each month from overseas shipments alone, supplemented by another river of profits from home distillery operations and illegal beer breweries. There was so much money that in 1923 Luciano thought nothing of spending $125,000 to buy two hundred ringside seats for the Dempsey-Firpo heavyweight championship fight to distribute to his friends. But he was always aware that the old habits of greed and the inclination to shoot rivals threatened this cornucopia. He and Lucchese began to discuss ideas of how to create some kind of structure to protect the business. Lucchese agreed, "We've got to get organized."

It required several years for Luciano to convince the underworld that organization was the key to continued success. Finally, in 1929, everyone agreed to convene in Atlantic City in a secret Luciano-sponsored meeting of the main criminal groups involved in the liquor business. During several days of intense negotiations, elaborate divisions of territories and responsibilities were worked out to prevent the kind of blood-letting that had marked past disputes. The impetus for this kind of organization was best summarized in Lansky's memorable phrase, "Ford salesmen don't shoot Chevrolet salesmen." There was plenty of money for everybody; old-style shooting wars over spoils were bad for business. One prominent example was the notorious incident which had occurred in February of that year when Al Capone, the crime boss of Chicago, arranged for the murder of seven rivals. The St. Valentine's Day Massacre, as it became known, had the unfortunate double effect of arousing public revulsion (people were willing to buy liquor from criminals, but didn't like bodies littering the streets) and alienating what had been a cooperative political establishment.

To prevent such infamies, Luciano arranged for the creation of what was called "the Combination," a board of directors composed of the seven leading criminal organizations involved in bootlegging operations, that would settle disputes and rule on territories. Its first order of business was to order Capone, one of the summit meeting's attendees, to stop killing people in Chicago.

Pointedly, Joe the Boss Masseria had not been invited to Atlantic City. He would not have attended in any event; a man of limited imagination, he saw no reason to cooperate with any other criminal organization. He became progressively more irritated by Luciano's insistence that the future of crime lay in large-scale organization, involving all crime groups, with territories and profits to be carefully divided and disputes adjudicated without recourse to violence. Masseria replied dismissively, "An outfit runs on its own and knocks off anybody in its way."

There were other things about Luciano that began to irritate Masseria. Technically, Luciano's job was to serve as field manager of bootlegging operations for Masseria's Mafia organization. But Luciano's striking business talents had made him something much more than that, an innovator whose ideas had earned vast amounts of money and made him the most highly respected figure in the criminal world, an astonishing achievement for a man only twenty-nine years old. Masseria did not like being overshadowed. Then there was the matter of the kind of people with whom Luciano was dealing. An ethnocentric, Masseria despised Jews and saw no reason why his people ought to have any contact with Jewish criminal leaders. He wondered aloud how a *paisano* like Lucchese could attend the bar mitzvahs and weddings of his Jewish criminal friends, and why other Italians in the 107th Street Gang had actually invited Jews to Italian weddings. And, Masseria complained, he had actually seen Jews and Irishmen in the Venezia Restaurant on East 116th Street, the Masseria organization's favorite hangout, laughing and joking with Luciano's people. To Masseria's shock, one of them, Frank Costello, had actually married a Jewish woman.

For the moment, Masseria tolerated these transgressions, because Luciano was earning the organization a lot of money ($12 million in 1925). But he continued to keep a close watch on Luciano and the rest of the 107th Street Gang, unaware that he was looking at a revolution. What Masseria did not understand was that Luciano and the others represented a generation of Italians very different from that which had brought Masseria and the other "Mustache Petes"—Luciano's derisive term for old-time Mafia leaders—to America. Masseria's generation arrived as mature young men, already formed by the old Sicilian traditions. But Luciano's generation arrived as children (Luciano at age ten, Lucchese at age eleven), and, despite the power of tradition in their immigrant neighborhoods, they were essentially Americanized. Instead of tradition, they were drawn to the distinctly American business values of pragmatism, efficiency, organization, specialization, and the drive to dominate or monopolize certain markets. An entirely new force in crime had emerged. To this new force, Masseria was an anachronism, a throwback to a time no longer relevant to the conditions of modern America.

Just how irrelevant was proven in 1927, when, at the height of the Masseria organization's success, a crisis arose in the person of Salvatore Maranzano, who was among the leading mafiosi driven out of Italy by Benito Mussolini. Then forty-three and relentlessly ambitious, Maranzano had fled Italy with a few loyal adherents. After arriving at Ellis Island, he took one look at New York City and decided that he would take over the local Mafia.

That required the elimination of Masseria, of course, a task

Maranzano immediately began to organize. Masseria reacted, typically, by shooting his rival's supporters, and soon another shooting war—just the kind of old lunacy Luciano had warned against—was underway, threatening the orderly flow of profits. The Masseria-Maranzano struggle, which became known as the Castellammarese War, put Luciano and the new criminal generation in a dilemma, for it would only be a matter of time, as the war intensified, before they would be forced to choose sides. "Greaseballs," Lucchese called both of them contemptuously, noting that Maranzano's own ethnocentrism made even Masseria look like the very acme of tolerance. Maranzano, born in the seaside Sicilian city of Castellammare, selected only men born in the same city for his gang, and tended to regard all other Sicilians as inferior for the error of being born elsewhere. When one of his men was killed, Maranzano would scream in rage, *"E una sporca macchia anl'onore di Castellammarese!"* (It's a dirty spot on the honor of the Castellammarese). Occasionally, he would order someone killed for the crime of insulting his birthplace.

Despite such murderous tendencies, Luciano and Lucchese had to admit that from a personal standpoint, at least, Maranzano represented something of an improvement over Masseria. A thin man who wore what appeared to be a perpetually worried expression, Maranzano dressed in conservative business suits that made him look like a banker. Armed with a small fortune he had smuggled into this country after fleeing Italy, he set up an import-export business and a real estate company as cover for his criminal activities, mostly bootlegging. A former seminary student with a university education, he was fluent in Greek and Latin (though his English was poor). He maintained an extensive library in his home, much of it dealing with his hero, Julius Caesar, whom he sought to emulate. His men learned that at some point they would have to undergo the ordeal of a dinner at the Maranzano home, where the post-dinner entertainment consisted of their boss delivering seemingly interminable lectures about Caesar, followed by recitations of long passages in Latin from classical literature. His guests, usually men with grade school educations and low IQs, would listen with apparent absorption, then say politely, "Yeah, you got a point there, boss."

The Luciano faction concluded that only one solution was possible: the old order represented by Masseria and Maranzano would have to go, and in a way that would not disrupt profits. A tall order, but Luciano developed a plan that, reduced to its essentials, amounted to joining with Maranzano as a temporary expedient to destroy Masseria, then in turn destroying Maranzano. "To deal with Sicilians, you gotta think like a Sicilian," Luciano counseled Lucchese before dispatching him on a mission to contact Maranzano and pledge the support of organized crime's younger generation in return for significant pieces of the action.

It is a tribute to Lucchese's powers of duplicity that the suspicious Maranzano—who had taken to riding around with a machine gun mounted on a swivel in the back seat of his car, along with several pistols and knives concealed under the seats—enthusiastically welcomed Lucchese and the rest of the Luciano faction into his fold. It was not long before Masseria discovered this treachery, which Luciano explained away by claiming he was running an infiltration operation to divine Maranzano's plans. Luciano did not tell him those plans included killing Joe the Boss himself. On April 15, 1931, Luciano invited his boss to a lunch at a noted Italian restaurant in Staten Island, ostensibly to discuss plans to murder Maranzano. Unaware it was his last meal, Masseria ate with his usual gusto, devouring an antipasto, a heaping platter of spaghetti, lobster *fra diavalo,* and an entire quart of Chianti. Three hours were required to polish it all off, but Masseria was still looking forward to dessert. Luciano excused himself to go to the bathroom. In the dining room, absorbed in the temptations of the dessert tray, Masseria may have failed to notice that other diners in the place had quietly left and that the waiters had disappeared. A fatal lapse: four gunmen, including Bugsy Siegel and Vito Genovese, suddenly burst in to the restaurant and pumped six bullets into Masseria, who fell, appropriately enough, in a clatter of dishes and eating utensils.

"I was washing my hands," Luciano explained to police, an explanation that would come to rank as the greatest alibi in history. Even the humorless Maranzano found it funny, but at the same time he was determined to keep a wary eye on his new ally. As a veteran of the Sicilian Mafia and its long tradition of double cross and triple cross, Maranzano was perfectly aware that a man who had betrayed his boss was just as capable of betraying the successor.

As if to checkmate such a betrayal, Maranzano carried out one of his own. Shortly after Masseria's murder, he convened a summit of all Mafia leaders in a Bronx meeting hall and proceeded to announce a new organization for crime. To Luciano's shock—and contrary to what Maranzano had promised—the Combination, crime's board of directors, was to be eliminated and replaced by one man, the *capo di tutti capi* (boss of all bosses). And that man would be Salvatore Maranzano, who would henceforth receive a percentage of every dollar earned by organized crime. Maranzano then demanded that the nearly one hundred attendees at the meeting immediately produce a tribute to their new *el supremo*. Some $100,000 was laid on the table.

For Luciano, there was further bad news. The cooperative of organized crime that he had so carefully put together to include all ethnic groups was replaced by five "families," as Maranzano termed them, Italian Mafia-only criminal organizations that would replace all the Mafia gangs in New York City. All other non-Italian organized crime groups were on their own, although Maranzano made it clear that the Mafia would now rule organized crime. Presumably, the non-Italians would be permitted only crumbs from the criminal banquet. All the new families, Maranzano decreed, would be organized along the lines of a Roman legion, with a boss of unquestioned authority, aided by an underboss (chief executive), who would in turn administer *capodecine* (ranks of ten), street crews that would carry out the bulk of the work. Each of the capodecine would be ruled by a *caporegime,* a junior executive roughly equal to the rank of captain in a Roman legion. In order to prevent tensions among these families and within each organization, Maranzano ordered that the following rules would be put into effect: *omerta,* under pain of death, for all Mafia members; unquestioning obedience by the lower ranks; no mafioso could strike another mafioso; and no mafioso would be permitted to covet the wife of another mafioso. The families would operate along strict geographical lines and would not be permitted to conduct any criminal activities in the sphere of influence of any other family. As a final flourish, Maranzano announced that he was now in charge of *all* Mafia gangs in the United States.

On Maranzano's new organization chart, Luciano was given control of the old Masseria organization and restricted to northern Manhattan, while his chief aide, Lucchese, was assigned as underboss to Gaetano (Tom) Gagliano, a talented criminal who had risen through the ranks from 107th Street (his predecessor, Giacamo Reina, was a 1930 casualty of the Masseria-Maranzano war). The new Gagliano family was given the Bronx. For Luciano and Lucchese, it was not much in the way of reward for all they had done to bring organized crime to its current status of wealth and power. But there were even more serious problems with Maranzano's reorganization.

For one thing, Luciano noted, it froze out the powerful Jewish organized crime groups, especially the one headed by Louis (Lepke) Buchalter, who dominated the Garment Center, and it ignored such essential contributors to the success of Italian organized crime as Meyer Lansky and Bugsy Siegel. Luciano was always careful to include both Italian and Jewish organized crime groups on his organization chart. For another, the idea of strict geographical limits was idiotic; modern crime—bootlegging was a prime example—did not follow strict geographical lines. For example, one of Luciano's business partners, Arthur (Dutch Schultz) Flegenheimer, among the leading Jewish criminal leaders, had a number of illegal beer breweries that serviced markets all over the country. Based in the Bronx, Flegenheimer's trucks crossed several state lines while making deliveries; how could that kind of operation be restricted to one area on the map?

Maranzano became aware of a growing restiveness in his new organization, but concluded it all resulted from the machinations of Luciano, whom Maranzano had come to regard as a threat. To eliminate the problem, he planned to lure Luciano to a meeting, where a notorious Irish gunman named Vincent (Mad Dog) Coll, hired for the specific purpose, would kill him. Then, in a massive stroke designed to solidify his hold on all organized crime in the United States, Maranzano planned on murdering sixty top hoodlums he perceived were either actual or potential threats to his rule, including Al Capone.

Luciano knew all about this mad scheme because Lucchese, his master spy, had infiltrated Maranzano's inner circle. Posing as a disaffected member of Luciano's organization, Lucchese won the confidence of Maranzano's lieutenants. Plied with liquor, they boasted to Lucchese of the master plan to wipe out all of their boss's enemies in two bloody steps. Lucchese immediately informed Luciano and added a warning: time was running short.

Luciano already had some inkling that matters were coming to a head. He had received a visit from an infuriated Louis Buchalter, who reported that Maranzano was moving to displace him as czar of the Garment Center rackets. Maranzano had dispatched several goons to a dress manufacturer in Brooklyn, informing him that he was now to pay tribute to Maranzano. The manufacturer balked, so the goons broke all the windows in his plant. When a union business agent called Maranzano to complain, the boss ordered his goons to murder him. They proceeded to kill the wrong man, an innocent worker, and the Garment Center was in an uproar.

As Luciano considered how to solve the problem, his hand was forced. Maranzano called him on September 9, 1931, ordering a meeting the next day in Maranzano's real estate office near Grand Central Station. Aware he was being summoned for his execution, Luciano set to work. With Lansky's help, he enlisted four Jewish gunmen—shooters whose identities Luciano was certain would be unknown to Maranzano—and then placed Lucchese at the very center of his plan as the man who would finger the victim for the shooters. The next day, it all went off without a hitch. Shortly before the scheduled Maranzano-Luciano meeting, just as Vincent Coll, packing a machine gun, was climbing the building's back stairs for his mission, Lucchese burst into Maranzano's office unannounced. Claiming he had urgent business to discuss, Lucchese began to lead Maranzano into an inner office, past five hulking bodyguards. At that moment, four men entered the outer office, announced they were Internal Revenue Service agents, and demanded to see Maranzano's books. Two of them pulled guns and told the bodyguards and Lucchese to face the wall. Lucchese nodded toward Maranzano, who was then shot and stabbed to death. As the hitmen fled, Lucchese calmly got into an elevator and descended to the ground floor. The killers fled eight flights down the back stairs, encountering Coll coming from the other direction. "Too late, Coll," one of them said. "He's dead." Coll, who had already been paid $50,000 as down payment for what was supposed to be the murder of Luciano, considered a moment, then turned around and left the building, having earned a lot of money without having to work for it.

As Maranzano died alone in a pool of blood, the man now known as "Charley Lucky" (because he had miraculously survived a vicious stabbing a year before) became de facto head of organized crime in the United States. But that was precisely what Luciano did not want to be. He had something more important in mind, which he unveiled several weeks after Maranzano's murder at a crime summit he convened in Chicago.

Attendees from all over the country had arrived in that city fully expecting Luciano to proclaim himself the new el supremo to whom they must now pay tribute. Even Al Capone, the conclave's host, assumed his share of the tribute would cost him upwards of $100,000. Eager to get on Luciano's good side, Capone had spared no effort to make him and the other delegates comfortable: the finest hotel rooms, catered food, beautiful women to play with, and the highest quality liquor.

But, to everyone's surprise, as the first order of business Luciano told everyone to put their wallets away; he had no intention of asking for any tribute. And, for that matter, Luciano added, the whole idea of a *capo di tutti capi* ought to be scrapped. No single man, not even himself, should ever rule crime again, he said; instead, there should be a national commission whose members would include the leaders of all the major criminal organizations in the country. Lucky Luciano would be only one vote on the new commission, which would arbitrate all disputes; its word would be final. There would be no further recourse to the gun and the knife as a method of solving business disputes. The new commission would meet regularly—perhaps every year or so—with an agenda of disputes that had been brought before it for resolution. He left the Maranzano "family" system of organization for individual Mafia groups largely intact, but eliminated the strict geographical limits.

"It's time we grew up," Luciano lectured. "Let's use our brains instead of our guns." Interesting talk from a man who had contrived to murder two criminal leaders, but he meant it. Luciano was convinced that the Maranzano killing, followed by imposition of organizational methods on the way crime did business, would finally end the many years of bloody feuds. From now on, he insisted, the new organization would deal with problems as a corporation would. And to ensure that members of criminal organizations could get a fair hearing on their grievances and disputes with other gangsters—another source of tension that tended to erupt into shootings—he recommended that each criminal organization appoint a consigliere (counselor), a respected senior member with the requisite talents of diplomacy and judiciousness, who would arbitrate disputes among members and hear any grievances.

As for murder, Luciano as a criminal recognized its occasional necessity as an instrument of business, but sought to organize that, too. In 1934, he convened another summit at which he recommended the creation of a special unit that would handle all murders. Requests for murder would have to be submitted for approval to the commission; if that body approved, the task—known as a "contract"—would be passed to a special unit of Jewish and Italian killers that would carry out any killing. Eventually, this unit became known as "Murder Incorporated."

All in all, the 1931 convocation amounted to the supreme triumph of an organization man. The attendees enthusiastically approved Luciano's proposals, whose larger meaning was that from now on, the organization was preeminent in organized crime; the whole was always to be greater than the sum of it parts. Among the more enthusiastic was Meyer Lansky, crime's other great organization man, whose very presence at the conclave represented an important political signal Luciano was sending: the Jews were equal partners with the Italians in organized crime.

All those who attended sensed they had participated in an important event. An entirely new structure for organized crime had been created, one which promised a businesslike system that would guarantee the millions of dollars flowing into its coffers each week without the disruption and violence of gang wars. But, at the same time, everyone understood they were members of a *criminal* organization, something that could not be formally named, as would a business corporation. And certainly not something that could be discussed publicly. Various groups evolved different, deliberately vague names for it, to be used in private conversations. Guys from Chicago called it "the Outfit." To New Englanders, it was "the Office." Many Italians preferred the vaguest reference of all: "Our Thing"— la Cosa Nostra.

Whatever the name, organized crime had now sunk deep roots into the American system. Millions of Americans were virtual coconspirators, happily dealing with organized crime to secure a commodity forbidden by law. The bribes paid to police and politicians created a systemic, endemic corruption that stained law enforcement agencies all the way to the top. The corruption also had a deep impact on the political system. The Great Depression had dried up many of the usual sources of political contributions, so politicians began turning to the one institution with plenty of ready cash to invest. Men like Luciano funnelled millions of dollars to politicians who could be expected to protect organized crime's interests—mostly in the form of appointed judges and senior police officials willing to look the other way.

But the new organized criminals also understood that there was a tacit quid pro quo in this arrangement. Organized crime must conduct business out of the public eye so as not to arouse the voters' disquiet: no gun battles in the streets and no violent crime to threaten ordinary citizens. Further, organized crime must not become involved in crimes most voters would not overlook, such as narcotics and child pornography.

East Harlem represented the perfect example of how the new system worked. Frank Costello, Luciano's chief corruptor, proved to be a near-genius at selecting up-and-coming politicians for largesse—district leaders, politically connected lawyers who might become judges in the future, political activists who would later become heads of various city departments. With Costello's bottomless bankroll, virtually any candidate for public office in New York City could win an election. (The Manhattan District Attorney's Office was shocked, after installing a wiretap on Costello's phone, to hear a newly elected criminal court judge gush his thanks to Costello for securing his nomination. "When I tell you something's in the bag," Costello purred, "you can rest assured." It did not require much imagination to predict what would happen if Costello or any of his colleagues appeared before the grateful judge.)

Costello, Luciano, and Lucchese maintained what they called a "buy bank," a fund of $5 million from which bribes to politicians and police were made. Those taking the bribes, ranging from the head of Tammany Hall, the Democratic political machine that ran the city, down to the cop walking the beat, guaranteed there would be no interruption to the river of money that flowed from loan-sharking, illegal gambling, bootlegging, prostitution, and a wide variety of criminal scams.

Given the tight political control over such matters as appointments to the judiciary, district attorneys' offices, and the high ranks of the police department, much of the buy bank money found its way into the hands of politicians. A high percentage of local elections were decided on the basis of which candidate the organization had decided to support with the kind of money to overwhelm an opponent. When bribery didn't work, the organization could exert a little muscle, as in the case of a district leader bodily evicted from his office because he wouldn't support an organization-backed candidate, or, more seriously, the election worker beaten to death in front of thirty witnesses because he sought to complain that the organization was paying bribes to voters to vote in a certain way. All the eyewitnesses later claimed they had seen nothing.

Despite the best efforts of Luciano and his friends, they were unable to derail the political career of a particular man they didn't like, East Harlem's noted native son, Fiorello La Guardia. He was an extremely popular congressman who later served as the city's most famous mayor, when he would cause the organization much grief. But there was a sufficient number of corrupted politicians to provide virtual immunity for the organization. Each week, a bagman for Tammany Hall with the resonant name of Joseph (Joe the Coon) Cooney picked up $20,000 in cash from Frank Costello for distribution to various politicians. In the police department, a deputy police commissioner had been assigned, with much public fanfare, to form a twelve-man "elite" squad that would root out gambling and corruption. In fact, the squad had been formed for the specific purpose of systematizing payoffs from the organization. Each week, the deputy commissioner would conduct extensive negotiations with Costello to determine how much money was to be paid to protect organized crime operations, with a sliding scale of bribes depending on the severity (and profitability) of any given crime. Further, an elaborate system was devised to ensure that *all* cops got their cut, ranging from the police commissioner himself to lowly patrolmen.

The intersection of politics and crime produced some unsettling statistics. By 1933, the New York Democratic County Committee had twenty-five ex-criminals on its payroll. Eight of the city's twenty-two full-time election inspectors, responsible for ensuring the honesty of all elections, were convicted felons. The judicial system became a joke: in 1932, of more than four thousand people arrested for illegal gambling, only 175 were actually held for trial (and subsequently got off with slaps on the wrist). Chief clerks in district attorneys' offices were notorious for "losing" criminal records, so that when a career criminal with a long rap sheet appeared in court, he could claim leniency as a first-time offender. To satisfy public relations demands that there be at least an appearance of effort against organized crime, police periodically conducted highly publicized raids against gambling parlors, houses of prostitution, cash stashes for numbers operations, and anything else guaranteed to earn some newspaper headlines. But almost all these raids were what the cops involved called "tipovers," meaning deliberate violations of the Constitution—such as smashing in a door without a warrant—so that corrupted judges later could cite these violations as rationales for dismissing all charges.

This sordid lesson in civics ran in tandem with another, the corruption of ordinary citizens. For example, illegal gambling, a crime that did not particularly upset most citizens, was a perfect operation for organized crime, since its success largely hinged on how well organized it was. It became very successful indeed, largely because criminals were able to enlist non-criminal citizens to help out. In East Harlem and other New York City neighborhoods, hundreds of noncriminals were enrolled as runners and couriers for "numbers" or "policy" (illegal lottery) operations. Many others, owners of mom-and-pop delicatessens, candy stores, and soda shops, were recruited, for up to $150 a week, to allow criminals to use their phones for bookmaking or let their stores be used as a dropoff point for betting slips. Some businessmen covertly rented out vacant warehouses or stores for illegal gambling parlors. The cash for such services, unreported to the IRS, was welcome in the hard times of the Depression. And it was easily rationalized; after all, the law-abiding citizens weren't moving drugs or concealing guns, so what was the harm? For further rationalization, some of these upright citizens could later point to their lawyer sons and doctor sons whose college educations had been underwritten by the stipends from organized crime.

The real winners in this game, however, were the criminals themselves, most prominently Gaetano Lucchese.

The career of Lucchese was nothing short of meteoric. From teenage street punk robbing pushcarts, he had risen in less than fifteen years to the very pinnacle of organized crime, one of its most important leaders. He first ran afoul of the law in 1921, when he was arrested for stealing a Packard touring car. Sentenced to three years in jail, he was paroled after just thirteen months. (Six years later, all records of this case disappeared in a mysterious fire, effectively erasing his criminal record.) By the age of thirty, he was a millionaire, a financial success who seemed amazingly immune to any attempt to bring him to justice.

The thirteen-month jail sentence would turn out to be the only prison time Lucchese ever served. It also provided him with a nickname that pursued him the rest of his life: "Tommy Three Fingers." While being fingerprinted after his arrest in the car theft case, one cop said, "Hey, it's Tommy Three Fingers," referring to Mordechai (Tommy Three Fingers) Brown, a popular three-fingered baseball pitcher of the era. Lucchese's friends subsequently began calling him "Tommy," but omitted the "three fingers" part; Lucchese was extremely sensitive about his left hand.

During the Maranzano-Masseria war, Lucchese committed a number of killings, including a 1925 murder for which he was indicted. The case looked unbeatable, since he had committed the murder in front of the victim's wife and mother. But before Lucchese was due to go on trial, the eyewitnesses suddenly recanted, claiming they could not remember what the murderer looked like. Five years later, Lucchese was indicted for another killing, but again an eyewitness had a convenient lapse of memory. No mystery why: Lucchese had a reputation as a stone-cold killer, and in a time long before the Witness Protection Program, there were not many people with suicidal tendencies strong enough to be willing to testify against Tommy Three Fingers.

Still, Lucchese, unlike some of his criminal friends, had no fondness for killing. He often complained to Luciano, no slouch himself at disposing of inconvenient humanity, about having to murder men with whom he had no quarrel, to put bullets into the head of someone merely because "Joe the Boss" Masseria had decreed the victim must die. Like Luciano, he came to conclude that all the killing was pointless and self-defeating; there were better ways to settle the disputes that inevitably afflict any organization without littering vacant lots with dead bodies. It was not a good way for a business organization to solve personnel problems.

Business, especially the criminal variety of it, was something for which Lucchese had demonstrated an early aptitude. Thanks to his partners (and close friends) Lucky Luciano and Meyer Lansky, arguably the two greatest criminal capitalists who ever lived, he had gone on to learn a great deal about the subject. And now, with the Maranzano-Masseria war over and crime organized to a degree that promised an end to gang wars, Lucchese was ready to expand his horizons. Having already predicted the imminent demise of Prohibition—and of its attendant profits for organized crime—he began searching for an alternate source of income. By 1932, he had found virgin territory in which to demonstrate his talents. In the process, he would provide organized crime with an invaluable lesson. The chosen target was chicken.

The kosher chicken business in New York City during the 1930s was a $50-million-a-year enterprise, divided primarily among a number of competing slaughterhouses, the critical components of the industry. On tight profit margins, the slaughterhouses competed for business from retail outlets that in turn sold to one of the world's largest Jewish communities.

As Lucchese observed, the kosher chicken business was in fact composed of several distinct but interrelated businesses; as with the individual cars on a train, knocking out one car would bring the entire train to a halt. There were fifteen steps in the preparation of kosher chicken, beginning with the trucks that brought the live poultry from farmers in upstate New York and New Jersey, down to the *shochetim* (kosher killers), the highly specialized workers who slaughtered the chicken according to strict Jewish dietary laws.

Lucchese's idea was to gain control over at least one phase of this process, which he would then use as a lever to bring the rest of the industry into line. Unlike the black hand days, Lucchese did not intend to simply extort protection money from the industry. His goal was much more sophisticated—to take over the industry and force it to pay him regular tribute for the privilege of operating. And make them like it.

Fortunately for Lucchese's plan, not only was there a labor union that represented key workers in the industry (Local 167 of the Teamsters), but the union's business agent, Arthur (Tootsie) Herbert, also happened to be a crook. Enlisted by Lucchese as a partner, Herbert provided the key weapon: threats of labor troubles for those who did not cooperate. Co-operation meant the various components of the kosher chicken industry were to join a new entity called the New York Live Poultry Chamber of Commerce. Membership benefits would include a guaranteed, preset portion of the chicken business, and a guarantee of labor peace. In return, members would pay the association a "tax" of one to seven cents for each pound of chicken sold.

In other words, a cartel. In Lucchese's conception, the new organization's primary function, aside from making a lot of money for Gaetano Luchese, would be to fix prices. There wasn't much the retail stores could do about it, since there were no alternate sources of kosher chicken. Moreover, the association would enforce stability over what traditionally had been a chaotic, cutthroat industry, parceling out business among the various competitors on a sliding scale dependent on their prevailing share of the market. And since Lucchese controlled the association, he would decide who sold what to whom, in what quantity, and at what price.

For the industry, this arrangement would not only offer the advantage of labor peace in a business notorious for labor-management turmoil, but it would also hold the promise of regular increases in price (and thus in profits), since the competition would have been removed. As for the association's "tax," that would be passed on to the consumers. Customers might complain, but ultimately they would pay; for observant Jews especially, there was no other source of kosher chicken. These consumers would be paying the first "crime tax" in American history, soon to be joined by many more.

It was all quite illegal, of course. Federal law had long prohibited economic cartels, and there were plenty of state laws barring labor extortion. But nobody complained. The simple fact is that the industry welcomed the new arrangement, which is why there was virtually no violence in organized crime's takeover. No bomb blasts, shooting, or other violence marked a crime that took place almost invisibly. Lucchese's takeover of kosher chicken set the mold for organized crime's infiltration of legitimate business. Over the next sixty years, organized crime, aided by its partnership with corrupt unions, would follow the pattern established by Lucchese in its infiltration of construction, restaurant supplies, wholesale foods, and a dozen other industries.

For Lucchese, the legal risk was minimal. Although he was committing a federal crime, there were no federal agents sniffing around, no surveillance teams watching, no wiretaps or bugs to catch him in incriminating conversations. He could talk unconcernedly on his phone and could meet openly with some of the most notorious criminals in the United States.

Certainly he had no fear of the government agency that was supposed to end what many had called "the lawless decade," the newly resurgent Federal Bureau of Investigation. The FBI was just then beginning its assault on what it claimed to be America's underworld: kidnappers, bank robbers, and gangsters. But as Lucchese well knew, such infamous figures as Pretty Boy Floyd, Bonnie and Clyde, Ma Barker, and John Dillinger represented only a tiny segment of crime in America.

The *real* criminals like himself, the organized racketeers who were making all the money, were delighted to see the FBI expend its energies on the unorganized gangsters who got a lot of newspaper headlines but were essentially amateurs. The "most wanted" posters on Post Office walls did not include mug shots of Gaetano Lucchese or the other premier criminal capitalists just then entering the golden age of their careers— Lucky Luciano, Meyer Lansky, Albert Anastasia, Carlo Gambino, Frank Costello, Joseph Profaci, and Joseph Bonanno.

While they were sinking deep hooks into the American economy, the agency that should have been their main enemy became preoccupied with a very different foe, one that was not much of an enemy at all.

• TWO •

"The Kiss of Death Wants to Talk to You"

Keep your friends close but your enemies even closer.

GAETANO LUCCHESE

"**W**e are in big trouble," FBI Special Agent Ed Shaughennessey said morosely, staring at the blank report form. His partner, Special Agent Edward Miller, reacted in mock horror. "What's this we shit, white man?"

Shaughennessey didn't laugh at the punch line of one of the era's favorite jokes, for he was quite right: the two agents were behind the eight ball. Four months earlier, they had endured a severe rebuke from J. Edgar Hoover himself, who indicated displeasure with their performance. Now, Shaughennessey was preparing to type a report certain to further incite the FBI director's wrath. And in the FBI of 1956, at the height of Hoover's power, he was not somebody to aggravate.

The problem was a man named Gus Hall, very high on Hoover's list of villains. Thanks to a double agent planted in the inner councils of the Communist Party of the United States of America (CPUSA), Hoover was aware that Hall, one of its top leaders (he would become head of the party in 1959) was handling millions of dollars in covert aid from Moscow. The stipend was to keep the party going, for, as Hall was only too aware, CPUSA was on life support. Reduced to a few thousand adherents, the party was an ebbing flame on the fringe of American politics.

But Hoover saw a very different CPUSA, a cunning Communist conspiracy busily at work undermining every American institution. Communism had been a lifelong obsession to Hoover, who diverted a large portion of FBI resources toward making life hell for American Communists. Now he saw a golden opportunity. Suspecting that Hall would not be able to resist the temptation of dipping into the subsidy, he assigned two agents in the Bureau's New York office the task of collecting evidence of this presumed embezzlement which, Hoover was certain, enabled Hall to maintain a lavish living in Manhattan. Hoover believed that evidence of Hall's lifestyle, so at variance with the party's demands for sacrifice by its members, would, when made public, once and for all destroy the party's credibility.

But as much as Hoover was convinced that Hall was living high on the hog from Moscow's gold, his agents could find no evidence. Hall, they reported, lived frugally. Infuriated, Hoover rebuked the agents and ordered them to try again. The agents went back to work, exhaustively tracking virtually every cent Hall spent. Months of work produced the intelligence that Hall took the subway back and forth to party headquarters, washed his own clothes in a laundromat, and habitually ate meals in a greasy spoon. Mrs. Hall was equally frugal.

Faced with the career-threatening prospect of telling Hoover that his preconceptions were wrong, the agents prepared a lengthy report which detailed how they had left no stone unturned in investigating Hall's finances. The conclusion was unavoidable: Hall wasn't dipping into Moscow's subsidy.

As they feared, their report lit Hoover's fuse. He angrily ordered the two agents transferred out of the Bureau's career-enhancing Intelligence Division—the agents assigned to counterintelligence duties, including Hoover's war against the CPUSA—and exiled to the Criminal Division. There they would spend most of their time handling the FBI's highest priorities of the time, bank robberies and interstate auto theft. These priorities had been set by Hoover years before, mainly as a means of inflating the Bureau's statistics; both were easily solved crimes (bank robberies, for example, always take place in front of eyewitnesses).

There was one other investigative task assigned the Criminal Division: the Mafia. But it was easily the most career-stunting task in the entire Bureau. For one thing, J. Edgar Hoover himself had proclaimed that the Mafia didn't exist. No surprise, then, that in 1956 there was a grand total of four agents in the New York office assigned to investigate what they could only call "Crime, Organized," since the word *Mafia* was forbidden in any FBI written communication. Meanwhile, nearly four hundred agents were assigned to intelligence duties, many of them concentrated against Hoover's pet obsession, the Communist menace.

No better circumstance can be imagined for organized crime to flourish—as Gaetano Lucchese and his friends were to prove.

Coincident with his success in the kosher chicken industry, Lucchese had begun an apprenticeship in labor racketeering in the Garment Center, where the Jewish gangs had established a foothold. The Garment Center, where some two hundred thousand people worked, stretched over forty square blocks in midtown Manhattan, a jungle of apparel firms, garment manufacturers, and cutting and trimming rooms that operated in a constant cacophony—the blare of horns from streets choked with trucks, the clatter of coatracks full of clothes pushed down crowded sidewalks, a thousand street corner business discussions. To the uninitiated, it was a strange, mysterious place of arcane, unwritten rules, a secretive world where handshakes represented inviolable business contracts, personal contacts meant everything, and time seemed out of joint: summer clothing was designed and manufactured in the winter, while winter clothes were produced in the summer. The men and women who worked there often described it as a giant crapshoot at the mercy of American clothing tastes. Dozens of entrepreneurs, large and small, bet all they had (usually borrowed money) each season that their designs would strike the fancy of clothes buyers. Successes and failures both tended to be spectacular.

In the 1920s, faced with the new demand for ready-made clothes, the Garment Center was created to consolidate the network of sweatshops that existed all over New York City.

But it also consolidated the industry's biggest ulcer, bitter labor disputes. A series of violent strikes brought in the criminals from Jewish organized crime. Hired as strikebreakers by the manufacturers or as goons by the unions to intimidate management, criminals became an integral part of the unique Garment Center environment. One of them, a criminal visionary named Louis (Lepke) Buchalter, realized that labor racketeering promised much greater profit than head-breaking.

One of eleven children from a devout Lower East Side Jewish family, Buchalter quit school at fifteen to go into crime. His partner from that moment was his close boyhood friend, Jacob Shapiro. They made an odd pair: Buchalter was thin, with large doe-like eyes, and was noted for his shyness and very quick mind. Shapiro was a Neanderthal, a hulking, dimwitted hood known as "Gurrah" for his habit of growling, "Get outta here" in an impenetrable Yiddish accent that made it sound like a single word. Shapiro hated most of humanity, save Buchalter, to whom he was slavishly devoted.

Together, they were a devastating crime combination. The soft-spoken Buchalter presented the image of a reasonable businessman who at the same time managed to convey the implied threat that if reason didn't work, the inevitable alternative was Shapiro, a violent man who carried lead sash weights in his pocket to cave in the skulls of the recalcitrant. Shapiro liked to terrify prospective victims by summoning them in Yiddish to an encounter, *"Malchamus vil redentzu dir"* (The kiss of death wants to talk to you).

Buchalter, an original thinker in the business of crime, had a critical insight, the very same one that had occurred to Lucchese at roughly the same time: the key to profit lay in the unique nature of any particular industry. In the case of the Garment Center, the industry amounted to a series of separate, interconnected enterprises that depended on each other. The trick was to find the most vulnerable link in the chain and use it to extort the entire industry. Buchalter found it in one of the smallest unions that represented Garment Center workers, Local 4 of the Cloth Cutters Union. By 1933, the union only had 1,800 members in the Garment Center, but they were indispensable to the industry. These highly skilled workers, who required years of apprenticeship to perfect their craft, cut the actual designs in cloth, the result to be assembled later by sewers, who joined the pieces into finished garments.

Buchalter's takeover of Local 4, abetted by its corrupt leaders, gave him a supreme weapon, for any strike by the cutters would bring the industry to its knees; those workers could not be replaced by scabs. With such leverage, Buchalter was able to construct an elaborate system of payoffs by manufacturers for "labor peace." By 1932, he was raking in $2.5 million a year, with Shapiro and dozens of other hoods on his payroll to enforce the system. Ever on the lookout to work new angles, Buchalter began to consider further ways to tap in to the economic flow of the Garment Center. One innovation was to bring him into a fateful partnership with Gaetano Lucchese.

As Buchalter realized, the garment industry was held hostage twice each year when buyers for department stores, chain stores, and wholesalers arrived in the Garment Center to inspect the new lines and decide what they would buy. Obviously, these visits were critical: a manufacturer who had bet all his chips on a line that did not attract buyers faced ruin, while a popular line which the buyers snapped up with big orders meant instant wealth. So the buyers were assiduously courted—with sex, drugs, liquor, bribes, anything that might sway them. During Prohibition, the one commodity most prized by the buyers was high-quality liquor, and manufacturers began begging for access to the best stuff. Buchalter approached Lucky Luciano, who put him in touch with Lucchese, who in turn soon was providing a steady flow of cases of the finest imported whiskey. In the process, Buchalter and Lucchese struck up a close friendship. Impressed with Lucchese's criminal mind, which worked in ways very much like his own, Buchalter ushered him into the Garment Center rackets, a move that immediately paid dividends when Lucchese devised a number of innovations.

One centered on the vast sums of money that poured into the Garment Center twice yearly, when capital had to be raised for the new lines. How to tap into it? The answer was loan-sharking.

For decades, people unable to secure bank loans—a category that included most immigrant Americans—had been using neighborhood lenders willing to advance cash in return for relatively modest interest. Often, such deals had no written contracts; payment was largely contingent on the honor of the borrowers, who dreaded the shame they would have to endure in the neighborhood if they became known as deadbeats. Lucchese was among the first mafiosi who refined that old immigrant tradition into a thriving business, which featured two important changes: money would be lent at usurious rates to people who had no other recourse, and repayment would be guaranteed by the Mafia's most powerful weapon, muscle.

Lucchese became active in advancing money to Garment Center manufacturers who for various reasons could not raise capital anywhere else. He pioneered the so-called "knock-down loan," typically $50,000 for twenty weeks at five "points," meaning weekly interest of $2,500. The interest had to be paid first, which meant that a borrower could pay $2,500 for each of the twenty weeks, and still owe the principal. The profit to Lucchese was enormous.

However usurious, these loans amounted to salvation for a number of Garment Center entrepreneurs who had commitments from buyers, but wouldn't actually get the cash for another thirty days, the standard deal. But if they were already deeply in hock just to get the line prepared in the first place, they faced bills that had to be paid before any money from the buyers arrived. Enter Lucchese, who had the cash at hand to solve the problem. And in the event of nonpayment, he offered to wipe out the debt in exchange for a piece of the business, an apparently reasonable alternative to broken knees. Within a few years, he would come to own chunks of a dozen Garment Center firms, and at least seven of them outright. He then worked a further twist to the game by using nonunion labor in his newly acquired firms, enabling him to offer goods at lower wholesale prices than his unionized competitors.

Lucchese ensured a steady flow of loan shark customers by still another innovation, bribing bank officers to let him know when any Garment Center manufacturer had been denied a line of credit. Aware that the manufacturer would become desperate, Lucchese then showed up at the man's office, offering an "easy" way out.

As if all this were not enough, Lucchese went on to take control of another critical Garment Center function: trucking, the vital artery that moved finished goods from the shops to customers. Control of the trucking outfits—achieved via corrupted Teamsters Union locals—provided him with a lucrative subsidiary source of income, for he could charge whatever he wanted for trucking services. Because a squad of goons made sure no competing trucking outfit entered the Garment Center, there was no alternative. A pure monopolist, Lucchese later repeated this pattern in a number of other industries, including bakeries, wholesale food, and meat. (Lucchese guaranteed the highest possible quality of meat, although there were occasional slipups, such as the day one of his underlings, confronted with a question from a supermarket manager whether any horsemeat had been slipped into a shipment of allegedly prime beef, admitted, "Well, some of it moos, and some of it doesn't moo.")

All these operations, which featured close cooperation between Italian and Jewish organized crime groups, involved surprisingly little violence, a hallmark of Lucchese enterprises. The same, however, cannot be said for another and much more notorious operation in which he played an important role. Ironically, given Lucchese's reputed distaste for murder and violence, it would become the most infamous killing machine in the history of crime.

Originally conceived by Lucky Luciano as a way to systemize murder for organized crime, the cadre of killers that became known as Murder Incorporated began operations in 1936. Eventually, its roster had two hundred men, recruited primarily among Jewish and Italian criminals from the Ocean Hill section of Brooklyn, whose mean streets tended to produce criminals with rougher edges. The organization's recruits were first assigned as apprentices at a salary of $50 a week. If they showed promise, they would be promoted either to "finger men" (who gathered intelligence on the movements and habits of targeted victims); or "wheelmen" (who stole the cars used in hits, then later made the cars disappear); or "evaporators" (who made the bodies of victims disappear, usually by hacking them to pieces and encasing them in cement). Eventually, they might achieve the highest rank, "hit men," who for weekly salaries of $100-$250 carried out the actual killings.

Murder Incorporated, a name invented by a newspaperman to describe an organization that for security reasons had no name, tended to attract some truly frightening characters. They included Vito (Chicken Head) Gurino, who honed his talent with a pistol by shooting the heads off live chickens; Philip (Pittsburgh Phil) Strauss, whose hair-trigger temper once compelled him to jab a fork into the eye of a waiter who failed to serve him his dinner dessert quickly enough; Seymour (Red) Levine, a devout Jew who refused to kill anyone on Yom Kippur; Louis (Pretty) Amberg, a psychopath who liked to enter restaurants and spit into diners' soup, emptying the bowls onto their heads if they objected; and the group's most famous killer, Abraham (Kid Twist) Reles, noted for his ability to slip a rope around a victim's neck and strangle him to death with only one twist. When not engaged in murder, the killers liked to hang around in Midnight Rose's, an all-night Brooklyn soda shop, sipping egg creams while discussing various killing methods—such as jabbing an ice pick into a victim's ear, which would scramble the brains and convince an unwary medical examiner that the deceased had died of a cerebral hemorrhage.

Murder Incorporated was managed by Buchalter and Lucchese, with Albert Anastasia, an alumnus of the 107th Street Gang who had become an important Mafia leader in Brooklyn, serving as on-site supervisor. How many murders the three of them arranged before Murder Inc.'s demise in 1940 is not known with certainty; estimates run anywhere from four hundred to over a thousand. Whatever the total, the important point is that the mere existence of Murder Incorporated was a powerful aid to organized crime's infiltration and takeover of certain industries. Minds of the difficult or the stubbornly defiant in those industries were concentrated by the knowledge that a large number of people who had run afoul of the racketeers for one reason or another seemed to have mysteriously disappeared.

Murder Inc.'s reputation was also handy for another criminal enterprise in which the Jewish and Italian organized crime groups were involved: narcotics. An enterprise notorious for betrayal and double cross, it frequently required homicide to serve as an example of the consequences of failing to play by the rules. But as both sides learned, the business of narcotics was very difficult to organize and control. That was to cause organized crime no end of trouble.

The first recorded instance of drug-smuggling in the United States occurred in 1868, when one Wah Kee, a merchant in the Chinatown section of lower Manhattan, was arrested for smuggling opium to supply an opium den he ran for addicted countrymen. Rich people discovered this vice, creating the first narcotics market in the United States. In 1898, another market was created when heroin was introduced as a cough suppressant, followed by cocaine, sold as a tonic. Widespread abuse led to the 1914 Harrison Act and other measures that prohibited the sale and possession of all narcotics. Like Prohibition, those measures presented organized crime with a perfect business opportunity: addicts with money were willing to pay *anything* to get narcotics.

Jewish organized crime groups were the first to grasp the significance of this development and were soon organizing operations to smuggle narcotics from the then-leading source, China, building laboratories to dilute and package the narcotics for retail sale, and forming distribution networks to get the product into the hands of addicts. (By 1919, there were two hundred thousand addicts in New York City alone.) The profits were staggering: in 1923, a kilo (2.2 pounds) of pure heroin costing $3,000 at the Chinese source, its purity later adulterated and divided into 15,500 multi-grain capsules, would return a profit of $300,000. The leading trafficker, Irving (Waxey Gordon) Wexler, made so much money that he used only a portion of his profits to build a huge castle in New Jersey, complete with moat. Wexler and other traffickers operated with little fear of the law: until 1956, federal law set a maximum sentence of ten years in jail for narcotics smuggling, although in most cases the sentences were one or two years. Suspended sentences were common, even for veteran traffickers, and bail was usually set at $1,000—pocket change for men like Wexler.

Buchalter became deeply involved in narcotics, reinvesting some of the profits earned in the Garment Center into drug trafficking operations, including one ring that bribed ordinary tourists to carry kilos of heroin and opium in specially marked suitcases waved through by U.S. Customs inspectors whom Lepke had bribed. He brought his friend Lucchese into the business, an act of friendship he and the rest of Jewish organized crime would come to regret.

Lucchese organized a number of successful narcotics operations, including one that smuggled opium and morphine from Mexico to be converted into heroin, but he was always careful to respect operations run by Buchalter and other Jewish criminals. Not so the rest of the Mafia; to Lucchese's distress, they began to rush pell-mell into the narcotics business. Having heard of the vast profits to be made, all the careful arrangements under Pax Luciano were trampled as mafiosi of high and low rank surged into narcotics. Eager to replace the vast bootlegging profits lost when Prohibition was repealed in 1933, the Mafia fastened on narcotics as the instant, and equally profitable, replacement. It deliberately lowered prices to drive out Jewish competitors, took over distribution networks, and with help from the Sicilian Mafia, began to dominate the Middle East production areas. In only a few years, the American Mafia not only managed to elbow aside its Jewish counterpart, it also vastly expanded the narcotics market by moving into the inner slums, creating what became a heroin epidemic. By the end of the 1940s, the five New York Mafia families were responsible for ninety-five percent of all heroin smuggled into the United States, moving an alarmed Frank Costello to warn that the Mafia's deep involvement with narcotics threatened to destroy the public's live-and-let-live attitude toward organized crime. To its eventual detriment, the organization paid no attention to his warning.

The Mafia rush into narcotics marked the beginning of the precipitate decline of Jewish organized crime. Essentially, it was a one-generation phenomenon. The Jewish immigrant community had always been ashamed of its criminals, all the more incentive to sacrifice in order to make sure their sons went to college and became the kind of successes that would bring respect and pride to the community. There were few Jewish families who hadn't heard the gossip about Meyer Lansky's wife, who after giving birth to a son with cerebral palsy, screamed at her husband, "God is punishing you for all the rotten things you're doing!'' Then too, the federal government played a key role: the 1924 Reed-Johnson Act cut immigration of Jews from eastern Europe to a trickle, drying up the pool from which the Jewish gangs drew young recruits. As Israel (Izzy) Schwarzberg, a leading figure in Jewish organized crime, summarized it, ''We lost our farm system.''

While the Jews faded from organized crime, the Mafia acquired exclusive control of the narcotics trade. But this triumph came with a disadvantage: unlike racketeering, which thrived in in an atmosphere of police corruption, public tolerance, and political indifference, narcotics was the focus of a federal law enforcement agency free of such shackles. That agency would mount the first serious attack on organized crime, in the process divining its greatest secret: the organization itself.

The Federal Bureau of Narcotics (FBN) was formed in 1929 to combat the growing problem. A year later, a Prohibition agent named Harry J. Anslinger was selected to head the new agency. An energetic and skilled bureaucratic infighter, Anslinger was determined to make the FBN the premier federal law enforcement agency. That immediately set him at loggerheads with another bureaucrat who had precisely the same ambition, J. Edgar Hoover, director of the FBI. For the next thirty years, they would jockey for dominance in a bitter rivalry that would help paralyze the government's war against organized crime for a long time.

Hoover won most of the battles with Anslinger. Thanks to his clout with Congress, Hoover was able to offer salaries that attracted the best recruits, while the FBN, whose salary scales were one-third lower than the FBI's, had to settle for less qualified recruits. But Anslinger got more street-wise recruits (ex-cops, mostly) who were willing to get their hands dirty in the trenches. They pioneered many of the techniques adopted years later by the FBI: networks of paid informants, undercover operations, grants of immunity to criminals willing to testify against other criminals, and sting operations. (However, the FBN was notorious for its lack of attention to constitutional niceties. It tapped telephones without court order, routinely dragged in suspected traffickers for interrogations that often involved rubber hoses, and smashed through doors without warrants.)

It was not long before the FBN discovered that the Italian Mafia had taken control of the narcotics trade. Aided by the Mafia's precipitate rush into the business without its customary attention to secrecy and security, the FBN was able to pinpoint the organization's traffickers. More significantly, it was able to uncover the organization's structure. Within a few years, the FBN effort resulted in two thick books. One, with a green cover, was distributed to other law enforcement agencies, describing in broad terms how the Mafia was organized and the breadth of its operations. The second, in black, was much more detailed; based on intelligence the FBN had gathered from its high-level informants in the Mafia, it was given a very limited distribution (including a copy to J. Edgar Hoover, who ignored it). The so-called "black book" was a virtual Mafia encyclopedia, detailing the organization's history, its structure, its operations, and dossiers on eight hundred leading mafiosi.

Among those names was Gaetano Lucchese, who had become a figure of consuming interest to the FBN. His dossier not only included details about his racketeering in the Garment Center and other industries, but also outlined his role as one of the country's major narcotics traffickers. The FBN dossier noted how tantalizingly close it had come to nailing Lucchese—his presence at a meeting of top Mafia narcotics traffickers at a New Jersey restaurant (a bug failed to record Lucchese saying anything incriminating), and undercover informants reporting his contacts with Corsican and Sicilian heroin wholesalers. Most potentially damaging of all, the FBN had managed to recruit Eugene Giannini, another 107th Street Gang alumnus, whom Lucchese had enlisted as contact man with the Sicilian Mafia. But Giannini had no sooner begun cooperating when he was murdered. The FBN learned that Lucchese had ordered the hit after learning of Giannini's betrayal, probably through officials he had corrupted in the U.S. Attorney's office in Manhattan—a suspicion heightened when three other informants were murdered coincident with their identities becoming known to the same office.

Although the FBN began jailing Mafia traffickers, top mafiosi like Luchese escaped the net. Their immunity to justice stemmed from the Mafia's greatest strength, its central doctrine: the organization is supreme, far more important than any one man. People could be replaced; the organization could not. So long as the organizational system remained intact, with its layers of protection and lower-ranking members willing to observe *omerta* even in the face of prison sentences, the Mafia's upper echelon would remain beyond reach. Just how effectively the system worked was demonstrated in another serious law enforcement threat that arose at the very moment the Mafia was entering its golden age.

Thomas E. Dewey was remembered in the small Ohio town where he grew up as a combative, nasty bully whose temper constantly got him into fights. Later, as he went to law school and felt the first stirrings of political ambition, he grew a little brush mustache to hide an indelible impression from his youth, a split lip suffered in a street fight.

A Republican, Dewey had served as U.S. Attorney in the Southern District of New York during the Hoover administration, a job that provided him with a panorama of the Mafia's grip on a dozen industries and the vast corruption that protected what had become an empire of crime. Given the lack of federal laws on organized criminal enterprises, there wasn't much he could do about it before he was forced to resign his post in 1933, following the election of Franklin Roosevelt. But a year later, he was to get a new job that very nearly made him president of the United States.

Fiorello La Guardia, a Republican who was elected mayor of New York City the year after Roosevelt's landslide, took office in 1934 and immediately announced his intention of cleansing New York City of organized crime. Born in East Harlem, La Guardia knew all about men like Luciano and Lucchese, scum he felt had stained the image of the Italian-Americans. Fortunately Democratic Governor Herbert H. Lehman agreed with him. Lehman was shocked to read a grand jury report on organized crime in the city which strongly hinted that the criminals were being protected by corrupt police and equally corrupt district attorneys.

The result was the appointment of Dewey as special prosecutor. Setting up headquarters in a nondescript suite of offices near City Hall in Manhattan, Dewey was off to a running start. He recruited dozens of the sharpest lawyers he could find—"young tigers," he called them, men and women willing to work eighteen-hour days for low pay. Dewey's reputation was so high that some three thousand lawyers applied for twenty jobs, and seven hundred accountants applied for ten slots whose job description promised the challenge of uncovering the secrets of organized crime's finances. (Dewey became a hero to the Jewish community for hiring Jewish lawyers and accountants at a time when many prominent accounting and law firms would not.)

Those who signed up for what Dewey called a "crusade" encountered a man with a remarkable legal mind. He would sit quietly, staring into space as lawyers outlined their cases to him. When they finished, Dewey would minutely pick their presentations apart, having managed to memorize every single word as it was spoken. Often, he would quickly scan a thick document, then summarize all its important points from memory. Presented with a case announced as ready for trial, Dewey would listen, then brilliantly argue both the prosecution and defense sides of the case with equal facility.

Dewey set his sights high, against the top racketeers. These promised to be difficult cases, given the legal help such men could afford, and the layers of insulation with which they had surrounded themselves. But Dewey had decided on an integrated approach, marshaling experts on his staff into teams that attacked targets from several angles at once. For example, Dewey's prosecutors couldn't prove that Irving (Waxey Gordon) Wexler was a narcotics trafficker, but his accountants could prove that in a year when Wexler had declared to the IRS an income of just over $8,000, he actually *spent* nearly $2.5 million. Wexler went off to prison for tax evasion, and was scheduled to be followed by another prime Dewey target, Arthur (Dutch Schultz) Flegenheimer. But Flegenheimer decided to solve his legal problems by murdering *Dewey*. He made the mistake of announcing this colossally stupid idea to Luciano, who had him murdered.

Flegenheimer didn't understand that the murder of the highly popular Dewey would gravely threaten the organization, a lesson Louis (Lepke) Buchalter also had to learn the hard way. When Dewey indicted him for violations of the Sherman Antitrust Act, Buchalter jumped bail and went underground. In hiding, he announced his intention of murdering thirty-five actual and potential witnesses against him. Worse, his flight had ignited one of those "most wanted" episodes that dominated the newspapers, the kind of attention the organization did not like. Lucchese tried to solve the problem by meeting secretly with Buchalter, during which he told his friend that the Buchalter criminal empire would be put in temporary escrow "until you beat the rap." Buchalter exploded, telling Lucchese he wasn't giving up anything, and repeating his determination to carry out the thirty-five murders as his sole legal strategy to defeat Dewey's case. Lucchese said nothing, but later told Luciano that Buchalter was out of control. In such a mood, who knew what damage he could cause?

A beautifully Sicilian solution was devised. Buchalter was induced by Lucchese to surrender—to J. Edgar Hoover, of all people—on the promise that Dewey would drop a pending plan to charge him with murder. But, too late, Buchalter learned that no such deal had been struck; his old friend Lucchese had betrayed him. Ultimately, Buchalter was convicted of murder and executed in 1944, thus attaining the distinction of being the only organized crime leader in American history ever to suffer the death penalty. Also executed at the same time were Louis Maione and Mendy Weiss, two of Buchalter's Murder Inc. hit men who demonstrated their loyalty even in the face of death by ordering the same last meal as their master: chicken and shoestring potatoes.

Dewey's biggest target was Luciano himself, a glittering catch that even some of Dewey's most aggressive prosecutors doubted could be achieved. Luciano clearly was a criminal genius whose position atop the hierarchy of organized crime sheltered him behind multiple layers of protection. Undoubtedly, he was receiving regular tribute amounting to millions of dollars as his cut of the vast panorama of rackets he had largely devised, but there wasn't a scrap of paper to prove it. Luciano met regularly with minions to receive this money, but issued strict orders that nothing be committed to paper; his remarkable mind was able to keep track of every single operation and its profits, down to the penny. He was extremely careful never to discuss sensitive matters on the telephone, and anyone calling him was answered by the greeting, "This is 312 speaking." And the chance that there might exist any human being insane enough to testify against Luciano in court was completely out of the realm of possibility.

But, as Lucchese was the first to realize, Luciano had made himself vulnerable. As his empire grew, Luciano was becoming careless. He held court each morning in his $800-a-month suite at the Waldorf-Astoria, luxury accommodations that always featured several prostitutes lounging around. (Luciano had organized prostitution into a single enterprise controlled by himself as chief executive, although an assistant named David Petillo was in charge of day-to-day operations.)

Lucchese was appalled. He tried to convince Luciano that perhaps it was not a bright idea to have prostitutes in attendance when sensitive business discussions with organized-crime sachems took place. "Ah, whores is whores," Luciano replied. Surely no prostitute's testimony would ever be taken seriously, even if any of them had the brains to understand what they were hearing.

But, as it turned out, the prostitutes understood well enough. When Petillo, a knuckle-dragging hood, decided to enforce discipline within the ranks by beating up some of them, they became determined to exact revenge. Dewey's cooperative prosecutors provided just the revenge they were looking for; later, in court, witnesses pointed to Luciano as the overlord of the prostitution business. Contrary to Luciano's belief, the jury found prostitutes' testimony very credible indeed, especially when one of them remembered hearing Luciano say in her presence, "I'm gonna organize the cathouses just like the A&P."

Luciano uncomplainingly went off to prison in 1936, an act that solidified the organizational principle he had established just a few years before: the organization remains supreme. Before departing, Luciano ceded the reins of power—although his influence would remain strong during his prison years—and like a virus that has absorbed a violent attack and expelled the invader, the structure of organized crime continued undisturbed, under rearranged management. The organization's ability to withstand the assaults of the FBN and the even more serious attack by Dewey underscored its strength. True, the FBN had put a lot of Mafia dope dealers in jail, and Dewey had secured some spectacular convictions. But, taken as a whole, what was the real impact on organized crime? Not much, really; Flegenheimer and Buchalter had been sacrificed in the name of keeping the organization intact, and narcotics traffickers were easily replaced. Even the departure of Luciano caused not a blip in the smooth functioning of the machine. Individuals had gone to jail, but the enterprise itself went on.

How the organization handled other threats to its existence provided further evidence of its resilience. For example, there was the matter of Abraham (Kid Twist) Reles, the star killer of Murder Incorporated, who in 1940 decided to evade a murder charge by telling all. A man with a photographic memory, Reles filled twenty-five stenographic notebooks with blood-curdling details on how Murder Inc. had shot, hacked, bludgeoned, ice-picked, stabbed, strangled, and crushed a long list of victims. But when Reles began to get into the more sensitive area of the leaders who had directed this slaughter, the organization reacted.

Reles had been talking to the Brooklyn District Attorney's Office, whose head, William O'Dwyer, was a crook, long a part of organized crime's roster of bribed public officials. O'Dwyer alerted the organization that Reles was about to provide critical information concerning Albert Anastasia, Murder Inc.'s chief operating officer, and would almost certainly reveal even more damaging details on other leaders. A special fund of $100,000 was collected by Frank Costello for the purpose of bribing the police detail guarding Reles at a Coney Island hotel. One night, Reles was thrown to his death from the window of his room, entering Mafia legend as "the canary who could sing, but couldn't fly."

Thus insulated, the organization's ruling commission met regularly with impunity, including a 1946 session in Havana, Cuba, when a hundred crime leaders convened to decide a number of weighty matters, chief among them the problem of Bugsy Siegel. On the recommendation of Meyer Lansky, who had established organized crime's grip on the growing business of casino gambling, Siegel had been bankrolled with $3 million of the organization's money to establish a casino in the dusty little town of Las Vegas, Nevada. But Siegel was skimming some of the money, an unforgivable lapse that was punished with three bullets in his brain. As an indication of just how efficiently the commission handled such matters, within ten minutes of Siegel's death, three men walked into his casino, announced they were in charge, and in less than an hour had things running smoothly, just as though Siegel had never existed.

In 1951, organized crime shrugged off the first serious congressional investigation of its activities. It began when Tennessee Senator Estes Kefauver in 1950 spoke to the American Conference of Mayors and was bombarded with demands from city mayors that Congress do something about organized crime. Corruption had become pervasive in their cities, and was beyond the capabilities of local law enforcement to stop it. Later, Kefauver attended a conference of U.S. attorneys and was astounded to hear them claim there was no organized crime problem in the cities or anywhere else, and that no such thing as the Mafia existed. Crime was carried out by disparate gangs of hoodlums, Kefauver was told.

Obviously something was wrong, and Kefauver organized a special Senate committee whose mandate was to investigate organized crime—if it even existed—and to recommend any necessary changes in federal law. During the next sixteen months, traveling from city to city, the committee heard six hundred witnesses. The hearings, among the first such events to be televised live, fascinated the public. When they were over, the committee's final report concluded, "There is a sinister criminal organization known as the Mafia operating throughout the country."

But in terms of impact on organized crime, there wasn't much to show for all the effort. The committee recommended nineteen new federal laws, but only one was passed. A small organized crime racketeering section was created in the Justice Department, but, with only a few investigators and faced with J. Edgar Hoover's refusal to cooperate, it accomplished nothing.

From the Mafia's standpoint, the only real impact was on Frank Costello. He had been the star of the hearings, with his raspy voice and refusal to have his face photographed on television—so the cameras had to photograph his hands nervously twitching and clenching as senators accused him of being a racketeer. Costello not only lost face within the organization for this episode, but it cost him a lot of money. The IRS, intrigued by testimony about the vast wealth of Costello and other mobsters, formed a fifty-man task force and began digging into the finances of several major organized crime leaders in New York, chiefly Costello and Lucchese. Hoping to repeat its most famous success, nailing Al Capone for tax evasion nearly two decades before, the IRS auditors began burrowing underneath the grand facades of legitimate income the criminal leaders had constructed to conceal the mighty river of illegal cash. To the auditors' frustration, even the most pain-staking examination failed to catch Lucchese in a single slipup—his sprawling network of nearly sixty apparently legitimate businesses and interests in dozens of others filed meticulous returns without even a penny out of place. Initially, Costello's finances appeared as unassailable, but then the IRS discovered that for all his caution as a criminal capitalist, he was only human. Costello, it turned out, had a mistress he supported in fine style in a Central Park West penthouse, and anytime his wife discovered he was dallying there, she would exact revenge by embarking on massive spending binges—that Costello ignored to avoid possibly more serious consequences of her anger. However, those spending sprees constituted a paper trail the IRS followed to discover that she had spent around $570,000 over six years—money Costello hadn't declared on his tax returns. That cost him five years in jail and a $30,000 fine.

While Costello was undergoing his travails at the Kefauver hearings and the IRS auditors were busy at work, his old friend Lucchese was sitting in his modest Garment Center office, calmly presiding over the empire he had created. He was not subpoenaed before the hearings for the simple reason that the committee's investigators didn't know about him. As a further sign of his ability to keep a low criminal profile, the investigators asked the FBI for the names of prominent New York racketeers the committee should summon. Lucchese was not among the half-dozen names the FBI provided.

To outward appearances, Lucchese was the successful

owner of six dress factories in New York and Pennsylvania; a businessman noted for his remarkable ability to raise money for a number of charities. The charities sought to take advantage of that ability by convincing him to become finance chairman of fund-raising efforts; he always managed to meet or exceed the targeted amount. He was especially talented at fund-raising dinners, selling off all the seats at prices ranging up to $1,000 each. (At one charity dinner, twenty-two judges bought entire tables.)

That was one Gaetano Lucchese. The other was the highly respected criminal innovator whose counsel in the inner sanctum of organized crime was avidly sought. By 1951, although still a relatively young man, he was regarded as a Mafia senior statesman, a criminal genius on a par with Luciano. The breadth of his criminal empire was impressive—illegal gambling, hijacking, labor racketeering, race fixing, loan-sharking, and narcotics. He also had pieces of restaurants and profitable slices of the wholesale food and liquor distribution industries. How much money he made from all this was anybody's guess; it was not a topic he discussed publicly.

That same year, Tom Gagliano, head of one of the five families that ruled the Mafia in New York—Lucchese was its underboss—died of a heart attack. There was no question who his successor would be; Lucchese was immediately selected. He was ushered into the Mafia's innermost council, the Commission. Although the Commission represented the twenty-four major Mafia organizations from around the country, with each having an equal vote, in practice the five New York families, the most powerful and wealthy, tended to dominate that body. At the time of Lucchese's accession, those five equals-above-equals consisted of Joseph Bonanno, who had taken over the old Maranzano organization; Frank Costello, who headed what had begun as Luciano's old 107th Street Gang; Vincent Mangano, who was boss of a group that included such noted mafiosi as Albert Anastasia and Carlo Gambino; Joseph Profaci, who headed a family whose ranks included an ambitious young hood named Joseph Colombo; and Lucchese himself.

Lucchese's new role as godfather formalized his reputation throughout the entire Mafia as one of its great criminal minds.

When Santo Trafficante, Sr., head of the southern Florida Mafia, wanted to instruct his son Santo Jr. in the intricacies of organized crime, he sent him north to stay with Lucchese for a few weeks of instruction. An awed Santo Jr. returned to tell his father that not only did Lucchese appear to have his finger into everything, he seemed to enjoy absolute immunity because of his extensive contacts in the political, judicial, and law enforcement establishments. Some time later, Trafficante's lawyer and his wife visited New York. They were taken out for dinner by Lucchese, who asked the lawyer's wife if she owned a mink coat. Not necessary in Florida she replied, laughing, but Lucchese said he wanted her to have one. The next day, he escorted her to one of New York's fanciest fur salons and told her to take anything she wanted. She selected a full length black mink whose cost she estimated was somewhere around the price of a small house, noticing that the obsequious salon owner, practically bowing and scraping in Lucchese's presence, made no effort to mention cost. Clearly, he was ready to give away the whole salon, if necessary, to please so august a presence.

Within the Mafia's inner councils, Lucchese became close friends with Carlo Gambino, an extremely shrewd capo in the Mangano organization whose ferocious earning power had already marked him for future criminal greatness. Lucchese and Gambino were remarkably alike. Both had been born in Palermo, had come to this country as young boys, and disdained all signs of flashiness. They dressed in off-the-rack suits, lived in modest homes, and worked hard to keep very low profiles. (Lucchese, however, liked to twit his friend about his sole concession to vanity, a license plate on his car that read "CG-1.") They were also similar physically: both were small, thin men who seldom had to raise their voices to get results. The one difference was that Gambino was invariably calm, the very picture of the confident Sicilian patrician, despite a habit of drinking a dozen cups of strong black coffee each day. Lucchese was nervous and fidgety; he constantly scanned a room, as if searching for hidden enemies.

Actually, he had very few enemies because if there was ever a man who knew how to buy influence and friendship, it was Gaetano Lucchese. Indeed, he was legendary for his ability as a corruptor. In 1945, he arranged for a political hack named Vincent Impelliteri to become the Democratic candidate for city controller—equivalent to election in a city with a nine to one Democratic enrollment edge—an investment that paid off five years later when Impelliteri became mayor. Impelliteri, whose announced ambition was to "get my pitcha in de paper," saw his job exclusively as hosting visiting foreign dignitaries, including "What's her name, the queen of Greece." As Lucchese knew, Impelliteri was not about to order the police department to crack down on organized crime. Four years later, Lucchese pulled off an even greater feat, actually dictating who would become the U.S. Attorney for the Southern District of New York. He trumped that by arranging for an old crony to be nominated for a federal judgeship. These triumphs of corruption soon inspired whispers around the federal legal establishment that Lucchese had managed to corrupt the entire system in New York, possibly the reason why one U.S. attorney actually set up his own private mailroom to handle confidential mail and documents to keep them away from staff members he was convinced were on Lucchese's payroll.

Given this sort of high-level corruption, there was no mystery why Lucchese felt secure. He walked around without bodyguards or entourage, projecting the image of a moderately successful businessman. A man of regular habits, he stopped each night at a fancy restaurant in which he had a hidden interest (to satisfy a loan shark debt) for a pre-dinner cocktail. He stood precisely at the same spot every night at the restaurant's bar, which prior to his arrival was polished to a high gleam; any glass he might use was washed and rewashed, and his cocktail was prepared beforehand, chilled to the exact temperature he preferred. The space where he stood to sip his cocktail was kept clear; every few minutes, somebody would be introduced to him. Lucchese would shake the man's hand, immediately conferring instant respect on the recipient, whose reputation would soar on the mere fact that he had been permitted to be seen with Lucchese and had actually shaken the great man's hand.

Despite his wealth and power, Lucchese followed a conventional path of immigrant upward mobility. Early in his criminal career, he left East Harlem when he married a local

woman, Concetta Vassallo, in 1927. They moved up to the
next rung in the immigrant ladder, a small house in a middle
class New Jersey bedroom suburb just across the Hudson
River. In 1951, coincident with his elevation to godfather, he
built a $60,000 custom home in the upscale Long Island bed-
room community of Lido Beach. The neighbors knew little of
the new arrival, although they were impressed by the steady
stream of judges and politicians who visited his home. They
were further impressed when this "dress manufacturer," as he
described himself, picked up a phone one morning and arranged for a sick neighbor to go to the Mayo Clinic the next
day—after the neighbor had been told he would have to wait
three months to get in. Another neighbor, suffering from a
severe kidney ailment, complained to Lucchese about the difficulty of traveling to see specialists for treatment. Lucchese
picked up a phone and the next day a prominent Park Avenue
specialist actually made a house call at the man's home. Still
another neighbor, facing eighteen months in prison for tax
evasion, lamented to Lucchese about his misfortune. Lucchese
advised him to change lawyers and then apply for resentenc-
ing. "You will receive a much smaller sentence, trust me,"
Lucchese said. The neighbor did just that and sure enough, his
sentence was reduced to one month.

Not all the neighbors were so impressed. Some were disturbed in 1952 when they picked up their newspapers one
morning to read that their "dress manufacturer" neighbor had
been summoned to a public hearing of the New York State
Crime Commission investigating organized crime, during
which he had taken the Fifth Amendment sixty-seven times to
questions about his criminal career. In these neighbors' eyes,
Lucchese was a lower class Mafia hood who didn't really belong in a community like Lido Beach. Others whispered gossip
about Mrs. Lucchese, who had the tendency to wave her arms
and scream when agitated. "She thinks she's back on 110th
Street," one neighbor sniffed. Not even the graduation of
Lucchese's son Baldassare from the West Point military academy impressed the neighbors who looked down on the Lucchese family. They much preferred to exchange gossip about
another seminal event in the Lucchese household, the marriage
of Lucchese's daughter Frances to Thomas Gambino, the son

of Carlo Gambino. This union, which in terms of Mafia politics resembled the joining of two royal households, was marked by an elaborate wedding that for atmosphere could only be compared to the wedding scene in *The Godfather*.

Aware of the whispers, Lucchese made efforts to adopt a cloak of respectability. He joined the Knights of Columbus, evading the organization's strict requirement that applicants be of "sound moral character" and have no criminal background by obtaining a "certificate of good conduct" from the New York State Parole Board—a virtual pardon, obtained through his political contacts, which eliminated the only criminal conviction on his record, the 1921 auto theft. The same document came in handy when Lucchese, suddenly aware that his parents had never bothered to apply for American citizenship, feared he might become the target of a deportation effort. The state parole board's certificate eliminated the single barrier to citizenship, a criminal record. (He became naturalized by means of a so-called "private" bill in Congress.)

Within the Mafia, Lucchese didn't have to worry about gossip. What counted in that world was respect, and Lucchese got plenty of that. In addition to his reputation as one of the Mafia's most prodigious earners, he also acquired a reputation as a model godfather. "Everybody gets well in this organization," he often said, by way of explaining his theory of decentralized management. He kept his family small—just over a hundred made members—and allowed his capos wide authority to run their fiefdoms as they saw fit. These middle executives gradually became de facto bosses of specific territories, and the Lucchese Family evolved into a number of semi-independent satrapies—northern New Jersey, the Bronx, Long Island, and Brooklyn. Immensely wealthy, Lucchese disdained all forms of tribute from his underlings, encouraging them to allow the foot soldiers in the organization to keep the bulk of the money they earned.

As a result, Lucchese was the Mafia's most popular godfather, a benevolent leader who loved to devise new ways of earning money illegally and pass them to his adherents in the form of handy little tips. For example, he revealed that some doctors and dentists, hiding large amounts of unreported cash from the IRS, were looking for ways to invest that money at high return without having to use such conventional means as stock brokerages, which might inspire awkward questions. Lucchese enlisted them as criminal capitalists, offering the astonishing (and unreported) return of one percent a week on their money—which he put on the street at five points a week. Other tips could mean immense profit, such as the advice to his troops in 1964 to bet the farm on an upstart underdog named Cassius Clay in his heavyweight bout against then-champion Sonny Liston. There was no guesswork involved; one of Lucchese's underlings, Frank (Mr. Gray) Carbo, had taken over whole sections of professional boxing (at one point, three of five heavyweight contenders were in his pocket). Liston was entirely controlled by Carbo, so when Lucchese advised heavy betting on Clay, he knew that Liston had been ordered to take a dive. The fight began at 7-1 odds in favor of Liston, who inexplicably sat on a stool and refused to come out for the seventh round, giving Clay—later Mohammad Ali—a technical knockout. At those odds, the bettors on Clay made a killing. (Clay, it should be emphasized, knew nothing of the arrangement.)

Like a pirate kingdom centuries before, the Lucchese organization and the rest of the Mafia grew more powerful and wealthy during the American economic boom of the 1940s and 1950s, largely because there was nobody to stop them. And a large part of the credit for that priceless immunity goes to J. Edgar Hoover.

Even in a capital full of singular characters, there never was anybody quite like Hoover. His ascent to near-legendary status in the pantheon of law enforcement represents a tribute to the skills of a consummate bureaucrat, for in truth Hoover was no great shakes as a law enforcement officer. An inept, excitable mama's boy, he began as an obscure government lawyer and found his niche when he was given the thankless task of rehabilitating the scandal plagued Bureau of Investigation. Hoover demonstrated the talents that would make him a master of the Washington bureaucratic game—brilliant self-publicist, skilled infighter, master politician, seducer of Congress and presidents.

He dedicated every waking moment of his existence to the

new FBI he created; his mission was to protect and expand an organization that was his very life. At the same time, he wanted to perpetuate himself. He carefully fostered the legend of omniscience and indispensability, serving every president, Republican or Democrat, in whatever way the president wanted. If they wanted dirt on their political enemies, he provided it. If they wanted him to solve a crime problem that was disturbing voters, he did it. An unsurpassed master of congressional politics, the inflated appropriations Hoover won for the FBI guaranteed its existence—and his own.

The FBI that Hoover created was very much in his own image. Tightly controlled from its Washington headquarters, the Bureau liked agents who functioned as near-robots. The middle managers under Hoover who ran the FBI's field operations were selected primarily for their unquestioning obedience to their imperious chief. Almost exclusively, they were dull, small-town southerners or midwesterners who had started out as clerks in the Bureau, demonstrated sufficient obedience to be considered for higher rank, and fulfilled the agency's requirement for a college degree by attending some third-rate night school. Their knowledge of urban life was virtually nil, as was Hoover's, so they had no inkling of the crime revolution that was occurring in America's cities in the decades after Prohibition.

Street agents contemptuously called them "Gandy dancers," a play on the old term for railroad builders that referred to the bureaucrats' fawning attention to Helen Gandy, the redoubtable, ill-tempered spinster who served as Hoover's secretary for nearly fifty years and had supreme authority over who would be allowed to see him. One negative word from Gandy to Hoover was enough to destroy a man's career. Her boss ruled his FBI like a Florentine prince from the equivalent of a medieval castle turret, a thirty-five-foot-wide, mausoleum-like office dominated by a huge desk. A man of precise habits, Hoover arrived at that office at exactly the same time every day, and spent hours sitting there quietly, poring through stacks of cables from field offices. With a heavy pencil, he would mark comments and orders on the reports, occasionally frowning at a page whose typing had strayed a few characters beyond the rigidly prescribed borders. "Watch borders," Hoover would scrawl in thick letters. He broke for lunch at precisely the same time every day, when he would eat the same meal he had eaten for the past thirty years.

Hoover's chief aide and constant companion for all this time was Clyde W. Tolson, and the close relationship between the two unmarried men inspired much gossip. Many years later, rumors would surface that they were homosexuals fond of dressing in women's clothes. According to one especially salacious rumor, Frank Costello and Meyer Lansky somehow had obtained a photograph of Hoover and Tolson cavorting in drag. They quietly let Hoover know about the picture, which is why Hoover for many years kept away from investigating organized crime. This persistent rumor, however, isn't true; no such picture exists. The real reason for Hoover's avoidance of organized crime stemmed from a much more complex set of reasons, having to do with the law, the nature of the FBI itself in the early years, and the personality of J. Edgar Hoover himself.

The salient fact is that the FBI in the early years of its existence really had no mission. It had a vague mandate to serve as the investigative arm of the Justice Department, but at the time there weren't that many federal laws, and even fewer violations of them. It was Hoover who created the FBI's jurisdiction, always with a careful attention to politics. He first went after "subversives," since that's literally where the money was; Congress was willing to lavish funds on an antisubversive crusade because the voters were concerned and wanted something done. In 1932, a wave of kidnappings hit the country. Responding to a public outcry, Congress passed new laws making kidnapping a federal crime. That provided Hoover with the legal basis to attack kidnappers, in turn creating more goodwill with a grateful White House and Congress. In the same decade, Hoover conducted a crusade against notorious gangsters, most notably John Dillinger, for the simple reason there was growing political concern about such public menaces. Later, Hoover focused the FBI's energies and resources on Communists, again because that's what concerned the public, and Congress.

In effect, Hoover wrote the FBI's operational mandate as he went along, selecting targets for maximum political impact.

Concurrently, he created an image for himself and the "G-men" that he strictly controlled. He was perfectly aware that there was such a thing as organized crime, but it was not an area in which he wanted to involve his organization. There were five major considerations that governed his thinking: First, there was no real public outcry or congressional concern on the subject. Second, there were no federal statutes governing interstate racketeering. Third, combating organized crime would require working with other agencies that Hoover could not control. Fourth, and most important, even acknowledging the existence of organized crime would represent a concession to his most bitter rival, Harry J. Anslinger of the Federal Bureau of Narcotics. The more Anslinger insisted that organized crime existed and that it represented a severe danger to the country, the more likely it was that Hoover would claim the opposite. Fifth, Hoover preferred to concentrate the FBI's resources on easily solved crimes that he could use to bloat the tables of statistics he provided to Congress each year to obtain still greater appropriations. (The number of stolen cars recovered was one of his favorite crime statistics.) He did not want to jeopardize these statistics by getting into the business of investigating organized crime, an endeavor not very conducive to statistics.

Besides these bureaucratic considerations, Hoover—who in fact had very little grasp of criminology—subscribed to a very strange theory about the nature of modern crime. He was convinced that organized crime exists only in an environment of failure by local law enforcement, a failure that inevitably produces "celebrity criminals." Therefore, organized crime—and all crime, for that matter—was always a local problem, and had to be solved locally. The FBI's function was to offer local law enforcement technical assistance, when necessary, and provide a "model of professionalism."

As a result, the FBI's knowledge of organized crime was virtually nonexistent. In 1946, for example, FBI agents in Chicago moved against an illegal interstate wire that flashed race-track odds around the country for the convenience of bookmakers. They quickly encountered the organization behind the wire, the Chicago Mafia. Having no idea of who these men were, the agents submitted reports referring to the "reactivation of the Capone gang,'' as though Capone's old gang had stirred themselves from their Florida retirements to return to Chicago and recommence shooting down rivals in the streets.

The deepest pool of the Bureau's ignorance about organized crime existed in New York, the Mafia's primary stronghold. The man most responsible for the Bureau's ignorance was the New York field office's chief throughout much of the 1950s and early 1960s, John Malone. A former FBI firearms instructor, Malone looked as though he had just stepped from an FBI recruiting poster: tall, handsome, and silver-haired, he had a military bearing and steady gaze that suggested efficiency and intelligence. In fact, he was quite stupid.

Called ''cement head'' behind his back by his own agents, Malone was a Hoover acolyte eagerly responsive to his boss's every whim. From behind a magnificent carved desk in a converted warehouse on East Sixty-ninth Street, Malone was in charge of several hundred agents, the Bureau's largest field force. As Hoover directed, Malone had deployed most of them against the Communist menace, including men who spent their nights pawing through the garbage cans of Communists, presumably looking for secret messages from the Kremlin the recipients had carelessly discarded in ordinary trash.

Malone had a number of sensitive and secret duties in connection with this crusade, including liaison with Francis Cardinal Spellman, head of the New York Archdiocese. Spellman, unaware that Hoover's secret gossip files were loaded with details of the cleric's homosexual dalliances, was a fanatical anticommunist who volunteered devout members of his flock to serve as spies and ferret out secret Communists. Malone had to patiently winnow through piles of reports from these amateur sleuths, some of which recounted alleged overheard conversations seeming to suggest Soviet intelligence agents had taken to publicly discussing their plans in crowded bars.

When he wasn't hunting Communists, Malone was providing his agents with a rich store of ''dumb Malone stories,'' such as the time he introduced a visiting congressman to a black agent with the words, ''This is one of our black agents.'' Agents found him a pleasant man without any hard edges, but they learned not to present him with anything too complicated.

On the subject of organized crime, which was flourishing all around him, Malone knew absolutely nothing, and had no wish to learn. Hoover had said there was no such thing as the Mafia; therefore, there wasn't. Shortly after becoming U.S. Attorney General, Robert F. Kennedy made a courtesy call on Malone, and took the opportunity to ask, "Mr. Malone, could you please bring me up to date on what's happening with organized crime?"

Malone paused for what seemed a full minute, then replied, "Mr. Attorney General, I'm sorry, but I can't, because we've been having a newspaper strike."

Malone's preeminent moment came not too long afterward, when his agents conducted a rare assault that involved organized crime, arresting Charles (Ruby) Stein, a non-made associate of the Mafia who served all five families as New York's most accomplished loan shark. Stein, who had millions on the street at any given moment, was an intellectual who liked to read foreign policy journals. In 1960, curious to see the Red Menace firsthand, he traveled to Moscow, where he bribed a guard to allow him to take part in the annual May Day Parade. As he passed the reviewing stand atop Lenin's Tomb, he took a snapshot, then had another marcher take a picture of himself on Red Square to prove he had been there.

These snapshots were among the items seized by the FBI when agents raided Stein's apartment, looking for loan shark records. When he saw them, Malone went ballistic. Immediately convening a press conference, he brandished the snapshots and thundered, "I thought the Mafia was loyal to America! These pictures tell us that the Mafia is connected to the godless, atheistic Russian Communist Party!"

Gaetano Lucchese was among the mafiosi who laughed most uproariously at this episode, for it confirmed his organization's belief that it had nothing to fear from a law enforcement entity that seemed to have sprung full-blown from a Keystone Kops episode. But appearances were deceiving, for in fact certain forces had been set in motion that would ultimately change everything. Lucchese didn't know it yet, but seismic forces were already causing hairline cracks in the vast edifice of crime he and his friends had so carefully built.

THREE

Pontifex Maximus

This Cosa, Nostra, it's like a second government. It's too big.

JOSEPH VALACHI

They would begin arriving late each night, strutting male peacocks. From his vantage point behind the bar of the Playboy Club in midtown Manhattan, Charles Rose thought the procession of swaggering men looked something like a tribal rite, the male warriors showing off their fancy feathers and body paint. They performed their little gestures with all the seriousness of a solemn ritual—the hug and kisses on both cheeks for the most favored, the handshake and squeeze on the arm for those lower in the pecking order, the brief handshake and folded twenty-dollar bill for the fawning servant class, the jovial greeting for the unannointed, the grand gesture of generosity for the hangers-on.

As if uniformed, there was a remarkable similarity about them: $500 Italian suits, Hermés ties, $50 razor haircuts. Almost all were accompanied by a bimbo, also distinctively uniformed: tight, short skirt, low-cut blouse, bouffant hairdo, and heavy eye lining. These women all seemed to be named Sherry or Toni, and had a vacant, wide-eyed look. They were beauticians and manicurists, mostly, dolled up for a night on the town, clearly thrilled at being squired around from one hot spot to another and permitted, however briefly, to exist in the same orbit as these powerful male warriors of the Lucchese, Genovese, Gambino, Bonanno, and Colombo tribes.

Charles Rose knew them all: Jackie Nose, Bobby Shorts, Tommy Loops, Joe Pineapples, Al Two Thumbs, and the rest of the guys with nicknames keyed to a prominent physical feature or some important event in their careers. They liked Rose, the sharp young college kid working his way through school by tending bar, and there was a five-dollar tip thrown his way every so often to let him know they looked favorably on the way he mixed the drinks and that fast little patter he dispensed. But they always made it clear that they were the superior beings, the men of respect who ostentatiously whipped out thick rolls of cash from their pockets to peel off a few bills for drinks and regarded people like Rose with that slightly condescending look that said, *sucker.* They knew Rose planned to go to law school, a career choice that amused them. Why would a sharp kid like Charlie invest his youth getting a shingle? To help some old lady draw up her will? In that boom year of 1963, a smart kid like Charlie could be out there on the streets making some real money.

Rose endured these underworld homilies with the friendly bartender smile that took no sides and remained studiously agnostic. The first night on the job, he had been carefully instructed by his bosses on the delicate art of accommodating customers, with special emphasis on "the boys," as the club management quaintly called them. The boys represented a special problem: be friendly to them, but not too friendly; never pry into their business affairs; be polite to whatever bimbo they had with them any particular night (*never* inquire about the guy's wife in such circumstances); do not antagonize them; and, above all, always make sure they pay for their drinks. Any freebies might create the impression that the bad guys had a piece of the place. The boys could be real touchy; even one free drink might give them the idea they had a permanent free ride. They tended to get mean when people said "no" to them.

Rose managed to conceal his distaste for the nightly parade of bombastic mobsters who liked to offer career advice as they waved diamond pinky rings in his face and brandished their great bankrolls of cash. "A nice kid," the boys concluded about Rose.

They could not have known that this "nice kid" some years later would make their lives hell. In the interim, however, the boys were to provide Rose with two object lessons on how things worked in their world.

It began one night when Rose, leaving work for home, saw a man being severely beaten by several other men. Rose rushed over and broke it up, pushing the assailants away. As a crowd gathered, the assailants left, glaring at Rose, who recognized them as mobsters who occasionally came into the club. Rose sensed he was in trouble.

The next night, the mobsters waylaid him outside. "Hey, cocksucker, don't you *ever* touch any of us," one of them said as Rose was pushed up against the wall. From their looks, Rose assumed they would now break every bone in his body or, perhaps, kill him. Aware how mob protocol worked, Rose decided on a desperate gambit.

"Listen, my uncle's not gonna like this," he said.

"Your uncle?" one of them asked.

Rose sensed their hesitation. "Yeah, you know. Tony."

"Who's he with?" In Mafiaspeak, this was a critical question, seeking to determine if Rose was related to a powerful mobster and to which Mafia group that relation belonged. If Tony was a powerful mobster, laying hands on Rose could prove to be a fatal mistake.

"I'd rather not say," Rose replied with deliberate ambiguity as their grip on him loosened.

Rose's assailants conferred, finally deciding there would be a sitdown between themselves and Tony. That provided a temporary reprieve for Rose, but he now faced a major problem. True, he had an uncle named Tony, but he wasn't a mafioso. Actually, he was an assistant director of the FBI.

A frantic call to Uncle Tony produced a plan. Tony, eager to keep his nephew in one piece, would fly up from Washington and participate in the sitdown. He arrived, to Rose's amusement, in full Mafia regalia, including garish jewelry, the very image of the topflight mafioso.

While Rose watched nervously from the bar, Uncle Tony and the mobsters met at a table in the back of the club. Rose noticed that the discussion seemed animated; to his disquiet, he saw Tony at several points gesture with his thumb and forefinger in the sign of a gun, while some of the mobsters made gestures that seemed to signify how they wanted to tear various organs from Rose's body.

At last, the sitdown was over. "Everything's okay," Uncle Tony told Rose. "Who did you say you were with?" Rose asked him.

"I didn't. That's for you to figure out." With that, Tony left.

Rose was trying to think how he would answer this inevitable question when the mobsters, now apparently eager to be his friends, approached him. "Hey, no hard feelings, Charlie," one of them said, shaking his hand. "It's all straightened out. Uh, listen, who's your uncle with? You know, what organization?"

"Well," Rose replied carefully, "he's big in his organization, believe me. He's an assistant director of the FBI." The mobsters stared at him a moment, then started to laugh.

But not too long afterward, they weren't laughing anymore, and Rose was given another lesson in the way the Mafia did business. That one almost cost him his life.

He had arrived at the club one night to begin work when a car screeched to a halt at the curb. "Get in the fucking car," one of several mobsters in the car commanded.

Inside the car, the mood was grim. As they headed downtown, Rose began thinking frantically, trying to deduce why he was in this car, with men who clearly intended taking him on one of the Mafia's notorious one-way rides. They were ominously silent.

Possibly, Rose deduced, their somber mood was related to events of that morning, when the roof had caved in: three men had been indicted in a bribery scheme involving the Playboy Club's liquor license. Rose's knowledge of that episode was confined to what he had read in the newspapers. His companions on the automobile ride, however, had different ideas.

"Somebody's a rat, Charlie," one of them said, breaking the silence.

"Really?" Rose said, suddenly aware why he was being taken for a ride. "I guess so. I wouldn't know."

"Yeah, well, maybe it was you, Charlie."

Rose, now thoroughly alarmed, began talking as fast as he could, desperately trying to deflect their suspicion. "Me? That's crazy. I'm just a bartender, for God's sake. I don't know anything." He pointed out that in his lowly position, he never even saw the club's books, much less know what was in them. And he would hardly be aware of such sensitive matters as any bribery deals between politicians and club executives. (He carefully avoided mentioning any of their organized crime connections.) Finally, to his relief, the mobsters appeared to relax.

Rose played his last card, arguing that while he knew the mobsters who hung out at the club and bantered with them, he didn't know anything about their business dealings—certainly not enough to reveal anything of consequence to the authorities. Why, he had even scrupulously ensured that all drinks ordered by mobsters were paid for, just to be sure that no questions could arise.

At that, the mafioso behind the wheel turned to stare accusingly at Rose. "Yeah, that's one of the things we gotta discuss with you, Charlie. How come we never get no free drinks? You don't like us?"

Rose started to reassure him, but was interrupted by the command, "Get the fuck out." The car pulled up to a curb and Rose was unceremoniously evicted.

However dangerous, the episodes were instructional for Rose. He was struck by a simple fact: these alternately terrifying and Runyonesque characters made no attempt to conceal who they were, nor did they try to hide the big "Mafia wads" in their pockets, nor their expensive "Mafiamobiles" (black Cadillacs and Lincolns) they seemed to park wherever they liked. To be sure, they did not discuss publicly how they came by such wealth, but everybody knew they were criminals—hijackers, extortionists, labor racketeers, dope dealers, pimps, killers, loan sharks, bookies, gamblers, smugglers, strongarm artists. But they betrayed no sign of worry about being arrested as they swaggered into places like the Playboy Club as though they had not a care in the world. And if they felt like beating up someone on a busy midtown Manhattan street, they just went ahead and did it (to say nothing of picking up people in cars preparatory to disposing of them).

These were the men most often called "wiseguys," New York slang for men who existed in an entirely separate and mysterious parallel universe and seemed immune from the law. Certainly, some of them went to jail on occasion, but they were swiftly replaced. Somehow, no matter what happened, their organization endured, more powerful and untouchable than ever.

What made this air of untouchability all the more amazing, Rose realized, was that it existed at a time when the organization, most frequently called by the generic term "the mob," had just undergone the gravest crisis in its history, and the aftereffects were still playing out. Judging by newspaper accounts, it had been a deadly melodrama of power and ambition whose furies virtually tore the organization apart. Yet, to judge by the air of apparently unworried arrogance with which guys like Joe Pineapples and his goombahs continued to swagger around such places as the Playboy Club, the organization had managed to repair itself. How was that possible?

The simple answer, Rose concluded, was that the organization, as it had done on other occasions in the past, was able to absorb the kind of threat that would have destroyed any other kind of organization. So the key to its success was the organization's structural integrity, which also happened to be its most impenetrable mystery.

The crisis came from within and began in 1956. Initially, it was a crisis invisible to the outside world, for the weight of expert opinion had concluded that there was no such thing as the Mafia. Prominent sociologists like Daniel Bell, echoing J. Edgar Hoover, decried what he called the "myth of the Mafia," and even people who should have known better, such as Brooklyn prosecutor Burton Turkus, insisted that the organization did not exist. Turkus, who had prosecuted Murder Incorporated, displayed some curious logic for his conclusion, arguing that if there was such an organization, some law enforcement agency "would have tripped it up."

Meanwhile, the organization they said did not exist was thriving. Its unwritten treaty with the political establishment that had been brokered nearly two decades before—no violent crime that threatened ordinary citizens, no gang wars in the streets, no narcotics-dealing—had remained largely intact. To be sure, there were recurring problems over the Mafia's involvement in narcotics, but the organization's chief liaison to the outside world, Frank Costello, continued to drop strong hints that he was taking steps to stop it. Costello had become known as the organization's "prime minister" for his sub rosa contacts with the political establishment, a part he played well. To many politicians and police officials, Costello was the "reasonable" mobster who was keeping the animals in check, an illusion Costello did nothing to contradict.

Such an illusion served Costello well, for the bulk of his criminal profits came from illegal gambling, which required at least a degree of cooperation from politicians and police. To further foster his benign image as a businessman involved in harmless, nonviolent activities, Costello hosted intimate soirees at his Manhattan penthouse apartment for influential politicians, police officials, artists, writers, and newspapermen. The very picture of the gracious host, Costello urged his guests to try their luck at some slot machines he had spotted around the apartment. Those who decided to risk a quarter got a pleasant surprise: just one play, and the machines would gush hundreds of dollars in quarters. The winners would marvel about their amazing stroke of luck, not realizing Costello had fixed all the machines.

The host, looking cool and relaxed in Japanese silk pajamas as he lounged in front of a huge art deco bar, feigned amazement as the quarters gushed forth. Two hulking hoods in blue serge suits served drinks while Costello expounded on various issues of the day, trying hard to match the sophistication of some of his guests. The intended effect didn't quite come off, for despite Costello's best efforts—his constant study to improve his "dese-dem-dose" vocabulary and regular visits to a psychiatrist to overcome what he called "feelings of inferiority" that occurred when he was in the company of educated people—every word out of his mouth marked him indelibly as a street punk from East Harlem.

Costello's affability on such occasions concealed his deep worry over the strains his organization was beginning to undergo. The immediate cause was narcotics. Despite Costello's warnings against the trade, the Mafia continued to be deeply involved. To make matters worse, the Mafia leader most directly involved was Gaetano Lucchese, Costello's childhood friend, who simply laughed off pleas by the prime minister that he get out of the business. Lucchese said that the heroin the Mafia was producing by the ton was going "into the veins of niggers," and so long as none of it was distributed in Italian neighborhoods—and thus violate one of the Mafia's sternest strictures—dope was "good business."

The simple fact was that Lucchese, like many other mafiosi, found narcotics (heroin, primarily) irresistible as a vehicle for profit. His chief henchman for heroin, another East Harlem gang alumnus, was John (Big John) Ormento, who by 1954 was overseeing a $300 million-a-year business. Ormento, blissfully unconcerned about any legal consequences, openly called himself a dope dealer and liked to advertise his success with such touches as a huge wristwatch bordered in diamonds, belt buckle and tie clasp embedded with the same precious stone, along with three huge diamond rings on his fingers. His career illustrated one of the major reasons why the Mafia was so active in narcotics. Ormento had been convicted twice of narcotics trafficking in the years 1937 to 1941, yet when he was caught again in 1952, he was sentenced to only two years in prison. Another of Lucchese's traffickers, Frank Callace, also was sentenced to a mere two years, despite being caught red-handed with thirty-four kilos of heroin. As pointed out by an infuriated Harry Anslinger, head of the Federal Bureau of Narcotics, "A guy who robs a post office gets 15 to 25 [years]."

Such judicial gentleness was hardly a deterrent, and the Lucchese organization became even more brazen, turning an East Harlem street called Pleasant Avenue into a virtual open-air narcotics flea market. Traffickers hung around the street, openly making multi-kilo deals by an established system: big-time pushers would drive up, conclude a deal, then park their cars on an adjacent block. Local teenage boys, enlisted for up to $500 a day, were assigned the task of carrying cardboard boxes of heroin to the cars and putting them in the trunks, returning with other cardboard boxes they took from the cars, these full of cash. To dampen the temptation that one of the boys would simply run off with one of the cardboard boxes—which might contain up to $1 million in cash—occasional examples of the consequences of such thievery had to be meted out. One such example was the body of a boy found with his hands chopped off and a firecracker jammed up what remained of his rectum. He had made the error of dipping into one of those cardboard boxes, and his broken body was left in the gutter for all to see as a vivid warning. Traffickers chalked up these slayings to the "advertising budget."

Such drastic measures were considered essential to protect an enterprise that was earning money at a rate that even the most optimistic criminal capitalists hardly dreamed possible, not even during the golden days of Prohibition. As the heroin epidemic spread throughout the inner cities and the growing number of addicts continued to enlarge the market, large rivers of money flowed into the Mafia. By 1955, a kilo of pure heroin purchased for $30,000 from Corsican traffickers (known as the French Connection) would arrive on Pleasant Avenue and was taken to "laboratories" hidden in local apartments. There, women worked naked—to prevent them from secreting heroin in their clothes—mixing one part of the heroin to six or seven parts of milk sugar, then repacking the result into small glassine "nickel" (five-dollar) or "dime" (ten-dollar) bags. When all the bags were sold to addicts, the $30,000 kilo returned a $500,000 profit.

Obviously, this sort of open criminality could exist only with official connivance. In the case of Pleasant Avenue, Lucchese traffickers operated in actual partnership with the city police's narcotics squad; a system of payoffs—sometimes in the form of narcotics the corrupt cops sold on their own—ensured no legal interference. Occasional police raids were staged, usually against low-ranking dope dealers, to maintain the fiction that the cops were waging war against the drug menace. These raids were carefully orchestrated by Carmine Tramunti, Lucchese's on-site supervisor for Pleasant Avenue operations, who maintained what he called "the switchboard," a roster of corrupt police who instantly tipped him off about any approaching danger. Tramunti liked to brag, "I can buy any cop or judge in this city."

Perhaps, but as Costello constantly argued, it would only be a matter of time before public unrest over the heroin epidemic would set off a crackdown. The moment he dreaded came in 1955, when an obscure congressional committee, the Senate Judiciary Committee's Subcommittee on Improvements in the Federal Criminal Code, held a series of little-publicized hearings. The key witness was Anslinger, who recited the statistics of the heroin epidemic: a tripling of heroin-related deaths to over a thousand a year, entire inner city neighborhoods laid waste by heroin, and a fivefold increase in heroin addicts to nearly five hundred thousand. The result was the Narcotics Control Act of 1955, which set mandatory sentences of five to twenty years for a first trafficking offense, and ten to forty years for a second offense.

Anslinger's agents went to work, and among their first catches was a big fish: John Ormento, Lucchese's chief wholesaler, who had just finished a brief sentence for heroin trafficking. Ormento anticipated another short sentence, but after being convicted, he was shocked when the sentencing judge threw the new book at him: forty years in jail. Another prominent Lucchese trafficker, Natale Evola, got twenty years. Ormento and Evola were among a rich haul of Mafia traffickers the FBN was reeling in; within eighteen months of the passage of the 1955 law, 206 of them had been arrested and convicted.

The consequences of this disaster dominated the agenda of the ruling Commission's annual conclave in 1956. Costello had already forbidden narcotics dealing by any member of his family, and he urged that the ban be made Mafiawide. But the best he could accomplish was a general ban that carried no penalties. Without a penalty, Costello—and every other mafioso—was aware that a rule missing teeth had no hope of ending a money machine that could earn $500,000 on a $30,000 investment.

The narcotics problem exacerbated some already tense relations within the Commission itself. There was already growing tension between Lucchese and Costello over narcotics; Costello suspected, correctly, that although Lucchese paid lip service to the new rule, he had no intention of adhering to it. At the same time, Costello had another worry: his underboss, Vito Genovese, had begun demonstrating symptoms of vaunting ambition, and there were whispers that he intended to take over by getting rid of his boss. In turn, that created tension between Genovese and Albert Anastasia, who had become head of Vincent Mangano's family organization when Mangano disappeared in 1951. It was widely assumed that Anastasia had gotten rid of Mangano, and there were suspicions he intended to take control of the entire Mafia by the same method. The rest of the Commission was afraid of Anastasia, and with good reason. A psychopath, Anastasia was known as "the mad hatter" for his preference of wearing a hat while killing people. How many people he had murdered was a matter of speculation; given his fondness for murder, estimates ran into the dozens. Lucchese particularly despised Anastasia, who threw the 1956 summit meeting into turmoil by openly accusing Lucchese of plotting to murder him. Lucchese denied it, and accused Anastasia of trying to murder *him*. Meanwhile, Anastasia's second in command, the ambitious Carlo Gambino, was quietly putting out feelers about a deal under which he would be given leadership of the Mangano organization in exchange for getting rid of the increasingly unstable Anastasia. The developing plot was regarded cautiously by Joseph Bonanno, who intended to take control himself—once he got Anastasia, Lucchese, Costello, and Genovese out of the way. It was, Lucchese observed, like a dinner party at the palace of the Borgias in Renaissance Italy, where all the guests were afraid to sample the soup because they assumed their fellow guests had laced it with poison.

An absolute mess, and all the intrigue made the next sequence of events inevitable. On May 2, 1957, Genovese dispatched a dimwitted hood named Vincent (The Chin) Gigante to shoot Frank Costello. Gigante managed to get within a few feet of his target, but the shot entered Costello's scalp just below the skin, traveled around his entire head, and came to rest in his hat. An unusual wound, but sufficient to convince Costello it was time to retire. Already a multimillionaire and sick of the intrigue, he walked away from the organization which he had done so much to elevate to wealth and power and spent his last days on his Long Island estate. Nearly six months later, on October 25, Albert Antastasia was not so lucky. Relaxing in a chair at a Manhattan barber shop, he was blown apart by a four-man hit team of Brooklyn hoods whose leader later liked to joke, ''From now on, you can call us the barber shop quartet.''

The deadly sequence of events mandated another Mafia summit. Unfortunately for the organization, it took place on November 14, 1957, at the Apalachin, New York, estate of Joseph Barbara, a senior capo in the Buffalo Mafia. The sprawling estate had been used for the 1956 summit, but the 1957 conclave, designed to resolve all the pending problems and tensions, had a larger than usual turnout—113 men from every corner of the country. So sudden an infusion of strangers into the small town's limited hotel space attracted the attention of the New York State Police, which began checking up on the backgrounds of the guests. Meanwhile, as flunkies broiled steaks and sausages on an outdoor grill, the hierarchy of the American Mafia convened in Barbara's mansion.

There were a number of important items on the agenda, chief among them the recurring narcotics problem. The consensus was that the new narcotics law made drug dealing too dangerous, so the 1956 ban was given teeth: henceforth, any made member found to be dealing in narcotics was to be killed, with no appeal. Lucchese was among the attendees who voted for the hardened ban, although his colleagues assumed his organization, the Mafia family most actively involved in narcotics, would somehow find a way around it. The meeting had progressed to other items on the agenda—including the elevation of Carlo Gambino to replace Anastasia, the confirmation of Vito Genovese as successor to Costello, and a vow that Commission members would stop shooting each other—when the alarm went up: the State Police had arrived. Mafiosi scattered in all directions, but sixty-three of them were arrested on vague charges. Lucchese was among those who evaded the raid.

The police heard all kinds of interesting explanations from those detained on why they had traveled so far from their homes to attend a barbecue. The most fascinating reason was offered by Paul Castellano, an important capo in the Gambino Family, who claimed he suffered heart problems (although he was only forty-two years old). He went to Barbara's place, he said, because he wished to consult with him about what measures he took to ease his own cardiac problems.

Given the unwelcome glare of publicity and the grave embarrassment the episode had caused the organization, not many mafiosi found this kind of flippancy funny. Two other men would find it even less funny, and they were in a position to cause the organization some real problems.

One was Robert F. Kennedy, the young counsel to the Senate Rackets Committee. Repeatedly told by J. Edgar Hoover that the Mafia did not exist, Kennedy now learned that a nonexistent organization had somehow managed to hold a summit meeting. He burst into Hoover's office—"without an appointment," a shocked Hoover later reported—and asked what information the FBI director had on the names of seventy Apalachin attendees, including Gaetano Lucchese. Hoover meekly replied that the Bureau had files on only forty of them (not including Lucchese), and these files consisted mostly of newspaper clippings. Kennedy stalked out of Hoover's office, his mood further worsened when he read that day's newspaper reporting the comment of the FBI's Buffalo SAC (special agent in charge) that the Apalachin summit was "just a picnic." He went on to say it could not have been a Mafia summit meeting because the Mafia didn't exist.

Kennedy knew better, for during the past several years his committee had gathered a small mountain of evidence that provided unmistakable indications that such a thing as the Mafia did indeed exist, and was busy robbing the country blind. Among the more helpful witnesses was Harry Anslinger of the Federal Bureau of Narcotics, who provided Kennedy with details from the agency's vast files. After his encounter with Hoover, Kennedy went to see Anslinger, who happily gave him the files on the seventy mafiosi about whom Hoover knew virtually nothing—including a six-inch-thick file on Gaetano Lucchese. Thus armed, Kennedy subpoenaed Lucchese before the committee. "I am a dress manufacturer," Lucchese said, then took the Fifth Amendment to Kennedy's next eighty-seven questions, most of them concerning labor racketeering and narcotics.

Hoover regarded this course of events with alarm. He did not like being embarrassed, and, even worse, his hated rival Anslinger had suddenly become the government's specialist on organized crime. To redress the balance, Hoover ordered a crash program. One of his deputies, William C. Sullivan, the Bureau's expert on American communists, was told to drop everything and find out everything there was to know about the Mafia. With no FBI files to work with, one of Sullivan's underlings, a research specialist, plunged into the back issues of the *New York Times* for the past hundred years, then read two hundred books on the subject. After months of sixteen-hour days that wrecked his health, he emerged with a two-volume study which concluded that the Mafia indeed existed. Confronted with the evidence, Hoover finally gave up. He didn't even bother reading the study, but sent a brief memo to Sullivan that read, "It is not now necessary to read the two-volume monograph to know that the Mafia does exist in the United States."

His next two moves were pure Hoover. First, he ordered every FBI field office in the country to begin a "Top Hoodlum Program." Each office was to prepare a list of ten "top hoodlums"—no more, no less—and target them for investigation and prosecution. The arrival of this order in such disparate FBI field offices as Butte, Montana, and New York City created two very different reactions. In Butte, where the last significant violation of federal law had occurred forty years before (and where, in any event, there were no mafiosi), the field office desperately searched for hoodlums to put on the list. Finally, it listed ten local juvenile delinquents and vowed a full investigation of their "criminal activities." Headquarters praised Butte for its diligence. New York, however, had a much different problem. Ten hoodlums represented a drop in the bucket; from an embarrassment of riches, whom to select? The New York office finally selected ten low-ranking hoods at random, and was also praised for its diligence.

The second Hoover move was to have much more serious consequences. He ordered "eleurs" (Bureau jargon for electronic bugs) in "strategic places," meaning not telephones; mobsters long ago learned that phones were unsafe, and tended not to discuss anything sensitive over telephone lines. Hoover wanted the bugs planted in the secret places where the mafiosi talked business. But very few of his agents had any idea of where such sensitive discussions took place. Finally, extensive surveillance by a group of aggressive young agents in Chicago spotted such an inner sanctum: a room above a tailor shop that seemed to attract an unusual number of visitors, all of them members of the Chicago Mafia. One agent, William Roemer, was asked to install a bug under "Mission Impossible" conditions: the bug would be installed without court order, and since it was illegal, Roemer, if caught, would be declared a rogue agent and prosecuted. Roemer, who later said he was "just young and stupid enough" to agree, dutifully installed an electronic bug in the room's baseboard, then waited to see what it produced.

The result was pure gold. It turned out that the room was used by the Chicago organization's new boss, Salvatore (Momo) Giancana, for his most sensitive business discussions. Tape reels were soon filled with talk about "points" the Chicago and New York Mafia organizations were taking out of Las Vegas casinos, gossip about various Mafia leaders, and, most intriguing of all, references to something called "the commission."

The spectacular success of the Chicago bug, code-named Little Al, led to the installation of other bugs around the country. They began to gush further evidence, if needed, that the Mafia indeed existed, and was being administered by a secret entity known as the Commission. Gradually, as the tape transcripts piled up, a picture of the Mafia's internal structure and the breadth of its operations began to come into focus. But Hoover appeared more intrigued with less weighty matters the bugs were collecting: gossip about politicians or prominent people.

Few in the FBI knew that for many years Hoover had maintained what he called a "personal file," actually several filing cabinets' worth of derogatory or incriminating material culled from FBI reports about leading public officials and assorted movers and shakers. This collection of dirt, gossip, and rumor was intended as potential blackmail material to perpetuate himself in office; those in power were reluctant to challenge Hoover when they heard—and Hoover made sure they heard—that the FBI director might have secret files on them, reputedly chock-full of whatever misdeeds they had ever committed.

Hoover paid special attention to the transcripts of one particular bug, which had been planted in Meyer Lansky's home. The bug was unproductive (the veteran mobster was very careful of what he said, even in the privacy of his own home), and the tape transcripts were mostly idle conversations with his wife. But among those conversations was one in which Lansky told his wife of hearing "rumors" that Robert Kennedy was having an affair with an unnamed woman in El Paso. "Oh, dear," a shocked Mrs. Lansky replied. "And he has seven children!"

Actually, the rumor was false, but the tidbit was added to a new secret file Hoover had opened on Kennedy. Hoover had begun the Kennedy file on the assumption that Kennedy at some point would become important in the life of J. Edgar Hoover. He turned out to be right.

However inane, the Top Hoodlum Program nevertheless had the effect of diverting an increased number of FBI agents into organized crime investigations for the first time. Added to the numbers of agents involved in Hoover's secret program of bugging, there was at least the nucleus of a force of agents who had begun to acquire some expertise on the Mafia.

How to combat this criminal menace, however, was a different matter. The agents operated with a number of handicaps, including a lack of specific antiracketeering federal laws that would form the basis for investigations. Additionally, there were several Hooveresque dictates from headquarters: no cooperation with local police, no contact with the hated FBN, and no deviation from the FBI's strict codes governing agent conduct—including the Bureau's rigid dress code of white shirt and dark suit, hardly the kind of outfit suitable for agents to get down in the trenches with the mafiosi.

The agents weren't getting much help from the Justice Department, either. In response to the publicity generated by the Apalachin episode, the following year the department created the Attorney General's Special Group on Organized Crime. It sounded impressive, but Hoover ordered his agents not to have anything to do with the group, which meant that the two dozen lawyers assigned to it had no investigative resources. And since they had very little knowledge of organized crime in the first place, Hoover's stricture put them completely in the dark.

Their first and highly publicized "attack on organized crime" was to indict twenty of the attendees at the Apalachin meeting on charges of "conspiracy to obstruct justice," notably the mobsters' refusal to tell a grand jury what went on during the meeting. A federal jury bought this legally dubious case, but all the convictions were later thrown out by appeals courts, which warned the Justice Department that if it wanted to crack down on organized crime, it had better find some real evidence.

Despite the obstacles, a small cadre of FBI agents began trying to find that evidence. To a large extent, they were operating in the dark. There was no manual on how to conduct organized crime investigations, so the agents began writing one as they went along. But in order to do so, they had to evade some of the more rigid and archaic FBI traditions, evasions that if discovered by Hoover would have meant the end to their careers. In New York, agents Guy Bernardo and Paul Brana began to devise the first undercover operations against the Mafia, despite the Bureau's longstanding antipathy toward such operations (Hoover feared undercover operations would expose his men to corruption). When headquarters rejected their ideas for undercover work, making it clear they would not authorize any money for such essentials as sharp suits and the kind of expensive jewelry an agent posing as a criminal would wear, the two agents approached friendly jewelers and the owners of unscaled men's stores to lend the necessary props of expensive suits and diamond pinky rings. (They didn't bother telling headquarters what they had done.)

Others, including a young agent in Detroit named Neil J. Welch, took the grave risk of establishing secret contact with FBN agents. When Welch asked an FBN agent with whom he had become friendly whether the FBN had any intelligence on Mafia membership, the agent replied, "Are you kidding?" He then gave Welch a five-page list, with four columns to a page, containing the names and relevant backgrounds of three hundred top mafiosi from around the country. Welch made copies of this list and covertly distributed it to other agents involved in organized crime investigations; copied and recopied, the list assumed the status of *samizdat*, the underground literature of Soviet dissidents secretly passed hand to hand. Like a dedicated band of medieval monks, the agents pored over the list as if it were a sacred document, all the while aware of what would happen should headquarters learn they were actually reading a document prepared by that tool of Satan, the Federal Bureau of Narcotics.

In addition to the covert contacts with the FBN, some agents in New York had established another forbidden relationship by connecting with a New York City Police detective named Ralph Salerno. Considered law enforcement's leading expert on the Mafia, Salerno was among a unit of thirty handpicked detectives who worked for a secret police intelligence unit that was supposed to keep track of organized crime. Their task was frustrating because the police department clearly did not attach a high priority to their work—they were given very little money (the entire police budget for paying confidential informants was $30,000 for a force of nearly thirty thousand cops), and had to make do with old unmarked cars with which they were supposed to conduct surveillances on mafiosi zipping around in Cadillacs and Lincolns.

Nevertheless, the always optimistic Salerno had managed to accumulate a massive data bank on the Mafia and its operations—the fruits of surveillances, some wiretaps, a few confidential informants, and Salerno's own unique background. Born in East Harlem, he had known many mobsters from childhood, such as Lucchese and Costello, and had grown to hate them all. A master of the unique rhythms and codes of the street, Salerno knew the Mafia world cold, and he was one of the few cops the mafiosi actually feared. (For one thing, he was incorruptible.)

Nevertheless, Salerno was endlessly frustrated because his own department and the district attorneys demonstrated very little interest in using his information. He was especially vexed by the sight of arrogant mobsters walking around the city as if they owned it (to a large extent, they did), and shrugging off a rare legal assault—a $100,000 bail bond raised with a phone call, the city's best legal minds enlisted for a defense, and, the final act in the farce, the crumbling of a case in court when witnesses demonstrated a sudden forgetfulness.

Salerno was more than willing to be helpful when FBI agents approached him, although they had to endure his teasing about the organization he called "La Feebia." He would inquire after the health of *capo di tutti capi* J. Edgar Hoover, then wonder aloud if the FBI director was wearing a dress or a suit to work that day. The FBI agents tolerated these barbs, for Salerno was taking the FBI to school, opening the vast system of his files and patiently instructing them in the art of divining what was going on inside the Mafia. It was Salerno who let the FBI in on a simple but valuable technique: always conduct surveillances on Mafia social rituals. Like the clues that revealed the latest shifts in the Soviet Politburo—such as the size of type used in *Pravda* for the name of a Politburo member—changes in the Mafia power structure could be read and interpreted, provided the watchers knew what they were looking for. The Mafia was a rigid social organization, Salerno pointed out; who stood next to whom at the funeral of an important Mafia leader and which man received the most elaborate shows of respect would reveal much about shifts in leadership. For all their attention to security, mafiosi were imprisoned by an ancient code which required them to make elaborate gestures of respect to higher-ups and mandated specific roosts in the pecking order, decreeing their precise role and position in every possible social occasion.

As the FBI agents began to acquire a much better working knowledge of the Mafia's world, la Cosa Nostra became aware that there were new players in the game. While most mafiosi considered the guys sniffing around their territory just new, minor irritants to contend with, some mobsters took special umbrage. In Cleveland, for example, the local Mafia was so annoyed that one of its senior capos vowed to kill an agent he had spotted taking pictures of his mansion. The threat was overheard by an FBI wiretap, and agents decided the Cleveland Mafia would have to be taught an object lesson. Aware that the mafioso had a prized collection of indoor plants inside his mansion, agents broke in one night and urinated on all of them. A few days later, as the puzzled mobster considered his wilted specimens, he received a call from an FBI agent asking him politely how his beautiful plants were doing. There was no further talk in the Cleveland Mafia about killing FBI agents.

Meanwhile, the FBI's wiretaps provided priceless insight into the Mafia's structure and how it operated, along with an unvarnished portrait of la Cosa Nostra. No one listening to mafiosi sitting around in what they thought were their inviolable sanctums, discussing crime and mayhem with the casual air of ordinary citizens chatting about crabgrass, could ever doubt the real nature of these men and their organization. A bug in Chicago recorded several hoods laughingly reminiscing over the four-hundred-pound loan shark they had been ordered to murder. They accomplished the task by stripping him naked, impaling him through his rectum on a meathook, then spending the next several hours torturing him to death with a cattle prod. In New Jersey, a bug concealed in the hangout of a local mobster named Angelo (Gyp) DeCarlo heard even more grisly reminiscences that showed the inner workings of the Lucchese Family.

DeCarlo liked to talk about his close friend, a Mafia legend named Riccardo (Richie the Boot) Boiardo, noted as a virtual one-man murder machine. Boiardo was a leading light of the Lucchese Family's New Jersey faction and a friend of Lucchese, for whom he disposed of murder victims (and those of other families). For bodies that were supposed to disappear—as opposed to those left in plain view as an object lesson—Boiardo burned them in a large crematorium hidden in a corner of his hundred-acre estate. The rest of the estate featured a thirty-room mansion and lifesize statues of Boiardo and members of his family. Boiardo also used the crematorium as an execution chamber for certain victims he wanted to kill personally, usually by beating them to death with the assistance of his son Anthony, an apprentice in the murder trade. For amusement, the elder Boiardo occasionally liked to dispose of live victims by tying them to an iron grill in his oven and slowly roasting them to death. When not busy killing, he liked to putter around his vegetable garden, which contained a large sign reading GODFATHER'S GARDEN, apparently meant to deter the local raccoons.

Boiardo's crematorium was a chamber of horrors, as recalled in one of DeCarlo's overheard conversations when he was reminiscing with Anthony Boiardo.

"How about the time we hit the little Jew?" the younger Boiardo prompted.

"As little as they are, they struggle," DeCarlo said.

"The Boot hit him with a hammer," Anthony recalled. "The guy goes down and he comes up. So I got a crowbar this big. Eight shots in the head!" While DeCarlo laughed uproariously, Anthony went on to relate how the victim, despite his face smashed to a pulp, somehow managed to spit and curse at his murderers before the mercy of death.

As horrifying and revealing as these tapes were, there was a problem in that they could not be used as evidence because the bugs that produced them were illegal. That obstacle, combined with the paucity of federal laws on interstate crime, meant that for all the post-Apalachin publicity about the FBI's new war on organized crime, there was little to show for it. By 1960, a grand total of thirty-five mobsters in the United States had been convicted of various federal charges, most of them low-level hoods. The prison terms were short. The Mafia's middle and upper ranks remained untouched, a fact which did not bother Hoover in the slightest. In his view, he had already achieved important victories, all bureaucratic: he had apportioned some of his resources to the crusade while avoiding the necessity of working with other law enforcement agencies (thus solidifying the FBI's independence), displaced the hated FBN as the government's spearhead against organized criminals, and, thanks to the Bureau's efficient publicity machine, had assumed primacy in the public's mind in the war against organized crime.

But Robert Kennedy wasn't impressed, and in 1961 what must have been the FBI director's worst nightmare came to pass: he became Hoover's boss. Kennedy's elevation suddenly complicated Hoover's life, for the new U.S. attorney general announced his intention to eradicate organized crime. He surrounded himself with a platoon of bright young lawyers and proceeded to make Hoover's life difficult. There wasn't much Hoover could do about it. His usual strategy was to go over the attorney general's head to the president, an option closed so long as the attorney general's brother occupied the White House.

Hoover not only disliked Robert Kennedy, he was puzzled by a man whose life seemed improbable. Considered for most of his early life a weak man thoroughly dominated by his powerful father, Joseph P. Kennedy, Robert Kennedy had drifted through Harvard and the University of Virginia Law School, then was given a job in the Justice Department through his father's influence. He handled loyalty and security cases without much enthusiasm, managed his brother John's successful senatorial campaign, then reluctantly took a job as counsel (again arranged by his father) on Senator Joseph McCarthy's investigating committee. McCarthy's eclipse compelled Robert to look for another job, and he found one as counsel to the U.S. Senate Select Committee on Improper Activities in Labor or Management Field, a new investigating committee headed by Senator John McClellan. Joe Kennedy didn't think much of the job because McClellan's committee, charged with investigating organized crime's influence on the labor movement, would not garner many headlines and was thus a backwater for a son destined for greater things.

But Robert Kennedy found his true calling in that committee (on which his brother John served) and began to make a name for himself as an energetic and aggressive proponent of new federal laws to combat racketeering. As chief counsel, he became noted as a tormentor of mobsters and crooked labor leaders who had been dragged before the committee—most prominently James Hoffa, head of the Teamsters Union. No one, least of all Hoover, understood the transformation of Kennedy into crusader, but from the FBI director's standpoint, the important point was its practical effect. Put simply, he was driving Hoover nuts.

Impervious to Hoover's usual tactics of bureaucratic end run or outright intimidation, Kennedy presented a real problem. As attorney general, he was no respecter of traditions, among them the longstanding one under which his predecessors left Hoover alone. From the first day he took office, he made it clear he was Hoover's boss. He besieged the FBI with around-the-clock phone calls demanding information or action, and periodically dropped in to confront Hoover personally. (In one afternoon visit, he announced his intention of interrupting Hoover's regular 2 P.M. "security conference." Barging into Hoover's office past the furious protests of the director's secretary and gatekeeper, Helen Gandy, Kennedy discovered the "conference" was in fact Hoover's regular afternoon nap.)

Ever the master bureaucratic tactician, Hoover realized he

had to give ground. To mollify Kennedy, he announced the creation of a new Special Division for Organized Crime, and appointed as its head an agent named Courtney Evans, who knew the Kennedy family. He also informed Kennedy that he had ordered a "top priority" effort against thirty top Mafia leaders, including Kennedy's longtime obsession, Gaetano Lucchese.

But Kennedy was not mollified, and demanded that Hoover do more. By way of demonstrating what he wanted, Kennedy more than doubled the strength of the Justice Department's Organized Crime Section from seventeen to fifty lawyers, with orders to draft new legislation against organized crime. He also created a Labor Racketeering Section and unleashed it on Jimmy Hoffa, the most notorious labor racketeer in the country. His prosecutors began cutting a wide swath through the Mafia; by the beginning of 1963, they had won 288 convictions, many of them high-ranking mafiosi. Among them was Joseph Aiuppa, a senior executive of the Chicago Mafia organization, who learned that Kennedy was prepared to use *any* statute, however obscure, in his crusade: Aiuppa was arrested for exceeding the legal hunting limit for mourning doves while hunting on federal land. To his acute annoyance, the incident gave him a permanent Mafia nickname of "Joey Doves."

The more Kennedy pressured Hoover, the more antipathy the FBI director felt for his new boss. Convinced that Kennedy and his chief aides were plotting to remove him, he had the private Justice Department elevator that Kennedy and his aides used slowed down, so that a bug he planted in it could record their conversations. For his part, Kennedy came to loathe Hoover, whom he regarded as an overrated, power-mad, petty bureaucrat who would not do anything decisive against organized crime unless some one held a gun to his head. He also disliked Hoover personally; informed one day that Hoover's close aide (and rumored lover) Clyde Tolson had been hospitalized, Kennedy snapped, "For what? A hysterectomy?"

Despite the mutual antipathy, the two men were to unite in a case that produced no convictions, yet was to have a profound impact on the Mafia. Ironically, it began as an FBN case involving a low-level Mafia narcotics trafficker. His name was Joseph Valachi.

Another product of the East Harlem talent pool for the Mafia, Valachi in his youth was a friend of Gaetano Lucchese, to whom he turned in some desperation in 1962. Valachi, serving a twenty-year sentence in the Atlanta federal penitentiary for heroin trafficking, wrote a letter to Lucchese begging his intercession to solve a problem. He was under pressure by the FBN, which wanted him to become an informant. Valachi had invoked *omerta* in response, but the prison grapevine had reported his meetings with FBN agents. Among Valachi's fellow inmates was Vito Genovese, also serving time for narcotics, whose suspicious mind concluded that those meetings meant only one thing: Valachi was a snitch. Valachi vehemently denied it, but, as he told Lucchese, there were accumulating clues that Genovese had ordered his murder.

Actually, this scenario was precisely what the FBN agents hoped would happen; among their standard techniques was calling convicted traffickers to prison meetings that, although unproductive, would create the impression the inmate was cooperating. Usually, the result was a death sentence, which would force the inmate to turn to a sympathetic FBN for protection (in return, of course, for information).

Lucchese, wary of causing complications with Genovese, did not reply to the plea for help from his old friend. It would turn out to be the worst mistake Lucchese ever made. An increasingly paranoid Valachi, one morning spotting another inmate he thought was stalking him preparatory to murder, beat the man to death with a pipe. Now facing a homicide charge, Valachi saw only one way out: he agreed to talk.

He would do his talking to the FBI, which Kennedy ordered to take over the case. In Kennedy's perception, Valachi's potential extended far beyond narcotics; as a lifelong mafioso, he could reveal much of the organization's inner secrets. And that is exactly what Valachi did *not* want to discuss, as FBI Special Agent James Flynn discovered at his first meeting with him.

One of the small number of FBI agents who had been assigned to organized crime, Flynn had studied the subject carefully, including intense analysis of the tapes from the Chicago bug. He had also become something of an expert on the mentality of lifelong mafiosi. Valachi, he realized, was a typical example: stupid in the intellectual sense, yet very street-shrewd, a man who was proud of his calling in an organization that had given meaning to his life. He took his blood oath of *omerta* very seriously; he did not want to betray la Cosa Nostra, but did want to exact some revenge on Genovese, whom he felt had betrayed the honor of the organization by preparing to murder him without any proof that he had become an informant. Therefore, he was justified in betraying Genovese. But it was only Genovese he wanted to betray.

Flynn played his prize catch carefully. He patiently worked months to establish a close rapport with Valachi, bringing him Italian delicacies and chatting about sports and movies—any subject but the topic he really wanted to discuss. The right moment would come. Aware that Valachi fancied himself an unmatched handicapper of horse races, Flynn began a contest to see which man could pick the most winners from a slate of upcoming races. Flynn made sure he picked losers, allowing Valachi to crow about his superior ability. Flynn also played mind games, at one point telling Valachi the FBI knew everything there was to know about the Mafia. Valachi snorted; there were secrets the FBI couldn't possibly know.

"Cosa," Flynn said, as Valachi's mouth dropped open in shock. "You know what the next word is, don't you, Joe?"

"Yeah, but I don't want to say it."

"Let me say it: Nostra. See? I told you, we know everything." He went on to rattle off dozens of tidbits about various Mafia leaders that he had gleaned from the Chicago tapes. Valachi was astounded. Flynn carefully drew him into a discussion about these details, sometimes deliberately garbling an incident to encourage Valachi to correct and amend. And, before he quite realized what was happening, Valachi became an informant about the Mafia.

The voluble Valachi provided a panorama of the entire organization, with much detail on its early evolution. There was, however, not much in the way of anything useful for prosecuting anybody. Flynn suspected, correctly, that Valachi was carefully limiting what he had to say to ancient history and general details on the Mafia's structure without providing specific information that would get a fellow mafioso arrested. Above all, Flynn realized, Valachi did not want to think of himself as a rat; he was willing to defect from the organization, but not to inform on specific members.

Judged narrowly by the standards of prosecutable cases, Valachi's information was useless. But Hoover grasped the larger significance: for the first time, a member of the Mafia had provided details on the mysterious organization's inner workings. Hoover sought to use this for the FBI's advantage: he ordered that his aides ghostwrite an article under Valachi's name, entitled, "The Inside Story of Organized Crime and How You Can Stop It," to be published in *Parade*, the nationally distributed Sunday newspaper supplement. And coincident with release of the news of Valachi's defection, Hoover planned an article under his own name that would claim Valachi's testimony "corroborated and embellished facts developed by the FBI as early as 1961."

An appalled Robert Kennedy vetoed the idea and substituted a better one: Valachi would testify at a public hearing of the McClellan Committee. Valachi's subsequent appearance in the fall of 1963 was a sensation. In what would later become staples of popular culture, he talked about la Cosa Nostra and such terms as blood oaths, families, *omerta*, consigliere, godfather, underboss, soldier, *caporegime*, respect, double-dealing, and hits. For a fascinated television audience he helped the FBI draw up huge organizational charts showing how the various Mafia families were structured—and he identified 317 of their members.

A bravura performance, but most of the Mafia was unruffled. What Valachi had to say was embarrassing to the organization, but he had avoided providing any kind of legally damaging testimony against anybody. However, a number of shrewder mafiosi saw the real danger, among them Momo Giancana, who warned that the government would use Valachi as justification for new laws targeted strictly against organized crime. Giancana turned out to be right: bolstered by new public opinion polls which reported that a majority of Americans now considered the Mafia a "significant problem" the government had to combat (a clear result of Valachi's testimony), a package of new federal laws was approved. They included bans on interstate travel "for racketeering purposes," interstate shipment of gambling paraphernalia, and the use of interstate communications "for gambling purposes."

Valachi had energized the war against organized crime, but just as Kennedy prepared a renewed offensive, three rifle shots in Dallas on November 22, 1963, suddenly changed everything.

"It couldn't have happened to a nicer guy," Gaetano Lucchese said with deadly sarcasm when informed of President Kennedy's assassination. He might have been surprised to learn that Hoover's reaction was not far different, along with an elation that he was careful not to show. The bullets fired from a Dallas book warehouse suddenly ended all of Hoover's bureaucratic problems: the President rumored to have seriously considered his removal was gone, and his brother, who had caused the FBI director so much trouble, would be certain to leave his post soon.

A devastated Robert Kennedy would in fact eventually resign as attorney general, and with his departure the new war on organized crime began to fizzle. "In another two months from now," confidently predicted Giancana, the Mafia's resident seer, "the FBI will be like it was five years ago. They won't be around no more."

The FBI agents who heard this conversation over their bug planted in Giancana's lair realized, all too sadly, that Giancana was correct. It was among the last such conversations they would hear, because newly sworn-in President Lyndon Johnson, worried about the possible consequences of all those warrantless FBI bugs, ordered Hoover to shut them down. The pipeline into the Mafia fell silent. Meanwhile, as Kennedy's prosecutors and lawyers drifted off to other jobs, the FBI effort against organized crime was sharply cut back. The sigh of relief around the Mafia was almost audible.

Things gradually returned to normal. In New York, Manhattan District Attorney Frank Hogan was shocked when, during a conversation with the city's fire commissioner, he learned the firemen were demanding hefty pay increases to bring them to parity with police "bonuses," meaning the systemic graft from organized crime that was swelling the income of most cops. That was only a single symptom of organized crime's resurgence. Another was its ability to survive still more internal crises.

One of them, which became known as the "Gallo-Profaci War," involved the Gallo brothers, three Brooklyn hoods who had carried out the execution of Albert Anastasia but had not received their promised reward in the form of larger slices of street rackets. Their boss, Joseph Profaci, refused to listen to reason, and a full-fledged shooting war broke out. It ended only when Profaci died of cancer.

The second was the so-called "Banana War," named after Joseph Bonanno, whose Mafia nickname was "Joe Bananas." Bonanno, seized by the same overreaching ambition that had once captivated Vito Genovese—to become *capo di tutti capi*—began plotting against his fellow Commission members. It ignited a war between various factions in his own family, a senseless conflict that claimed a dozen lives before the whole problem was solved by the Commission's expulsion of Bonanno from the ruling body.

"This is getting out of hand," Carlo Gambino complained, and floated an old idea: create a sort of Commission chairman whose main function would be to stand as high-level consigliere for the Mafia's upper level, a highly respected boss who would adjudicate disputes among the other bosses before they degenerated into serious conflict. Gambino suggested that Gaetano Lucchese, the most highly respected boss in the entire Mafia, would be the natural choice. But mutual suspicion among the Commission members killed the idea before it got any further.

In fact, Lucchese would not have taken the job under any circumstances because his health was beginning to deteriorate. By 1963, he was spending an increasing amount of his time at a vacation home he had built in Florida, hoping the distance from Mafia tensions in New York would help his worsening cardiac troubles. He was suffering from dizzy spells, and as his health got worse, he began to lose interest in the intricacies of Mafia politics.

Although a relatively young man, Lucchese's frame of mind was darkened by the reminders of his mortality. He had other reminders, for his Mafia generation was dying off. A year earlier, his old friend Lucky Luciano had suddenly dropped dead of a heart attack in his Italian exile. His death climaxed the last sad years of his existence. Luciano had begun his exile supported by $25,000 in cash delivered each month by emissaries from the organization as a sign of its immense respect for the man who was most responsible for their success. But as the years went by and new leaders came into power, the cash tribute got smaller and smaller. By 1961 Luciano was so desperate for money he signed a deal with a movie producer for a film based on his life. An alarmed Commission dispatched a messenger with a blunt message: drop the movie idea or get killed. Lucchese, ever loyal to the organization's strictures even at the expense of his friends, had concurred in the dispatch of this threat.

Still, as he sadly noted, he thought he'd never see the day when Lucky Luciano himself would be threatened with death by the organization. There was an even sadder moment to come. Luciano's body was returned to the United States for burial in the family plot at a cemetery in the New York City borough of Queens. FBN and FBI agents, along with cops, showed up in force, anticipating a big mob turnout, but only a few family members and friends showed up for a graveside service. Neither Lucchese nor any other member of the Mafia attended.

However sad or brutal, the nature of Luciano's passing underscored, once again, the supremacy of the organization as the first operating principle of la Cosa Nostra. Whatever the organization's debt to Luciano—and that debt was almost incalculable—he was not exempt from its rules. The Mafia's nonattendance at his·funeral made the point: Luciano had violated an important rule by agreeing to a movie based on his life, and not even the founder himself could expect to get away with it.

No one believed more fervently in this guiding doctrine than Lucchese, a confirmed Mafia traditionalist. That belief led him to reveal to the Commission in early 1966 that, in addition to his heart troubles, he had been diagnosed with a brain tumor. It was terminal, and in only a year or so—perhaps even less— he would be dead. Lucchese wanted an orderly succession, a transition in which the Commission should fully participate in order to guarantee that the organization would suffer no disruption.

By guarded calls from pay phones, whispered conferences in secret meetings, and the exchange of messages via trusted couriers, the process began. Who would replace the man they all called Tommy? It was during this process that the Mafia, confident it had been restored to its former strength and power after the disruption of the Kennedy years, performed an arrogantly contemptuous public gesture that was meant to signal how invulnerable it had become.

On a crisp September day in 1966, Carlos Marcello, boss of the New Orleans Mafia, and Santo Trafficante, Jr., boss of the southern Florida Mafia, made their way to New York for a meeting with several of their New York counterparts to discuss the Lucchese succession. They met at an Italian restaurant in Queens. As Marcello and Trafficante sat down with the New York mobsters—Carlo Gambino, head of the family that would later bear his name; Thomas Eboli, the new head of Frank Costello's organization, now called the Genovese Family; and Joseph Colombo, the recently appointed chief of Joseph Profaci's organization—flashbulbs suddenly went off. To Marcello's shock, the table was surrounded by news photographers. Then police arrived and arrested everybody at the table on charges of "consorting with known criminals"—each other.

It turned out that Marcello, a notorious narcotics trafficker, had been trailed by FBN agents northward from New Orleans. When they saw him sit down with a number of Mafia leaders, they notified the police, who in turn tipped off the newspapers so they could record the drama of cops dragging off bigtime mafiosi.

They were held overnight on $100,000 bail as the Queens District Attorney's Office announced plans to hold them further as material witnesses to testify before a grand jury that, conveniently enough, was being empaneled at just that very moment. But the next day, a judge decreed that all this amounted to "harassment," dismissed all charges, and ordered the accused released.

One week later, New York newspapers were astonished to receive a call from Marcello inviting them to record a reunion of sorts: all the mafiosi would reconvene at the very same restaurant in which they had been arrested the week before, and would sit at precisely the same table in precisely the same chairs. The photographers, along with a frustrated posse of police, arrived at the restaurant to record the mobsters indeed sitting at the same table in the same chairs. Having ordered the same meal that was interrupted by the previous week's raid, they were happily eating away. As the photographers snapped pictures, several of the mafiosi raised their glasses of wine in a toast. "*Salud!*" Marcello shouted.

For anyone failing to get the point, an even more significant demonstration of the Mafia's fearlessness was made some months later when Lucchese died. Aware that his funeral would attract strong law enforcement attention, Lucchese's family announced they would understand if the deceased's "friends" chose not to attend. But they came, all of them. More than a thousand people showed up to pay their respects, including virtually the entire hierarchy of the Mafia and, more disturbingly, dozens of judges, public officials, politicians, and prominent businessmen. Not since the Frankie Yale funeral nearly four decades before had a mobster's funeral drawn so many mourners.

No one who attended seemed worried about the lurking detectives and federal agents busily carrying out the standard Mafia surveillance duties of jotting down license numbers and taking pictures of some of the mourners. It was as if nobody in attendance had the slightest concern about being seen at the funeral of one of the most notorious criminals in the history of the United States.

And so Gaetano Lucchese passed into criminal immortality, the event noted in extensive newspaper coverage the next day. Among the more interested readers of the accounts of Lucchese's passing was a student at Brooklyn Law School. Like a number of other readers, Charles Rose was astonished at the sheer effrontery of it all. Criminals were rubbing shoulders with judges and politicians in public, confirming what the cynical whispers had insisted for many years: it was big, so big nobody could do anything about it. What happened at Lucchese's funeral, Rose understood, was a graphic demonstration of the dangerous nexus between politics, business, and crime. It confirmed what he had experienced firsthand, to a certain degree, while working his way through college, and what he saw growing up on Manhattan's West Side, the clues to a hidden world that every city kid at one point or another would come to encounter. The local candy store known as a work site for bookies. The bars with big-stakes poker games in the back rooms that paid off the cops. The guy trying to lay low because he was late on his shylock vig. The store whose below-wholesale prices meant it was peddling hijacked goods. The occasional hit victim lying in the street.

And there was a more personal connection. Rose's father was a cop who had joined the police department in 1931, when the training for new cops consisted, in the main, of being handed a nightstick and a gun, along with instructions to report to a veteran (usually Irish) cop who would teach the new kid the ropes. Rose's instruction was simple: "You see anybody coming at you, deck 'em with your nightstick." The first night walking a beat, a man rushed at Rose, who knocked him cold with one blow. The next day, his agitated supervisor was almost beside himself.

"Are you crazy?" he demanded. "That was the local policy [illegal lottery game] guy who was trying to make sure the new cop on the beat got the regular two dollars."

As things turned out, the local mobsters assumed that Rose had decked their man for the act of trying to hand him his cut of the local precinct's graft (known as the "pad"). They gave him a wide berth, and for the next thirty-eight years of his police career, no mobster ever again tried to offer Rose a bribe. In the mob world—and its satellite world of corrupt cops—Rose became known as an oddball, a rare species of incorruptibility.

Rose passed his sense of stern moralism to his son, along with a bookshelf's worth of insight on how the great clockwork of organized crime and pervasive corruption was turning New York City—and everywhere else crime thrived—into a cesspool. Something had to be done, and Rose hoped his son would follow him into the police department. But, as his son progressed through his education at Cornell, graduate work at the state university, and finally law school, it was clear that wouldn't happen.

The younger Rose had a very different career path in mind, but as things turned out, his father could not have been more delighted. The reaction of la Cosa Nostra was quite something else.

FOUR

"We'd Go for Your Eyeballs"

You can't be a thug forever if you want to get ahead. Somewhere along the line, you have to learn to be a racketeer, as well.

SALVATORE (SAMMY THE BULL) GRAVANO

By noon, the awning at the hotel's poolside seemed to be wilting in the fiercely tropical Puerto Rican sun. Underneath, the five men sipping their piña coladas glanced at the pool where several shapely young women were cavorting in the water.

"Hey, Jim, why don't you get out of that suit and take a little swim?" said one of the men to a stocky man in a blue pincord suit. "You could maybe play a little water sports with that little piece of ass in the red bikini. I think she's had her eye on you." He winked broadly as the other men laughed.

"Nah," replied James O'Brien, with a wave of his hand. "To tell you the truth, I'm a, uh, little overweight, you know what I mean? I'd look like a fucking white whale in there. I'd scare the bejesus out of her." The men laughed again.

The teasing banter was relaxed, as could be expected among this close circle of men of the world's most powerful criminal organization, la Cosa Nostra. O'Brien was not a full member, but as a trusted associate, a non-Italian cooperating criminal, he was treated just as though he had taken the same Mafia blood oath as the other four men. That trust had brought O'Brien into their circle as a partner in crime and as an invited guest to a working vacation at a seaside hotel in Puerto Rico. There, they spent most of their time lounging around the pool, discussing the details of a great crime, which happened to be the theft of several million dollars.

In the languid heat, the five men ordered another round of piña coladas. One of them stared at O'Brien sweating in his suit, hand inside his shirt, apparently scratching his chest. ''You believe this fucking guy?'' he said, squinting at O'Brien. ''You know, Jim, you look like an Irish cop. I'll bet you're a fucking cop, right?'' Four pairs of eyes turned toward O'Brien with the faint glint of suspicion that searched for so much as a millisecond's hesitation.

''Fuck no,'' O'Brien replied instantly. ''Actually, you dumb shit, I'm an FBI agent.''

The four men laughed uproariously. What a joke: O'Brien was a tall, flabby guy who drank too much, ate like a pig, and spoke a rough street argot that made him sound like a mafioso himself. Besides, he had a prison record, a five-year stretch for labor racketeering.

O'Brien laughed too, while, under cover of scratching his chest, he checked the Nagra tape recorder taped there, hoping his sweat hadn't shorted out the batteries. The last thing he wanted was a malfunctioning tape recorder failing to pick up some very interesting conversations.

Some months later, the men who were with James O'Brien that day would be sitting somewhere else, in a New York courtroom, facing trial on charges of labor racketeering. O'Brien was not with them. Shortly after the trial began in 1972, he entered the courtroom, took the witness stand, and, in response to the prosecutor's request to identify himself, replied, ''I am James Abbott. I am a Special Agent of the Federal Bureau of Investigation.''

For the next several days, Abbott provided an unprecedented look at a Mafia labor racketeering operation from the inside. A fascinated jury heard him recount how he had successfully posed as ''James O'Brien,'' whom the Mafia knew as a ''labor consultant'' adept in the ways of helping mobsters bend an industry to their will. The chosen target in this case was the construction industry, and the technique followed the blueprint first drawn up by Gaetano Lucchese many years before. As in all other such operations, its appeal lay both in its simplicity and relatively low legal risk, along with the ultimate appeal of great profit.

The operation which Abbott had managed to infiltrate amounted to shaking down construction firms in New York and New Jersey for labor peace. "Jim O'Brien" was the front man for the scheme, explaining the facts of life to contractors. Those facts were easy to grasp: a number of big rehabilitation projects were underway in the New York metropolitan area, involving $25 million in federal funds. The Mafia intended to grab a share of that money.

In his conversations with contractors, O'Brien would never mention the word "Mafia." He didn't have to; contractors with experience in the rough and tumble world of the New York construction industry instantly understood the meaning of the phrase "labor peace" and what O'Brien meant when he told them that this peace could be guaranteed by O'Brien's "friends" and "partners." And the contractors also immediately grasped the significance of O'Brien's mention of Ted Maritas, a name instantly recognizable to anyone in the New York construction business.

Maritas, head of the 25,000-member New York District Council of Carpenters, controlled every union carpenter in the metropolitan area. A walkout by any of his locals would bring a construction site to a halt, because no other union—the Teamsters, the Concrete Workers, and a dozen others—would cross the picket line. Hiring nonunion help was no alternative; any construction site using nonunion help was subject to picket lines by carpenters protesting the use of "scabs," lines that would cut off deliveries. The corrupt Maritas, who had entered into a partnership with the Mafia, was the fulcrum of the entire scheme. The looming threat that he could ring a construction site with pickets in a matter of minutes by simply picking up a telephone was sufficient to convince contractors seeking to bid on major construction projects that it was wise to pay the "fees" to O'Brien's "friends."

There were further refinements to the racketeers' plan. To guarantee that there would be enough money earned on any given job to provide a profit for the contractor and the necessary cash for the "fees," the contractors were organized into a cartel. Bids on jobs were parceled out among the contractors, so that any given bid could be fixed; four contractors might bid, but three would bid deliberately high so that the lower bid would win. Any contractors refusing to go along were subjected to labor unrest until they saw the light.

But very few contractors refused to go along, and that was the beauty of the scheme. Judged strictly as a business deal, it was perfect. Any contractor guaranteed a winning bid could confidently tack on whatever was needed to handle the "fees," along with his profit margin. Even better from a contractor's standpoint, the scheme removed every contractor's biggest ulcer, the process of trying to come up with competitive bids. The process was a nightmare: unaware of how low competing bids were, contractors had to come up with bids they thought might win, often by slicing their profit margins so perilously thin that they might disappear altogether in case of delays caused by bad weather, labor troubles, or unexpected problems in the construction project itself.

From the Mafia's standpoint, this sort of mutual back-scratching could not have been more useful. It meant there was little likelihood of complaint to authorities, very little violence or muscle necessary to make it work, and the lowest possible criminal profile. And the relatively modest "Mafia tax" (a small percentage of projects costing $1 million or more) was small enough not to attract undue attention, but cumulatively returned immense profit, considering that some $200 million worth of construction projects was involved. So long as the scheme operated to the mutual benefit of both sides, no one was prepared to blow the whistle. In fact, the only real complication was in the Mafia itself. Because three different Mafia families were involved in the scheme, including the Lucchese organization, smooth operation required careful attention to how the money was collected and split, for any suspicion that one family was receiving a disproportionate share or was cheating the other families could ignite a very nasty confrontation.

In addition to tapes he had recorded himself, Abbott came armed with even more devastating evidence: tapes from a bug

Abbott had contrived to plant in Maritas's office. They detected the corrupt union leader putting the fear of God into contractors who had either unwittingly or deliberately fouled up the scheme. For example, there was one contractor who was not a member of the "club," as Maritas liked to call the Mafia-controlled cartel, and who made the error of innocently bidding on a project. His honest bid for a major rehabilitation project in the Bronx was some $1 million below the fixed bid. As a result, the $800,000 that Maritas and the mobsters were to split was now in jeopardy. Martitas summoned the honest contractor to his office, where the sinister figure of Vincent DiNapoli, a four-hundred-pound capo who represented the Genovese Family in the scheme, sat glowering.

"You know," Maritas told the contractor, "you took a million dollars out of people's mouths."

The puzzled contractor said he had no idea of what Maritas was talking about, whereupon the union leader explained it to him in no uncertain terms, ending with this little homily: "You have no idea what goes on in this town ... You know, we steer these things. You think things just fucking happen out of the sky?"

Obviously not, but Maritas later encountered another problem contractor, a man who had the temerity to announce that he would have nothing to do with the cartel. Worse, he had submitted an honest low bid for a job, unaware that the mobsters and Maritas had the fix in. He won the bid and was summoned to Maritas's office for a discussion of the matter.

Maritas immediately bared his fangs. "I don't know if you understand what you're into," he said. "You're in a lot of hot water."

When the contractor professed not to understand, Maritas made it plain what was at stake: "Everybody got together, okay, specifically to see a certain guy got the job, okay, and people had it set up that way, okay? I mean, like everybody had submitted a bid was in on it, and you came along ... and come in a million less than the low bidder."

The contractor held his ground. "Listen, this is my ship ... I got a kid going to college."

In response, Maritas turned up the heat a few degrees. "These guys," he said, lowering his voice a threatening octave, "feel like they blew a million dollars, all right? If you were just some guy we didn't know, you would have problems. *We'd go for your eyeballs!*"

His mind suddenly set right by this analysis, aided in no small part by a baleful stare from Vincent DiNapoli, the contractor hurriedly assured Maritas he would withdraw his bid. He considered himself lucky to leave Maritas's office in one place.

But it was to be Maritas's last success. He had brought Jim O'Brien into the scheme as the labor consultant with the right contacts in the construction business who could get things moving along. When a suspicious DiNapoli raised the possibility that O'Brien might be some kind of undercover agent, Maritas assured the mafioso that O'Brien was "good people," only to discover he had opened the door to an FBI agent. Neither the Mafia nor DiNapoli forgive such lapses, and after the indictments of twelve men—including DiNapoli—were handed up, Maritas disappeared. He was later found floating near the Throgs Neck Bridge with a bullet in his head. His most prized possession, a silver Lincoln Continental he loved to show off as emblematic of his success, was never found.

The remaining defendants were involved in a landmark case, for it marked the first time that the FBI had managed to penetrate a major Mafia criminal conspiracy. And that signified nothing less than the beginning of a revolution in the crusade against organized crime.

At the time of J. Edgar Hoover's death in 1972, the FBI he had created and enlarged during the more than forty years of his reign had degenerated into a tangle of rival cliques, united only by fear of their increasingly failing director. By that point, Hoover had built the Bureau to a force of 8,631 agents.

Hoover had reluctantly assigned a small percentage of these agents, the most highly trained in all law enforcement, to investigating organized crime during the Kennedy administration, a modest effort that faded after John Kennedy's assassination. The Bureau then got back to Hoover's dominating obsession, the communist menace—now enlarged to include all forms of domestic dissent that Hoover felt supported the Kremlin's master plan. Hoover's pattern for many years was to hook the Bureau into whatever concerns his presidential patrons expressed. Beginning in 1964, Hoover was to service a pronounced streak of paranoia that afflicted both Lyndon Johnson and Richard Nixon.

The domestic unrest set off by the civil rights revolution and America's deepening involvement in Vietnam brought out the worst in Hoover. He hardly needed White House encouragement—and there was plenty of that—to pounce upon both these fault lines in American society. Entire platoons of agents were deployed against political dissidents, including a squad with the sole assignment of investigating John Lennon's influence on the antiwar movement. Many others were assigned to Hoover's deepest secret, a program of outright disruption of civil rights and antiwar groups called COINTELPRO (for "counterintelligence program"), which sought to create turmoil inside these organizations and destroy them from within.

This assault on civil liberties assumed its worst form in the Bureau's New York field office, where a slavishly devoted Hooverite with the unlikely name of J. Wallace LaPrade took command from John ("cement head") Malone. LaPrade made Malone look like a civil libertarian; he was convinced that all forms of political dissent were secretly underwritten by communists, and determined to prove it. To that end, he created a secret unit called Squad 47 and assigned seventy agents to such tasks as tracking down fugitives from the radical Weather Underground. Unable to find them, Squad 47 agents went after relatives and friends of the fugitives, tapping their telephones, reading their mail, and breaking into their homes—all without warrants. In the process, much of the FBI had become a virtual secret police agency, spying on thousands of Americans merely on the suspicion that they were COMSYMP, Bureauspeak for "Communist sympathizer."

LaPrade had no interest in organized crime, much less in doing anything about it, a philosophy which could not have delighted that subculture more. Granted another reprieve, it entered a new golden age, epitomized in that ultimate American monument to fame, a movie. *The Godfather* was pure myth (the word "Mafia" is never mentioned once in the movie), portraying a world of oppressed Italian immigrants who reluctantly become "men of honor" in a new world where everyone and everything is corrupt. Mafiosi of all ranks professed to have seen the movie a dozen times, although there were some interesting exceptions. A puzzled Carlo Gambino, the most powerful and respected family boss after the death of Lucchese, was once serenaded with the movie theme as he entered the reception hall during an elaborate union dinner. He asked what song it was; when told it was the theme from *The Godfather* (whose main character Vito Corleone is a thinly veiled portrait of himself), Gambino said he had never seen the movie. Then he gently stroked his nose, the very same gesture Marlon Brando used in his portrayal.

While a union was paying homage to Gambino, several of his hoods had tied the eighty-year-old owner of a linen supply company to a chair. He didn't want to cooperate in Gambino's takeover of the industry, so the hoods sought to change his mind by slowly passing a lit propane torch in front of his eyes. Having practiced beforehand with a piece of paper to determine how close they could come with the torch before setting the paper aflame, they knew the precise point to place the torch without actually burning the man's eyes. As Gambino noted before dispatching his goons on their mission, actually blinding the man would not secure his ''cooperation.''

Each day, in a thousand different ways, something like this scene was enacted in a thousand different places in the course of conducting business. The enterprise thrived anew in an atmosphere of official disinterest and, more dangerously, corruption. There were any number of statistics that underscored the virtual legal immunity under which the Mafia had come to operate. One of the more revealing was this fact: during the years 1960 to 1969, nearly forty-five percent of the 1,762 organized crime-related cases that reached the indictment stage in New York State's court system were dismissed by state judges, more than four times the normal rate. As anyone familiar with how that system operated knew, a small tribe of mob lawyers played the system like a board game, maneuvering to get their clients' cases before certain ''right'' judges known for granting constant postponements that tended to dim witnesses' memories (or made them disappear altogether).

For the rare mafioso to see the inside of a prison cell, the experience was hardly a deterrent—or much of a punishment, for that matter. Like everything else it touched, organized crime organized the prisons. Mafia inmates entered a system in which corrupted guards were able to provide everything a prison sentence was supposed to deny—sex, special food, and drugs. Every prison had its "Mafia Manor," a special section where Mafia inmates were housed. Considered the most orderly and trouble-free section of a prison, it was run by the senior Mafia prisoner present, with all the rules and customs of the organization kept intact. Even the most minor disputes were subjected to sitdowns, during which the senior mafioso would act as a no-appeal judge. Inmates in "Mafia Manor" spent most of their time discussing the finer points of organized crime and teaching younger inmates the ropes.

For prisons where certain things could not be obtained, even from corrupted guards, ingenious solutions were devised. At the federal penitentiary in Atlanta, for example, Mafia prisoners organized a flourishing heroin business by means of tennis games. Players became terribly careless, constantly hitting balls over the walls. The prisoners could not scale the walls to retrieve the errant balls, but by remarkable coincidence, kindly citizens always seemed to be walking by outside. They helpfully threw tennis balls back over the wall—each one of which was filled with heroin.

Bosses rarely went to prison, but when they did, every effort was made to ensure their comfort. Vito Genovese, sent to prison in 1959 for heroin trafficking, had weekly visits from a hair stylist and manicurist; similarly, Lucky Luciano in his prison days had a cell with an electric stove, curtains on his cell door, and a prison uniform that consisted of a custom-made silk shirt and tailored pants. More importantly, Mafia bosses in prison ran their organizations as though they were back home. They passed on orders via visiting family members, but for more important matters requiring instant decisions, they would place collect calls to their lawyers. Legally, inmate-lawyer calls cannot be monitored, so mob lawyers would take the calls, exchange a few words, then hand the phone to one of the jailed mobster's underlings, who would then conduct the rest of the conversation.

No wonder the Mafia began to regard itself as invulnerable, especially when the FBI's early, limited offensive slackened after the Kennedy assassination. From that point until Hoover's death in 1972, the Mafia saw the FBI as only a minor problem. Indeed, the organization on occasion openly tried to intimidate the Bureau. In 1963, an FBI agent conducting a surveillance at the funeral of the father of Mafia capo Carmine Lombardozzi was pistol-whipped by four hoods. A year later, Joseph Colombo, who had taken command of the Profaci organization, became annoyed when he spotted several FBI agents following him and taking his picture. Further angered when the Bureau arrested his son for a major jewelry heist, Colombo conceived an extraordinary counterattack. He formed the Italian-American Civil Rights League, whose major theme was a denial of the existence of the Mafia, termed an ''FBI invention'' meant to sully the honor of all Italian-Americans. The irony, of course, was that Colombo, whose mobster father had been garrotted in the back seat of his car with a girlfriend for antagonizing the hierarchy, was a pure Mafia thug, with a record for murder and loan-sharking. True to his tradition, he skimmed the proceeds of the organization's dues and carefully split them with other members of the Commission. Meanwhile, he set up picket lines of protesters around the FBI's New York field office headquarters, and managed to convince the Justice Department to ban the word ''Mafia'' from its lexicon.

Arrayed against this power was a ragged line of combatants. It did not include the Federal Bureau of Narcotics, once the Mafia's most dangerous enemy. The agency began to fade into irrelevance by the 1960s, largely because its head, Harry Anslinger, made several serious political mistakes. One was his strange obsession over marijuana, which he tended to equate in seriousness to heroin. The famous cult movie *Reefer Madness*, regarded as high camp by a generation that saw marijuana as harmless, was an Anslinger-inspired production. Its central theme of marijuana as life-threatening was laughable to all those casual users. Anslinger's more serious tactical error concerned his attempt to emulate his rival Hoover by pandering to White House politics. But Anslinger lacked Hoover's skill at the game, and lost credibility when he claimed that Communist China was masterminding a massive conspiracy to produce heroin for the U.S. market as part of a plan to undermine American youth. (It was an echo of his World War II-era attempt to curry favor with the Roosevelt administration by claiming that the Japanese controlled all the opium trade in China and exported the drug to the United States to weaken American youth.) After Richard Nixon took office, the FBN was dismantled, to be replaced by a new agency called the Bureau of Narcotics and Dangerous Drugs (BNDD), which in turn was reorganized into the Drug Enforcement Administration.

As for the FBI, its frontline forces arrayed against the Mafia consisted of a few squads of veteran street agents whose immersion in the underside of American society tended to produce characters very much different from the conventional image of G-men. After years of exposure to a distinctly separate culture, they spoke and acted like veteran street cops. Operating in an atmosphere of low priority (or sometimes disinterest) from their organization's headquarters, they improvised, fighting to establish an FBI presence at a time when many mafiosi had no respect for the Bureau. "Take that badge and stick it up your ass," was a frequent response when agents confronted mobsters.

One agent who did not get that kind of reaction was the Bureau's most noted agent in the New York street wars, Bernard Welsh. A giant of a man whose back-slapping bonhomie and baby face concealed an extremely aggressive agent, Welsh was noted for a rollicking sense of humor and a relish for combat in the trenches. He liked to go face to face with mafiosi, who nevertheless regarded him with affectionate respect. Invariably called "Bernie" by the mobsters, Welsh was fearless, often strolling into Mafia social clubs and announcing he was there to collect evidence of criminal wrongdoing. One of his favorite tricks was to barge into mob hangouts and ostentatiously greet a mobster with a warmth that raised the suspicion in other mobsters' minds that their colleague might be an FBI informant (Welsh was noted for his uncanny ability to recruit underworld informants.)

Other agents involved in organized crime investigations developed their own little tricks. One was to put a paper bag, with holes cut out for eyes, over the head of an agent, seat him in the back of a car, then drive slowly past a Mafia hangout while the hooded agent ostentatiously pointed out several men. The stunt, as intended, ignited paranoia inside a Mafia group over which of their fellow mobsters was the secret informant concealed by a paper bag hood.

The street agents tried to use electronic surveillance whenever possible, but even when they were able to secure the necessary court orders, they lacked the advanced equipment jealously guarded by the Bureau's counterintelligence experts. They still were able to make a few significant penetrations, aided by some street agent tricks. In one case, they planted a bug in a social club patronized by Matthew (Matty the Horse) Ianello, an important capo in the Genovese Family. But raucous background noise rendered the bug useless, so the agents wanted to get Ianello to move, somehow, to an office he maintained nearby for business discussions—an office already wired up for sound. The agents began a deliberately ostentatious surveillance operation against the social club. As the agents hoped, a jittery Ianello concluded the club was no longer safe for sensitive discussions, so he adjourned to his office, where the lack of background noises produced clear tapes.

But too much of the FBI's effort was concentrated on illegal gambling operations of the interstate variety. It was a priority decided by headquarters, which wanted arrests for that crime to bolster the Bureau's statistics it liked to brandish before Congress each year around appropriations time. Headquarters exerted pressure on field offices to increase gambling arrests each year so that the Bureau could show steady progress— and justify its request for increases in appropriations. Congressional committees that did not look too deeply were impressed when informed, for example, that the FBI had made 1,075 arrests involving members of organized crime in 1970, a nearly thirty percent increase over the previous year. But almost all these arrests were for violations of the federal statutes involving interstate gambling. They resulted almost exclusively in light prison sentences or fines. Such statistics represented the triumph of quantity over quality, for as every street agent knew, gambling arrests were useless as any kind of indicator of progress against crime, much less organized crime. Illegal gambling was simple to prove, since it is among the most visible of crimes (no one can practice it secretly). But illegal gambling was almost universally regarded by the judicial establishment as the classic "victimless crime" that did not merit stiff jail sentences. Many agents had the experience of watching newly arrested gamblers walk out of courtrooms on low bail before the ink was even dry on their arraignment papers. Mafia gamblers tended to regard occasional arrests as the costs of doing business, and so long as millions of Americans wanted to gamble, they were willing to undergo the modest risks of helping them do it.

Frustrated agents who had established covert pipelines with police detectives discovered that the cops shared the same frustration: their department and district attorneys, eager to demonstrate to voters their aggressiveness toward organized crime, routinely staged highly publicized raids against bookie joints, horse parlors, and numbers banks. When the dust settled, those arrested were back on the streets within hours, only slightly slowed by the inconvenience of a small fine. On the rare occasions when those caught in a raid actually wound up in jail, it caused not even a speed bump's worth of disruption to organized crime's illegal gambling operations. Within minutes of an arrest, an operation would be switched to a new location, with new men in charge. It was something like a football team's depth chart, with every position staffed three and four men deep so there is always an instant substitute for an injured or nonperforming player.

The shared frustration created a number of close relationships between some FBI street agents and their police counterparts, but they remained strictly unofficial. During the Hoover years, any cooperative effort with local police departments was officially discouraged on the grounds that agents might become tainted by contact with police agencies, regarded within FBI headquarters as universally corrupt. Then too, there was a great cultural divide between the FBI and police. Veteran street cops regarded the FBI as overrated as a law enforcement agency, and snidely called the Bureau "Famous But Incompetent." They were also bothered by the Bureau's bad habit of appropriating evidence gathered by police and claiming it as its own. For their part, FBI agents could spend hours recounting stories about the "meateaters" they had encountered in police departments, cops so greedily corrupt they would steal the pennies off a dead man's eyes.

Among some of the men on both sides, however, there was a growing realization that their respective organizations somehow would have to overcome the mutual antipathy. For neither the FBI nor the cops had any hope of making inroads against organized crime without some sort of cooperative effort. Nobody knew how that could be achieved, but a clue emerged in 1972 in Brooklyn. It was a case that became known as ''The Gold Bug,'' the first serious assault against the Lucchese Family.

The two main characters in the case were Captain John Nevins, head of the Brooklyn District Attorney's Squad, and his star detective, Kenneth McCabe. Nevins, regarded by the Mafia as an implacable enemy, was a highly aggressive detective squad commander who made organized crime his highest priority. McCabe, a football tight end–sized detective who had spent most of his career battling mafiosi in the streets of Brooklyn, was equally aggressive. Nevins in particular came to be loathed by local mobsters, largely because of the round-the-clock pressure he ordered his detectives to conduct. McCabe, known to mobsters as ''Kenny the Giant,'' was noted for an in-your-face approach that mafiosi found especially annoying.

The bitterest enemy of the two cops was Paul Vario, an important capo in the Lucchese Family and one of the organization's prime moneymakers. Vario, known within the Lucchese organization by the diminutive ''Paulie,'' ran a sprawling empire that ranged from auto theft to narcotics, although his most noted activity was hijacking trucks from Kennedy Airport. He had been in and out of jail, but remained largely untouchable. Nevins made him a priority target, unwelcome attention that led Vario to christen his chief tormentor ''Captain Cocksucker.''

Nevins was one of the rare detective commanders who advocated close cooperation with the FBI in organized crime investigations. He had established connections with several FBI agents, who one day presented him with a gift: an FBI informant had revealed, in the course of discussing an entirely different matter, that Vario was running his criminal enterprise from a trailer parked on the grounds of a Brooklyn junkyard he owned.

The FBI's tip led to an extensive surveillance operation, headed by McCabe, to determine if Vario was indeed using the trailer as a criminal command post—the essential basis for a court order to achieve Nevin's goal of getting bugs inside. Operating from a Catholic school just across the street (one priest, a police buff, happily volunteered to write down the license plates of interesting cars parked near the junkyard), McCabe detected a steady parade of criminals into Vario's trailer. Either the underworld had a sudden need for auto parts or the criminals wanted to talk to Vario about an entirely different subject.

The subject was crime, as the cops discovered after managing to penetrate Vario's security screen of a fourteen-foot-high chain-link fence topped in barbed wire, a watchman, and three attack dogs to install several bugs in the trailer ceiling, along with taps on three telephones in the trailer. The result was called "The Gold Bug," partly in honor of Brooklyn District Attorney Eugene Gold, and in tribute to the sheer quality of what gushed forth—discussions about narcotics, robbery, counterfeiting, gun-running, hijacking, labor racketeering, stolen cars, arson, illegal gambling, robbery, burglaries, assaults, payoffs to politicians and judges, and references to some two hundred legitimate businesses in which Vario had hidden interests. The bug also detected Vario's constant complaints about how his nemesis, "Captain Cocksucker," and "that pain in the ass Irish giant motherfucker" were making his life miserable.

Eleven months later, when Nevins made the decision to end the operation and begin making arrests, he led McCabe and a police posse to the trailer. Nevins pounded on the door.

"Who is it?" Vario asked from inside.

"Captain Cocksucker," Nevins replied. "Open up!"

Vario opened the door. "What is it now, you fucking pain in the ass?"

"You're going to jail, that's what," Nevins said as Vario was dragged away.

As Nevins predicted, Vario did indeed go off to jail, there

to delight fellow prisoners and guards with his unsurpassed skill as a cook, particularly his masterpiece, a *a pasta fagiole* regarded as the best in New York. But if Vario was suffering a relatively benign prison term, a larger point had been made during the "Gold Bug" operation: although the cooperation between the FBI and police in that case was on a small scale, it could lead to significant results.

Not too long afterward, an even more extensive experiment in such cooperation was carried out. Almost coincident with the death of Hoover, police and FBI agents got together and created a joint task force to attack one of the pillars of organized crime, its grip on the Garment Center. Code-named Project Cleveland, the joint operation was specifically targeted against the Mafia's control of Garment Center trucking firms. The FBI had managed to convert an ex-con into an informant, and he agreed to set up a phony trucking firm wired for sound. The idea was to attract mobsters to his office, where it was anticipated they would deliver assorted incriminating threats against the independent trucking firm as it began to compete for business.

The operation began promisingly, but soon the inexperience of both the FBI and police in running joint operations began to show. Squabbling between agents and cops broke out, and an operation originally designed to run for five years was aborted after only seventeen months. An anticipated rich haul of mobsters resulted in thirteen indictments and only four convictions, none of which resulted in any significant jail time. It had virtually no impact on the Mafia's dominance of the Garment Center.

Still, both the FBI and police learned a great deal, and not all the lessons concerned the nuts and bolts of running intricate organized crime investigations that involved different law enforcement groups. The FBI learned that not all cops were corrupt, and cops learned that not all FBI agents were incompetent. Perhaps even more important, both sides learned they complemented each other: the FBI needed the cops' encyclopedic knowledge of the streets, while the cops needed the FBI's unsurpassed expertise on how to investigate large-scale economic conspiracies. Fundamentally, the Mafia was precisely that kind of conspiracy, with roots in the streets.

At the same time, both the police and FBI began to draw another important and much broader deduction from the course of events: there was something *something seriously* flawed with the entire law enforcement approach. Essentially, the law required that law enforcement catch organized criminals in the act, and very few of them were careless enough to do so—certainly not at the higher levels of the Mafia. What made organized crime possible was organization, and unless the organization could be attacked as a criminal entity, putting mafiosi in jail—especially for relatively short terms—would have no impact on the organization. As Luciano had established years before, so long as the organization remained intact, organized crime would survive. A criminal enterprise thrived so long as the enterprise itself continued functioning.

The "Gold Bug" case was a perfect illustration of the problem. It produced 677 subpoenas, resulting in sixty separate criminal cases, but when they were parsed out into provable, specific criminal acts, the results were meager. To be sure, Vario went to jail for three years, but it was the kind of sentence a veteran mafioso could do standing on his head. Considering the breadth of his criminal activities—which he continued to oversee from his prison cell—three years wasn't much to show for eleven months of hard work.

There was an even smaller return for investment in a similar case, a result that caused an FBI agent to wonder whether he may have wasted his time and effort. It was an unsettling thought that would come to be shared by a federal prosecutor. Their doubt would form the nucleus of a dramatically different approach to attacking organized crime.

The important thing to remember about FBI Special Agent James Abbott, those who knew him would say, was that he was a man who straddled both worlds of law enforcement, and knew both cold. An ex-New York City cop, he had become appalled by the department's rampant corruption and institutional politics. He quit and went off to college to earn a master's degree in public administration. When the idea of spending the next twenty years of his life as a bureaucrat paled, he joined the FBI—"for a greater challenge," as he later put it. First assigned to the Atlanta field office, he was bored to distraction and badgered his superiors to be transferred to his native New York. Once there, to his delight, he was assigned to the small band of agents targeted against organized crime. In that small world, he would become one of the FBI's legendary agents.

A complex character with a short fuse, Abbott was unmistakably a product of the New York streets. In his youth, he had worked summers on construction projects, a field he came to know well. Later, when Abbott was busy in the FBI's New York field office attacking Mafia loan sharks, he encountered a contractor for whom he had once worked. After reminiscing over old times, the contractor suddenly unburdened himself, complaining about the Mafia's steady inroads into the construction business and how nobody seemed to care. Abbott listened quietly, then replied that if he had anything to say about it, the FBI was going to do something.

That something was Lil Rex, code name for an undercover operation that would feature Abbott as the key man in a force of ten handpicked agents. The operation was conceived by Abbott and fellow agent Kenneth A. Giel. But after drawing up what they thought was a well-planned operation to infiltrate the Mafia with an undercover agent and use electronics that would in effect get the mafiosi to convict themselves out of their own mouths, they discovered that headquarters welcomed the plan with all the enthusiasm, as Abbott phrased it, of "a fart in church."

Part of the problem had to do with the mentality of senior Bureau officials still nervous about agents coming into contact with organized crime, an interface they remained convinced would inevitably lead to corruption of the agents. But another part of the problem was the fact that Giel and Abbott were the agents who had proposed the operation. The two men had the reputation of "wild men" in the insular world of headquarters, street agents regarded as semisavages whose years on the streets had transformed them into something very much like the Mafia hoods they were chasing. Their plan was rejected.

An infuriated Giel traveled to Washington, burst into headquarters, and in an imitation of some of the worst Mafia street hoods he had encountered, confronted the official who had decided to reject the proposal for the Lil Rex operation. "Kiss my ass!" Giel screamed at the terrified man cowering in a corner of his office while enumerating the way he planned to rearrange the official's face. Giel swept up papers from his desk and took them to a more sympathetic supervisor who agreed to approve the operation. But given the overall distaste in headquarters for undercover operations against organized crime, the best he could get was an appropriation of $10,000 for six months.

"You've got to be fucking kidding," Giel said, but, aware that that was as far as headquarters would go, he reluctantly agreed to go ahead with what he knew was a paltry amount for an undercover operation of the dimension he and Abbot planned to carry out. (He turned out to be right: later, the two agents had to borrow $7,000 from a Mafia loan shark to keep Lil Rex going. Somehow, they forgot to inform headquarters about it.)

Abbott set the operation in motion by contacting his contractor friend, who provided the key: he knew Ted Maritas, the corrupt carpenters' union head who was working with the mobsters, and agreed to vouch for "James O'Brien," a veteran labor racketeer operating as a "labor consultant." If anybody checked (and somebody did), there was a file at the federal penitentiary in Atlanta on O'Brien, a real bad apple who had served five years there for labor racketeering. The file was an elaborate forgery prepared by the FBI.

Abbott slipped into his new identity and proceeded to patiently work his way into the center of the conspiracy. Supported by a backup team of agents ready to pounce if the mafiosi were to learn of O'Brien's identity and try to dispose of him, Abbott set up a phony labor consulting firm. It was called, wickedly enough, "James Rico Construction Consultants." Fortunately, mobsters didn't catch the joke: "Rico" was the name of the character memorably portrayed by Edward G. Robinson in the classic gangster movie, *Little Caesar*. The movie's famous last line, "Mother of God, is this the end of Rico?" perfectly summarized Abbott's intention.

Claiming to be a bachelor, Abbott set up residence in an FBI-provided apartment, where any phone calls were automatically routed to his real home in suburbia. Over the next year, as Abbott gained the mobsters' confidence, he had a number of narrow escapes—such as the day in a restaurant when, on his way to the men's room he encountered an old friend who shouted out, "Hey, Jim, how are things in the Bureau?" Fortunately, the mobsters with whom Abbott was sharing lunch were out of earshot. There were enough similar, heart-stopping close calls to cause Abbott a stress-induced severe colon problem that later required a colostomy to correct. The rest of his health also suffered: he put on sixty pounds in the course of sharing gargantuan lunches and dinners with mobsters, whose preferred venue for business discussions was a restaurant table.

The infiltration operation itself unfolded much as Abbott and Giel had scripted it. In the process, they were writing the book on how to conduct such operations, especially the tricky part concerning how undercover operatives manage to live in two separate identities at the same time. Given the impact on his health and the severe mental strain it caused, Abbott was pleased when the operation was pronounced ended. But as the case moved into court, he was much less pleased with the final result.

Encountering Vincent DiNapoli shortly after the case had broken in the newspapers, Abbott braced for an explosion. But DiNapoli, an old-line mafioso, made it clear he harbored no ill will toward the FBI agent, resignedly telling Abbott that the agent was "only doing your job." That out of the way, DiNapoli asked for similar courtesy: "Listen, Jim, do me a favor, please. I don't want to be arrested at home in front of my daughter. She's very religious, you know." When Abbott agreed, DiNapoli arranged to surrender some distance from his home.

Possibly one reason for DiNapoli's relative calm even after learning the FBI had the electronic goods on him was his realization that a worst-case scenario, conviction on all charges, would cost him only a few years in jail, the kind of sentence mobsters regarded as a routine cost of doing business. He was right: a guilty plea sent him to prison for five years and he was out after serving just over three years. Naturally, he went right back to labor racketeering.

Not much of a deterrent, Abbott realized, and he became

very depressed. Although Lil Rex proved that undercover operations targeted against organized crime could work, the problem was that all the investment of time, manpower, and money produced not much in the way of a serious legal threat. And without a serious legal threat, there was no hope of making any kind of deep inroads against organized crime, no matter how well-run an FBI penetration.

Never a man to mince words, Abbott had often criticized prosecutors in the U.S. attorney's offices in Manhattan and Brooklyn for what he perceived as a lack of imagination and willingness to take on tough organized crime cases. There must be *something* in the statutes, Abbott insisted, that could be used more effectively in prosecuting such cases. He did not make himself popular among prosecutors by constantly hectoring them, nor were they thrilled to hear Abbott suggest that perhaps they demonstrated something less than zeal in handling organized crime cases because they were either lazy or timorous.

For their part, the prosecutors regarded Abbott as an overzealous agent embarked on some sort of quirky crusade. Unconcerned about what prosecutors thought of him, Abbott had inspired much talk around the U.S. attorney's offices by stomping into the office of one prosecutor and demanding that he do something about the loan shark case that had been laying on his desk quite some time. When the prosecutor indicated he didn't think the case was worth much of his time—the victim was just as bad a scumbag as the mobster who beat him up for late payments—an infuriated Abbott scooped up the case file from his desk and began looking for another prosecutor to take the case. When prosecutor after prosecutor turned him away, a desperate Abbott decided on one last attempt, a real long shot. Not really expecting much, he carried the case file into the office of the most junior member of the prosecutorial team, a young lawyer who had just joined the U.S. Attorney's Office in Brooklyn. From experience, Abbott knew that prosecutors new to the job tended to be cautious and reluctant to deal with any case they knew had been passed over by more senior prosecutors. New prosecutors learned quickly that it was not politically wise to go against the grain at the very beginning of their careers.

But from the first moment, Abbott realized that the new kid on the block, named Charles Rose, was not the average rookie prosecutor. For one thing, Rose shared his zeal about organized crime cases and had a surprisingly sophisticated grasp of that world. For another, he made it clear he was not afraid to step on toes, even his superiors'. As Abbott sat in the new prosecutor's office, sipping Diet Pepsi as part of his program to lose the pounds that put him over the FBI's weight limits, he began to develop an affectionate respect for one of the more interesting men he had ever met. Rose put on no airs (he invariably padded around his office in his socks) and seemed unfazed about any difficulties in the loan shark case—or the inherent problems of any other kind of organized crime case, for that matter. Abbott was most struck by Rose's odd combination of Ivy League intelligence and down-home casualness, along with the interesting dichotomy of a mind that could alternately discuss the more esoteric points of the law and recount funny goombah stories from the street.

"Ah, I see the accused has mightily abused the Decalogue," Rose said as he scanned the case file. "In other words, we can safely assume that at some point, he told his victim, 'I'm gonna rip your fucking face off!' "

Abbott laughed, but as he came to realize, Rose's characteristically Baroque swoops through the English language signified an important personality trait: Rose was a moralist whose geniality masked a very deep antipathy for mafiosi and all they represented. He shared Abbott's loathing for the Mafia, along with a similar frustration over how ineffectively the law enforcement establishment was combatting it.

"We are going to prosecute this case," Rose said. "Extortionate extension of credit, as our federal criminal code so euphemistically describes it, is a crime. And we are supposed to prosecute crime. I don't care how wretched or unsympathetic the victim is."

Abbott watched in astonishment as Rose first took on the judge assigned the case, Jack B. Weinstein, who in pretrial hearings tried to deflect the prosecutor. "In all candor, Mr. Rose," Weinstein told him, "this is the most unsympathetic 'victim' I have ever seen." In other words, a trial would be a waste of time because the jury, confronted with a chief witness who was even more disreputable than the defendant, would probably declare a pox on both their houses. Rose argued that the kind of people who dealt with loan sharks tended toward the shadier side of society, and if only cases involving sympathetic victims were prosecuted, there would be precious few prosecutions. Loan-sharking was organized crime's most important source of working capital, and must be prosecuted.

Weinstein gave in and the trial went forward, resulting in a conviction. Rose had made his point, but as he and Abbott agreed, it was a hollow victory. The case involved only one low-level loan shark in the Lucchese Family, just a single casualty in a brigade. The successful prosecution had taken one soldier off the street for a few years, but he had already been replaced. More significantly, it made hardly a dent in loan-sharking as an enterprise. High-level mafiosi continued to lend out money to their underlings at a point a week, repaid from the five-points-a-week "street price." Bosses, underbosses, consiglieres, and capos with even relatively modest six-figure amounts working each day on the street had a blue-chip (and tax-free) investment returning several thousand dollars a week in profit. And there was no risk: under prevailing Mafia rules, the street soldiers were required to pay that one percent each week without fail, even if their own street investments went sour. The legal risk was also minimal; as long as prosecutors went after individual loan sharks—the ones actually caught red-handed—the casualties were bearable, because the underlying system could easily absorb such losses and continue. As Rose summed up the problem, it was like trying to kill a dragon by stepping on its tail.

Rose and Abbott had only to look to the Lucchese Family's structure for confirmation. Despite such prosecutorial victories as Lil Rex and Rose's loan shark case, the Lucchese organization had grown more powerful and unassailable than ever. Its power grew despite a leadership vacuum, one that was resolved when the organization reached deep into its roots to find a successor to Gaetano Lucchese.

Although Lucchese had planned an orderly succession after his death, a number of circumstances had made that process more complicated than he anticipated. Ironically, the problem was not a lack of a qualified successor, but an embarrassment of riches. Thanks to Lucchese's theory of decentralized management, the organization produced a number of criminally talented senior executives, any one of whom had become perfectly capable of assuming the role of boss.

As Lucchese's health began to deteriorate seriously in 1966, there were whispers around the organization that he had decided on one of his capos, John (Johnny Dio) Dioguardi, as his favored successor. The choice made sense: Dioguardi was one of the family's biggest earners, specializing in labor racketeering in the Garment Center and Kennedy Airport. Moreover, he was from East Harlem, and as everyone in the organization knew, Lucchese tended to bestow favor on men who shared his roots.

Dioguardi had been a protégé of Lucchese, who recognized his criminal talents early. In 1930, at the age of fifteen, he was already apprenticing under Lucchese in the Garment Center as a leg-breaker. He later served a stint in Murder Inc., and in 1935 Thomas Dewey listed him among the most dangerous hoods in New York. By 1955, at age forty, he was a multimillionaire, admired and respected throughout the Mafia as a gargantuan earner from labor racketeering. An apt pupil of Lucchese's pioneering methods in organized crime, Dioguardi was making so much money (more than $100,000 a week), his standard Christmas gift each year to his wife was a shoebox stuffed with $50,000 in cash, accompanied by the instruction, "Go buy yourself some nice clothes, honey." He lived and entertained in the grand style, cruising around in a chauffeur-driven limousine, living in luxury hotel suites, and eating out six nights a week with friends, never spending less than $200 for a meal. On Sundays, he liked to show off his own considerable culinary skills to friends and family invited for dinner by preparing Italian meatballs so perfect, they actually floated in the sauce.

Emulating Lucchese, all this money—according to his scrupulous tax returns—was from several highly profitable clothing factories he owned in Pennsylvania. And yet, the Commission made it clear that Dioguardi would not assume the mantle of the Lucchese Family's boss for one simple reason: he had a single unforgivable blot on his otherwise sterling criminal career. That blot was made on the night of April 5, 1956, when a low-level hood walked up to Victor Riesel, labor columnist for the *New York Daily Mirror*, and threw a vial of acid into his face, permanently blinding him. Suspicion immediately focused on Dioguardi, since Riesel had been writing about his labor racketeering. The suspicion further hardened when the hood who carried out the attack later was found murdered, obviously to forestall the possibility he might talk. The assault on Riesel was never solved, and although Dioguardi vigorously denied to both police and his own organization that he had ordered the attack, no one believed him. In terms of his career plans, however, it hardly mattered; the Commission decreed that his "lack of judgment" as demonstrated in the Riesel attack demonstrated his unfitness to become a boss. (Some years later, the Commission's judgment was vindicated when Dioguardi stupidly became involved in stock fraud, something he knew little about. He was caught and drew a twenty-year sentence in prison, where he died.)

Paul Vario of "Gold Bug" fame was another leading candidate. He rivaled Dioguardi in earning power, but had the disadvantage of being personally disliked by Lucchese, who was repelled by his notorious crudity. A fat, multijowled mobster who often communicated in grunts, Vario was noted for such table manners as devouring a large shrimp cocktail by tilting his head back and letting the shrimp slither into his mouth. He was a loud, often drunken brawler who called too much attention to himself by some of his wilder public escapades—such as the night when his wife, angered over his attentions to a young woman in a nightclub, stripped naked and paraded through the club, only to be knocked cold by her husband in retaliation for such disrespect. The low-profile Lucchese disliked such public notoriety, and was displeased that much of the flamboyant Vario's business seemed to be public knowledge. (Too many people in Brooklyn, for example, seemed to know that Vario's murder victims were taken to his auto junkyard and included in the next cube of scrap metal shipped to auto manufacturers. As a joke, some Brooklynites would occasionally bow their heads in mock respect to a passing Chevrolet or Ford on the assumption that a missing person they knew was probably a part of the car.)

Even without Lucchese's personal animosity, Vario became ineligible for the top job when, almost coincident with his boss's death, he suddenly got into income tax trouble. Vario had laughably claimed an income of exactly $7,280 in each of the tax years 1965 and 1966 as a florist. At his trial for criminal tax evasion, the government easily proved his actual income was somewhere in the millions during those two years. To make matters worse, Vario insisted on testifying in his own behalf. Prosecutors tore him to pieces, a humiliation that severely reduced his stock in the Mafia. The Commission ruled that Vario was too stupid to serve as boss, although he was awarded the consolation prize of consigliere in tribute to the vast piles of money he had made for the family.

That left a number of other worthy candidates known to enjoy Lucchese's favor, including Vario's predecessor as consigliere, Vincent Rao. But Rao was serving a twenty-year sentence in prison, having been caught up in the same FBN net that ensnared Lucchese's main operative for narcotics, John Ormento. Paul Correale, another highly-regarded capo under consideration, suddenly dropped dead of a heart attack. Carmine (Mr. Gibbs) Tramunti, Lucchese's second in command, ordinarily would have been guaranteed the post as boss upon his leader's death, but he was almost seventy years old and suffering from a variety of physical ailments.

Attention then focused on Lucchese's other capos for a possible candidate, one of whom immediately stood out: Antonio Corallo. Called "Tony Ducks" for his amazing ability to avoid conviction, Corallo had a number of criminal qualities that caused his name to be mentioned with increasing frequency at Commission meetings. He was from East Harlem, and thus enjoyed Lucchese's favor. More significantly, he was a tremendous earner, primarily in labor racketeering. He was fifty-three years old and in good health in 1967, considered the perfect age for a Mafia middle executive to move up in rank. He was shrewd, enjoyed the loyalty of the crew he supervised, and was very much a disciple of Lucchese, sharing his boss's preference for low profile. By early 1968, the Commission had just about decided that Corallo would become the new boss of the Mafia's crown jewel.

But there was a problem. In one of the rare instances where

Corallo was actually convicted of a crime, he was facing jail time for his role in a bribery scheme. A New York City commissioner fixed a multimillion-dollar contract for cleaning the city's reservoir system so that a Mafia-connected outfit's inflated bid for the job was accepted. Corallo, who had a conviction for heroin trafficking on his record, was looking at a five-year sentence. The Commission rethought Corallo's selection; five years was too long to keep the Lucchese Family's top leadership position vacant while waiting for him to come out of jail.

Despite his record, Corallo was sentenced to three years. With time off for good behavior, he would probably serve about two years. The Commission reconsidered, and this time the decision was that Corallo would receive the designation as the new Lucchese leader, and would actually take command after his prison sentence concluded. Meanwhile, the aging Carmine Tramunti was named as interim boss to keep the seat warm until Corallo walked out of prison. (Events later developed with uncanny precision: Corallo got out of jail at the very moment Tramunti was convicted on stock fraud charges. Corallo gave him a lavish going-away party.)

It is a tribute to Corallo's vaunting reputation that the Commission made such an extraordinary arrangement. But no one who knew Corallo was surprised, for even in an organization full of talented criminals, Tony Ducks was already something of a legend.

"One of the scariest and worst gangsters we ever dealt with," Senator John McClellan once said of the short, stocky man with piercing blue eyes who had snarled his way through several uncooperative appearances before McClellan's Senate committee. By that point, in 1958, Corallo already was one of the top labor racketeers in the country. A close working partner of John Dioguardi, he had first come to Lucchese's notice in 1930, when, as a violent street punk, he was recruited for the 107th Street Gang. Five years later, he was in the underworld's big time, dealing heroin. Federal agents caught him selling of $150,000 worth of the drug, but, thanks to his organization's corruption of the judiciary, he was given a slap on the wrist: six months in jail. During the next twenty years, he would be arrested twelve more times on charges ranging from extortion to murder, but all the charges were dropped before trial. "Tony ducks again," Lucchese joked about still another amazing Corallo escape from the law, creating a permanent nickname.

When Corallo had finished his short prison sentence in 1935, he was recruited by Lucchese for labor racketeering and served an apprenticeship in the Garment Center, the Mafia's graduate school for learning the arts of corrupting labor and management. Lucchese took off some of the rough edges from his protégé, patiently instructing him that he had to act and look like a businessman. Within six months, the transformation of Tony Ducks was complete: stylish dark suits, shirts with French cuffs, a pair of black horn-rimmed glasses, and a smooth way of speaking when engaged on such business matters as collecting tribute from Garment Center manufacturers.

But the glossy veneer only barely concealed the inner thug. Even in a Brooks Brothers suit, Corallo *looked* scary; with that deadly stare, he was noted for an ability to convey an ominous message. Lucchese found him useful for face-to-face sessions with Garment Center businessmen late on their shylock payments, or who were being uncooperative in some way. In one instance, workers at a Garment Center factory were becoming restless over a sweetheart contract their corrupted union had negotiated with their employer, part of a deal that Lucchese had arranged (for a healthy cut of the resulting savings in labor costs.) He sent Corallo to "get their minds right," which meant that Tony Ducks for the next two weeks each morning would appear on the factory shop floor, silently glaring at the workers. He never said a word, but at the end of the two weeks, there was no further restiveness.

By 1943, only thirty years old, Corallo was promoted to capo, a rare achievement for so young a hood. The promotion was a recognition by Lucchese of Corallo's brilliant ability in labor racketeering. The centerpiece of Corallo's efforts was his control, with John Dioguardi, of five Teamsters Union locals, along with the Toy and Novelty Workers Union, the Painters and Decorators Union, the Conduit Workers Union, and the United Textile Workers. He held executive posts in all these unions, giving him a combined—and ostensibly legitimate—income that made him a millionaire. Seven years later, he and Dioguardi struck up a partnership with an ambitious young Teamsters local head from Detroit named James Hoffa. To aid Hoffa's rise to power as head of the entire Teamsters Union, Corallo created a number of "paper locals" (union locals, staffed by Mafia hoods, that existed only on paper) that voted for Hoffa in union elections. A grateful Hoffa let Corallo do whatever he wanted with the Teamsters locals in New York. Tony Ducks had a number of interesting ideas for those locals, including staffing them with "ghost workers," salaried employees carried on a company's books who did not in fact exist. Corallo collected their salaries, kicking back some of the proceeds to companies that participated in the scheme. Corallo could afford to be generous in such circumstances, since at one point he was making $69,000 a week on the deal.

Obsessively security-concious, Corallo gradually increased his empire with hardly a whisper of publicity. That changed in 1958, when he was summoned for the first of several public appearances before the McClellan Committee to discuss labor racketeering, especially his alliance with Hoffa. He was distinctly uncooperative, leading a frustrated committee counsel, Robert Kennedy, to accuse him to his face of being "the worst kind of racketeer this country has produced." Corallo shrugged off the insult, although privately he called Kennedy "that snot-nosed fucking punk."

Corallo got some additional unwelcome publicity in 1966, when horrified British authorities discovered he was deeply involved with several major gambling casinos in London. Corallo headed up an elaborate operation to lure high-roller American gamblers on overseas junkets to the casinos, where the gamblers were separated from their money. Corallo got a cut of every dime the gamblers lost. Even after expenses were paid—complimentary air flights for the gamblers, among other amenities—Corallo was earning a very high profit. On one of his visits to London to check up on the operation, Corallo was barred from entering and unceremoniously booted out of the country.

Aside from these incidents, Corallo operated out of the glare of any spotlight, secure in the knowledge that whatever he did was protected from prying eyes and ears by the layers of security that his organization had spent decades perfecting. In that atmosphere, he unworriedly held a series of meetings to put together his management team. His security screen was so tight, it would take law enforcement nearly two years to learn who these men were.

As his chief aide, Corallo selected Aniello (Neil) Migliore, thirty-six years old at the moment of Tony Ducks' accession, but already a Mafia legend. Born in Queens, as a teenager he demonstrated remarkable aptitude for running illegal gambling operations. He had been recruited by a local Lucchese soldier, Joseph Lorato, who quickly devolved on him virtually total control of all Lucchese gambling operations in the borough. Arrested ten times, he served only a nine-month prison sentence. By the time he was twenty-one, in 1957, Migliore was earning $50,000 a day, an astounding earnings record that made him the most talked-about young mafioso in the entire organization. That year, he was invited to serve as one of the Lucchese Family's delegates to the Apalachin summit, a rare honor for someone so young. The invitation signaled that he had been marked for future greatness, but to the organization's puzzlement, he made it clear he had no ambition to rise to a senior leadership position. Migliore, a placid, easygoing man, disliked the often-deadly politics in the higher ranks. He was a close friend of Corallo, and agreed to become his chief executive only on the understanding he would not have to participate in such duties of the Mafia's executive ranks as those interminable sitdowns.

Christopher (Christy Ticks) Funari, whom Corallo selected for underboss, was another legendary earner, mostly in loan-sharking. By 1962, when he joined the Lucchese Family at the relatively advanced age of thirty-eight, his record indicated no hint of future criminal talent. A Brooklyn hood from the age of fifteen, by the time he was nineteen he had already served two prison terms for armed robbery and was entering prison for a third stretch, a sentence of fifteen to thirty years for the gang rape of a sixteen-year-old girl whose broken body Funari dumped into a muddy road. Released on parole in 1953, he dabbled in heroin trafficking and gambling, but discovered his true calling in the loan shark business. Corallo, who had been assigned by Lucchese to establish the family's presence in Queens, spotted Funari's talent and recruited him to build up Lucchese Family gambling operations in that borough. By the time of Funari's formal induction into the Mafia, he was earning $25,000 a day.

The man selected as Corallo's consigliere was not able to immediately assume the post because he was in prison, a circumstance that would come to represent a tribute to the redemptive powers of the federal narcotics trafficking laws. Salvatore (Tom Mix) Santoro was still another alumnus of the 107th Street Gang from East Harlem, and like many of his fellow alumni had gone into the heroin business as the quickest road to riches. Beginning in 1934, as a nineteen-year-old trafficker, he served three brief prison sentences for selling heroin. In 1959, he was caught with a hundred kilos of heroin, and discovered that the new federal laws had teeth: a twenty-year prison sentence. Released in 1978, he became friends with Corallo and declared he had been permanently cured of heroin trafficking. Corallo had an alternative career: labor racketeering, a field in which Santoro demonstrated inborn talent. Soon he was Corallo's chief point man for a dozen different labor rackets, known for his ability to keep them all running smoothly—and the money flowing.

During the three years he spent in prison, Antonio Corallo depended mostly on Funari and Migliore as his main sources of intelligence on developments from within and without the organization. In terms of the organization, there was actually not much to report: following the turmoil of the Gallo and Bonanno wars, things had settled down. Carlo Gambino, head of the family named in his honor, had risen to become the most powerful and influential member of the Commission, an influence aided by the fact that the new heads of the Bonanno and Colombo organizations were his protégés. Business was booming, and if the various components of the organization could stop fighting each other, everybody was going to get very rich.

As for the outside world, Corallo learned that family operations remained largely immune, although, as Migliore noted, there appeared to be signs that the FBI was becoming more active. Funari added a warning: since Corallo was about to assume command of the Lucchese Family, it seemed likely he would become a target. So perhaps it would be wise for the new boss to adopt an extremely low profile. Funari phrased this warning carefully; he was aware that Corallo planned to celebrate his new status by building a $900,000 custom home on Long Island, a flash of ostentatiousness that Funari thought might wave a red flag at law enforcement. But he was also aware that Corallo was determined to build his dream home and would not react kindly to any suggestion he abandon the idea.

Corallo understood the real focus of Funari's argument. He had long been amused by Funari's obsession with a low profile, including living in a modest home and keeping two cars— a used Chevrolet for business travel, and a Mercedes for non-business driving. What Funari had done with all the millions he earned was a matter of speculation; he sure didn't spend much of it.

Corallo made it clear that while he was as security-concious as necessary, he thought Funari's caution went a little too far. Besides, he argued, given the low level of danger the organization faced from law enforcement, there was no real need for the kind of near-invisibility Funari practiced. "Hey," Corallo said, laughing, "with the kind of assholes they got on the other side, I got nothing to worry about."

But events taking place simultaneously in a classroom in Quantico, Virginia, a conference room at FBI headquarters, and at a small Justice Department office in Washington would prove him wrong.

FIVE

The Sun Luck Mafia

After all, when you've got three million dollars, you can't be too secretive.

ILARIO ZANNINO

Promptly at 8 A.M., as an icy wind howled outside on a typically frigid Washington winter morning in 1977, the parade began. One after the other, the men entered the conference room in the Justice Department, there to confront a somber-looking group of men and women seated around a large oak table piled high with personnel files. Each man summoned to that room sat in a large winged armchair and answered a series of questions, climaxing with this one: "How would you improve the FBI?" The people at the table listened quietly to the answers, took a few notes, then thanked the interviewee for coming.

Somewhere around 10 A.M., a lantern-jawed man with riotous eyebrows and what seemed to be a permanently grim expression entered the room. Neil J. Welch, SAC of the FBI's Buffalo field office, answered several questions about his FBI career, then was asked the climactic question: what would he do to improve his organization?

"Sandbag Bureau headquarters and rip out the phones," he replied instantly, without the slightest change in his grim expression.

133

There were a few suppressed titters as Welch was excused and thanked. When he had left, some of the people around the table exchanged bemused glances. Welch certainly had lived up to his nickname of ''Jaws,'' one of the toughest agents in the entire Bureau, and a man notorious for his bluntness. But among the 235 candidates the panel would interview, he was unanimously regarded as the right man for the job they were trying to fill: Director of the FBI.

The blue-ribbon panel had been appointed by newly elected President Jimmy Carter to find a successor to Clarence W. Kelly, who was retiring after beginning the job of repairing the post-Hoover Bureau's tattered reputation. The panel's mandate was to recommend to Carter a miracle worker— someone who had a spotless background, a sterling record of achievement in law enforcement, a reputation of sufficient size to inspire respect, and the guts to change an ossified institution. All three qualities would be needed for a Herculean task, defined by Carter as taking the FBI apart and rebuilding it. The FBI was in bad shape following the battering it took during congressional investigations of the American intelligence community, which uncovered such ugly secrets as the COIN-TELPRO program. Two Bureau officials were facing indictment for violating the civil rights of domestic dissidents. The FBI's reputation was at its lowest ebb.

Despite the panel's unanimous conclusion, Carter decided not to submit Welch's name for congressional confirmation. Carter agreed with the panel's assessment of Welch's abilities, but felt he lacked an essential political component. In Carter's calculation, a post-Watergate Congress, determined to radically overhaul the entire American intelligence community, would only approve a candidate who not only had an impeccable background, but also had no connection to the FBI. Carter's easily confirmed alternative was a distinguished federal judge of unquestioned probity, William H. Webster of St. Louis.

It was an inspired choice, for Webster, armed with a blank check from the White House to rebuild the FBI in any way he saw fit, immediately made it clear he intended nothing less than a revolution. Armed with one of the first post-Hoover reforms in the FBI, mandatory retirement at age 55, Webster conducted a drastic housecleaning, ordering deadwood in headquarters and field offices all over the country to submit their retirement papers forthwith (among them J. Wallace LaPrade in New York). Webster then announced he intended to fill these vacancies with "ass-kickers" who would carry out his drastic reorientation of FBI priorities. He ordered the Bureau to stop spying on domestic dissidents ("We are out of that business forever") and directed that all those agents snooping into people's garbage be reassigned into the kind of work they should be doing—such as investigating organized crime.

The key vacancy Webster had to fill was in New York, the Bureau's largest and most important office (its SAC is the only one in the Bureau to carry the rank of FBI assistant director). New York was also the epicenter of organized crime, and he wanted a man with a record that indicated a strong anti-Mafia commitment and hard-nosed enough to restructure an outpost notoriously resistant to change. Webster didn't hesitate a second: only Neil J. Welch was the man for the job.

To the small band of agents involved in operations against organized crime, the appointment of Welch could not have signaled more clearly the seriousness of Webster's intention to revolutionize the FBI. Welch, one of the Bureau's legendary agents, not only had a reputation as an innovative anti-Mafia fighter, but he also was noted for an open contempt of headquarters. There were many stories about his take-no-prisoners style, such as the time when, as SAC in Philadelphia, he discovered one of his supervising agents phoning a friend in FBI headquarters to complain about an order from his boss. Welch picked up a pair of scissors and cut the line in mid-sentence. "This is what I think of headquarters," he said. On another occasion, he had to be physically restrained from strangling one of the Bureau's senior officials, who had made the mistake of telling Welch that his "obsession" over the Mafia was pointless: "It's just some guys shooting each other, so what?"

Within the Mafia, Welch was regarded as one of its most dangerous enemies. He had devised a number of innovations to make the mobsters' lives uncomfortable, such as extensive "sting" operations and the first use of videotaped evidence, which tends to impress juries. To the dismay of headquarters, he ordered his street agents to stop wearing the standard FBI uniform of white shirt and business suit, substituting a more grungy look that helped them blend into the street world. When he worked as SAC in Buffalo, the local Mafia organization, long accustomed to being left alone by the cops and the city's FBI unit, reacted in outrage when Welch ordered tight surveillance of known mafiosi and began arresting some of its senior executives. An angered Stefano Maggadino, the Buffalo Mafia boss, ordered his men to conduct their own surveillance against Welch's agents and his office; some mobsters began following agents in their cars and writing down their license plate numbers. The counteroffensive ended when Welch passed the word that unless it stopped, the Buffalo Mafia's existence was about to become a nightmare whose horrors would make everything that had happened to date seem like a Sunday school picnic.

In New York, Welch hit the ground running. "This place is a fucking mess," he announced to a gathering of the field office's agents the first day of his arrival. "I am going to rebuild it brick by brick." He made it clear his first priority would be to reorient street agents toward organized crime, but immediately encountered some indications that would be no easy task.

For one thing, Welch was astounded to learn that the New York field office had a grand total of fifteen agents assigned full-time to organized crime investigations, a modest resource further diluted by the emphasis on the pursuit of illegal gamblers. He got another shock when one of those agents, soon-to-retire Paul Cummings, told him, "When I leave, Chief, you can turn out the lights, because I'm the last agent in New York with any information in la Cosa Nostra."

Welch received still more unsettling news when he made the obligatory round of courtesy calls on the various components of the law enforcement establishment in New York. At the U.S. Attorney's Office for the Southern District of New York—the job once made famous by Thomas E. Dewey—the U.S. Attorney, a dim bulb named Robert B. Fiske, told Welch that the FBI would find no official corruption in New York, since there wasn't any. Managing to hide his incredulity,

Welch politely did not mention the fact that the Southern District during the past ten years—a time when New York City was a cesspool of corruption—had not prosecuted a single case of political corruption. Worse, it had little interest in the subject, and seemed to have even less interest in organized crime cases.

Welch met a far different reception when he traveled across the East River to the Brooklyn headquarters of the U.S. Attorney's Office for the Eastern District, where prosecutors like Charles Rose laughed hysterically when informed what Fiske had said. Among the more amused was Edward McDonald, chief prosecutor for the Eastern District Organized Strike Force. McDonald's organization was one of seventeen such units created in 1968 following an idea first articulated by Robert Kennedy. The idea was to concentrate the various federal law enforcement agencies, ranging from the FBI to the IRS, in a single, coordinated effort targeted against specific organized crime figures who were committing federal crimes. But the concept had only modest success, largely because there were not enough FBI agents assigned to the strike forces. The Eastern District unit was an exception—with meager resources, it had managed to convict over two hundred mafiosi since 1969—and McDonald wanted more FBI agents and more aggressive FBI efforts to infiltrate organized crime operations.

Welch agreed, and had just the plan in mind. A devotee to sting operations, Welch in 1978 conceived one code-named Abscam, originally designed to infiltrate the connection between corrupt politicians and Mafia-controlled industries on Long Island. Unexpectedly, the operation detected something juicier: corruption in Atlantic City. Refocused on New Jersey, the operation ultimately ensnared a number of corrupt politicians, most prominently the state's senior U.S. Senator, Harrison Williams.

In terms of organized crime, Abscam had only limited impact, but it was an essential proving ground for some of the techniques Welch wanted to use in other assaults. Abscam built on the success of an earlier undercover operation, Unirac, which was targeted against organized crime's grip on the East Coast waterfront industries. Some two dozen convictions resulted, although as with Abscam and the more modest Lil Rex operation, the real value was in the lessons the operation taught on how to integrate undercover investigations with a potent new tool the law had now provided the FBI: electronics. The 1968 Omnibus Crime and Safe Streets Act included Title III, which allowed the FBI to seek a warrant for installation of a bug or wiretap on the basis of "probable cause," somewhat loosening the previous standard of direct evidence. In practical terms, that meant the FBI could go into court and get a bug installed merely on the basis of information provided by an informant, whose affidavit would attest he had witnessed criminal matters being discussed at a certain place. Even better, Title III created a chain reaction: if a bug at one location provided "probable cause" that crime was being discussed or carried out at another location, then the first bug would provide sufficient basis for another warrant for the new location. Strict time limits were set for Title III warrants—usually thirty, sixty, or ninety days—but as the FBI learned, a bug operating for even thirty days could pick up a tremendous amount of valuable intelligence, in addition to the "probable cause" it might produce for further warrants.

Title III eventually would prove to be a devastating weapon against organized crime, but, as Welch noted, for the moment it was nearly useless unless the FBI significantly improved its intelligence and did a much better job at recruiting top-level informants. A number of agents told him that the only effective way those two requirements could be met lay in cooperation with the police, whose street detectives had a roster of informants and knew all the players in the game. Although there had been unofficial contact between some cops and FBI agents, these tended to be intermittent. What was needed, the street agents insisted, was some kind of official and permanent joint setup between the two law enforcement agencies. The problem was that nobody had been able to figure out how to do it, given the two very different cultures each side represented, along with bureaucratic politics, further worsened by years of mutual suspicion.

Just as Welch was considering how such a joint effort could be achieved, a spectacular criminal event took place at Kennedy Airport, a crime whose aftereffects proved the urgent need for an FBI-police partnership. It was a very deadly lesson.

In December 1978, a gang of seven masked men held up the terminal of Lufthansa Air Cargo at the airport and escaped with $8.5 million in cash and jewels, the largest cash robbery in American history. The robbery was organized and directed by James (Jimmy the Gent) Burke, an infamous criminal who was a member of the Lucchese Family crew led by the equally notorious Paul Vario. A good chunk of the proceeds went to Vario, who sought to anticipate any possible loose ends that would lead back to himself by a typically Mafia solution: arranging the murder of fourteen people connected in some way with the heist, including six of the seven men who actually carried it out. (An alternative theory was that Vario actually arranged all those murders not because he wanted tight security, but because he wanted a larger share of the proceeds for himself.)

Since the theft involved money from an interstate shipment, primarily bank funds transferred from European to American banks, FBI jurisdiction was clear. But the police were also intent on solving what some newspapers were calling "the crime of the century," and both agencies found themselves working at cross-purposes. They jealously guarded promising leads, did not share intelligence from their respective informants, and generally acted as competitors. In such an atmosphere, it was not surprising that with the exception of two Lufthansa employees who had provided inside information to the robbers, none of the perpetrators was ever arrested, nor was one cent of the loot ever recovered.

No one was more frustrated by this development than an FBI supervisor named Steven Carbone, who directed the New York FBI's investigations of major robberies. Carbone, the Bureau's most avid student of the crime, developed a theorem of big heists, which postulated that the larger and more complex a robbery, the more likely organized crime was behind it. Only organized crime, Carbone came to learn, had the kind of resources that could recruit experienced criminals, provide whatever technical help necessary, and, most important, arrange for the laundering of the proceeds (a vital step because the serial numbers of large-denomination bills are routinely recorded by financial institutions). Additionally, organized crime had the requisite muscle to enforce any necessary discipline, especially among robbers who in the event of dissatisfaction with their cut of the proceeds might be tempted to exact revenge by talking to law enforcement.

Within twenty-four hours of the Lufthansa heist, Carbone knew that it was a Mafia operation. A so-called "top echelon" informant—Bureau jargon for a valued informant of proven reliability—confirmed it, adding the interesting information that Paul Vario of the Lucchese Family was in overall charge of the robbery operation, which had been carried out by Jimmy the Gent Burke's gang. But since the informant was not a participant in the robbery and was only repeating what he had heard secondhand, he would be of no use in proving what he had revealed.

As things developed, neither Carbone nor the police ever did get that proof. Despite the remarkable total of 125 agents put at Carbone's disposal, all they found were dead bodies and suggestive wisps of clues: Still, there was some justice in the case: Jimmy the Gent Burke, the robbery's mastermind, was convicted in an unrelated case and was sentenced to life in prison, while Paul Vario also was convicted in another unrelated matter and went to jail for five years. These consolation prizes came about because Carbone managed to recruit Henry Hill, a low-ranking, drug-addicted member of Burke's gang as an informant—and, later, as a prosecution witness. Hill provided the ammunition that destroyed Burke and what remained of his gang while temporarily derailing the criminal career of Vario. (In the process, his experience provided the raw material for the Martin Scorsese film *Goodfellas*.)

Carbone took scant comfort from either development; as he pointed out, the overall Lucchese Family enterprise remained untouched, now further enriched by over $8 million, not to mention the fact that the greatest cash robbery in American history remained officially unsolved. From a procedural standpoint, there was even worse news: the fragmented investigation starkly underscored the great chasm between the FBI and police, and, to a large extent, revealed the shortcomings of both. On balance, Carbone concluded, the Lufthansa episode was a disaster for law enforcement. Something had to be done.

The New York police establishment had reached the same conclusion, also because of the difficulties that arose in the Lufthansa case. Just emerging from the worst scandal in its history—revelation of a systemic corruption that reached into every precinct—the New York City Police Department had begun to stir, cleaning out corrupt cops and bringing in new leadership that was open to new ideas. In the process, a number of cops who had long complained about the way the department handled the problem of organized crime suddenly found that their new bosses were actually listening to them. Among the more pleasantly surprised at this development was Detective Joseph Coffey, one of the department's star detectives. Coffey, whose accomplishments included heading a team that broke the famous ''Son of Sam'' serial murder case, for years had criticized what he called the ''half-assed'' approach of his department and district attorneys toward organized crime. For too long, he had seen district attorneys combat the Mafia by dragging individual mobsters before grand juries under grants of immunity, demanding they reveal what they knew of organized crime, and, when they refused to talk, charging them with contempt. Mobsters had come to accept the process as a cost of doing business; as they were well aware, legally they could only be sentenced to jail for the term of the grand jury, usually thirty days. So they showed up for their grand jury appearances with toothbrushes in their pockets, fully prepared for an enforced vacation in a ''Mafia Manor.'' They tended to treat these appearances casually, such as the time Jimmy the Gent Burke was dragged before a grand jury and asked what he knew of his friends, the Gallo brothers of Brooklyn, an infamous team of Mafia hitmen. ''Are them the guys what make the wine?'' Burke asked in wide-eyed innocence, and was immediately clapped in jail for contempt (or, more accurately, for being a wiseass). As a crime-fighting tool, the grand jury appearance earned district attorneys a lot of publicity, apparently the main point of the exercise, but in terms of practical effects the whole process was a waste of time.

In 1978, as Welch was tearing apart the New York FBI office, Joseph Coffey was called in by the new police heads and given what appeared an impossible assignment. Tired of publicity over unsolved mob hits—there were thirty current cases on the books—the top brass ordered Coffey to solve them. He was given an elite unit of eight handpicked detectives and told to do whatever necessary to get the job done. Within three years, "Coffey's Gang," as they became known, solved twenty-one murders (a number that grew to fifty-two by 1983). It was an extraordinary achievement in an area of police work traditionally regarded as impossible. The achievement was a tribute to the talents of Coffey and his team, but some credit was due to Coffey's decision to set up a liaison with Welch's FBI agents, who shared their intelligence and resources on organized crime with the cops.

The result demonstrated what could be achieved when both law enforcement organizations worked together, a lesson that had its greatest impact on the New York office of the FBI. In fact, it landed there with a bang.

The FBI agent had seen the dangerous miscreant trying to make a run for it, but was able to get off a shot that drilled him in the head, killing him instantly. "Last time that son of a bitch steals any food from *this* place," Kenneth J. Walton said as his fellow FBI agents stared, open-mouthed.

Walton nudged the body with his foot. "Got him right in the head," he said, proud of his marksmanship. He picked up the body of the dead rat by the tail, wrapped it in several sheets of newspaper, and dropped the corpse into an incinerator chute.

And with that dramatic entrance, Walton marked his arrival as head of the FBI's New York office to succeed the retiring Neil J. Welch. Such dramatic gestures were not entirely unexpected from one of the Bureau's most famous agents, a man who had been involved in a number of spectacular cases during a twenty-year career in the FBI's counterintelligence and criminal divisions. He was that rarity in the Bureau, a certifiable character who, it was whispered, actually once told off J. Edgar Hoover himself and lived to tell about it.

He didn't look like the typical FBI agent. He was always dressed in tailored suits of the latest fashion, with shirts handmade by his wife (she made the left sleeve one inch shorter so that her left-handed husband would never have to endure the indignity of an arm action making one sleeve show an inordinate amount of cuff). With his gold cigarette case and a year-round deep tan, periodically maintained with a sunlamp, Walton's overall effect, other agents thought, was of a Florida real estate hustler.

But despite the foppish appearance, Walton was one of the toughest street agents in the Bureau. "We are here to kick ass," he announced to the assembled troops as he took command. Having already solved the rat problem in the office's East Side headquarters (apparently, news that some kind of homicidal maniac was loose in the building caused the other rats to leave), Walton turned his attention to the next priority on his agenda, organized crime. From now on, he ordered, the FBI's approach to crime would be coordinated with police. He created the FBI's first permanent joint task force on organized crime, joining his best agents with their police equivalents, and issued orders that his agents were to cooperate fully with the cops. The task force was the most important of several such units he created, including those for bank robberies, auto theft, and terrorism. And to emphasize the importance of such cooperative efforts, Walton used one meeting of the new joint organized crime task force to severely berate one of his agents for failing to work closely enough with police members of the team, the worst dressing-down agents had ever seen administered to a fellow agent.

As Walton intended, word of his reprimand quickly spread along the police jungle telegraph, convincing the remaining skeptics that the FBI was indeed serious about a joint effort against organized crime. That sea change in the FBI's approach was welcome within police ranks for another reason: it helped solve the nagging problem of jurisdiction.

The simple fact was that organized crime had outgrown the various jurisdictional boundaries that had been created a century before, when no one could have conceived of criminal conspiracies that would cut across city, county, and state lines. New York's district attorneys—each of the state's sixty-four counties had one—served as the chief criminal prosecutors, but could only prosecute crimes that occurred within the boundaries of their counties. (New York City had five district attorneys, one for each of the city's original counties, subsequently renamed boroughs.) Police departments had similar jurisdictional boundaries, not very useful at a time when organized crime had moved out of its old ethnic neighborhoods.

One solution was an entirely new entity in the New York law enforcement establishment, the New York State Organized Crime Task Force (OCTF), mandated to investigate organized crime activities throughout the state without regard to local jurisdictions. Initially, the OCTF was a failure. Led by political hacks and staffed by untalented ex-cops whose political connections got them jobs to supplement their police pensions, the task force was a joke.

All that changed in 1981 when Governor Hugh Carey, tired of reading newspaper accounts about how organized crime was running wild in his state—and fed up with excuses by district attorneys that they lacked the resources to do anything about it—went looking for a new OCTF director to revitalize the agency. Carey found the ideal man: Ronald Goldstock, an ex-prosecutor from the Manhattan District Attorney's Office, where he specialized in organized crime cases. Later, he worked on labor racketeering cases at the U.S. Labor Department.

"I want this mess cleaned up," Carey instructed Goldstock, then backed up that order by granting his new OCTF director's first request: a sevenfold increase in the agency's budget and personnel. Given carte blanche by Carey, Goldstock dismissed the "empty suits," as he called them, and went recruiting to fill 125 slots for investigators. Trolling among the state's police departments, Goldstock concentrated on enlisting veteran cops with impeccable records of incorruptibility and extensive experience working against organized crime who were either about to retire or who were looking for new challenges. And he wanted investigators who were willing to work with the FBI; Goldstock was among the more passionate proponents of the principle that unless law enforcement agencies cooperated and shared their leads and intelligence unreservedly, there was no hope of accomplishing anything. Within a few months, he had recruited an impressive pool of talent, including such luminaries as Detective Joseph Coffey. (Sick of his department's relentless office politics, Coffey had retired.)

In Goldstock's conception, his task force, freed of jurisdictional concerns (the law creating it allowed free rein anywhere in New York State), could work with the FBI, also free of any jurisdictional boundaries, to investigate large-scale Mafia enterprises that sprawled across the entire state. First, however, they had to learn the dimensions of their hidden enemy.

An early disciple of the theory that the key to defeating organized crime was attacking its greatest strength, organization, Goldstock ordered the newly revitalized OCTF to create an intelligence data bank on just how organized crime was organized—a detailed picture of where it operated, who ran it, how it worked. What emerged was a picture of a great clockwork, an interconnected mechanism that was almost breathtaking in scope, with tentacles that extended from the streets to the boardrooms of dozens of industries. It was supremely adaptable, fastening on whatever it could infiltrate or dominate, and corrupting whatever could not be pushed out of the way. Some of the tentacles were visible; many were not. Cutting off individual tentacles had no lasting effect, for most invisible of all was the central directing mechanism that simply grew new tentacles.

As Goldstock and the OCTF learned, no group of organized criminals better illustrated the power and durability of the system than the Lucchese Family. Accordingly, the family became a priority target—and a formidable one, as it turned out.

Geographically, by 1978 the Lucchese Family extended over a wide territory. Its central base was Long Island, where Tony Ducks Corallo and his chief aides lived and operated. Following Lucchese's example of semi-dependent satrapies, Corallo loosely oversaw the other strong family branches in northern New Jersey, Brooklyn, Manhattan, the Bronx, and Queens. Each of these areas was under control of a senior capo who was given wide latitude by Corallo to run things pretty much as he saw fit. This management style allowed the capos to keep the bulk of their earnings, since Corallo demanded only a relatively modest annual fee instead of the traditional heavy percentage of earnings that in other families was forwarded to a family boss. Corallo's fee bore no relation to the annual profit of the various subsidiaries, witness the $10,000 the northern New Jersey branch paid each year in tribute to Corallo, a real bargain considering the $30 million it earned annually.

Corallo's most profitable subsidiary was in Brooklyn, mostly because it was run by the premier criminal capitalist, Paul Vario (until he went to jail). Vario created a money machine that gushed the proceeds from narcotics, loan-sharking, illegal gambling, labor extortion, auto theft, hijacking, and at least two dozen other assorted felonies. His steadiest source of income was from the numbers operations he ran in Brooklyn's black communities. Each afternoon, Vario's minions would watch in awe as relays of runners brought in the day's proceeds, which he would carefully count out; many days the total would reach $25,000 or more.

Vario devised a number of criminal innovations to return even more profit, including a network of chop shops throughout Brooklyn that cut parts from stolen luxury cars for sale to crooked auto suppliers and service centers. Vario liked to brag that his chop shop network was so extensive and efficient that he could provide any part for any luxury car on only ten minutes' notice. Vario's crews of auto thieves that cruised the streets each night, stealing cars with the most potentially valuable parts, were the biggest contributors to New York City's unwelcome ranking as the auto theft capital of the U.S. (In New York City, most cars are parked on the streets, rather than in garages, making them that much more vulnerable to professional thieves who can hotwire a car in a matter of seconds.)

Like his role model, Tony Ducks Corallo, Vario was a generous boss, letting the nearly fifty made men and associates who worked for him keep the bulk of what they were able to hustle. But he was also a man not to be antagonized; he surrounded himself with tough hoods who carried out stern retribution against those who had crossed him in some way. Among them was the homicidal maniac Thomas (Two-Gun Tommy) DeSimone, so named for his habit of packing two pearl-handled pistols; a strongarm artist named "Bobby the Dentist" (because he liked to smash all the teeth of his victims); and Vario's favorite hood, Jimmy Burke, who once broke every bone in the face of a man for the sin of being late on a loan shark debt.

Equally profitable was the Lucchese Family's northern New Jersey branch, run by another talented criminal, Anthony (Tumac) Accetturo. A protégé of Corallo, Accetturo had built the Lucchese tentacle from a small slice of the Italian neighborhood in Newark into a sprawling complex of crime that spread into the New Jersey suburban bedroom communities just across the Hudson River from New York City. He had also staked an early claim in Atlantic City, an investment that paid off when gambling was legalized in that city and a market for prostitution, loan-sharking, and narcotics was created. By 1978, Accetturo was making so much money, primarily from narcotics, loan-sharking, illegal gambling, and construction industry racketeering that he opened a suboffice in Florida and began building an extensive loan-sharking and gambling operation. (He subsequently extended operations even further, into Haiti, where he had a hidden slice of several gambling casinos whose take was regularly skimmed.)

Accetturo was a personal favorite of Corallo, and very much in his boss's image. He kept a very low profile (he was virtually unknown outside of law enforcement circles) and demonstrated an amazing ability to avoid conviction. In one case, charged with murder, he balked prosecutors by fooling an entire staff of doctors into believing that he had Alzheimer's disease. When the government dropped the case, Accetturo suddenly had a miraculous recovery from the disease, which he said occurred when he fell and hit his head in the shower. Enraged prosecutors put him back on trial, only to suffer another reverse when the chief witness against Accetturo took the witness stand, began to tremble at the sight of the defendant glaring at him, then dropped dead of a heart attack.

Accetturo was always grateful to Corallo for the very cheap price charged for the immensely profitable franchise in northern New Jersey. It may not have been strictly a case of altruism, because the fact was that Corallo could afford to be very generous. He was making a ton of money in the territory he directly controlled—so much money that he hardly needed to demand much in the way of tribute from any of his subsidiaries.

Corallo was solely responsible for his own success. In the early years of his criminal career during World War II, when Gaetano Lucchese had dispatched him to the New York City borough of Queens to establish a family presence, Corallo looked even further east, toward the flat plains of Long Island. There did not seem to be much in the way of potential profit in a largely rural area then dominated by potato farms, but Corallo was looking far ahead. In the not too distant future, he told Lucchese, millions of veterans would return home to start families. They would need houses to live in, and places like Long Island, with all those acres of potato farms, would become dotted with housing developments. And that meant construction, a lot of it. Further, all those houses would produce garbage which somebody would have to pick up. Corallo's rise to criminal greatness lay in those two facts of suburban life.

Corallo's prediction was proven correct: at war's end, vast housing developments sprung up on Long Island, and Corallo had a piece of every house that was built. He achieved that by the tried and true method first devised by Lucchese: allying himself with a small but critical union to serve as a lever for extorting the entire industry. In the case of Long Island, Corallo entered into a partnership with the corrupt leaders of Local 66 of the Laborers International Union, which represented some 1,200 construction laborers. These were the men who poured and spread the concrete used in foundations. They were among the least skilled workers in the construction trade, but they were critical: any work stoppage or even a slowdown would bring a construction site to a halt as tons of unspread concrete hardened into a useless mass. With that lever, Corallo forced contractors to pay up to $2,000 a week in tribute to him to prevent any strikes by Local 66. Those contractors refusing to cooperate could expect a visit from the head of the local, Peter Vario (nephew of Paul Vario), who warned of major labor trouble. The contractors got the message and were soon organized into the classic Mafia cartel, with major contracts (over $1 million) awarded to participants on a schedule decided by Tony Ducks. As a result, the price of concrete on Long Island jumped to $55 a cubic yard, some twenty percent higher than prices prevailing elsewhere. That extra twenty percent was the Mafia tax.

Not satisfied with the river of cash the scheme produced from the great construction boom that would cover Long Island with housing developments, shopping malls, office buildings, and highways, Corallo invented a number of other twists to the concrete game. One involved crushed stone, the essential ingredient for manufacturing concrete. Crushed stone was produced almost exclusively in Connecticut and shipped to concrete production plants on Long Island. Corallo's friend and working partner Aniello Migliore gradually took over the single port facility on Long Island through which the crushed stone was shipped. In short order, the price of a ton of crushed stone nearly tripled to $18.28. Since there was no alternative, every concrete producer paid the inflated price; like the ripples from a rock thrown into a pond, the bloated cost was passed down the line in the form of increased prices for just about any product in which concrete played a role.

Corallo devised still further refinements to his flourishing construction racket. One of his favorites involved imposing onerous provisions on the contracts between construction unions and contractors, who signed them under pressure of eternal labor disruption. For example, a contract would require a construction company to have a "compressor operator" on a construction site, which consisted of a highly paid union worker assigned the sole and not very taxing duty of turning on a compressor in the morning and switching it off at the end of the workday. Another required construction firms to hire "gatemen," whose job was to open the gate to the fence surrounding a construction site each morning, and close it at night. As Corallo planned, these contract provisions virtually invited contractors to cut a deal, and he was prepared to offer one: in exchange for a "labor management fee," he would arrange it so that the union agreed to overlook such provisions.

While the construction companies were building all those houses on Long Island (more than 17,000 in the first major development, called Levittown), Corallo made arrangements to trump his construction racket with another innovation. Farseeing as usual, Corallo predicted that in the future garbage disposal would be a major industry. Organized crime had never paid much attention to garbage collection in the suburbs since that promised little profit. But Corallo predicted the throwaway society (He was proved right: by 1970, America was a disposable, packaged world in which each man, woman, and child generated 6.8 pounds of garbage every day).

Somebody had to haul all that garbage away. For many years, when Long Island was a sleepy rural backwater, local guys with trucks would earn a few extra dollars taking people's garbage to the local town dump. But by the 1970s, some two million people lived on Long Island (not counting the New York City boroughs of Brooklyn and Queens), generating tons of garbage each day. To handle the enlarged demand, hauling companies were formed. The business was intensely competitive because, unlike other areas of the country, Long Island municipalities left all garbage collection to private companies. Each town and village awarded the exclusive franchise within its boundaries for what local bureaucrats called "refuse collection" to the company that offered the lowest prices for its service.

Corallo's idea was that if he could get control of the process, he could fix prices and impose a Mafia tax. Corallo repeated the standard pattern, first seeking out the lever by which he could impose a cartel. He found it in a man named Bernard Adelstein, head of Teamsters Local 813, which represented almost all the drivers of garbage trucks on Long Island. Adelstein had been in bed with mobsters for many years, so he and Corallo came to a quick business arrangement. In exchange for a cut of the proceeds, Adelstein served as the club with which Corallo cowed haulers into a cartel called the Private Sanitation Industry Association. The association fixed prices, dividing the various municipalities among its members and deciding which ones would get which contracts. The losers in this racket were the citizens of Long Island: by 1978, the rates they paid to have their garbage collected had increased over 50 percent. The winners were Corallo, who was making $400,000 a year from the garbage operation, and the individual haulers, who were part of a system that guaranteed them work (and profit) without the hassle of competitive bidding. And to ensure that the system kept going, Corallo corrupted a dozen municipal officials who could be counted on to approve exclusive franchises for predesignated haulers.

Corallo was always alert to any changes in the business that might affect his profits. One example was toxic waste. When new laws decreed that hazardous materials and other such toxic garbage had to be disposed of separately in special landfills (haulers were permitted to charge very high rates for such specialized disposal), Corallo set up a network of illegal dumps in Pennsylvania, Delaware, and Maryland. Toxic waste was dumped there, while the haulers pocketed the money they were supposed to pay in "dump fees" at special landfills. Of course, Corallo took his cut of that money. Other haulers, collecting sky-high rates to dispose of such environmentally hazardous garbage as medical waste and deadly chemicals, split their fees with Corallo, who arranged to have their deadly cargos dumped all over the eastern seaboard, and in the Atlantic Ocean.

Corallo repeated the same pattern in another enterprise that returned even greater profit, Kennedy Airport. Once called Idewild until it was renamed in honor of the late president, Kennedy Airport was a beehive that stretched over five thousand acres, with planes arriving or departing every few seconds and over $50 billion worth of air freight moving through each year. And it was in air freight where Corallo contrived to carry out one of the biggest ripoffs in the history of crime.

This time Corallo did not need to find a corrupt union; there were already two in existence, created by the Lucchese Family some years before. They had been brought into being by John Dioguardi in partnership with Jimmy Hoffa—Local 295 and Local 851 of the Teamsters Union. Specifically formed for the purposes of organized crime, the locals organized 3,500 cargo handlers, truck drivers, and other air freight workers (Local 251), and several hundred office workers in air freight companies (Local 851). The next step was a repetition of a familiar pattern: with the locals as levers, the Lucchese Family extorted payoffs for labor peace from air freight and trucking companies, then herded them into an "association" that rigged bids and fixed prices. By 1978, shipping costs had more than tripled, another Mafia tax passed on to every consumer in the United States who bought anything that had moved via air freight. Shipping companies meekly went along, especially after Corallo provided a graphic example of what would happen to anyone not willing to cooperate. One airline, tired of paying inflated rates to a Corallo-controlled trucking firm, decided to hire an outside trucking outfit. The new outfit ignored warnings of trouble from Corallo's emissaries, and one night found the tires on thirty-eight of its trucks slashed. The next night, one of the outfit's trucks careened out of control when the rear wheels fell off (all the lug nuts had been loosened). A day later, another truck's wheels fell off, at which point the trucking company gave in.

The airport racket provided all sorts of subsidiary opportunities. Corallo filled a number of union jobs with some of his hoods, who conducted extensive loan-sharking operations among airport workers desperate for ready cash (usually because they were addicted gamblers). Even more profitable was the hijacking of valuable goods. Mobsters on Local 295's payroll had advance notice of such valuable shipments as computers, designer clothes, and jewels—intelligence they conveyed to Paul Vario's hijackers. A good percentage of the "hijackings" in fact weren't hijackings at all; truck drivers deep in debt to loan sharks would be forgiven their debts if they carelessly left the ignition keys in their trucks while stopping at a diner for a cup of coffee.

There were still other gushing sources of cash for Corallo, most prominently the Lucchese Family's old stomping grounds in the Garment Center. "Well, you got the Garment Center," the Gambino Family underboss Aniello Dellacroce told Corallo shortly after he took command of the Lucchese Family. It was a simple statement of fact: Corallo owned the Garment Center because he had a stranglehold on its most vital artery, trucking. No one could move so much as a stitch in or out of the Garment Center without using one of several trucking firms that had the exclusive franchise to ship goods. And all those trucking firms were controlled and organized into a cartel by Corallo, thanks to the alliance he had forged years before with Jimmy Hoffa's Teamsters Union. As at Kennedy Airport, Corallo worked an extra twist, seeding mobsters among the Teamsters locals that controlled the truckers. None of these mobsters drove trucks, but instead spent their time running loan-sharking and bookmaking operations among Garment Center employees—all to great profit.

There was one other major Lucchese Family enterprise that returned the most lucrative profits of all, but it was not one that Corallo wanted. In fact, he wished it would go away, somehow.

Ever since his arrest for heroin trafficking many years before, Corallo had seen the light. He was convinced that the narcotics business was a dead end, not worth the trouble no matter how much money the Mafia earned selling it. Like a reformed smoker, he constantly hectored fellow mafiosi to get out of the business. "The problem with the junk business," he lectured his chief aides, "is that you get exposed; you got to go out on the street to sell it." Unlike labor racketeering, he noted, selling narcotics was not an invisible crime. Besides, the public did not like narcotics. Neither did judges, who were routinely imposing forty and fifty-year sentences on major traffickers.

Corallo was an enthusiastic supporter of the Mafia's official ban on dopedealing by made members, but to his frustration, he couldn't get his own people to stop. Within the Mafia, they were called "sneakers," guys who paid lip service to the ban on drug dealing, but covertly made millions in the trade. For many mafiosi who lacked Corallo's talent for the criminal arts, narcotics offered a simple route to riches requiring very little mental agility: in the 1970s, ten kilos of raw opium could be purchased from Turkish farmers for the bargain price of $350 and converted into one kilo of pure heroin worth $225,000. And that kilo, diluted for street sale, would realize another $1 million in profit.

Even the threat of death for any made member of the Mafia caught dealing narcotics failed to deter dozens of mafiosi from the narcotics trade. Corallo tried reason, constantly arguing to his followers that the record was clear: everybody dealing dope eventually got caught. And those caught, facing huge prison sentences, were vulnerable to blandishments from law enforcement to ease their jail sentences by giving up fellow mafiosi.

Corallo had in mind such turncoats as Robert Molini, a

Lucchese associate who had borrowed $200,000 from loan sharks to get into the heroin business. Already too flamboyant for his own good (he kept a seventy-pound adolescent mountain lion as a pet in his apartment, occasionally taking the cat for a walk that terrified neighbors), Molini turned out to be not very good at selling heroin. When he couldn't meet his debt obligations, angry loan sharks pressed a gun to his head, threatening to use it unless he came up with the money the next day. Molini immediately ran to police and gave up every Lucchese dope dealer he knew.

Corallo was also worried about the tendency of many Mafia dope dealers to sample too much of the product themselves. As proof, he cited the disastrous events of 1972, when a special elite unit of honest police detectives, working in conjunction with federal drug agents, rolled up the "Pleasant Avenue Connection," arresting sixty-five Mafia drug dealers (half of them affiliated with the Lucchese organization). Also rolled up was a corrupt police narcotics unit that protected them, the Special Investigations Unit (SIU), whose corrupt deeds were later chronicled in the movie *Prince of the City*. Forty-three cops in the sixty-man unit went to jail for corruption.

All of them got caught, Corallo lectured, because they were too visible and because they couldn't resist the temptation of dipping into the drugs they were selling. Some of them would pass the time between drug deals by rubbing cocaine on their penises to induce three-hour-long erections for what they called "matinees" with prostitutes in nearby apartments. It was only a matter of time before they got caught.

"You cannot be in the narcotics business and put it on your fucking stomach," he fulminated one day to his top capos. "You can't hide it. You gotta be exposed to it, you gotta go out on the street, you gotta sell it. You can't be in the fucking junk business without going in the fucking streets and selling this cocksucking shit. We should kill them! We should make some examples! Now, I couldn't be plainer than I was with some of these guys. . . . Anybody fucking with junk, they gotta be killed, that's all. Fuck this shit!"

For anyone thinking that a low profile in the dope business was an answer, Corallo cited the case of Louis Cirillo, at one time the New York Mafia's chief middleman with French and

Sicilian narcotics wholesalers. In 1971, at the height of the heroin flood, Cirillo had shown up in Paris for a business meeting with French heroin wholesalers and casually handed over $12 million in cash for hundreds of kilos of pure heroin that he contrived to smuggle into the United States in the false bottom of a Canadian oil tanker. Cirillo took extraordinary efforts to keep the lowest possible profile, working days as a humble bagel maker as cover and concealing the millions he was making by living with his mother in a modest Bronx house. He drove around in an old car, and never visited flashy nightclubs or took expensive vacations. But federal drug agents eventually found out about him, arriving at his house one morning with a search warrant and shovels, which they used to find $1 million buried in his back yard. Cirillo went off to prison for thirty years.

The Cirillo case, Corallo insisted, was the final proof, if any was needed, that no matter how careful a dope dealer is, no matter how low the profile, eventually he'll become exposed. There were any number of members of his organization who nodded solemnly in agreement with this analysis—and then went out and made more heroin deals. And even when some of them were killed on Corallo's orders *pour encourager les autres* (to encourage the others), in Voltaire's famous phrase, it made not the slightest difference: many Lucchese Family members and associates continued to sell narcotics.

Despite his concern, the ongoing narcotics problem was one of the few frustrations Corallo was experiencing as a criminal supremo. His organization was functioning smoothly, churning out piles of cash with clocklike regularity, and steadily expanding its operations and influence. At a time when most Americans were concerned about "violent crime"—political code words for street criminals who sallied forth from inner-city ghettos to prey on the white middle class—the Lucchese Family was conducting the real criminal depredations. But it operated almost invisibly; the bulk of its profits came from operations that did not present the same threat that purse-snatchers, muggers, burglars, and street-corner dope dealers presented in the public imagination.

In that atmosphere, Corallo began to regard his criminal empire (and himself) as virtually invulnerable. He was unruffled when one of his men came to him one day with a newspaper clipping reporting that Corallo was in the process of taking over the entire toxic waste business in New York. "They're right," Corallo said with a shrug. "So?"

He was equally unfazed when Christy Ticks Funari told him that there was something funny going on: there appeared to be increased surveillance around the Lucchese Family, apparently by cops. More ominously, the FBI seemed to have become more aggressive lately; Funari had spotted what he was certain were some FBI agents sniffing around big construction projects. Corallo airily waved off the warning: "Ah, these cocksuckers. You know, they're always trying something."

If there was in fact increased interest in Corallo by law enforcement, he saw no danger. He wasn't called "Tony Ducks" for nothing; the Mafia leader with the lowest profile, Corallo had spent years perfecting a security system he believed made him untouchable. He did not hang around Mafia social clubs, he avoided Mafia sitdowns, seldom dealt personally with outsiders (even coconspirators), said nothing of any consequence over any telephone line, and did not discuss business at home. To prevent any possible infiltration of his ranks, he closed the books for his organization in 1976. For business meetings, Corallo would huddle with a few key aides in diners or parking lots, with a different location chosen for each meeting. Any meeting site was carefully checked out beforehand for signs of surveillance teams lurking about, and Corallo would never drive anywhere without conducting extensive "dry cleaning" to balk anyone from trying to follow him. Those seeking a meeting with Corallo could never reach him directly; they first had to contact the man Corallo called "switchboard," a hood named Richard DeLuca who took the message, arranged a meeting site, and made sure the site was "clean" (free of law enforcement surveillance). For especially sensitive business discussions, Corallo used a rolling office—a Jaguar owned by Salvatore Avellino, his capo who oversaw the garbage collection racket. As Avellino drove aimlessly around New York while dry cleaning with such techniques as driving up the wrong way on a one-way street to detect anybody trying to tail him, Corallo discussed business with invited passengers sitting in the back seat.

Cloaked with this kind of security, Corallo had no concern that he might have become a focus of renewed attention. But as the watchers discovered, it was one thing to look at organized crime's most elusive ghost, and quite another to actually catch him doing something incriminating.

It had snowed all night, and by dawn there was a foot of it on the ground. Just after 7 A.M. a large stretch limousine equipped with a snowplow cut its way up the winding road in the Long Island community of Oyster Bay Cove, a distinctly upscale area with huge luxury homes on multiacre miniestates.

The limousine stopped before a sprawling stone house and plowed the driveway. When that was finished, three bulky men got out of the car carrying brooms and shovels. They cleaned off the walk and entranceway. As they finished, Antonio Corallo emerged from the house. He suddenly stopped and frowned at two small spots of snow near the front door. The men furiously attacked the offending spots. When they finished, Corallo imperiously walked to the limousine through a door held open by one of the men. Another carefully brushed Corallo's shoes before he got into the limousine, lest any flakes of snow get tracked into the vehicle.

The limousine, looking somewhat odd with a snowplow attached, proceeded to Corallo's official place of business (and, according to his tax returns, his main source of income), a Brooklyn dress factory. What happened there subsequently depended on Corallo's schedule. On some days, he would be picked up in a black Jaguar driven by Salvatore Avellino that would then disappear from view in a series of evasive maneuvers, not to reappear for several hours. On other days, Corallo might appear at his favorite Italian restaurant in the Long Island community of Huntington. He would enter with an expensive camel hair coat draped over his shoulder in the company of two hulking bodyguards; as he entered, he shrugged off the coat, confident that one of the men would catch it before it hit the floor. Before sitting down for lunch, Corallo would receive a hug and a kiss on both cheeks from the restaurant owner, a devoted admirer who had properly prepared for the occasion by telling any other diners who he thought might be FBI agents or police detectives, "Get the fuck out."

On another day, Corallo might take a sentimental journey into his past, traveling to East Harlem to sip a few glasses of wine with his friend Anthony (Fat Tony) Salerno, second in command of the Genovese Family. The trip represented one of the rare occasions when Corallo was ever seen in the company of a fellow mafioso. The two men would meet in Salerno's hangout, the Palma Boys Social Club, in a neighborhood where Corallo and Salerno as boys ran around the streets stealing from pushcarts. There were no pushcarts now, and almost all the Sicilians who once lived there were long gone, having advanced, like Corallo, several rungs up the immigration ladder. The old neighborhood had become almost completely Hispanic.

Both men would lament the passing of old times, bemoan the new generation of mobsters who showed no respect for their elders (one had actually called Salerno "Fat Tony" to his face), vow drastic action to stop the drug dealing by young mafiosi, and generally bewail the complicated state of Mafia politics. As old-time mafiosi who proudly regarded themselves as hoodlums, Salerno and Corallo had a close affinity, although Corallo liked to twit his dour friend about some of his more interesting habits—such as sending Christmas cards that consisted of a color picture of himself, posed before a Christmas tree, in blue bathrobe, white pajamas, and baseball cap while wearing a sour expression and a huge cigar stuck in his mouth. When the visit was concluded, Corallo would hoist a last glass of Italian wine in a toast: "Well, here's to your health and fuck everything."

On his way back home each evening, Corallo would pass the home of his close friend and chief executive, Aniello Migliore, just a block away from his own. Migliore had built both houses—out of stone, naturally. The houses looked very much alike except for one extra touch on Migliore's house, a large cage on the roof that contained his two hundred racing pigeons. The upscale neighbors were appalled ("You can take the man out of Queens, but you can't take Queens out of the man," some of them sniffed). They were further upset when they picked up their morning newspaper one day to discover that their neighbor, whom they thought was a wealthy tile manufacturer, had been named by the New York State Crime Commission as one of the state's leading Mafia racketeers. They were even less pleased to read in the same account that another neighbor, Antonio Corallo, supposedly a very successful dress manufacturer, was an even bigger racketeer. Still, they had to admit there were a number of benefits to having such men in the neighborhood: no crime, and unsurpassed garbage collection service that did everything short of coming into the homes of Corallo's neighbors and actually bagging their trash for them.

None of these people would ever think of entering into any kind of business arrangement with so infamous a neighbor, but there were people from Corallo's old neighborhood who did. One day, a husband and his wife from the East Harlem days of Tony Ducks approached him and reenacted a scene straight out of *The Godfather*. Their young son had been raped by a Lucchese hood named Michael DiCarlo, known as "Mikey Muscles" for his body-building hobby that had bulked him up into a massive strongarm artist. They demanded justice in the time-honored Mafia tradition.

"You will have justice," Corallo told them. It took the form of several of Corallo's hoods seizing DiCarlo, then hideously torturing him for several hours. When they finally tired of abusing their victim, the hoods shot him in the head and began dismembering the body preparatory to disposing of the pieces that were to be placed in garbage bags and scattered in a landfill. They had chopped off DiCarlo's legs and were in the process of severing his head when, incredibly, DiCarlo rose up and tightly gripped one of his tormentor's arms. The grip was released only when the hoods smashed in his head with hammers, finally killing him.

After what remained of DiCarlo disappeared, Corallo summoned the couple to announce that justice had been done. "We shoved a broomstick up his ass," he told them. Each of them dropped to one knee and kissed his hand.

A Mafia traditionalist, Corallo took much satisfaction from the episode, for it represented an echo of a time long past when Italian immigrants, scorned by the political and judicial establishments, could only obtain justice in the New World by recourse to the sole method that worked in the Old World—la Mafia. It was, moreover, a case of life imitating art: *Don* Antonio, like Vito Corleone the wise, benevolent Mafia patrician, dispensing justice to his grateful people. Corallo eagerly sought such moments as anchors in a time when so much in his world appeared to be out of joint. The old immigrant neighborhoods were just about gone, the second and third generations scattering to take root in suburban worlds of two-car garages and Little League; a declining percentage of them even knew a word of Italian. The ordered world he had known was shattering: adolescents took over university administration offices, women publicly burned their bras, and there were actually men who spoke of ''getting in touch with their feelings.''

Closer to home, it was becoming progressively more difficult to find street punks of Italian background willing to apprentice in the Mafia. And the ones recruited out of this declining talent pool were not the eagerly ambitious, respectful kids Corallo once remembered; now, they were most often sullen, disrespectful punks who openly scorned the idea they were expected to serve years of low-paid apprenticeship before even being considered for the honor of becoming made.

Corallo had the sense that the world of his enemies was changing, too. He had heard the Mafia gossip that reported an encounter between a mafioso and Kenneth J. Walton, the new FBI chief honcho in New York. Spotting Walton in a restaurant one night, the mobster sent a waiter over with a drink and his best regards. Walton exploded, and in a voice loud enough to be heard in the entire restaurant, said, ''Tell him if this were a desert, and this constituted the last water on earth, I wouldn't drink it!'' Then he picked up the glass and smashed it against the wall.

Actually, the changes were running far deeper than Corallo suspected. The most significant of them were taking place at the New York field office, where an entirely different breed of young agents was moving into jobs vacated by the deadwood the new FBI regime was cleaning out. (Walton, an enthusiastic proponent of the purge, had his own way of making his displeasure known to agents of Hoover's generation he thought should retire. He approached one of them, slipped a ten-dollar bill into his hand and told him, "Go get me a cup of coffee." Walton then took back the money, telling him, "Never mind; you'd probably fuck that up, too.")

The new generation of agents was born in a classroom at the FBI Academy in Quantico, Virginia. In 1968, James Flynn, the FBI agent who had converted Joe Valachi into a star witness, was assigned as a training officer at the academy; among his duties was a course on undercover operations. Flynn converted that course into a class on how to infiltrate Mafia organizations, along with his own insights about the Mafia in general—and implied criticism of the FBI for failing to do much about it. A year later, his most attentively devoted students began to arrive.

Many of them were Vietnam veterans, a very different kind of FBI recruit. Their experiences had formed men who were skeptical of perceived wisdom, even more skeptical of the government, and did not have a high opinion of what they had seen so far of Hoover's FBI. (As one of them, James Kallstrom, an ex-Marine Corps captain who had been at Khe Sanh, put it, "I have the bad feeling that the guys in Washington running the FBI are the same guys who ran the war in Vietnam.")

Strikingly unlike the earlier generations of agents, this new generation was eager to get into the FBI for the specific purpose of changing it. They found their sense of mission in Flynn's shared lore about the mysterious world of the Mafia—and how it could be destroyed if the FBI decided to take on the job. A number of these new-generation agents wound up in New York, where, to their satisfaction, they were assigned to organized crime. But the early enthusiasm paled as they found themselves wasting their time on what the Bureau called "IGB" (illegal gambling business) cases. Such cases had a depressingly routine air about them: an arrest, an arraignment, a release on law bail, a plea bargain, and, rarely, a short jail sentence (more likely, modest fines). Any connection between this parade of gamblers in and out of federal court and combatting organized crime seemed remote.

By 1970, a clique of frustrated agents from the new generation gathered in a sort of support group to share war stories about a new conflict that was as ineptly run and as unwinnable as the last conflict in which they had fought. They called themselves "the Sun Luck Mafia" for their habit of convening in regular after-hours seminars at the Sun Luck Chinese restaurant on the East Side of Manhattan, just a block away from FBI headquarters. The main topic of discussion was organized crime, and what the FBI was doing about it. Not nearly enough, they agreed, as they exchanged horror stories about misplaced priorities and boneheaded leadership. One classic involved Jules Bonavolonta, an ex-Green Beret officer, who had developed a pipeline into a major Mafia gambling operation. Bonavolonta, a strapping product of the New York streets who could do a perfect imitation of a Mafia hood, wanted to infiltrate the operation posing as a big-time gambler. Higher-ups approved his proposal, and then allotted the grand sum of $100 for a bankroll for Bonavolonta to flash.

To Bonavolonta and the other members of the Sun Luck Mafia, the entire well-publicized "war on organized crime" that Hoover was conducting amounted to a bad joke. On paper, of course, the crusade looked impressive: a steady increase each year in "organized crime arrests," and more agents assigned to organized crime investigations. The reality, however, was that almost all of them were wasting their time. Complaints up the chain of command by street agents that the FBI was missing the boat went unheeded, and reports that deviated from perceived wisdom went unread. Some of them took the dangerous step of ignoring official strictures and developing their own policy. For example, Tom Sher, street agent and former Marine, thought the FBI's obsession with bank robberies was a waste of time, especially since local police departments were perfectly capable of handling them. But the Bureau wanted exclusive FBI jurisdiction over this easily solved crime. Sher found that FBI agents and cops actually raced to see which of them could get to a bank robbery first and establish territorial imperative. Sher worked out an unofficial arrangement under which he invited the cops to make the actual arrests (so they would get credit for them), then have cases prosecuted federally, so the FBI would get the credit for the conviction. The cops and FBI happily worked together in what became the most successful such unit in the entire country. Among themselves (but never on paper), they called their joint success the "Joint Bank Robbery Task Force," with J. Edgar Hoover never the wiser.

The Sun Luck Mafia held on, their patience finally rewarded when the revolution arrived at the FBI in the wake of Hoover's death in 1972. For agents like Bonavolonta (who years later would become head of all organized crime investigations for the Bureau), Kallstrom (eventually head of the New York field office), James Moody (later the field commander leading squads of street agents), and James Kossler (later head of organized crime investigations in the New York office), it was as if the sun had broken through after a long period of gloom. Now they wanted nothing less than an all-out, military-style assault on organized crime. As Bonavolonta summarized it, the FBI should take the attack into the streets where the Mafia made its money, into the homes where its leaders lived, and destroy its nerve center by decapitating the mob's entire top command. Amazingly enough, the Bureau's new leadership, the "ass-kickers" busily transforming it, were actually listening when the agents outlined this audacious plan. They were not only listening, they were providing the necessary weapons, most importantly an electronic one.

Among William Webster's first actions upon taking command of the FBI was to order the Bureau's counterintelligence unit to loosen the tight control over its Aladdin's cave of surveillance technology—transmitters concealed in olives, wall clocks with television cameras, night vision binoculars, miniature recording studios inside a briefcase, laser detectors that recorded conversations in a room from the vibrations on windows, and quarter-sized electronic bugs that could transmit intercepted conversations to receivers two miles away. The counterintelligence people had always feared that allowing the Criminal Division access to this wizardry would inevitably lead to revelation of such devices during the discovery phase of a criminal trial at some point (and thus tipping off Soviet spies), but under orders from Webster, they reluctantly introduced street agents to the wonders of their electronic arsenal.

The chief beneficiary was Kallstrom, who had been ordered to create an entirely new electronics and surveillance unit targeted exclusively against organized crime. The energetic

Kallstrom, who began the assignment with less than a layman's knowledge of electronics, plunged into the task. He taught himself the esoterica of the new technology the counterintelligence people had provided, then formed special teams that would covertly penetrate organized crime's inner sanctums and plant electronic ears. At the same time, he organized intensified surveillance operations to be conducted against the entire Mafia leadership in New York.

By the time Kallstrom finished, he had created an empire with a $20 million budget and a force of 350 agents divided into special teams of lock-pickers, break-in experts, and sharpshooters—this latter group recruited by Kallstrom from the "quarter-inch club," agents who could put three shots in a small circle less than a half-inch in diameter at a range of two hundred yards.

There was an even more powerful weapon available, although, ironically, the FBI had not yet grasped its significance. This weapon, which would eventually prove fatal to the Mafia, was created by the most unlikely looking anticrime crusader, a soft-spoken, scholarly lawyer named G. Robert Blakey.

In 1961, just out of law school, Blakey joined Robert Kennedy's Justice Department and began studying organized crime with the aim of devising new laws to fight it. Not too long thereafter, he arrived at a critical insight, summarized in the mantra he constantly repeated: "Organizations make organized crime possible." And the only way to combat such organizations, he argued, was to create what amounted to organized law enforcement.

The idea had been inspired by Blakey's study of Thomas E. Dewey's organized crime prosecutions in the 1930s. Although Dewey had little in the way of federal antiracketeering laws to work with, he nonetheless had managed to achieve a number of important convictions, thanks to his concept of uniting teams of experts to attack a specific criminal enterprise, such as Luciano's prostitution racket.

A devoted acolyte of Robert Kennedy, Blakey quit the Justice Department in 1964 when the anti-Mafia crusade of his hero slackened in the wake of John Kennedy's assassination. "They're not thinking of organized crime as organized crime,'' he complained of Kennedy's successors. In 1970, however, Richard Nixon's ''war on crime'' brought Blakey back to the Justice Department, which wanted him to draft an entirely new legal approach for attacking organized crime. The result was the Organized Crime Control Act, swiftly approved by Congress, that represented a complete overhaul in the government's approach. The law included funds to relocate and support witnesses, expanded wiretapping statutes, and what would prove to be the Louisville Slugger for all future prosecutions of organized crime, the Racketeer-Influenced and Corrupt Organizations (RICO) Act. For the first time, it made the senior leaders of organized crime legally vulnerable: the new law said that any member of a ''racketeering organization'' (for which read Mafia) who participated in planning organized crime (defined as ''enterprise'') or even discussed it was just as guilty as a low-ranking underling who carried it out. In other words, if a family boss discussed loan-sharking operations with a low-ranking soldier who actually put the money on the street and broke legs of recalcitrant debtors, both men were equally guilty of the same crime, ''racketeering enterprise.'' And each violation carried a penalty of twenty years in prison. Committing just two of the twenty crimes defined in the statute over a ten-year period could convict a defendant of being a ''member of a racketeering organization.'' And conviction on those counts meant forty years in prison. To a large degree, the RICO law made membership in the Mafia itself a crime.

But to Blakey's frustration, the federal law enforcement establishment was reluctant to use the new weapon. There was concern whether some of the new law's provisions would survive a constitutional test, and indeed many federal prosecutors said flatly the RICO statute was unconstitutional. The law was not actually used in an organized crime case until 1975, in Philadelphia. But the rest of federal law enforcement waited to see how appeals of that case would be decided before testing the constitutional waters. Moreover, even the newly overhauled FBI was skeptical that the law would work. It preferred its traditional method of concentrating agents against one case at a time, involving specific violations of the law.

Blakey became something of an itinerant preacher, conducting seminars at law schools all over the country to which he invited prosecutors and FBI officials to hear discussions about the Organized Crime Control Act—which were in fact platforms for Blakey to sell his idea of using the RICO statute to attack the Mafia. "Organizations make organized crime possible," he repeated, insisting there would be no progress until the Mafia was attacked as an organization.

Blakey wasn't getting anywhere until a hot August day in 1980, when he noticed two FBI agents from the New York field office sitting in the audience for his seminar at Cornell University. Aware that two of the attendees were from the FBI, the audience stirred uncomfortably when Blakey launched into an attack on the way the FBI had been combating organized crime. "Get off the merry-go-round, guys!" Blakey shouted, staring directly at James Kossler and Jules Bonavolonta. Arresting individual mafiosi wasn't achieving any results, he argued, for the simple reason that these casualties were being replaced while the organization remained intact.

The two agents listened quietly to Blakey's scathing analysis. When he had finished, Bonavolonta turned to Kossler. "You know," he said, "he's absolutely right."

At that moment, the New York FBI's war on the Mafia was transformed. Kossler, considered an organizational genius, went to work. He created five separate task forces of agents and police detectives, each targeted against one of the five Mafia families. Their new marching orders: gather evidence for the family's enterprise and take down the family's entire top leadership. Each task force would work closely with Kallstrom's surveillance and bugging teams to infiltrate the families, with the emphasis on using the bugs to gather evidence not of individual crimes, but of what Blakey called the "pattern of racketeering."

By the end of 1980, the great law enforcement offensive against the Mafia was ready to begin. Poised on the edge of their trenches, awaiting the signal to go over to the attack, were 270 FBI agents and a hundred police detectives, along with dozens of New York OCTF investigators.

But the opening shot in the battle did not come from this formidable array of law enforcement firepower. It came from a quiet community on Long Island, where the rutabaga crisis was in full swing.

• SIX •

The Jaguar That Talked

I like to be by myself. Misery loves company.

ANTONIO (TONY DUCKS) CORALLO

The problem, they learned, was lack of humus. As the small knot of concerned gardeners gathered, Robert Kubecka demonstrated how failure to properly prepare the ground that spring was now causing all kinds of difficulties. No wonder the Jerusalem artichokes and the rutabaga were just barely hanging on, spindly and unimpressive-looking. *This* is what they like, he said, drawing out some dark loam from the bottom layer of a compost heap.

Now inspired, the gardeners immediately set to work shoveling in the rotting results of the egg shells, coffee grounds, grass clippings, prunings, shredded leaves, and kitchen scraps that they had laboriously carted over from their homes to this little corner of a Long Island farm. With a slight smile, Kubecka watched them hard at work. These were serious people, the kind of white-collar yuppies who approached everything in their lives with a grim determination to to succeed—even here in the organic garden. The garden had been set up by the town of Huntington on some unused farm land for the benefit of suburbanites who wanted to have a vegetable garden, but lacked the space for it on their small home plots. For a few evenings during the week and on weekends, they showed up at the organic garden in their spiffy new Smith and Hawken outfits to happily dig in the pesticide-and fertilizer-free dirt on their assigned plots and add to their personal compost piles.

Officially, Kubecka was an environmental engineer for the town government, whose duties included management of the organic garden. In the process, he became the guru to suburbanites in its lore. They liked the slender, earnest-looking young man who had an apparently inexhaustible treasury of handy tips about such esoterica as how to sic ladybugs on the aphids. Invariably patient and pleasant, Kubecka was someone who gave every appearance of that rare man content in doing something he loved for a living.

But none of his devoted gardeners knew that behind the pleasant demeanor he was living a secret life, involving a violent struggle with a sinister entity. And in that unlikely atmosphere of staked tomatoes and lettuce, Robert Kubecka had decided on a way to win that struggle. In the process, he would play a key role in the destruction of the Lucchese Family of the American Mafia.

To understand what made Robert Kubecka tick, it is first necessary to understand his father. Like many other World War II veterans, Jerry Kubecka had settled in Long Island after the war to put down roots. He went to work for his brother-in-law's dairy, driving a milk delivery truck at a time when almost all milk was home-delivered. Eventually, Kubecka had a route that grew to four hundred customers, who asked him for a favor: when he delivered their milk, could he pick up and take away their garbage? Eager to earn some extra cash, Kubecka agreed, only to run afoul of local health departments which decreed that a truck used to deliver milk could not also haul garbage.

Kubecka sensed a business opportunity. He quit his job, invested $25 to buy an old fertilizer truck, and set himself up as a garbage hauler to service his hometown, the small bedroom community of Greenlawn, some fifty miles east of New York City. He charged $1 a week for weekly pickups, and supplemented that income by hauling hay from upstate to the remaining Long Island farms. As the young families surged into the new housing developments springing up everywhere on Long Island, Kubecka solicited their business, and soon had a small fleet of trucks—and a thriving enterprise.

But beginning in 1956, Kubecka noticed an ominous development in the garbage hauling business. Hauling companies were being approached by men who wanted to organize them into a "trade association." Kubecka heard stories about how haulers were being threatened with labor trouble by Local 813 of the Teamsters Union if they didn't cooperate, and how some haulers who refused to give in were experiencing broken windshields on their trucks, accompanied by warnings of even worse trouble.

Soon, it was Kubecka's turn. He was visited by two men with no necks who told him that the benefits of joining the Private Sanitation Industry Association were too good to pass up—the association would set prices among Long Island communities, assign inviolable territories to its member haulers, would guarantee that every hauler got a predetermined slice of the business, and would protect members from unspecified "trouble." What kind of trouble? Kubecka found out when he sent the two men packing: a few days later, the windshields on some of his trucks were shattered. Still later, when his trucks wouldn't start one morning, Kubecka discovered that somebody had poured honey into the gas tanks. Apparently operating on the assumption that Kubecka's mind had now been set right, the two goons paid a return visit. Kubecka told them to go to hell, and the next day, one of his shaken drivers told him he was quitting: three scary-looking guys had waylaid him on his route and threatened to break his legs.

Kubecka called the police, but the cops demonstrated little interest. They suggested he file a complaint against the two goons for threatening him, a suggestion that Kubecka found unhelpful; even assuming the case went to court, it would be a matter of his word against theirs. Kubecka had a strong streak of stubbornness, and despite the advice of fellow haulers to go along, he was determined not to give in, even as his windshields continued to be shattered, his drivers threatened, and his phone rang regularly late at night, usually with variations of the same message: "Listen, asshole, how'd you like to take a swim in a cement overcoat?"

In 1957, Kubecka received an even more graphic reminder

of the potential consequences of his refusal to "cooperate." Another hauler he knew, John Montesano, didn't want to co-operate either, and contacted the McClellan Committee to complain about how the Mafia was trying to take over the garbage hauling industry on Long Island. Nothing was done, and an angered Montesano took an even more dangerous step, announcing his intention of creating an entirely new (and hon-est) trade association that would combat the Mafia's trade group. He was under no illusions about the possible conse-quences, telling Kubecka, "They're going to whack me out, leave my brains in the street." He was right: one morning, as he left his home, several gunmen put thirteen bullets into his body. The murder was never solved.

If the mobsters intended the slaying as the ultimate warning to Kubecka, it didn't work, for he remained among the last holdouts as the Lucchese Family took control over the garbage hauling industry on Long Island. It was a lonely crusade; Ku-becka could not convince any of his fellow haulers to stand up to the mobsters. In fact, they began to regard him as some-thing of a nutcase whose obstinacy guaranteed him a meager existence on the fringes of the business—if he managed to stay alive. Although they were aware they had been shang-haied into a Mafia cartel, the haulers could justify their sur-render on the basis of simple economics. The cartel guaranteed them rapidly escalating prices, permanently assigned territories that included lucrative commercial customers, and stability in an industry noted for intense competition. True, there was a price to be paid: the $5,000-a-year "membership fee" in the association, and the regular cash tributes that each hauler had to pay to the mobsters and Local 813 for "labor peace," but, as the cynics argued, it wasn't very different from what went on in any other business. Besides, whatever had to be paid was simply tacked on to the rates charged to homeowners and businesses. The customers might not like the steadily increas-ing costs of having their garbage hauled away, but to whom would they complain? To the politicians in Tony Ducks Cor-allo's pocket?

These arguments may have made perfect sense in the hard-headed world of garbage hauling, but they made no impression on Kubecka. A determined man even in the face of impossible

odds, he continued a defiance that was nothing short of quix-
otic. It was a cause of endless wonder among his fellow haulers how Kubecka was managing to hang on—and even more
incredibly, how he had managed to stay alive. Kubecka's survival may have been related to the fact that he was among the
smallest haulers on Long Island, with only eight trucks, and
thus was not in a position to compete with the larger haulers.
His nonunionized employees were loyal to him, as was his
roster of business customers who ignored occasional warnings
from Local 813 emissaries that there might be trouble if they
persisted in doing business with that "flake." A more likely
reason, perhaps, for Kubecka's continued survival was that
there was little point in disposing of him at a time when the
mobsters had taken virtual control. They didn't need any further graphic examples to get somebody's mind right.

The threats and vandalism, however, continued. Kubecka
tried to shelter his son Robert from the storm in his business
life, but Robert could see the tightening of his father's face at
night, when he would answer the telephone and immediately
hang up when he heard a threatening voice on the other end.
And despite his father's firm rule that business not be discussed at home, Robert sometimes overheard conversations
between his father and his workers who were reporting the
latest smashed windshield or slashed tires. Worst of all, he
could see the toll the struggle was exacting on his father's
health.

Kubecka Senior did not want his son anywhere near the
garbage business, and was delighted when Robert went off to
college, emerging with a graduate degree in electrical engi-
neering. Concerned over his father's worsening health, Robert
decided to stay close to home, taking a job as an engineer in
the town of Huntington's environmental department (Green-
lawn was one of the communities within town boundaries).
But as Jerry Kubecka's health continued to deteriorate—he
had developed a serious heart condition—his son made what
would prove a fateful decision: brushing aside his father's mis-
givings, he took over the family business. Joined by his
brother-in-law Donald Barstow, Robert announced his
determination to keep the business going, no matter what the
mobsters did.

The mobsters immediately subjected Kubecka to their form of a rite of passage, breaking the windshields and slashing the tires of all his trucks. That was followed by a visit from a man who described himself as a "labor consultant." For a payment of $20,000, Kubecka was informed, all his troubles would disappear. "Go fuck yourself," Kubecka told him, a rejection followed by a new wave of vandalism so serious that Kubecka hired a private security firm to guard his trucks and office around the clock. But it could not stop the late-night phone calls, the rough-edged voices of men who never identified themselves, warning him that if he persisted in not "cooperating," he could expect "big trouble."

The campaign of terror was designed to intimidate Kubecka and at the same time to test whether he had inherited his father's courage. He had, but there was an extra dimension: not satisfied with maintaining stubborn defiance, he decided he would go on the offensive. He was uncertain how he would do that until he read a newspaper account that the reinvigorated state Organized Crime Task Force was investigating organized crime conspiracies in a number of industries, including garbage hauling. Kubecka called the OCTF headquarters in suburban White Plains, just north of New York City: would they be interested in what he knew about the Mafia's takeover of the garbage industry on Long Island?

They certainly would, for at the moment Kubecka called, the OCTF had opened a major investigation into just that very subject. It began when Ronald Goldstock, head of the OCTF, read his unit's first analyses of organized crime's infiltration into legitimate businesses. Among the more blatant—and dangerous—was the mob's control of the garbage hauling industry. Goldstock was appalled to learn that the entire private sanitation industry in New York City and the suburbs of Long Island and Westchester had come under Mafia control, and there were active tentacles being established in northern New Jersey, Connecticut, and northern Pennsylvania. Working in league with corrupted union leaders and politicians, the Mafia was earning millions from inflated prices. In New York City, where municipal garbage collection services only residential buildings, major corporations learned that they were part of territories assigned by mobsters to specific carting companies and that any attempt to cut the outrageously high costs by hiring a competing hauler would be squashed by threats of "big labor trouble." (One new Garment Center firm that had just opened for business was visited by the representative of a hauling company, who announced that his outfit had the exclusive "franchise" in that area and that the company's annual garbage bill would be $200,000. Asked how he could possibly make such an estimate by merely looking around, the representative replied, "I can tell just by looking, believe me. And if you don't like that estimate, I've got friends who'll come here and estimate even higher. Take your choice.")

It was even worse in the suburbs. In Westchester, an entire development of homes had to be evacuated when it was learned that Mafia-controlled haulers had illegally dumped highly toxic waste into a nearby vacant lot. New Jersey beaches were littered with medical waste that had been dumped into the Atlantic Ocean by haulers splitting fees with mobsters. An interstate highway in Pennsylvania had to be shut down after toxic chemical waste dumped under a bridge by a Mafia cartel of local haulers exploded. On Long Island, homeowners dissatisfied with bad service and soaring prices discovered they were in a form of industrial servitude—they could not give their business to a hauler other than the one that had been permanently assigned to them.

"This must stop," Goldstock said, and ordered one of his senior investigators, Richard Tennien, another of the ex–New York City detective superstars he had recruited, to head up a team of investigators that would make a prosecutable case of criminal enterprise. The first target would be Long Island, Goldstock decided, where the Mafia's garbage racket was most blatantly at work. The initial target also had the advantage of being the main operating area of the Lucchese Family, an OCTF priority.

Tennien's handpicked team, which included some of the most experienced organized crime investigators in the state, had an early advantage: Robert Kubecka. He not only provided everything he knew about the garbage racket, he happily volunteered to wear a wire. With a tape recorder taped to his stomach under his shirt, he filled cassettes with talk from fellow haulers and assorted lowlifes about how the system worked—the payoffs, the assignment of territories, the corrupt leaders of Local 813, the inflated prices.

But just out of reach were the men the OCTF investigators knew were behind it all: Salvatore Avellino, the capo in direct charge of the entire Long Island garbage operation; Christopher (Christy Ticks) Funari, who oversaw the Lucchese Family's partnership with Local 813; and, most important of all, Tony Ducks Corallo himself, the criminal leader who had dreamed up the scheme in the first place. Kubecka tried his best, but could not get close enough to Avellino to ever get him on tape; as for Funari and Corallo, they never seemed to be in public view for more than a minute at a time.

The three mafiosi were like ghosts: everybody knew they were around someplace, but Tennien's investigators were having trouble pinning them down. The central mystery was how they were managing to run their assorted criminal enterprises without meeting—or at least without being seen meeting. Corallo and his henchmen had no social club or any other kind of hangout, as did most other mobsters, to use as a site for business discussions. They conducted no crime business from their homes, and were almost never seen in restaurants or nightclubs. How, then, were they functioning in a culture where sitdowns were a way of life? The answer was critical, because Tennien planned to install a bug wherever the Lucchese Family's top command gathered to discuss business, the essential basis for a racketeering case.

It was Robert Kubecka who provided the vital clue. In addition to collecting tape recordings, Kubecka was also keeping his eyes and ears open. Gradually, from bits of unguarded conversations, he came to realize that the reason why the OCTF investigators couldn't find the Lucchese Family's command post was because it was on the move—specifically, in Sal Avellino's $120,000 black Jaguar, the same car that mysteriously disappeared from the radar screens for hours at a time, apparently driving aimlessly all over New York while Avellino took elaborate measures to elude anyone who tried to follow him.

Heightened surveillance on the Jaguar confirmed that Kubecka was right. Each day, Avellino picked up Corallo, later joined by other members of the Lucchese Family top command, and drove around. Periodically, he would double back to where he had started and drop off some of the car's occupants.

So the command post had been pinned down, but that still left the considerable problem of how to bug it. Tennien ordered even more surveillance on the car, a three-month effort that produced only bad news. Avellino, the investigators learned, was as security-conscious as his boss. He never conducted or discussed business in any location that had even the potential to be bugged, confining such matters to his car, whose sanctity he guaranteed by detailing two thugs to watch it every moment he was not actually behind the wheel. At night, when the car was parked in the garage of his Long Island home, it was guarded by an elaborate security system that rivaled a bank's.

Nevertheless, Tennien was determined to plant a bug in that car. At some point, he was convinced, Avellino and Corallo would make a mistake, creating a narrow window of opportunity the OCTF could exploit. Almost certainly, that window would open when the car would be unguarded for some reason. The problem was that any security lapse probably wouldn't be a lengthy one, so the OCTF somehow had to figure out a way to get inside the car and plant a bug in a very tight time frame, which Tennien estimated might be only a few minutes. The most talented of the police bugging experts Goldstock had recruited for the OCTF were skeptical, pronouncing the task a very formidable one—perhaps even impossible.

In preparation for a possible penetration, Goldstock organized extensive practice sessions designed to get the necessary time down to the absolute minimum. Thanks to his contacts with the Drug Enforcement Administration, he managed the considerable feat of talking the agency into letting him borrow one of the luxury cars it had seized from convicted drug dealers: a black Jaguar of precisely the same type and model as Avellino's. Day after day for weeks, while Goldstock timed them with a stopwatch, Tennien and a team of bugging experts practiced entering the Jaguar, unscrewing the dashboard, planting a three-inch-long by half-inch-high electronic bug with a homing device, hooking it up to the car's electrical system for power, then replacing the dashboard and exiting the car. Many hours of practice enabled them to carry out the operation in about twenty minutes.

Meanwhile, a twenty-four-hour surveillance on the car looked for the opportunity to put all that practice into effect. Weeks went by, then months. Not a single chink appeared in Avellino's armor. But on the night of March 23, 1983, the Mafia made a small but costly mistake. Tennien was there to exploit it.

Avellino—trailed by Tennien, two of his best bugging experts, and a surveillance team—had driven to a Long Island catering hall for the annual dinner-dance of his Private Sanitation Industry Association, turning over his Jaguar to two of his hoods who were ordered to stand watch over the car while he was inside. It was a stormy night, and while Avellino was sipping his drink and chatting with fellow denizens of the garbage industry during the cocktail hour for the event, the two miserable hoods stood in the parking lot guarding the Jaguar as the rain poured down on them. The rainstorm blew with steadily growing force, finally convincing them there was no need to stand over a car that nobody was about to approach in so furious a storm. They ducked inside the catering hall to get warm and dry, leaving the unlocked car unguarded.

It was the moment that Tennien and the two bugging experts were waiting for. Huddled in the dark shadows at the far end of the parking lot, they quickly scaled a fence and, crouching low, dashed toward the Jaguar. In a practiced motion, one man opened the door and simultaneously doused the door light as another man crawled inside the front while Tennien, equipped with a walkie-talkie, clambered into the back seat. As the wind howled and the rain poured down, the two men in the front took off the dashboard and began to install the bug, all the while urged to hurry by Tennien. But the dashboard resisted all attempts at haste, and as the minutes ticked by, an increasingly frantic Tennien wondered if all the effort they had already invested in the operation was about to go to waste. With each passing second, he dreaded that his walkie-talkie would come alive with a warning from his surveillance team that the hoods or Avellino were about to return to the car, forcing Tennien and his two bugging experts to abort.

Finally, just over fifteen minutes later, the last screw was replaced. Behind the dashboard now lurked a bug with a transmitter that would send whatever it detected in the car to receivers up to a half-mile away. The three men exited the car the way they came, Tennien using a rag to frantically mop up rainwater that had blown into the car when they opened the door. (He feared that any water in the interior might alert the super-cautious Avellino that his car had been tampered with.)

Some time later, as the storm diminished, Avellino left the dinner dance and waited at the front entrance of the catering hall as his hoods pulled up in the Jaguar. They nodded at him, signaling that no one had been allowed anywhere near the car. Avellino frowned as he got in: there were a few wet spots on the floor around the front seat. Assuming the hoods had carelessly allowed some rainwater to get inside, Avellino scowled at them and drove away.

As usual, he carefully checked for signs of any police or FBI surveillance cars while he headed out of the parking lot and into traffic. He did not see the van, parked near the road, switch on its lights and enter a string of vehicles, some distance behind the Jaguar. Nor did he see a half-dozen nondescript sedans take up positions in the traffic to his front and rear.

The next morning, Avellino picked up Corallo at his home and they headed toward New York City. Avellino did not take the direct route; following his customary security procedures, he twisted and turned through a maze of side streets, service roads, and back streets, all the while checking his rearview mirror for any sign he was being followed. Occasionally, he would see an ordinary delivery van far behind him, but the van never seemed to be there when he rechecked a few minutes later. He would see other vans, all different, clearly just the normal delivery traffic.

"Those fucking stupid cops would have to be geniuses to follow us today," Avellino boasted as he took a tire-squealing turn into another side street. Tony Ducks Corallo laughed, a sound that could be heard clearly in the headsets of an OCTF team sitting in one of those delivery vans. Thanks to the homing signal connected to the bug, the vans and several sedans (which were equipped with electronic "repeaters" to boost the bug's signal) had no trouble following Avellino's circuitous route—and hearing every sound inside the Jaguar, even the soft ticking of the dashboard clock. And the tape recorders were running.

For the next several weeks, while Avellino and his passengers remained blissfully unaware, reel after reel of tape filled up with the most revealing conversations from inside the Mafia ever recorded. But just as this electronic cornucopia promised even greater revelations, Avellino did something no one could have anticipated: he decided to take a vacation in Florida. While Avellino sunned himself on the beach, Tennien's teams watched in frustration as the Jaguar sat in the owner's garage, the bug slowly draining the power from the car's battery. Since the OCTF warrant for the Jaguar bug did not include Avellino's garage, the investigators legally could not get inside and recharge the bug. Even worse, when Avellino returned and found a dead battery in his car, any mechanic checking the electrical system would easily spot the bug.

The investigators then came up with an ingenious plan. Avellino returned, predictably found the dead battery, and called his car dealer to come pick up the car and fix it. Thanks to a tap on Avellino's phone, the OCTF teams were aware of the call, enabling them to set up an ambush. A tow truck arrived at Avellino's home and towed the Jaguar away, but just a mile down the road, the tow truck driver suddenly found himself surrounded by an entire posse of uniformed police. They ordered him out of the truck and led him away to the side of the road to conduct what appeared to be an interminable "routine registration check." While he argued with the cops about why he was being subjected to this harassment, two OCTF investigators slipped into the Jaguar and removed the bug. The annoyed tow truck driver was sent on his way with the effusive thanks of the police for his "cooperation."

A day later, the Jaguar was returned to Avellino, who was told by his car dealer that the mechanics were mystified: nothing appeared wrong, yet somehow the battery had drained. To be on the safe side, they had performed a thorough check of the electrical system and installed a new battery. The following morning, Avellino set off on his daily rounds as the Lucchese Family's mobile command post. On the way to pick up Corallo, he decided to stop off for a cup of coffee at a diner, where he encountered a low-ranking hood he knew. Absorbed in chatting with the man, Avellino did not notice that an unmarked van had slid into the parking space next to the Jaguar, blocking his view of it from the diner. An OCTF team quickly put a new bug into the Jaguar, finishing just as Avellino exited the diner and prepared to get into his car.

Not even a glimmer of suspicion crossed the mind of a newly tanned Avellino as he drove around New York. All the while, the small bug only inches from him transmitted a running narrative of how the Lucchese Family was running its operations. It detected Avellino complaining to Richard DeLuca, Corallo's "switchboard," about having to carry piles of cash each week to the ungrateful Gambino Family, which shared some profits from the construction and garbage rackets with Corallo's organization: "Two thousand, five thousand, ten thousand, twenty thousand, fifty thousand. I can't even fucking carry them [envelopes]. And never a thank you; thank you would be too much to expect." It overheard Salvatore (Tom Mix) Santoro reporting to Corallo about a major loan shark deal involving $230,000 owed by a vending machine manufacturer. The debtor was having trouble coming up with the $5,000 vig each week, so Santoro recounted how he had magnanimously reduced it to $10,000 a month. "He owes me $230,000, this cocksucker," Santoro said, but admitted: "Of course, $110,000 of it is vig."

There was hardly a word spoken in the Jaguar that was not incriminating in some way. The conversations also represented something of a graduate seminar on organized crime, as in this exposition by Avellino on how the Lucchese Family intended to take over every garbage hauling operation on Long Island: "We're gonna knock everybody out, absorb everybody, eat them up.... Whoever stays in there is only who we are allowing to stay in there." And to Lucchese hoods Thomas Ronga and Emedia Fazzini, apprenticing in the garbage racket, Avellino explained how corrupting a union was the essential first step: "Whoever controls the employees controls the bosses.... Because the power is if you got twenty people and they're not gonna come to work tomorrow to pick up that fucking garbage, who you going to listen to? The victim will say to you, 'I'll give you $10,000, but leave me alone, I've got to work.' "

But the real nugget in all the hours of business conversations concerned something that neither the OCTF, nor the FBI, nor the police knew even existed, a golden river of cash that amounted to the Mafia's greatest secret. It concerned a rather prosaic substance: concrete.

As the Jaguar tapes revealed, the Mafia's ruling Commission, impressed by Corallo's successful concrete racket on Long Island, decided in 1980 to extend it to New York City. As usual, all the Mafia families (excluding the Bonanno organization, which had been evicted from the Commission as punishment for a number of transgressions) would share in the scheme. The first step, straight out of the playbook written by Lucchese and Corallo, sought a critical union that could be corrupted. That turned out to be the Cement and Concrete Workers District Council, an umbrella labor group that represented Teamsters who drove concrete trucks, laborers who poured the concrete at construction sites, masons who finished the poured concrete, and carpenters who built the wooden frames into which concrete was poured.

These workers were vital to any major construction project in New York City because skyscrapers and apartment buildings were made of concrete; without it, any building project would come to an immediate halt. Even a day's delay was catastrophic for contractors, who had millions of dollars invested in raw materials and a huge payroll of hundreds of highly paid workers.

The labor leader who went into business with the Mafia was Ralph Scopo, chief business agent for the umbrella union organization. An associate of the Colombo Family, with which he had done business for years, Scopo and his power to instantly call a slowdown or strike represented the stick in the scheme. The carrot offered by the Mafia to major concrete contractors consisted of a guarantee of a portion of all projects of $1 million or more via rigged bids that grossly inflated prices, along with labor peace. In return, the Mafia would receive one percent of every contract, plus an additional Mafia tax of $2 for each cubic yard of concrete poured. The six leading concrete contractors were organized into a cartel the mobsters came to call the "concrete club." By profitable co-incidence, the scheme was put together just as a major construction boom began in New York City. Within a year, the four Mafia families were splitting profits of $40 million, a spectacular success that led to talk of expanding the operation in New Jersey, Connecticut, and a number of other cities elsewhere in the country that had Mafia organizations at work.

The concrete scheme's Mafia tax was eventually passed on to every consumer, for the contractors included it in their bids. As a result, by 1983 the New York price of ready-mix concrete—the type used in construction projects—had soared to $80 per cubic yard, more than double the price charged anywhere else in the country. (Just a mile or so across the Hudson River, in New Jersey, the price was $35 a cubic yard.)

The sudden and mysterious jump in the price of concrete inspired whispers around the construction industry that something was not quite right in the concrete business. When bids were announced for the huge new Jacob Javits Convention Center, only two bids were submitted for the largest concrete construction project in the United States. Moreover, those suspiciously similar bids of $40 million for the concrete work on the $486 million project were about $13 million higher than the center's engineers estimated, even accounting for inflation. Similarly, the $100 million Trump Tower project, which should have drawn a large number of bids, attracted only two remarkably similar bids—and both of them greatly exceeded even the high end of engineers' estimates.

Despite the whispers, the concrete scheme rolled on, seemingly trouble-free. However, as conversations in the Jaguar made clear, it was causing the organization no end of trouble. And the trouble could not have come at a worse time, for the Mafia already was coming under great strain.

"Where the fuck are we gonna find good people?" Corallo asked aloud one day in his Jaguar mobile office. The question went right to the heart of the Mafia's biggest headache as the 1980s began: a distinct decline in the number of promising recruits. In years past, the Mafia had its pick of the most promising youth gang members and an apparently inexhaustible supply of aspiring talent from the Italian community. But, like every other institution in America, the Mafia was feeling the impact of social change. The youth gangs that once plagued nearly every inner-city neighborhood were now predominantly black or Hispanic, ineligible for membership in an organization that was strictly whites only—and Italian ones, at that. As for the traditional reliance on the talent pools in Italian immigrant communities, most of those old neighborhoods were disappearing: Little Italy in lower Manhattan, once containing the largest concentration of Italians outside Italy, was becoming resettled by Chinese immigrants.

There was a constant need for new blood in the Mafia, if only to fill gaps caused by prison and death (murder or the more natural variety). In 1975, short of personnel, the Mafia's Commission ordered the organization's books opened for the first time since 1958. In years past, news of available slots would have attracted many aspirants seeking the honor of "made" status, but the 1975 recruitment drive encountered difficulty in finding any worthy recruits. In fact, the paucity of qualified candidates was so striking that the Commission sought to broaden the potential pool of recruits by amending its long-standing rule that recruits had to be full-blooded Italians. Henceforth, the Commission ruled, a recruit only needed to have an Italian father. The change was a reflection of a modern social reality: given intermarriage over the generations between Italians and non-Italians, full-blooded Italians were becoming increasingly rare.

Even that change failed to increase the quality of recruits, and by 1982 there was a Mafiawide disquiet over the deteriorating quality of the men seeking membership. Too many of them were wild "cowboys," as senior mafiosi liked to call young undisciplined criminals. They included many who used narcotics; even worse, from the standpoint of Mafia traditionalists, they were openly contemptuous of old traditions, which they termed "all that Cosa Nostra bullshit."

Corallo, among the leading Mafia traditionalists, frequently lamented to a sympathetic Avellino about the wretched quality of potential recruits. For evidence, he needed to look no further than his own Mafia family, where one recruit caused him an annoying political problem. Corallo learned that the recruit on his own had tried to take a slice of a Gambino Family gambling operation, leading to angry complaints. A sitdown between Christy Ticks Funari and Paul Castellano smoothed ruffled feathers, and Corallo summoned the recruit for a scolding and a forceful reminder about the niceties of Mafia protocol. To Corallo's shock, the young punk listened sullenly, then, when his boss had finished, said, "Yeah, whatever."

Corallo and his fellow traditionalist, Fat Tony Salerno, shared their frustrations over the personnel problem during their regular get-togethers at Salerno's East Harlem headquarters. "I don't know what to do, I swear I don't," Salerno told his friend one day. He went on to fulminate about the "disrespectful punks" the Genovese Family was about to induct, despite what Salerno regarded as their unfitness for such an honor. But, Salerno added morosely, things had gotten so bad, the family would induct them anyway, for the simple reason that there were no better ones to recruit.

"Get rid of them, kill them," Corallo advised, but then realized that wouldn't solve the problem. "Well, then you can't go on . . . it's disgusting."

Another problem grew directly out of the concrete racket. The sheer scale of profit created a prevailing climate of suspicion that one family organization or another might be secretly getting a bigger slice than other families. It was a natural enough suspicion, since each family had certain private arrangements with various companies, particularly in the construction business, to extort payments for labor peace. These individual shakedown operations were kept "off the books," meaning the profits were not shared among all the families, as Mafia custom decreed. Tony Ducks Corallo, for example, was the focus of suspicion that the Lucchese Family was becoming enriched by its exclusive control over the stone business. He denied it with the same fervor that Paul Castellano denied rumors that the Gambino Family planned on building a huge concrete production plant that would produce virtually all the concrete used in New York construction. At the same time, Vincent (The Chin) Gigante, head of the Genovese Family, vigorously denied that his organization was secretly extorting money from individual construction companies as part of a master plan to eventually take over all construction industry rackets.

The atmosphere of suspicion and recrimination became so bad that Corallo proposed the creation of what he called a "little Commission," a subsidiary of the Commission, whose sole function would be to direct all construction industry operations and adjudicate any disputes. The participants would include the individual family capos in charge of those rackets; more intractable problems would be handled by family bosses at regular Commission meetings.

Corallo's plan alleviated much of the interfamily tensions, but created another problem. To iron out all the assorted squabbles, many meetings were required. The participants paid careful attention to security, meeting in out-of-the-way restaurants, pool halls, and a small home on Staten Island, but as some of them were aware, so many meetings increased the likelihood that the cops or the FBI would inevitably wonder what was going on. "The bubble is going to pop," warned Salvatore (Sammy the Bull) Gravano, the Gambino Family capo in charge of that organization's interests in the construction rackets. "All these fucking meetings are gonna put us in prison."

What made these tensions even more problematical was the rickety condition of the Mafia's ruling hierarchy. As Corallo reported to Avellino during their Jaguar jaunts, the Commission seemed to have become something like a collection of unruly juvenile delinquents who hated and distrusted each other. With the exception of Corallo's organization, all the families were in some form of turmoil.

The Colombo Family's head, Carmine (The Snake) Persico, was in jail for a brief stretch, but he wanted control of the organization passed temporarily to his son, Alphonse (Allie Boy), a moron who headed up a crew of untalented dopeheads (one of whom had died of a heroin overdose at the age of twenty-four). Meanwhile, bizarrely enough, Vincent Gigante had hit upon the idea of avoiding legal trouble by pretending he was insane. Gigante's "insanity" took the form of such acts as wandering the streets in bathrobe and slippers, mumbling to himself, and standing naked in the shower with an opened umbrella when served with a grand jury subpoena. His friend, Paul Castellano, head of the Gambino Family, had withdrawn into the splendor of his $3.5 million Staten Island mansion where, each morning, dressed in silk bathrobe and cravat, he presided over meetings of his increasingly resentful middle executives. His street crews, progressively more restive over their boss's remoteness and insistence on taking the lion's share of their earnings, were plotting his downfall under the leadership of a violent Queens hood named John Gotti.

The worst problem was the Bonanno Family, a mess whose ramifications would prove very costly to the rest of the Commission. The Bonanno organization had been banned from Commission membership (and thus did not share in such common enterprises as the concrete racket) for a variety of lapses, including outright stupidity by its progenitor, Joseph Bonanno himself. Bonanno's overweening ambitions had led to his forced retirement some years before, but instead of playing shuffleboard at his Arizona retirement home, he began planning a comeback in conjunction with his two sons, untalented dimwits who had delusions of Mafia grandeur. He carefully wrote out these plans on paper to aid his thinking, then threw the papers into the garbage—where FBI agents later retrieved them. The lapse cost him four years in jail. Not content with that unbelievably stupid error, Bonanno then committed another, one that would ultimately prove very damaging to the Mafia. He wrote his autobiography, in which he casually discussed the formation and functioning of the Commission, apparently oblivious to the fact that the Commission is a criminal organization. Since one of the Commission's charter members had admitted its existence, no other mafioso would ever be able to deny that fact.

As if all this weren't enough, Bonanno's inheritors in the family committed an even more unpardonable sin when they allowed an FBI agent named Joseph Pistone (posing as Mafia-connected jewel thief "Donnie Brasco") to infiltrate the family's best crew, led by Dominick (Sonny Black) Napolitano. An indictment of the crew for racketeering, with Pistone as chief prosecution witness, revealed the FBI penetration. Napolitano paid the price: his body was found with the hands chopped off, the traditional Mafia signal that the deceased had been executed for violating security. But the damage had been done.

The family's leadership vacuum was subsequently filled by the elderly and not very talented Philip (Rusty) Rastelli, who began an insistent campaign to get the organization readmitted to Commission membership. His application was rejected. Fat Tony Salerno summarized the Commission's judgment by telling Corallo, "No fucking way it will ever happen; they're all a bunch of fucking junk pushers."

There was even worse turmoil to come. One of the Bonanno Family's most violent capos, a vicious thug and heroin dealer named Carmine (Lilo) Galante, had been released from prison in 1974 after serving a twenty-year sentence for narcotics. Determined to restore his family's glory days—and its seat on the Commission—Galante decided to shoot his way to power. He dynamited the bronze doors off Frank Costello's tomb to signal his intentions, then announced he planned to take over all heroin dealing for the entire Mafia, and would kill all the other leaders if they tried to stop him. "I'll make Carlo Gambino shit in the middle of Times Square," he vowed.

Gambino died before the threat could be carried out, but when it became clear Galante planned to kill everybody else on the Commission, it was time to act. At Corallo's urging, Rastelli agreed to a murder plot to eliminate Galante. The chosen instrument to carry out the killing was the Bonanno Family's leading hitman, Anthony (Bruno) Indelicato, a psychopath with a $3,000-a-week cocaine habit. On a hot summer day in 1979, Indelicato and two other henchmen ambushed Galante as he sat in a Brooklyn restaurant.

But to the distress of the Commission, the hit was badly handled. An eyewitness jotted down the license plate number of the getaway car Indelicato used—a stolen vehicle later abandoned with fingerprints all over it. Indelicato fled to Little Italy to report to Gambino Family underboss Aniello Dellacroce on the success of his mission, unaware he came into view of video cameras set up by a police surveillance team keeping tabs on Dellacroce's base of operations, the Ravenite Social Club.

Infuriated over such incompetence, Corallo and Salerno convinced the Commission to order a hit on Indelicato, who went into hiding to get out of the line of fire. But Corallo still wanted his pound of flesh, so he settled for the murder of Indelicato's father, Alphonse (Sonny Red) and two of his henchmen—murders decreed, in Corallo's words, because "We have to make an example of *somebody*."

The strain of all this murderous Mafia politics began to affect Corallo's health. When he experienced heart pains, he checked himself into a Long Island hospital under an assumed name for a much-needed rest. As usual, he mandated strict security: not even his fellow Commission members were to know where he was, and his private room was guarded around the clock by several goons who allowed only his chief aides, doctors and nurses inside. Tom Mix Santoro and Christy Ticks Funari were his stand-ins at Mafia sitdowns, where they deflected any questions by saying that their boss was "unavailable" or "on vacation." Given Corallo's established near-invisibility, no one questioned the explanations.

Santoro and Funari were regular visitors to Corallo's bedside, there to receive his orders and pass on news of current events from the Mafia world. The news wasn't good: at the very time the Mafia should have been enjoying its greatest prosperity ever, thanks to the vast piles of money earned from such cash cows as the concrete racket, the turmoil was getting worse. Paul Castellano had found out that John Gotti, his murderously ambitious capo, was involved in heroin dealing and planned to have Gotti killed (in response, Gotti was planning to kill Castellano). Fat Tony Salerno was sick of the mess, and was dropping hints he might just give it all up and retire to his $4 million horse farm upstate. The Colombos were all at each other's throats; one of their more ambitious capos, Gerry Lang Langella vowed, "Those bosses, I'll make them eat shit; I'll blow their asses off!" The Bonannos had descended into lunacy, with various capos jockeying for dominance, shooting each other in the process.

It had all been summed up, Santoro reported, by the Gambino Family's consigliere, Joe N. Gallo, who said one day, "It's all turning to shit, isn't it?"

Actually, Gallo was more right than he knew, for the roof was about to cave in.

* * *

While the bug hidden behind Avellino's dashboard in 1983 continued to pick up incriminating conversations (eventually, a total of some one thousand hours), other electronic penetrations were underway. Among the most significant were the bugs the FBI planted in the dining room/office in the home of Paul Castellano, another in Fat Tony Salerno's East Harlem social club, and another planted in a television set beside the sickbed of Castellano's underboss, Aniello Dellacroce, who continued to conduct business as he lay dying of terminal cancer.

These bugs were the work of James Kallstrom's FBI teams, who were busy all over the city wiring up the Mafia. Not all their forays were successful—an enraged mistress of Vincent Gigante complained to the FBI when Kallstrom's attempt to plant a bug in her apartment went wrong, producing only a pile of plaster on her new rug—but a sufficient number of successful installations formed a remarkably detailed picture of precisely what was going on inside the Mafia's top command. It was almost as if the Mafia had decided to cooperate with a radio documentary that recorded even the most sensitive discussions.

There were enough leads in all the tapes to investigate a hundred felonies, but both the OCTF and the FBI's organized crime task force, their attention focused by a new appreciation of the RICO statute, concentrated on the concrete scheme. In terms of a RICO case, it was just about perfect, an "ongoing criminal enterprise" if ever there was one. Even better, the enterprise involved the New York Mafia's entire hierarchy, which meant there was a reasonable possibility that the organization's leadership could be decapitated in one blow.

Evidence other than the tapes was beginning to accumulate. The FBI grabbed the books of the six concrete firms mentioned most prominently in the recorded conversations. Assuming that the records reflected an elaborate effort to hide the money the firms regularly handed over to the Mafia, a former agent who had become a prominent CPA was asked to take a look at the books. He spent a few days going over the accounts, then sourly returned them to the FBI, clearly disappointed that he had not been given a greater challenge.

''There's no complicated money trail here,'' he reported. ''It's a joke; they didn't even take much effort to hide it.'' He pointed to one company's books, which contained nearly $3 million in checks made out to cash, with no explanation of what they were for. Another company had almost $2 million in cash checks, again with no explanation. Obviously, these were payoffs, almost certainly to mobsters.

Meanwhile, surveillance operations, working from clues provided by the Jaguar tapes and FBI bugs, were busy taking long-range telephoto pictures of some of the various Mafia conclaves convened to iron out difficulties in the concrete racket. Among the more interesting was the series of photographs FBI agents snapped of some of the Mafia's chiefs entering and leaving a meeting at a small, nondescript house in Staten Island. As Sammy the Bull Gravano had predicted, such pictures would prove very damaging; no jury would believe that these men convened in the small house so far from their own homes for a social occasion.

While the evidence accumulated, Kenneth J. Walton of the FBI went shopping for a prosecutor who shared his vision that a RICO case based primarily on the concrete racket promised to be the most successful assault on organized crime ever mounted. He went first to the U.S. Attorney's Office in the Eastern District of New York, where he gave one of his favorite prosecutors, Charles Rose, a glimpse of his evidentiary treasures. Rose shared Walton's enthusiasm, but the decision on whether to proceed rested with Rose's boss, U.S. Attorney Raymond Dearie. A notoriously cautious man—prosecutors in his office claimed that he consulted legal precedent before deciding to go to the bathroom—Dearie listened with growing skepticism as Walton made his pitch. After he was finished, Dearie announced he would not take the case, which he described as an ''FBI fantasy.''

''Your boss,'' an irritated Walton told Rose, ''has the vision and imagination of a termite. Fuck him. I know somebody who'll jump all over this case.'' He stomped out of the Eastern District headquarters and crossed the Brooklyn Bridge to lower Manhattan. The man who Walton was convinced would take the case had just taken the job as U.S. Attorney for the Southern District of New York following several years as a

Department of Justice official. Still earlier, he had served as prosecutor in the Southern District, when his dogged brilliance in the infamous *Prince of the City* police corruption cases made his reputation—and an unflattering portrait in the movie based on the case. His name was Rudolph Giuliani.

The man who came to be known as "the Torquemada of Foley Square" was a pale, ascetic-looking man who radiated intensity and aggressiveness. "Elliott Ness with an attitude," as defense lawyers liked to call him behind his back. The man who would later become mayor of New York City had once planned to enter the priesthood. He found a higher calling in the criminal statutes, and had a special animus for mafiosi. Raised in a middle-class Italian home, Giuliani had spent a childhood hearing tales from his parents about the evils of the Mafia, and how the mafiosi were shaming the Italian people.

Walton sensed that Giuliani probably would eagerly take the case, but, to make sure, he brought along some heavy ammunition: Ronald Goldstock. As Walton was aware, Goldstock had immersed himself in the intricacies of the RICO statute and was now among the leading experts on the law—which, by interesting coincidence, had just been upheld as constitutional by the U.S. Supreme Court.

The three men met in a conference room. "You should listen to this, Rudy," Walton said as Goldstock stepped to a blackboard. He drew a large circle, then sketched a smaller circle in the center and several straight lines from it to the outer edge of the larger circle.

"Think of it as a wheel," Goldstock said, writing the words "Jaguar bug" inside the smaller circle. "And this is the hub of that wheel." The revelations from the bug in Avellino's Jaguar, Goldstock lectured, tied in with the spokes of other bugs and evidence to form an almost perfect RICO case, the crux of which was the concrete scheme. That scheme was the "ongoing criminal enterprise" that any jury could easily grasp, Goldstock noted, especially with the accumulating evidence of how the four Mafia families ran it, profited from it, and forced everybody else to pay the Mafia tax.

"It is," Goldstock said, with a final flourish, "the mother of all RICO cases."

"I want it," the clearly enthused Giuliani said as Walton

beamed in satisfaction. But the prosecutor added a caveat: it would be nice, he noted, if they had a murder charge in the package of indictments he would put together. Juries tend to be impressed by murder charges. Was there a murder case anywhere in the stacks of tapes?

"No, but we'll get one," said the ever-optimistic Walton, as though he was discussing a trip to the corner newsstand for a pack of gum.

Although Walton's FBI agents had no evidence (or leads, for that matter) of murder in connection with the raw data collected so far, the cops on the task force did. They recalled the 1979 murder of Carmine Galante, the violently ambitious Bonanno Family capo, and its interesting sequel: one of the killers, Anthony (Bruno) Indelicato, had been spotted in Little Italy only a short while after the shooting by a police surveillance videotape. Because the videotape also recorded Indelicato accepting what appeared to be congratulations from the underboss of the Gambino Family and the consigliere of the Bonanno Family, was it possible the shooting was a Commission-ordered execution? If so, then members of that Commission were equally guilty of the RICO law's "predicate act" in furtherance of a criminal conspiracy.

The man who could answer that question was John Gurnee, one of the New York City Police Department's most noted organized crime detectives. Gurnee had spent much of his career in the organized crime section of his department's Intelligence Division, where he had made his mark tracking and surreptitiously taking pictures of mafiosi. In the process, he collected enough intelligence on them to fill an entire wall of filing cabinets—the unsurpassed data bank that was an essential resource for FBI agents and cops involved in organized crime investigations.

Gurnee had run the 1979 police surveillance operation in Little Italy into which Indelicato had stumbled. To his frustration, the Manhattan District Attorney's Office ignored the tape dealing with Indelicato's arrival, and paid only slightly more attention to the other evidence Gurnee and a team of detectives had collected over ten months. Although Gurnee argued that the evidence he and his team had collected—conversations among mobsters concerning at least a dozen major felonies—

constituted a racketeering case, the D.A. opted to convene a grand jury before which six mobsters (including John Gotti) were taken and asked what they knew about organized crime. Not surprisingly, five of them pleaded ignorance on the subject. A sixth refused to testify, and was sent to jail for a year for contempt. A paltry result for all that police work. As a discouraged Gurnee summarized it, "We're not getting anywhere."

Now, Gurnee could hardly believe what he was hearing. The FBI and police task force wanted to take a new look at the Galante murder; could Gurnee help them out? He sure could. First, he dug out the 1,200 feet of videotape that showed a sweating Indelicato rushing into Little Italy and meeting at the Ravenite Social Club with Aniello Dellacroce, underboss of the Gambino Family.

"Clearly," Gurnee pointed out as he ran his tape for an audience of cops and FBI agents, "Dellacroce had been assigned by the Commission as the direct supervisor of the hit. So that's why Indelicato, as his first action after killing Galante, rushes to Little Italy. He's reporting to Dellacroce that the hit has been successfully carried out. No other conclusion is possible; Dellacroce is Gambino, and Indelicato is Bonanno, so why else would Indelicato be in Gambino territory?"

Gurnee ran some more of his tape. "Now, look at this little scene. We have [Bonanno capos] Sonny Red Indelicato and Philip Giaccone arriving at the Ravenite in a tan Lincoln. Here's something even more interesting: Steve Canone, the Bonanno consigliere, emerges from the Ravenite. We can safely conclude he was inside, meeting with Dellacroce. We can also safely conclude the subject of the meeting was the murder of Galante, judging by the arrival of the shooter and the two Bonanno capos."

As the tape ended, Gurnee played his final card. "To me, the real clincher was what happened to Bruno Indelicato subsequently. We learned he received an immediate promotion to capo, and as you know, that kind of rapid promotion is quite unusual. So we can further conclude he was getting a reward for something very important. And we know what that was. Further, we know that he went underground not too long afterward because the Commission was unhappy over the mistakes he made in carrying out the hit. Now all you have to do is prove that Mr. Indelicato actually carried out that hit.''

That daunting task was entrusted to two star detectives whose talents had led to their recruitment for the task force. One of them, Kenneth (Kenny the Giant) McCabe of "Gold Bug" fame, had retired from the New York City Police Department and was immediately recruited by Giuliani for what he had come to call "the Commission case." The other was McCabe's friend, Joseph Coffey, the preeminent investigator of mob hits, who had been detailed from the OCTF to get Giuliani his murder case.

The two investigators confronted a four-year-old case whose components were a quasi-certain eyewitness, the license number of the getaway car helpfully jotted down by a passerby, and Gurnee's videotape. They went to work, gradually putting all the pieces together, and finally clinched the case when they caught a lucky break.

Although Coffey and McCabe assumed Indelicato's getaway car had been closely checked for fingerprints, they learned that when the D.A. had indicated a lack of interest in Gurnee's attempt to push a murder case against Indelicato, the police crime scene people hadn't bothered to perform the arduous task of trying to find a particular fingerprint among the many dozens found on the car. Now, under pressure from McCabe and Coffey, the crime scene experts went back to work, finally emerging with a match: Anthony (Bruno) Indelicato's palm print had been found on a door of the car.

The next problem was to find Indelicato. In hiding after learning the Commission wanted his head for making too many mistakes in the Galante hit, his rapid promotion to capo was just as rapidly revoked. He was not a man anyone wanted to be on the loose anywhere: when high on cocaine (with a $3,000-a-week habit, that must have been most of the time) he liked to kill people. His record included the attempted murder of a federal drug agent, and he was known to boast he could kill anyone with only one shot, since he dipped his bullets in cyanide.

To find this psychopath, the task force assigned a team of agents from the FBI, the organization whose strengths included finding people who did not want to be found. It took them a year, but they finally tracked Indelicato to his hideout, managing to press a pistol to his head before he could reach for one of the half-dozen guns he kept near him at all times.

With the arrest of Indelicato and the gathering of the remaining evidence, the case was ready for trial. The unsealing of the indictments took place on February 25, 1984, and it was clearly the Mafia's Black Day. Beginning at dawn, teams of FBI and police arrested the entire hierarchy of the New York Mafia, except Philip (Rusty) Rastelli, boss of the Bonanno Family, who was already in prison (gravely ill, he would die there a few years later).

Among the more shocked by this sudden and unexpected legal assault was Tony Ducks Corallo. Confronting an FBI-police posse at his home just after dawn, Corallo looked stunned as they announced he was under arrest for violation of the RICO statute. The cops and agents could almost see his mind working, trying to figure out how his security screen had been penetrated.

"You're in big trouble, Tony," one cop told him. "We got you on tape."

"Yeah, right," Corallo sneered. "In your fucking dreams."

"No dream; we put a bug in the Jaguar. We got terrific tapes, Tony; just wait till you hear them." The color drained from Corallo's face as his jaw dropped open.

Corallo would learn soon enough that he was not the only Mafia boss in trouble. At the arraignment, he found himself joined by his chief aides, Tom Mix Santoro and Christy Ticks Funari. (Aniello Migliore, Corallo's other chief helper, was indicted in a separate racketeering case.) The parade of hand-cuffed defendants was then joined by Fat Tony Salerno of the Genovese Family, Carmine Persico and Gerry Lang Langella of the Colombo Family, and Paul Castellano of the Gambino Family. They all looked at each other in shock, unable to actually believe such a thing was happening: the entire leadership of the world's most powerful and successful criminal organization suddenly brought to the bar of justice.

Also joining the parade were Anthony (Bruno) Indelicato, the killer of Carmine Galante, and Ralph Scopo, the concrete union official. Added to the others, they created something of a traffic jam, necessitating long waits while the arraignment process went forward. To pass the time, one FBI agent was working on a difficult crossword puzzle. Tom Mix Santoro looked over his shoulder and unhesitatingly provided the answers for all the unanswered clues. ''Not bad for a ninth grade education, huh?'' he said proudly.

Santoro would need more than a facility for puzzle solving to beat the legal equivalent of the sixty-ton weight that had dropped on his and other defendants' heads—thirty volumes of evidence, eighty-five witnesses, three hundred hours of surveillance tapes and photographs, and, most damaging of all, 150 of the choicest tapes from a collection numbering in the thousands (including, the defendants were now appalled to learn, recordings from a bug planted in Ralph Scopo's car, in which he had the bad habit of extorting bribes in the name of the Mafia from concrete contractors).

The trial opened several months later missing one key defendant and an unwilling witness. Defendant Vincent Gigante was among those swept up in the net, but checked himself into a psychiatric hospital, where doctors pronounced him insane and unfit to stand trial. The witness, presumably a hostile one, was to be Joseph Bonanno, whom Giuliani planned to summon to explain certain interesting passages in his book, notably the ones dealing with the Commission. Bonanno refused to testify, and was jailed for contempt. (Later, Bonanno was found to be suffering from senile dementia, and was released to return home, there to spend his days mumbling incoherently to himself about the Mafia's glory days.)

For the defendants actually in the courtroom, the proceedings among supremely practical men soon induced a sense of fatalism as Giuliani's evidence buried them. Corallo sat beside his friend Fat Tony Salerno at the defense table, looking barely interested as his voice boomed out over court loudspeakers while the Jaguar tapes were played. Salerno, aware that the tapes of his own voice meant he also was convicting himself out of his own mouth, was equally disinterested in the proceedings. To Corallo's annoyance, Salerno consoled himself by constantly munching chocolate-nut candy bars drawn from an apparently inexhaustible supply in his rumpled suit pocket while jurors stared in fascination. When an FBI agent helpfully offered him a granola bar, saying, ''They're really much better for you, Mr. Salerno,'' Fat Tony waved it away. ''Who the fuck cares? I'm gonna die in the fucking can anyway.''

Occasionally, Salerno tried to further enliven the proceedings with a few examples of Mafia humor, such as the time a flunky brought him a batch of his favorite cigars during a recess. Salerno stared at them a moment, then shouted out, ''Didn't you bring me a gun?''

It was among the few moments of levity for the defendants, for the proceedings amounted to a series of legal disasters for them. There simply was no defense possible against a mountain of evidence, especially the tapes. One of the defendants, Carmine Persico, made his hopeless case even more impossible by acting as his own lawyer, and managed only to prove anew the adage that the man who acts as his own lawyer has a fool for a client. Conversations during recesses tended to be glum, dominated by lamentations over how some of the shrewdest criminals in existence had managed to get themselves bugged. One recurring topic of conversation concerned the question of why Corallo didn't have Sal Avellino killed when he learned that his garbage capo had somehow let the cops plant a bug in his Jaguar. Corallo's perfectly logical response was that Avellino hardly could be held responsible for such a lapse, considering the fact that several Mafia bosses themselves were guilty of the same error. (Besides, Avellino was unavailable for disciplinary proceedings; he had been arrested for his role in the Lucchese Family's garbage racket, and was being tried separately in a case brought by the state.)

Given the overwhelming evidence they were confronting, the defendants were all the more surprised when Corallo one morning showed them that day's *New York Times* containing an interview with New York Governor Mario Cuomo in which the governor said, ''There is no such thing as the Mafia.'' Even the dour Corallo found this incredible assertion amusing. But there was a very different reaction at the FBI's New York field office, where Jules Bonavolonta, now heading up organized crime investigations, walked into a meeting of FBI supervisors, threw the newspaper on the table and announced, ''We are going to make this dumb son of a bitch governor eat his fucking words.''

Actually, twelve of Cuomo's constituents made an even

more potent refutation: after nine weeks of trial, they found on November 19, 1986, that yes, the Mafia indeed exists; that it is a dangerous criminal organization; that it utilizes murder and violence to accomplish its ends; that it is ruled by an entity called the Commission; that Corallo and his fellow defendants were guilty of belonging to this criminal organization; that they were further guilty of a number of criminal conspiracies, principally, taking over the concrete construction industry; and that they were collectively guilty of ordering the murder of Carmine Galante. (And Anthony Indelicato was guilty of actually carrying out that murder.)

Given the fact they expected the verdict, none of the defendants demonstrated any emotion. They showed the same lack of interest later when they appeared for sentencing. Each defendant learned the RICO law had very sharp teeth: one hundred years in jail, virtually a death sentence. Indelicato got forty-five years, also practically a death sentence for a thirty-three-year-old man.

The convicted were taken temporarily to the Metropolitan Correctional Center, the federal government's prison in lower Manhattan, pending transfer to their permanent prison destinations. They gravitated to the prison's Mafia Manor on the ninth floor, there to be greeted by fellow mafiosi in expensive warmup suits, $200 sneakers, and big cigars who gave them the obligatory kiss on both cheeks and expressions of regret over the "fucking frame" that had brought them behind bars.

During their first night in jail, Corallo and his fellow defendants decided to mark the end of their freedom by adjourning to one corner of Mafia Manor to share a bottle of fine Italian wine.

Fat Tony Salerno raised his glass in the traditional Sicilian toast, *"Cent'anni,"* shorthand for "May you live a hundred years."

"Cent'anni," Carmine Persico replied, then paused. "Jesus Christ, I guess we'll have to get some other toast."

To everybody's surprise, Tony Ducks Corallo laughed uproariously.

Paul Castellano was not among the participants in this little party. The previous December, out on bail as the Commission trial was about to get under way, he appeared at a Manhattan restaurant for a scheduled sitdown with his rebellious capo, John Gotti. But he never made it inside the restaurant; outside, five of Gotti's hoods shot him to death.

Ironically, Castellano's murder took place on the night that G. Robert Blakey, the man whose RICO law made the great new anti-Mafia offensive possible, was being honored at a cocktail reception for his singular contribution. As Blakey basked in the glow of praise from an audience of police detectives, FBI agents, and prosecutors, beepers suddenly went off all over the room, the sounds of their offices alerting them to the Castellano killing. The room nearly emptied as police and FBI agents left to go to work. Among the federal prosecutors who remained behind, a bemused Charles Rose considered the dramatic course of events.

"The old order changeth," he said. "The new order is coming in, and I have the funny feeling we're about to see a new and very violent turn of events. Of course, in an odd way, that may be very good news."

SEVEN

"Call Me Gas Pipe and Die"

> You know what life is all about? Not you, me, but your children—to leave them a pile of money.
>
> SALVATORE (TOM MIX) SANTORO

"**S**o the question is this, Gas Pipe," said New York City Police Department Detective George Marino of the FBI-police Joint Organized Crime Task Force. "Why did somebody put four bullets into you?"

Anthony Casso glared at the detective from his hospital bed. "I told you a million fucking times, I don't like being called Gas Pipe."

"Oh, excuse us," said Marino's partner, Detective Robert Hellman. "*Mr.* Gas Pipe, how come somebody tried to kill you?"

Casso scowled at him, then shrugged his shoulders, rattling several intravenous tubes stuck into his arms. "How should I know? There's nobody that doesn't like me, right?"

Marino smiled. "Well, I could give you a pretty long list of names, actually. But the point is, we'd like to know who shot you. See, we get very upset when people start shooting each other, which is very naughty. And we become very curious when we find out the victim is a member of organized crime. You see my point?"

"I don't know nothing about organized crime," Casso snapped.

The two cops laughed. "Oh, that's a good one," Hellman said. "So I guess our records are completely wrong when they say you're a button in the Lucchese Family, right? And I guess we got it all wrong when we hear you got some kind of a beef going and somebody doesn't want you to be a button anymore, correct?"

Casso shrugged again. "I don't give a fuck about your fucking records. I'm telling you I don't know nothing about organized crime, and I don't know who shot me. End of story."

The two detectives sighed and prepared to leave; clearly, Casso was not about to be helpful in any way. They had no real expectation that he would. As they understood, in Casso's Mafia universe, shooting victims do not discuss motives, the identities of their assailant(s), or anything else of interest to the outside world.

Nevertheless, it was worth a shot. The two cops knew that Casso's shooting indicated some kind of problem within his universe—the kind of problem that potentially could erupt into still another of those occasional Mafia shooting wars with bodies littering the streets, perhaps some of them innocent victims. The last thing the cops wanted in that summer of 1986 was a full-scale Mafia war. Things were unsettled enough in the wake of the destruction of the Mafia's ruling hierarchy; there was real danger that even one small spark—such as the shooting of an obscure Brooklyn mobster—would be the Mafia Sarajevo that might set off a general conflagration. So the cops and FBI agents were in all the mobsters' faces, hoping their demonstration of intense interest would head off any plans for general war.

In the case of Anthony (Gas Pipe) Casso, apparently none the worse for wear after being struck by four bullets the previous morning in the parking lot of a Chinese restaurant (the bullets managed to miss any vital organs), the demonstration of official interest had no effect. The two detectives were no sooner out the door of his hospital room than he began laying plans to kill the man who tried to kill him—and that death, Casso swore, would be a long and painful one.

Casso's mind was often preoccupied with thoughts of

deadly revenge against his enemies, real or perceived. An absolute psychopath, one of those rare blood types of humanity who really liked killing people (often torturing them horribly beforehand), Casso had already murdered more than two dozen people in his twenty-five-year Mafia career. He was a perfect example of a class of mafiosi known as street hood, the kind of soldier useful for an organization that occasionally had need of unquestioning, violent loyalists willing to do the dirty work of leg-breaking and murder. Usually of low mental capacity (as was Casso), they were enlisted by the organization strictly for their brawn, which meant they would occupy a permanent rank at the bottom of the organization chart.

But Casso, the penultimate hood, would eventually soar in rank, right to the top: boss of the entire Lucchese Family, successor to such criminal luminaries as Gaetano Lucchese and Antonio Corallo. How he got there and what he did once he achieved that pinnacle reveals much about what happened to the post-1985 American Mafia.

To a large extent, it self-destructed under relentless pressure from the outside, best illustrated by the strange course of events that were to occur in the Lucchese organization, a series of disasters for which the violent Brooklyn hood was largely responsible. It is no exaggeration to say that Anthony (Gas Pipe) Casso, the unquestioningly loyal Mafia worker ant who considered the Lucchese Family of la Cosa Nostra his very life, did more than anybody to destroy it.

The dispute that led to Casso's hospital stay was only the first in a series of disruptions that broke out in the turmoil that followed the legal assault against the New York Mafia's senior command in 1985. In addition to a leadership vacuum that ambitious mid-level Mafia executives were rushing to fill, removal of the bosses—and their strict system of sitdowns and imposed settlements to avoid trouble within the organization—created some anarchy in the lower ranks. Very quickly, a number of festering disputes between various hoods erupted into violence.

One of them went under the name of James Hydell, a wild Staten Island hood who as a non-Italian could only achieve associate status with the Mafia, specifically the Gambino Family. Hydell, the typical drugged-out "cowboy" who so concerned the older Mafia generation, ran a small gang (also non-Italians) of similarly inclined violent criminals. They were involved in narcotics, auto theft, murder, and hijacking, working under the direction of Michael (Mickey Boy) Paradiso, a Gambino capo. Paradiso's most profitable enterprise was a flourishing heroin business he operated in partnership with Casso, a knuckle-dragger with the quasi-independent Brooklyn faction of the Lucchese Family.

In early 1986, the arrangement between Paradiso and Casso went sour in a dispute over division of profits. Previously, such disputes would have been brought to the Commission for resolution, but with the senior leaders preoccupied with legal troubles, Paradiso opted for the old-fashioned street solution. He sent a three-man hit team of hoods, led by Hydell, to kill Casso. They waylaid him just as he finished lunch one day at a Chinese restaurant, but Hydell, the actual shooter, made the fatal error of failing to kill his target, despite four shots fired at near-point blank range.

Given Casso's reputation as a psychopath, there was not much doubt what would happen next. As soon as he was sufficiently recovered from his wounds, Casso set about to kill all three of the men dispatched to kill him, then Paradiso, the man who had ordered it. Hydell went into hiding while Casso tracked down and killed Nicholas Guido, one of Hydell's hit team. However, it turned out that Casso had murdered the wrong man, a law-abiding telephone installer who tragically had the same name and bore a strong physical resemblance to the criminal Guido. Casso shrugged off the error and redoubled his efforts.

Guido was out of reach, having fled after telling friends, "Gas Pipe will put me on a table, cut my heart out and show it to me." That left Robert Bering, the third member of the Hydell hit team. However, he opted to surrender to police, preferring whatever vengeance the legal system might exact to the more horrible revenge Casso would carry out. (Even behind bars, he was still terrified of Casso, and dropped dead of a heart attack in his jail cell at the age of forty not long after surrendering.)

Casso finally was able to get Hydell by inducing two corrupt cops to track him down and "arrest" him. What went through Hydell's mind can only be imagined as he realized, probably within a few minutes after he had been seized and handcuffed, that the unmarked car was definitely not taking him to police headquarters. The cops dumped him into a warehouse, where he encountered the smiling figure of Gas Pipe Casso and three of his friends.

"Hi, Jimmy, nice to see you again," Casso said, alternately caressing a gun, a knife, and a blowtorch. Hydell's ordeal lasted for the next twelve hours until he was finally granted the mercy of death. His broken body was dumped into a street to serve as warning for anyone considering the idea of challenging Gas Pipe Casso. As for Paradiso, Casso's ultimate target, the law anticipated him. Mickey Boy was arrested for heroin dealing, and in a trail that featured his own brother testifying as the chief prosecution witness in a tasteful outfit of white satin racing jacket, he was convicted and went to jail for the next twenty years.

It is hard to imagine such events taking place during the reign of Tony Ducks Corallo. A murderous battle costing several lives, one an innocent civilian, over the relatively trivial matter of heroin profits had caused a lot of disruption—and unwelcome publicity—to no real purpose. (Not to mention proof of the wisdom of the Mafia establishment's antipathy to dealing in narcotics.)

This kind of lunacy was becoming all too common as the new generation of mafiosi took the reins of power. The problem, simply, was that they were nowhere near the caliber of their predecessors—as events in the Lucchese Family would demonstrate.

While Tony Ducks Corallo sat in his federal penitentiary cell, he faced one last duty for the organization: select a successor. This was no easy task, for all the family's top leaders were either behind bars, or about to be. Corallo had long assumed that he would be succeeded by one of the three talented senior executives who functioned as his chief aides: Salvatore (Tom Mix) Santoro, Aniello (Neil) Migliore, and Christopher (Christy Ticks) Funari, men very much in his own image. But Santoro and Funari were in the same prison as Corallo, and

Migliore was in another prison following his conviction in a labor racketeering case. Salvatore Avellino, a Corallo protégé, might have been a candidate, except that he was on trial in Long Island in a state case for his role in the garbage racket. Since the crux of the prosecution case was the irrefutable Jaguar bug, Avellino was anticipating a prison sentence of some duration.

That left the Lucchese Family's roster of capos, none of whom, Corallo thought, had the record of accomplishment that would have marked an aspirant worthy of promotion to boss. Finally, Corallo decided on the best of an average lot, Anthony (Buddy) Luongo, one of the leading lights of the family's Brooklyn faction. In early 1987, the word was passed to Luongo that he had been anointed as Corallo's successor. A delighted Luongo informed his wife one night that he had to go out to an "important meeting." He was never seen again.

Corallo didn't know that Luongo had been lured to a meeting with his chief aide, Vittorio (Vic) Amuso, who killed him in the name of ambition. Shortly after the murder, Corallo began to receive messages from the Brooklyn faction urging him to appoint Amuso in Luongo's stead. The messages had been instigated by Amuso, who promised fellow mafiosi a considerable share of the family proceeds if Corallo selected him.

"It's a mistake, Tony," Tom Mix Santoro warned Corallo, "These [Brooklyn] guys are fucking nuts." He went on to note that Amuso had no real management experience, was a convicted heroin dealer almost undoubtedly still in the trade, and was not known for a criminal mind of any dimension. Moreover, his friend and chief henchman was Gas Pipe Casso, a violent time bomb that could explode at any second.

Corallo finally decided to appoint Amuso anyway. The reasons for that decision remain unknown, although his consultations with Santoro suggest that Corallo was concerned about rebuilding the family's fortunes, which were sagging. Amuso was known as a major earner (Corallo chose to overlook the fact that most of those earnings were from selling heroin), and had the reputation of a tough taskmaster over his crew, which, in Corallo's perception, meant that Amuso would be able to restore discipline to a decentralized organization in danger of falling apart. Somehow things would all work out, Corallo told Santoro.

It would turn out to be the worst mistake Tony Ducks ever made.

Control of the Lucchese organization had now passed to its Brooklyn faction, the family's most violent. Its power base was the community of Bensonhurst, a two-square-mile area that was among the last remaining bastions of Italian immigrants in the United States. First settled by immigrants moving out of Manhattan ghettos into what were then the suburbs, Bensonhurst was dotted with two-family brick houses guarded by white wrought iron gates; many of these homes had back-yard grottoes in honor of the Virgin Mary. The people of Bensonhurst were predominantly blue-collar workers who considered themselves more authentically Italian than their brethren of Little Italy and East Harlem. (They liked to cite the fact that the only "real" pizza in New York City was produced in their neighborhood because Bensonhurst pizza parlors still used wood-burning ovens.)

Judging by police statistics, street crime in Bensonhurst was among the lowest in the entire city, but there was plenty of organized crime. The Mafia arrived with the first wave of Italian immigrants who settled on what had been the farmland of early Dutch settlers, and by the 1980s, la Cosa Nostra was solidly entrenched. It survived with the tacit acceptance of the people of Bensonhurst, but only so long as the Mafia kept its end of the bargain: no violent crime in the streets, and no selling of narcotics in the neighborhood.

Vittorio Amuso and his chief aide, Anthony Casso (now consigliere), were only the latest in a long line of infamies bred in Bensonhurst, which tended to produce mobsters with a harder edge. Amuso, a short, slender man, was gruff and dangerous, almost like a wild beast. He had begun his criminal career as a strongarm thug and enforcer for the Brooklyn faction's extensive heroin operations, in the process coming to the attention of Carmine (Mr. Gibbs) Tramunti, chief executive officer for narcotics when the family was run by Gaetano Lucchese. Amuso became Tramunti's chauffeur and, by 1967, when Tramunti became temporary family boss after Lucchese's death, Amuso's career had an important patron. A big-time heroin dealer himself, Amuso invested the proceeds in a large-scale loan-sharking enterprise whose profits gave him a reputation as an earner. Despite Corallo's edict about narcotics, Amuso went right on peddling heroin until he was caught in 1977 and served several years in prison. By 1986, he was still selling heroin, albeit more cautiously, and was earning enough to afford a fancy house on a one-acre plot that also contained a big swimming pool and tennis courts. Not bad for a Bensonhurst street punk who had dropped out of ninth grade.

Amuso and Anthony Casso met in 1972, when Casso, another Bensonhurst street punk, was among the ranks of soldiers working as enforcers for gambling and loan shark operations. The two men shared several characteristics: explosive tempers, sinister reputations as stone-cold killers, and vaunting ambitions to become major Mafia leaders in the Tony Ducks Corallo mode. Casso was the more sinister-looking of the two; short and swarthy, he combed his hair straight back in a style that gave him a vaguely simian appearance. According to neighborhood legend, he had been a violent criminal from the age of nine, when he helped his father, a career Brooklyn hood whose specialty was tapping into gas mains for illegal hookups for people who didn't feel like paying gas bills. This created a nickname, "Gas Pipe," used for both father and son, that Casso would come to find especially irksome. (Later, when he rose to become Amuso's second in command, he warned other Lucchese mafiosi, "Call me Gas Pipe and die," although he would tolerate his closest friends addressing him as "Gas.")

Like his father, Casso aspired to become a Mafia soldier. Hoping to get into the business of fulfilling hit contracts, by the age of fifteen he was a dead shot, having perfected his aim by picking off his neighbors' racing pigeons in midflight with a .22-caliber rifle. The neighbors dared not complain, for Casso was head of a violent street gang called the Tigers, and had committed four murders by his seventeenth birthday. His violent reputation led to his recruitment by the Lucchese Family's resident overseer of gambling and loan-sharking operations, Christy Ticks Funari. Casso was assigned the task of ensuring prompt payments among longshoremen customers on the Brooklyn waterfront, but added a few touches Funari had not authorized—such as the day he took a forklift and dropped a five hundred-pound box of cargo on a new pair of steel-toed workboots worn by a longshoreman, crippling him for life. "I just wanted to see how good the steel toes in those boots were," Casso explained.

In 1962, when he was twenty-two, Casso was arrested for involvement in illegal gambling operations on the docks. The five-day jail sentence and $50 fine would be the only jail time he would serve for the next twenty-eight years. In the interim, he was arrested five other times, but all the cases collapsed before trial—including one case in which the chief prosecution witness was shot eight times as he walked up the courthouse steps on his way to testify.

Casso acquired a reputation as an earner for devising and running one of the most successful organized theft operations in U.S. history. It would come to be called the "Bypass Gang" for its ability to bypass even the most sophisticated security system and carry out robberies. Casso recruited the most talented safecrackers, cat burglars, and second-story men in the city; linked up with a band of talented electronics experts, they were sent to rob selected targets guaranteed to have a lot of cash around—major jewelry outlets, companies with large cash payrolls, and banks. The gang's preferred method was to cut a hole in the roof of a building, allowing the electronics experts to descend inside, where they deactivated the telephone lines, electronic warning devices, and burglar alarms. For the most formidable vaults and safes, Casso utilized the talents of Dominick Costa, rated as the best safecracker in the world, whose career included cracking three hundred safes and extracting $75 million. His favorite method was to make a hole in a vault with special diamond drills, then insert a tiny optical scope to read the vault's clock-driven alarm system, from which he would divine the lock combination.

By 1986, after five years in business, the Bypass Gang had stolen somewhere around $100 million, the bulk of which found its way to the Mafia—thanks to Casso, whose sinister reputation ensured that none of his thieves succumbed to the temptation of letting some of the money stick to their fingers.

That reputation also came in handy for another enterprise in which Casso was involved, although other criminal minds had dreamed up the scheme first. In the 1980s, men of the Russian Mafia—émigrés from the criminal world of the Soviet Union, now operating in the New World—had devised a ripoff that was at once simple and immensely profitable. They discovered a small loophole in the law that governed the collection of the 7.1-cent federal excise tax on wholesale gasoline: essentially, it was an honor system, with the tax paid by whichever wholesaler last had possession of the gasoline before being sold to a retailer. The Russian mobsters created a daisy chain of companies that passed wholesale gasoline through a bewildering series of paper entities, finally ending in what was called the "burn company"—the company that actually sold the gasoline to a retailer. That company pocketed the taxes and disappeared; the IRS would find only an empty shell. At first glance, the ripoff, amounting to a few cents a gallon, didn't look very impressive, but multiply that by several hundred million gallons of gasoline.

The success of the scheme ignited serious conflict among the Russians involved. One of them, Mara Balagula, had become friendly with Gas Pipe Casso. Early in 1986, he summoned Casso to his house. Casso found him hooked up to a makeshift intensive care unit recovering from a heart attack. A terrified Balagula told Casso he was afraid to check into a hospital for fear that his rival, Vladimir Reznikov, would kill him. The day before, Balagula related, Reznikov had put a gun to his head and demanded $600,000 while announcing that he was Balagula's new partner. Balagula won some time by having a heart attack on the spot, but begged Casso to do something to keep Reznikov away from him.

"No problem," Casso replied, without blinking an eye. A few days later, Reznikov was invited to a restaurant meeting with a Lucchese hood, Joseph Testa, who shot him to death. In gratitude, Balagula began passing a modest cut of his proceeds to Casso.

Casso's take from the Bypass Gang and gasoline operations, the first real money he had seen in his criminal career, ignited an orgy of conspicuous consumption, the kind of spending that men like Corallo had always warned his minions to avoid, since it tended to attract law enforcement attention. Keep a low profile in terms of lifestyle, Corallo advised: invest criminal profits carefully, gradually acquire stakes in legitimate businesses that could account for large income, fill out tax returns scrupulously, and never do anything out of proportion to declared income.

But Casso was from a different Mafia generation that saw money as something to be spent, the sooner the better. Not mentally agile, Casso was bored by talk of such things as investment opportunities. Instead, he acted like a child with a hundred-dollar bill let loose in a candy store. To reflect his new status, he acquired a 10.5-carat, $500,000 diamond ring, a new wardrobe (to the delight of one men's store, where Casso one day bought fifteen $2,000 suits), and prepared to construct a lavish home in Brooklyn. After investing $200,000 of his cash to buy a piece of waterfront property in the upscale Mill Basin section, he planned to build a $1 million custom home. He hired a local architect, Anthony Fava, to draw up the plans, carefully instructing the architect to include a number of details not ordinarily seen in waterfront homes—such as secret closets hidden behind false walls (he didn't tell Fava they were intended for use as weapons and drug caches), and bulletproof windows. Fava went to work and finally emerged with a beautiful design, then made the mistake of submitting a bill of $40,000 for his services.

Casso thought the bill excessive, a commercial disagreement he solved in typical fashion: Fava was lured to a meeting to discuss the matter, during which Casso and several of his hoods murdered and then dismembered him, but not before Casso underscored his displeasure by working over the architect with an acetylene torch and red-hot spoons to gouge out his eyeballs.

Having saved the cost of architect's fees, Casso completed the building of his new home, all of it paid with cash. The project, in conjunction with his Mafia promotion, elevated him from ordinary street hood to man of respect in his neighborhood. The new status led to one of those *Godfather*-like moments: a neighbor approached him for help in solving a problem he did not want to bring to the police. His daughter,

a "woman of purity and honor," had broken up with her fiancé, who had taken to harassing her. Among other things, he
was threatening to inform her new boyfriend, whom she intended to marry, that she was no longer "pure," meaning her
former fiancé was only one of many men who had enjoyed
her sexual favors. To Sicilian traditionalists, the idea of a bride
with so unsavory a reputation was unthinkable. Casso was
asked if he could solve the problem by "taking care" of the
ex-fiancé to keep his mouth shut. "No problem," Casso said,
in his best Tony Ducks Corallo imitation. "You and your
daughter can rest easy tonight; he won't bother you anymore."
It is probable that the neighbor intended only for the sinister
Casso to threaten the ex-fiancé, perhaps accompanied by a few
slaps to make the point. But Casso's solution, to the neighbor's
discomfort, was more draconian: the ex-fiancé was shot and
his body dismembered, the remains buried in several separate
graves.

Given his new status, Casso did not personally participate
in this murder, for he now had recruited his own crew of hoods
for such duties. They were very much in Casso's own image:
violent street hoods of low intelligence with a fondness for
killing. The most striking was Peter (Fat Pete) Chiodo, a 537-
pound enforcer of gargantuan appetites who periodically
weighed himself on a meat packing company scale to check
whether his constant round of crash diets was having any effect. Mostly, they weren't, although people who knew Chiodo
considered it politic to get on his good side by remarking,
"Hey, Pete, you look good; been losing weight, huh?"

Chiodo was a man nobody wanted to get mad, for his huge
size, combined with a hair-trigger temper and a pronounced
streak of violence, meant that somebody was usually guaranteed
to get hurt when he lost his temper. He had come to join Casso's
new crew after a fairly standard career path for a Mafia street
hood. A hijacker since his teens, Chiodo was recruited, not surprisingly, for strongarm work while moonlighting as a bodyguard, including a stint protecting comedian Eddie Murphy.
Known as the hood most likely to collect on an outstanding loan
shark debt, he was formally made in 1987 in a ceremony presided over by Vic Amuso. It included the standard blood oath
of knife, gun, and burning picture of a saint, followed by a

recitation of the rules. These rules were also standard, ending with the stern injunction against any made member dealing drugs, although Chiodo could not avoid noticing that the mention of the no-narcotics rule was accompanied by snickers from Amuso and other Lucchese mafiosi in the room. Even in Chiodo's dim brain, the meaning was unmistakable: whatever the Mafia's official position on dealing in narcotics, the new Lucchese organization was going to sell it.

Also attending the ceremony was Casso, who had received another promotion, to underboss, a strong signal of the trust and esteem in which Amuso held him. Casso made it clear that Chiodo and the rest of the crew he had recruited owed their unswerving loyalty to Amuso, their new boss, whose orders were to be regarded as the unquestioned word of God. Casso pledged his own undying loyalty, a vow he also extracted for himself from Chiodo and the other men he recruited. They unhesitatingly gave it; as lowly street hoods accustomed to earning the Mafia equivalent of nickels and dimes, they now were being ushered into the big time. The prospect of earning some real money in close alliance with the new powers of the organization was sufficient for them to guarantee their very lives, if necessary, to the greater glory of the new Lucchese Family leadership.

The new crew that would come to dominate Lucchese operations was a varied cast of characters, ranging from the truly scary to the buffoonish. Among the scariest was Richard (The Toupe) Pagliarulo, a vain and diminutive hood who sought to enhance his unimposing appearance with possibly the worst hairpiece ever worn and a pair of elevator shoes that made him look slightly out of balance. Despite a very low IQ, he was consumed by ambition to become a major Mafia leader, a career path he tried to enhance by becoming the hitman's hitman. He became pretty good at it, acquiring a reputation as the man to send when somebody had to be disposed of without any slipups. Equally frightening was another hitman, Frank Lastorino, and his fellow killer, Michael DeSantis, who was also known for his ability to use baseball bats on recalcitrant loan shark debtors or other people who required an "attitude adjustment." (DeSantis liked to talk shop with fellow Mafia hitters about whether baseball bats or golf clubs were the more suitable instruments for heavy work; DeSantis opted for bats because, he said, they made a more "satisfying" sound when swung at full force into a victim's skull.)

While Lastorino and DeSantis were unmistakably street hoods, another member of the crew, Alphonse D'Arco, presented the image of mild-mannered businessman. Called either "Little Al" (for his small size) or "Professor" (for his studious appearance), D'Arco was a veteran heroin trafficker who had struck up a friendship with Amuso during a prison stretch in the 1960s. In 1982, Amuso arranged for his induction into the Mafia, a ceremony, D'Arco liked to relate later, that included the serving of tea and cookies afterward. A born raconteur, D'Arco was the crew's clown prince, but this voluble hood had a dark side: in addition to his narcotics dealing, he was also involved in a dozen murders. He ran a small restaurant whose equipment included a store of body bags to use for disposals as the need arose. D'Arco's chief cook was an arsonist who might be asked to interrupt his cooking at any given time to burn down a building.

Another interesting character was Thomas (Tommy Irish) Carew, whose ethnicity thwarted his dream of becoming a made member of the Mafia. As an associate, Carew was regarded as a full-fledged mobster with a reputation for violence and modest talent as an earner (he had made a pile of money in an operation he worked with Russian mobsters to counterfeit expensive jeans). His friend, Corrado (Dino) Marino, though fully qualified ethnically to become a made member, had not managed to achieve that life-long dream ("Ever since I was a little kid, I wanted to be a mafioso," he liked to say) because he was breathtakingly stupid with not even a glimmer of promise as an earner. Nevertheless, thanks to his close friendship with Carew, he was enlisted for the new Amuso-Casso regime as an associate on the promise that he might demonstrate criminal talent at some point. Meanwhile, Marino worked as a barber, with a clientele dominated by mobsters, including Casso, who characteristically warned Marino that the slightest error in cutting his hair would result in the barber becoming part of the next highway project.

While Marino had been enlisted on the vague promise of

future talent, another member of the crew, regarded as a buffoon, was enrolled strictly for political reasons. Christopher (Jumbo) Funari Jr., son of the famed Christy Ticks Funari, wanted to be a gangster in the style of his father, but unfortunately for his ambitions—and to the anger of his father—he was not only an idiot, he had not an ounce of criminal talent. Eager to please Funari Sr., one of the most respected names in the entire Mafia, Amuso enrolled his son (without giving him anything important to do) and assigned him to Casso, who in turn gave him assorted gofer tasks to carry out. Funari appeared honored even to fetch a cup of coffee for Casso.

Amuso's first priority was to establish his leadership over the family's disparate tentacles. In meetings held at the family high command's new secure meeting site—the end of a deserted pier on the Brooklyn waterfront—Amuso dispatched his men to make contact with the various components of the family's criminal empire to pass the word of the transfer of power and plant the flag of the new regime.

Amuso personally handled the Lucchese Family's crown jewel, the union racket at Kennedy Airport. He met its current overseer, a 305-pound hood with a notoriously explosive temper, Frank Manzo. A protégé of Tony Ducks Corallo, Manzo ran his business from the office of a trucking firm he controlled, although he liked to conduct especially sensitive business discussions at a corner table in a diner near the airport. Amuso already knew Manzo by reputation, primarily for violence. He had heard the story about the Gambino mobster who ran afoul of Manzo's violent streak one day when, during a meeting in the diner, he raised the possibility that his organization was not receiving its due share of airport rackets, as a Commission agreement worked out years before had decreed. Manzo's face turned nearly purple as the mobster pointed an accusing finger at him. He seized the mobster's hand, pinned it to the table, then impaled it with a fork. "The last guy who pointed a finger at me," Manzo snarled as the man writhed in agony, "I cut it off and shoved it up his ass before I blew his fucking head off."

As Amuso discovered, Manzo had things well in hand, and piles of cash flowed into the family's coffers with regularity.

In addition to the millions earned from the organized shake-downs of trucking companies and air freight operations, Manzo also was running a flourishing loan shark business at the airport that was earning $4,000 a week in vig payments alone. Manzo was careful to forward the lion's share of this money to the family hierarchy. His cut of the proceeds was sufficient to provide a lavish lifestyle, although as a follower of Corallo's example of inconspicuous consumption, Manzo lived in a modest home and drove inexpensive sedans.

Manzo reported no problems with the great clockwork of crime at the airport, and recounted for Amuso the recent conversation he had with the chief executive of one air freight company, who wondered why his business should have to pay "labor management fees" to Manzo to guarantee no labor trouble from local 295 of the Teamsters Union. "I don't think he knows in his heart that we rule the airport," Manzo told Amuso with a laugh, shaking his head in wonderment that any company could be that naïve.

While Amuso was establishing his presence at the airport, Casso was assigned the task of auditing the organization's oldest operation, the Garment Center. He discovered that things were pretty well in hand, mainly through the efforts of Sidney Lieberman, who served as front man for the Lucchese organization's control of trucking firms. Lieberman, the son of Jack Lieberman, who had served as the original partner in crime for Gaetano Lucchese in the old days, oversaw the Lucchese interests, mainly insuring that the 7.5-cent Mafia tax on every garment shipped was paid regularly and conveyed to the family boss. The younger Lieberman had enjoyed a relatively trouble-free criminal career, except for a small interruption in 1981, when he had to serve a year in jail on reduced charges in a union bribery case. (It could have been a lot worse for him: Lieberman was facing more serious charges until the chief prosecution witness and his wife were found shot to death.)

Although things seemed to be running smoothly, Lieberman reported one festering problem: Michael Pappadio. A veteran Lucchese racketeer in the Garment Center, Pappadio had inherited Gaetano Lucchese's loan-sharking operations there and was dutifully forwarding a share of the profits upward in the family. But Pappadio had developed a sideline business, arranging arson for hire for Garment Center businessmen seeking to get out from under a failing business by torching it and pocketing the insurance money (a portion of which Pappadio took as a fee for arranging the arson, known as "Jewish lightning" in New York slang). The problem was that Pappadio hadn't bothered to inform his boss of this extracurricular activity, nor was he sharing its considerable income—serious violations of Mafia rules that came to light when one businessman was arrested for arranging to have his factory torched and revealed to Lieberman the arrangement with Pappadio. Amuso and Casso decided that the new regime would have to make an example of Pappadio so that other Lucchese mobsters would not be tempted to commit a similar offense.

Accordingly, Pappadio was lured to a Brooklyn warehouse, ostensibly for a meeting with Casso and Amuso. As he entered the building, Al D'Arco jumped out from behind a door and began to smash him in the head with a steel-jacketed electrical cable. *"What did you do that for?"* Pappadio screamed while D'Arco continued to hit him with the cable. As blood splattered all over the floor and walls, Fat Pete Chiodo and Richard Pagliarulo decided to put Pappadio out his misery by shooting him several times. They dumped Pappadio's body into the trunk of a car, preparatory to disposing of it, only to discover that Pappadio somehow was still alive and moaning in pain. They decided to cremate him, and took the body to a Lucchese-controlled factory with a huge incinerator and shoved it inside—but the apparently indestructible Pappadio was still moaning as the roaring flames licked around his body. Only after the fire completely consumed the body and Pappadio was a pile of ashes were the two killers finally convinced he was dead.

The new regime also decided that murder would be required to set minds right in another Lucchese enterprise, illegal gambling. Among the more profitable segments of that business was the numbers racket in poor neighborhoods. The man in charge of the operation, an associate named Robert Hopkins, had things running efficiently and was grossing $500,000 a week. Hopkins was making so much money that he had to hire armed guards to move all the cash, including the share for the Lucchese Family's high command. When he wasn't busy overseeing this flow of money, Hopkins lived in the splendor of a $2.2 million duplex in the Trump Tower, where neighbors like Johnny Carson and Sophia Loren knew only that he was a wealthy "businessman and investor."

Hopkins told Amuso that he had suddenly encountered a serious problem: a Cuban-American organized crime group known as *la Compania*, based in Jersey City, New Jersey, had decided that gambling operations in Hispanic neighborhoods should be controlled by Hispanic criminals. They were busy trying to drive the Lucchese people out of those neighborhoods. To nip this problem in the bud, Amuso decided an object lesson was in order. He had one of the *la Compania* leaders gunned down as he stood in a movie line, then announced that the only "sensible" solution was a compromise arrangement. Not prepared for a shooting war with the Mafia, *la Compania* quickly agreed to an arrangement under which they received a modest percentage of all gambling operations in Hispanic neighborhoods not under their direct control.

Having solved that problem, Amuso then confronted another, which arose in a less profitable but nonetheless important gambling operation. The operation was not strictly Lucchese; it was run by Spyredon (Spiros) Velentzas, boss of the small Greek Mafia that controlled organized crime among a community of Greek immigrants in Queens. Velentzas had a network of illegal gambling casinos that featured *barbut,* a dice game for high stakes, along with several horse parlors that used satellite dishes to pick up transmissions of races from all over the country.

Velentzas was paying tribute, in the form of a percentage of his profits, to the Lucchese Family for the right to operate in Queens, cash payments he believed included the implied guarantee of such services as elimination of intruders. When a rival for control suddenly arose (a fellow Greek mobster with lofty ambitions), Velentzas went to Amuso, the new Lucchese boss, for help. Amuso saw the logic in Velentzas's argument that the money he was paying in tribute entitled him to Lucchese executive services, and Casso was ordered to provide one. Shortly afterward, Velentzas's rival was found murdered, the handiwork of Richard Pagliarulo.

Another murder was required to restore equilibrium in an even more important Lucchese interest, this one in the construction industry. For many years, the family had a flourishing source of income from every stroke of a paintbrush in New York because of its hooks into District Council 9 of the Painters Union. The Luccheses' man in the council was its corrupt president, James Bishop, who shared extortion payments wrested from contractors and helped impose a ten percent Mafia tax on every major paint contract that used union labor. The union international, alarmed over reports that Bishop was in league with mobsters, sent a monitor to examine the union books. The monitor was beaten unconscious by several Lucchese goons wielding lead pipes, and Bishop was in trouble. As the union international put the council into trusteeship and the cops closed in, Amuso concluded that Bishop had not only outlived his usefulness, but almost certainly would roll over when confronted with arrest.

To forestall the problem, he dispatched Pagliarulo. The task turned out to be relatively easy: Bishop was a man of punctual habits, including showing up at his mistress' house at precisely the same hour each evening. Pagliarulo lay in ambush and when Bishop drove up and parked in the same parking spot he had used for years, his body was torn apart by several shotgun blasts at close range. Asked later by Amuso why he had shot Bishop so many times when a single blast would have done the job, Pagliarulo replied, "It was fucking cold out there waiting for him to show up, so I got really pissed off that this cocksucker caused me to get so cold."

The other important segment of the Lucchese Family's construction industry interests was an old reliable, Local 66 of the Laborers Union on Long Island. Peter Vario, its former head, had gone to jail for labor racketeering, but as was so often the case, he was simply replaced by another crook. The new man was Michael (Big Mike) LaBarbara, who decided that the racket for which he served as fulcrum was invulnerable to law enforcement and that he could afford to advertise his success. He had a palatial, 2,000-square-foot office built for himself with a private sauna and kitchen, and when Amuso and Casso arrived to check up on their newly inherited operation, LaBarbara was in the process of completing a personal golf course on the grounds of his union's headquarters. At the same time, according to the union's books, Local 66 was building a million-dollar "training school," although in fact it was a union-paid luxury home for LaBarbara.

There was another Lucchese hook into the construction industry, but this one was new, an opportunity that had dropped into Amuso's lap. It promised to rival the "concrete club" in terms of multimillion-dollar profit, and again concerned something quite ordinary: windows

As usual, the essential first step was a corrupt union leader. In the case of windows, he was John Morrissey, known as "Sonny Blue," head of Local 508 of the Architectural and Ornamental Ironworkers Union, whose members included workers who installed windows on office buildings and apartment houses. Their union chief was a wild, violent character who openly conceded, "I'm a thief and a hoodlum." He was a throwback to the days when union leaders were virtual thugs, fearless, violent men tough enough to face down company goons and strikebreakers.

There was no doubt that Morrissey was a tough guy. An ironworker by trade, he was an alumnus of a violent gang of Irish criminals known as the Westies, who dominated a rough ethnic neighborhood on Manhattan's West Side called Hell's Kitchen. It was perfect preparation for the violent battles between union and management that marked the union's organizing efforts among predominantly Irish and Italian immigrant workers. Morrissey's private life was equally violent. He had been arrested several times for brawling in bars, including one incident in which he had stabbed a bartender who tried to break up a fistfight, and another in which he had shot a man he thought was making a pass at his wife.

While in jail on one of his convictions for assault, Morrissey became friends with a fellow inmate named Vittorio Amuso. In discussions that centered on Morrissey's desire to get rich if he could get in on some kind of construction racket, they agreed to cooperate in the future on an unspecified operation, presumably to mutual profit. Some years later, just that kind of operation came to pass because a low-level mobster named Peter Savino got a bright idea.

Savino was unusual by underworld standards because he was intelligent (he had two years of college) and was known to actually read books. Fundamentally, however, he was a criminal. He had begun his career as a cigarette smuggler and pot dealer, working with the Lucchese and Genovese families. He needed to earn a lot of money because he had an insatiable desire for female flesh, a predilection that demanded cash to underwrite a string of girlfriends, alimony payments for two ex-wives, and the support of five children. He earned the necessary cash by becoming a big-time dope dealer, laundering his profits in a small window replacement company, a business in which he had worked some years before. He hoped the narcotics profits would allow him to build his company into a major contractor, at which point he could leave the dope business forever. That business, he realized, was becoming increasingly unstable, largely because of the worsening instability of his business partners, two Mafia dope dealers named Barclay Farenga and Gerard Papa. Both had the distressing habit of sampling their own wares. When high, Papa became a psychopath and liked to wave guns around, while Farenga appeared to be high most of the time, demonstrating his violent tendencies. They had been involved in at least six murders and had convinced Savino to bury two of their victims underneath the floor of his window company. To Savino's unease, Farenga and Papa dug a hole for the bodies, then calmly decided to break for lunch before tackling the job of covering the corpses. They consumed a takeout order of fried chicken, throwing the bones onto the bleeding corpses, then shoveled dirt over them.

Savino had made the mistake of enrolling Farenga and Papa as business partners in his window company. Eager to put some distance between himself and the two unstable hoods, Savino bought them out for $250,000 each. The price seemed high, but, as Savino was aware, an incredible moneymaking opportunity had just come knocking at his door, one he did not want to endanger by the presence of two doped-up mafiosi. He may have overlooked the fact that they already knew too much.

One essential thing they knew was that Savino was preparing to take advantage of a plan by the New York City Housing

Authority, which administered 318 public housing projects in the city, to save on rising energy costs—and tap into a pile of available federal aid money—by replacing all 1.5 million of the windows in those buildings with new, double-hung, double-glazed thermal windows that would save $6 million annually in heating and cooling costs. Savino had done some work for the Authority, earning a few extra dollars when he discovered that some of its officials were willing to take bribes to fix bids. Now they tipped him off about an even greater opportunity: the Authority would soon announce the staggering total of $143 million in bids for its massive windows project. Savino did the math. If the bids for those contracts could be fixed, even a modest Mafia tax of a dollar or two per window would return several millions of dollars in profit. And it had the virtue of being a virtually invisible crime: who would suspect criminal enterprise in so worthy a project as improving the lives of the poor people who lived in public housing?

Savino and his small company had no hope of handling so huge a contract, but he realized that if he could help the Mafia gain control of the bidding process—by means of organizing the dozen or so major window installation companies into a cartel—he stood to make a very considerable profit as a partner in the deal. Savino knew that the lever to achieve this goal would be Morrissey and his union local, which controlled all unionized window installers in the city.

Savino passed the word to his Lucchese and Genovese contacts that there was blood in the water, and soon the sharks began to gather. As Mafia working procedure decreed, so large a scheme had to be shared among the four families and administered by the Commission. But Savino failed to realize that the Mafia's organizational structure, severely rattled by the shock of the 1985 Commission case, was in very bad shape. To make things worse, the second-generation mafiosi who had moved up into the top command positions were simply not up to the task of administering a large-scale criminal conspiracy. What now passed for the Mafia's senior hierarchy was rent by divisions, mutual suspicion, murderous antipathy, and outright incompetence.

All these deficiencies would cause problems as the Mafia

sought to replicate the success of its concrete scheme with the windows operation. In the process, its organizational structure would finally collapse under the strain. Among the victims buried in the rubble would be Peter Savino.

The salient fact to remember about the new post-1985 Commission was that its senior member, according to Mafia protocol usually the most respected boss at the table, was spending most of his time trying to convince the outside world that he was insane. It was a circumstance that hardly inspired confidence in the organization.

Vincent (Chin) Gigante, boss of the Genovese Family, was the sole survivor of the 1985 disaster that had shattered the Mafia's top leadership. He appeared at meetings of the new Commission in pajamas, bathrobe, and slippers, the uniform in which he wandered the streets early each morning, mumbling incoherently to himself. This little routine was for the benefit of the FBI and police surveillance teams he knew were always lurking about, hoping to catch him behaving with enough lucidity that they could prove that he was in fact sane (as indeed he was). Meanwhile, a battle raged in court between prosecutors and Gigante's defense lawyers, who insisted their client was mentally ill and thus unfit for trial. Every so often, Gigante would be ordered into one mental health facility or another to determine his sanity. Psychiatrists were split on the issue, some concluding Gigante was quite sane and putting on an act, others finding that he was mentally deficient (one report noted Gigante's obsessive watching of children's television cartoon programs, especially any that involved "funny Martians"). The division of psychiatric opinion was sufficient to cause a legal stalemate that kept Gigante out of a courtroom, although prosecutors were constantly filing new motions to put him on trial.

"I gotta keep up appearances," Gigante would tell fellow bosses at meetings of the new Commission, half-jokingly explaining why he had shown up for a business meeting in nightwear. He often would go on to lament the years he had invested in his crazy act, a routine that thus far had kept him out of jail, but at a high price: "You know, if I had it to do over again, I wouldn't do it. I got all the money I need but I can't even spend it. I can't go anywhere.''

Despite his seniority, Gigante was not regarded with much respect by the other Commission members. ''A fucking loony old greaseball,'' John Gotti, the new head of the Gambino Family, called him behind his back. To Gigante's face, Gotti was barely polite; he despised the Genovese Family chieftain, whom he considered of the old Mafia generation, a fossil standing in the way of the new, younger generation like himself. Gotti intended to dispose of Gigante at some point, unaware that Gigante planned the very same fate for him.

A diehard Mafia traditionalist, Gigante had an acute animus for Gotti that was both personal and professional. In addition to his distaste for the swaggering, boastful new Gambino Family boss in $2,000 suits whose courting of publicity was regarded by Gigante as an invitation to trouble, he had never forgiven Gotti's violent seizure of power in the Gambino Family by murdering Paul Castellano. ''Big Paulie,'' as he was known, was a close friend of Gigante, but aside from the personal loss, Chin was upset over the fact that Gotti had ''raised hands'' to a boss—and gotten away with it. On a political level, Gigante had been around long enough in the Mafia world to immediately recognize the even larger ambition that lurked within Gotti, which involved nothing less than taking over the entire New York Mafia as *capo di tutti capi*. Gotti did everything but carry a neon sign advertising that ambition; as Gigante was aware, he often liked to refer to himself as ''God's gift'' to the new Mafia generation, in the process of assiduously courting soldiers and capos of other families in what clearly was an attempt to gather disciples.

The real significance of Gotti's violent accession to power, Gigante argued to other Commission members when Gotti was out of earshot, was that it had been carried out without formal Commission approval. Unauthorized murder, especially the killing of a boss, was just about the quickest way to destroy the organization; if any street punk got the idea he could dispose of a boss with impunity, the result would be anarchy. The idea behind creation of the Commission in the first place, Gigante pointed out, was to organize things, including ambition. In other words, if a capo like Gotti had grievances with his boss, the Commission was supposed to function as the court of first and last resort to resolve the dispute before it got out of hand. In effect, Gotti had made the Commission irrelevant. And without the Commission and its authority, Gigante insisted, the Mafia would be just another street gang, "like the niggers selling crack in Harlem."

Gigante the traditionalist had another problem with Gotti, this one involving one of the Mafia's most sacred strictures. Gotti had been involved in an affair with the daughter of his late underboss Aniello (Neil) Dellacroce, and she was married to a made man. Coveting a made man's wife was strictly forbidden under Mafia rules. When Gigante confronted him about it at one Commission meeting, Gotti coolly replied that the woman was in the process of divorcing her mobster husband, and besides, since she was the product of the relationship between Dellacroce and his mistress, "She's not Neil's real daughter." As an appalled Gigante noted, this kind of legalism made a mockery of the organization's rules. There was a sound reason for the rule barring men like Gotti from coveting the wives or daughters of other made members: nothing so provokes rage as the discovery by one mafioso that another has taken up with his wife. This type of behavior, too, if it spread, could lead to anarchy.

During Commission meetings in such secure sites as underground parking garages, Gigante tried to win support from the new heads of the Bonanno, Colombo, and Lucchese families for a solution, presumably violent, to what he called "the Gotti problem." But the Colombo Family was under the somewhat shaky leadership of Victor Orena, who faced the ongoing problem of a mutiny led by the forces of the imprisoned ex-boss Carmine Persico. The Bonanno Family, largely in disarray, was still barred from Commission membership, but, as Gigante realized, that made no difference in the context of the Gotti situation. The Bonannos had come under the command of Joseph Massina, a 350-pound heroin dealer, who also happened to be a close friend of Gotti. Busy trying to reorganize his family and restore its faded glory, Massina was in no mood to listen to anything negative about Gotti—the man, he had come to believe, who represented the very future of the American Mafia. Moreover, he needed Gotti's support for his eventual goal, restoring the Bonanno Family to full Commission membership.

That left the Lucchese Family, and, to Gigante's surprise, it was there that his fulminations against Gotti received their most sympathetic hearing. Vittorio Amuso and his shadow, Anthony Casso, eagerly agreed with everything Gigante said on the subject, and what's more, they volunteered their services for whatever solution The Chin might devise. The eagerness of Amuso and Casso to throw their lot in with Gigante had nothing to do with Gotti's violations of Mafia protocol—both men regarded such matters as trivial, at best—but had everything to do with politics. Amuso, gauging the weak state of the Commission, believed that the opportunity now existed to make his own move. In his calculation, getting rid of the dangerous Gotti would allow him to emerge as the de facto equal above equals, for Gigante was certain to be taken off to jail at some point; Orena would probably be consumed in the Colombo civil war; and Massina would be weakened without Gotti's patronage (assuming he wasn't arrested beforehand for his addiction to selling heroin). That would leave Amuso with a clear field to take control.

Gigante's solution to the Gotti situation, as might be expected, involved killing. The opening move came on April 13, 1986. On that day, the newly crowned Gambino boss Gotti planned to visit the Brooklyn social club owned by James (Jimmy Brown) Failla, an important capo in the Gambino Family. Gotti intended to press the flesh and generally make himself known to the Failla faction, part of his effort to solidify his leadership. He did not realize that Failla, a friend of Castellano, harbored deep resentment over the murder of Big Paulie four months before. Also a friend of Gigante, Failla made his displeasure known, and the two men came to an agreement: Failla would help get rid of Gotti, in exchange for Gigante's support of his own ambitions.

The plan was to blow up Gotti with a bomb as he entered his car in front of Failla's social club. Mafia protocol normally forbids the use of bombs in hits (too much danger of killing innocent civilians and causing public outrage), but bombs were a staple of the Sicilian Mafia. In Gigante's conception, the bomb that would kill Gotti would be blamed on the Sicilian faction of the Gambino organization, deflecting suspicion from the more likely suspect, himself.

Casso made the arrangements, and on the appointed day, a Brooklyn hood with bombmaking talents waited in ambush with a bomb and an electronic detonator. But Gotti canceled the appearance in favor of a more urgent appointment, and sent his new underboss, Frank DeCicco, in his stead. Unfortunately for DeCicco, he bore a strong resemblance to Gotti, whom the waiting bomber knew only by description. So when he saw the man he thought was Gotti park a car near Failla's social club, he planted the bomb, concealed in an ordinary paper bag, under the car. A short while later, as DeCicco returned to his car and opened the door, he set off the bomb. DeCicco was blown to pieces.

A severely rattled Gotti holed up in his Queens headquarters, the misleadingly named Bergin Hunt and Fish Club, and dispatched his underlings to find out what happened. They returned empty-handed: although suspicion naturally focused on Gigante, there was not even a trace of a clue pointing to him. Besides, DeCicco had met his end by the car bomb method, never before used in New York Mafia disputes. Most likely, Gotti was told, the bombing had been carried out by the Gambino Family's Sicilian faction angered over DeCicco's treason (formerly close to Castellano, he had betrayed his boss by allying himself with Gotti).

Even more alarmed were the FBI and police, who feared the outbreak of a new Mafia war, and they were determined to douse the brush fire before it spread to a conflagration. Cops and agents took direct action, invading Gambino and Genovese hangouts to warn they would not tolerate a gang war. One of them, the veteran anti-Mafia detective Kenneth McCabe, approached the Triangle Social Club in lower Manhattan, Gigante's chief headquarters.

"Open up! Police!" McCabe yelled, banging on the door. He heard heavy clunking sounds from within, the sound of guns being dropped on the floor.

"Ah, Detective McCabe," said one mafioso pleasantly as he opened the door. "What a nice surprise. Drink?"

"I don't drink with people like you," McCabe snapped.

"What's this?" He pointed to a pistol laying on the floor at the mobster's feet.

"Holy shit!" the mobster exclaimed in horror. "There's a gun on the floor. I wonder how it got there?"

Of course, no one would own up to the arsenal on the floor, so McCabe had no proof for charges of illegal weapons possession. The guns were confiscated. Meanwhile, similar visits to Gambino Family hangouts conveyed the same message: start shooting at your peril. It had the desired effect of dampening any enthusiasm for an all-out shooting war, but did not stop Gigante from continuing to plot Gotti's removal. Casso was the key player in the drama, arranging for the subsequent murder of Gotti's close friend and chauffeur, Bartholomew (Bobby) Boriello, and, still later, the murder of Gotti's chief narcotics trafficker, Edward Lino. Gotti suspected Gigante was behind the killings, but opted to retaliate not with killing. Instead, he ordered an aggressive program to take over chunks of Gigante's operations.

Gotti's counteroffensive caused real problems for the Genovese Family's New Jersey operations, which soon bombarded Gigante with demands that he eliminate the threat. In August 1987, Gigante approved their plan to solve the Gotti problem once and for all by killing him, his brother, and any other Gambino mafiosi who happened to be in the way. Six of the New Jersey faction's leading hoods met in what they believed was a perfectly secure site—the ladies' room of restaurant one of them owned—to map out precisely how the hit would be carried out. But the FBI had bugged the ladies' room and, aware of the murder plan, was morally obligated to warn Gotti, who reacted calmly when three FBI agents showed up at his door to inform him they had incontrovertible proof that he was the subject of a murder plot. Once the agents left, Gotti ordered his minions to redouble their efforts to take control of Gigante's operations as a means of impoverishing his most formidable Mafia rival.

For the moment, relentless FBI and police pressure ended any further overt moves in what had become the Gotti-Gigante war, but the intrigue continued. In 1988, during a Commission meeting in a Manhattan underground garage, the atmosphere was so tense that both Gotti and Gigante were convinced the meeting site was the place of their execution. Each boss seeded gunmen around the site, with orders to shoot everybody who emerged from the garage in the event they heard shots ring out from inside. The tension carried over into the meeting itself, as both men warily circled each other like two scorpions looking for a vulnerable place to strike.

Things grew even more tense when Gotti made his move: he asked that the Commission formally crown Joseph Massina as head of the Bonanno Family (and that the organization be readmitted to Commission membership), along with Victor Orena as head of the Colombo Family. Gigante spotted the danger immediately: Gotti had established friendships with Massina and Orena, both of whom he felt he could control; their presence on the Commission would guarantee Gotti's domination, since the alliance would represent three votes out of five.

Gigante parried the threat by counterproposing that the question of the Bonanno Family's readmission be deferred until a future Commission session, by which time the organization would be able to determine whether the Bonanno Family had reformed itself sufficiently to stop dealing heroin and avoid being infiltrated by the FBI. Gigante agreed to Gotti's request for the coronation of Orena, but as he well knew, it was largely a symbolic gesture: the weak Orena, he calculated, almost certainly would be consumed in the fire of the Colombo Family's worsening civil war. To Gotti's unease, the Lucchese Family's Vic Amuso fully backed Gigante, which meant a standoff: Orena and Gotti versus Gigante and Amuso. At that moment, Gotti undoubtedly realized that he faced not one enemy, but two.

The next item on the agenda concerned the matter of personnel. Continuing depredations by the FBI-police Joint Task Force were cutting wide swaths in the lower ranks. Gotti noted that each family might have to recruit up to forty men simply to make up the losses. Gigante sensed further danger: he was aware that Gotti had been actively wooing potential street soldiers, and suspected that his rival would arrange for at least a significant percentage of new recruits to be loyal to him. As if to signal his intentions, Gotti told Gigante he had inducted his own son. "Jesus, I'm sorry to hear that," Gigante replied, then won Amuso's support for a deferral on the question of how many new recruits would be admitted.

But the deferral was a mistake, for the problem of personnel in the Mafia was reaching critical mass. Not only was the organization still encountering problems in finding qualified recruits, but there were growing indications that the second generation mafiosi already at work amounted to a pretty sad lot. Amuso, no paragon of criminal statesmanship himself, could cite any number of serious personnel problems within his own family—as with a young street hood to whom he awarded a $1,000-a-week no-show job at a carting company, only to learn that the man he believed was an up-and coming mobster had quit, later telling an enraged Amuso that he didn't like the company's health plan. Then there was the more serious problem of Frank Manzo, the Lucchese capo in charge of the family's operations at Kennedy Airport, whose violent temper had boiled over in an incident that caused severe disruption at the Mafia's upper levels.

Manzo was sitting at his diner corner table one night, having dinner with Leonard Orena, son of the Colombo boss Victor Orena. For some reason, Manzo suddenly felt compelled to tell Orena, ''You know, your father is a worthless piece of shit.''

Orena erupted in anger, smashing a ketchup bottle over Manzo's head, then fled. Manzo ran home, got a gun, and enlisted a friend to help him find Orena. They later spotted him driving along a busy highway. Manzo leaned out the window of his car and fired five shots at Orena, all of which missed. Terrified motorists scattered in all directions.

It required several tense sitdowns between the Lucchese and Colombo organizations to cool things down without a shooting war breaking out, a peace largely achieved because Manzo was out of range, having fled to Europe to spend two years in hiding. (He was later ordered to pay significant compensation to Orena as a means of finally settling the matter.)

Even Casso, about the purest example of violent psychopathology around, found the Manzo incident unsettling. Like Amuso, he constantly fretted about the current tendency of street soldiers and capos alike to commit unbelievably stupid acts that drew attention to themselves (such as trying to kill someone on a busy highway). Too many of them had the risky habit of dressing in what had become the standard Mafia uniform: gray Armani jacket, black turtleneck and gold chain. The outfit lacked only a sign reading, INDICT ME.

Still, such lapses were only to be expected in an organization now run by men whose intellectual level was nothing to brag about, either. There were any number of examples, among the more prominent being Sammy the Bull Gravano of the Gambino Family, an astonishingly knuckleheaded street hood who had suddenly vaulted from lowly rank to the lofty post of underboss in the Gambino organization for the sole reason that he had thrown in his lot early to support the ambitions of another dumb street hood, John Gotti. Gravano's stupidity was legendary: years before, in a brief flirtation with legitimacy, he had enrolled in a barber school, from which he somehow managed to flunk (the school discovered that among his many failings was cutting the hearing aid wire of a customer while trimming the man's hair). Yet this was the man now put in charge of his organization's interests in various businesses and rackets, two subjects of which he had very little grasp. His inexperience and ignorance, however, ran no deeper than that demonstrated by his colleagues, including Casso and Amuso.

This was the distinctly turbulent atmosphere into which Peter Savino had brought the new golden calf. While all the squabbling and double-crossing went on, Savino worked tirelessly to put together the windows scheme. Morrissey was an enthusiastic partner, working directly with Casso to cow the window contractors into submission. Very quickly, the classic dimensions of the standard Mafia construction racket assumed form: a cartel of contractors, herded into subservience by the threat of labor disruption. The bids for the various contracts that the Housing Authority was about to advertise would be fixed, with the winning bids pegged deliberately high—but not too high—to guarantee handsome profit and the Mafia tax.

"This," Savino announced "will be fucking beautiful."

While Amuso and Casso waited for the flow of cash from the windows scheme to arrive, they embarked on an important diplomatic assignment, flying to Florida to deliver some bad news to Anthony (Tumac) Acceturo, boss of the Lucchese Family's New Jersey satrapy. The news was that from now on, Tumac had to come up with a lot of money for the privilege of running it.

Acceturo welcomed the visit with little enthusiasm, since he had a sense of what he was in for. The timing could not have been worse: by 1986, he had built the New Jersey organization into unprecedented heights of wealth and power. The organization ran so smoothly that Acceturo was now spending almost all his time in Florida, where he had established highly profitable enterprises in cocaine smuggling, extortion of major businesses, and fixing horse races (his favorite trick was spiking the water of chosen horses with amphetamines). Like his old friend Corallo, Acceturo was a master of security and low profile; very few people even knew of his existence, much less his role as a Mafia kingpin. Despite the millions he earned each year, Acceturo lived in a modest Florida home. He never went anywhere near Mafia hangouts, nor was he ever seen in public with mafiosi. Such attention to security had contributed to a remarkable statistic: in more than thirty years of a criminal career to this point, Acceturo had served only four months in jail.

Aware of the reputations of Amuso and Casso, Acceturo was not thrilled to hear of their arrival in Florida. Nevertheless, he did his best as a gracious Mafia host, putting them up at a top hotel and providing every other possible amenity. He disliked them instantly, an antipathy he concealed behind a friendly outward appearance as the three men shared several dinners at expensive restaurants while discussing business. Acceturo was displeased to see Casso play the Mafia bigshot, ordering rare $400 bottles of wine, stuffing one-hundred-dollar bills into waiters' front jacket pockets, and running up $1,000 dinner tabs that he paid by ostentatiously peeling off bills from a huge wad in his pocket. Acceturo, whose culinary tastes ran to *fettucine* prepared at cheap mom-and-pop restaurants, regarded the performance with discomfort: this kind of flashiness was almost suicidal.

Acceturo's mood further worsened when his two visitors from New York announced that there would be a change in the long-standing arrangement between himself and Corallo.

That $10,000 annual payment was a joke, Amuso said, and did not reflect the true value of Acceturo's operations. Henceforth, Acceturo would pay a percentage of his profits, which Amuso estimated would be somewhere around several million dollars each year. Trying not to show his shock, Acceturo mildly protested that this dictate violated an understanding that dated back many years. When Amuso curtly dismissed the point, Acceturo played for time, noting that his profits were not nearly what Amuso believed them to be. Besides, trying to come up with a fair percentage agreeable to both sides would require a great deal of work. Further meetings would be needed. In the meantime, Acceturo purred, the new leader of the Lucchese Family enjoyed his full support.

The three men parted on this soothing political note. As Vic Amuso and Gas Pipe Casso flew back to New York, they conducted an overview of what they had accomplished so far. They had firmly planted the flag in the family's various operations, and in a number of them had instituted firm measures to get things back on track. As for money, there would be a steady flow from the old reliables (including narcotics, from which the family prohibition had been removed), but the real profits would come in the gasoline ripoff, the windows scheme, and the take from Acceturo's New Jersey operation. Taken together, there would be more money than ever; by the time they had everything running at peak speed, they'd bring the family to a level that even Gaetano Lucchese or Tony Ducks Corallo couldn't achieve. Things looked very good.

Tony Acceturo had a very different perspective. While his new boss and chief aide flew back to New York, Acceturo convened a meeting of his senior aides to report on the results of his encounter. "Things look bad," Acceturo said morosely. There was no doubt in his mind, he said, that he had encountered two of the stupidest Mafia leaders in his forty-year career, guys he could hardly believe had been produced by the same organization that also produced a Gaetano Lucchese or a Tony Ducks Corallo. Worse, they were insanely greedy and believed that the answer to any given problem was to shoot somebody. Acceturo had no doubt that Amuso would not be satisfied with a mere slice of the Acceturo organization's profits, but would eventually take larger and larger pieces until there was hardly anything left. And given the kind of men Amuso and Casso were, there also was no doubt that they would simply take whatever they wanted, killing anybody in the way. Acceturo said he would stall for time until he figured out a way to fend off the pending assault from New York.

"I'll tell you what really worries me," Acceturo said. "These stupid bastards are gonna fuck it all up. Mark my words."

• EIGHT •

"How Come There's a Bomb on My Front Seat?"

Things change now because there's too much conflict.
People do whatever they feel like. They don't train their
people no more. There's no more respect.

ANIELLO DELLACROCE

If he hadn't known better, Charles Rose might have thought
that Everett Hatcher had pulled off that quiet road on Staten
Island to catch a little nap. Seen from the driver's side, head
back on the seatrest, eyes closed, the black Drug Enforcement
Agency agent looked at peace. But as Rose circled around the
car and peered inside from the passenger side, he could see
the dark hole on the side of Hatcher's head.

"Anybody tell his wife yet?" Rose asked.

"There's people over there now," said one of the somber-
looking DEA and FBI agents on the scene. Rose tried not to
think of how Hatcher's wife was taking the news, or how she
would tell her two small children. Sometime later in the day,
Rose realized, he would have to make the same sad journey
to the small, neat suburban house and give his condolences to
Mrs. Hatcher, offering what comfort he could.

"He was a real good guy," said one of the DEA agents to
Rose, who nodded solemnly. He led Rose to the rear of the
car and opened the trunk. "Charlie, we know you worked with
Everett. He thought a lot of you. So we think he'd want you

to have this." He reached into the trunk and extracted a leather case containing Hatcher's badge and pressed it into Rose's hand. Rose could see tears in his eyes.

"Let me tell you something," Rose vowed. "Some day, I'm going to take this badge and shove it into that son of a bitch's face."

Everyone there in the predawn hours of February 28, 1989, knew that Rose was referring to Costabile (Gus) Farace, a low-level Mafia heroin dealer. And they knew that Farace had murdered Hatcher. Shortly before his death, Hatcher had left his home for an important appointment on the road with the mafioso, when he hoped Farace would commit the one act the DEA agent had been working months to achieve: sell him some heroin. It was to be a critical move in a very dangerous game in which Hatcher had been playing, the role of a big-time black dealer trying to tap into Farace's source of supply. But something had gone wrong. Now, Hatcher was dead and Farace had disappeared.

A veteran agent, Hatcher was aware that even the slightest misstep in Farace's violent world would forfeit his life. Operating unarmed, his backup some distance away to avoid being spotted, Hatcher was nakedly alone with men like Farace, who murdered with the same casualness with which others swat flies. The only clue to Hatcher's real identity, his gold badge, was hidden beneath the carpet in the trunk of his car.

But for Hatcher and the DEA, the risk was worth the potential reward: penetration of the mob's "Sicilian connection," now the main source of high-grade heroin for the American Mafia. Thanks to dozens of mafiosi like Farace who were willing to flout the Mafia establishment's official (but laxly enforced) ban on narcotics dealing, the Sicilian-American partnership was flooding the United States with the best quality heroin anyone had ever seen. And the most profitable: a kilo of pure Sicilian-produced heroin, its quality assured by a stable of expert chemists that once worked for the fabled French Connection, could be bought wholesale for about $40,000, then reduced in purity to around six or seven percent for sale to street-level users for an eventual net profit of $1.4 million.

As the chief narcotics prosecutor for the Eastern District of

New York, Charles Rose was among the first to know of the resurgence of Sicilian-provided heroin. And he knew firsthand about a series of dangerous undercover operations the police, DEA, and the FBI were mounting to get at it. Men like Everett Hatcher literally had to put their lives on the line to sit in dark basement rooms with suspicious, violent men. Armed only with their wits, acting ability, and street smarts, they had to perform a high-wire act without a safety net, aware every moment that the slightest error—a second's hesitancy in answering a question, a momentary lapse in remembering the name of an important dealer, a tiny hole in a cover story—would blow an undercover operation (and might get them killed). In the world of narcotics enforcement, there was no alternate method: infiltrate a conspiracy, find out who was involved, uncover the sources of supply, then prove it all in court. Even under the best of circumstances, many of these undercover operations failed because among upper-level dope dealers, especially the Mafia variety, there was a heightened alertness to any attempts to infiltrate their operations. The tiniest suspicion was enough to abort the most elaborate operation; often, a major dealer would refuse to commit himself out of pure criminal instinct, because he didn't like the "feel" of a situation.

Under the unwritten rules of this high-stakes game, Mafia dope kingpins, as contrasted with the Colombians and other groups, usually would not murder a undercover agent. The mafiosi understood that such killing would not only be pointless—the dead undercover agent would simply be replaced by another—it had the more serious disadvantage of rousing their enemies. Killing an agent was like poking a stick into a hornet's nest, setting off a fury that was very disruptive for business.

But as Rose had discovered, the new Mafia generation moving into narcotics was much more violent and unstable than their predecessors. The gargantuan profits of the narcotics trade were attracting real crazies who would kill anybody in their way. Many of them were heavy drug users themselves, and, when high, became extremely unstable. Farace, for example, was a heavy steroid user to bulk himself up for what he considered a Mr. Universe physique. Without much in the way of brains, like many of his fellow street hoods who sought to take a shortcut to wealth by heavy dealing in drugs, Farace was an unguided missile. Just short of being an addict, he liked to dip into the stuff he was peddling, making him even wilder.

Why he had decided to kill Hatcher was a mystery, but the important fact was that a mafioso had murdered a federal agent. The entire law enforcement establishment regarded that as a direct challenge. Rose found himself quickly besieged with offers of help from what seemed to be every cop and federal agent in New York, all them volunteering their free time, in addition to their duty hours, to work the case.

In the end, Gus Farace would be brought to justice, although not quite in the form Rose intended. There was, however, an unforeseen side effect that Rose could not have anticipated: a severe impact on the Lucchese Family of la Cosa Nostra.

To the Mafia's unease, an infuriated law enforcement establishment, convinced that the Mafia was hiding Farace, began to exert furious pressure against every soldier, capo, and associate it could find. All of them got the identical message: give us Gus Farace, or your existence will become a living hell. Even the bosses felt the pressure. Robert Stutman, head of the DEA's New York field office, nearly unhinged over the grief and anger he felt about the murder of his agent, barged into the home of John Gotti and told him, "Farace whacked our guy. We want him." Otherwise, Stutman warned, Gotti could expect "pressure," the consequences of which he didn't even want to think about.

Gotti carefully replied that he'd do what he could, but added he didn't have the vaguest idea of where Farace could be located (true: Farace worked his narcotics deals for the Bonanno and Lucchese organizations). Joe Massina, head of the Bonanno organization, assured a detail of police detectives and DEA agents that he was very upset and certainly would do all he could to see that Farace was put into their hands. "I'd like to kill that stupid cocksucker myself," he said, adding that neither he nor anybody else in his organization knew where Farace was hiding.

Even more cooperative was another boss, Vic Amuso of the Lucchese Family, who hastened to assure his visitors he personally felt terrible shock at the news of Hatcher's murder.

And, of course, he didn't know where Farace was, but he would put all the resources of his organization to work in an effort to find Farace and turn him in to the authorities. "Anybody who does a thing like this," he said with apparent sincerity, "ought to be hunted down like a dog, that's my opinion."

The sentiment, as far as it went, was genuine. Yes, Amuso was appalled by Hatcher's murder, but in fact he had a pretty good idea of where Farace was hiding. It was also true that he wanted Farace brought to justice, but he meant his own particular variety. He did not want Farace in the hands of an angry law enforcement establishment: since Farace would be facing murder charges, there was at least the reasonable possibility he would seek to avoid a possible death sentence (for killing a federal agent) by bargaining his way out with relevant information—such as his narcotics dealings with the Lucchese organization, most prominently Vic Amuso himself.

Shortly after Hatcher's murder, Amuso learned that Farace had sought sanctuary with an old friend from his prison days, John (Johnny Boy) Petrucelli, a street hood with the Lucchese organization's Bronx faction. Amuso passed a grim choice to Petrucelli, either kill Farace or yourself. Petrucelli refused and warned Farace, who fled. Amuso made good his threat. Another Lucchese street hood, Joseph (Joey Blue Eyes) Consentino, who happened to be Petrucelli's best friend, was given the ultimate Mafia loyalty test: murder your lifelong buddy. Consentino did just that, but Farace was still loose.

It took several months, but Amuso finally tracked him to a hideout in Manhattan. One of Amuso's minions lured him out with the bait of money and a false passport to flee the country, but Farace never made it to the meeting site. He emerged from the apartment building where he had been hiding and was cut down in a fusillade of bullets fired by James (Jimmy Frogs) Galione, another street soldier from the Lucchese Bronx faction. Newspapers called Farace's killing "Mafia street justice," although Amuso knew it was in fact a fairly standard operation to eliminate a potentially troublesome witness.

News of Farace's execution caused an almost audible sigh of relief throughout the underworld, but the massive dragnet for the trigger-happy dope dealer had an unintended, and very damaging, consequence for Amuso and his organization. While the DEA was rooting around in the drug world for Farace, it began to uncover a number of narcotics operations that had previously escaped its notice. One of them was a large-scale cocaine smuggling ring, a Mafia operation run by Barclay Farenga. He was caught red-handed and now faced fifty years in prison.

Seeking leniency, Farenga announced he was willing to become a federal witness. Taken to Rose, he began to drop a few tidbits, none of which particularly impressed the prosecutor. Rose suspected Farenga knew a lot more. A few more days in jail, the longest drug-free span of time Farenga had undergone in quite a while, apparently cleared his thinking process, and he was back before Rose with more substantial goods to peddle. These consisted of two very intriguing questions: Would Rose be interested in some dead bodies? And, would Rose be even more interested in a guy who was fixing window-installation contracts for the city Housing Authority on behalf of the Mafia?

Rose certainly was interested, and a few days of conversation with Farenga produced a team of FBI agents, armed with a search warrant, that showed up at the Brooklyn office of the Arista Windows Company. Its owner, Peter Savino, expressed shock that they wanted to dig up his factory floor to look for bodies. ''Bodies? What bodies?''

''Look,'' one of the agents told him, ''we're not here to play games. We've got a pretty good idea there's two dead bodies buried here. If we have to, we will dig up every goddamn square inch of this place. We'll take everything apart, and maybe we'll put it back together, and maybe we won't. Let me guarantee you something: if there are bodies buried anywhere in this building, we will find them. You can either cooperate with us and make things easier on yourself, or force us to do a lot of work, which will piss us off. So make up your mind.''

Savino did some fast calculation. Clearly, the FBI agents were there looking for bodies because somebody told them where to look. And that meant his worst nightmare had come true: one of his drug-addled ex-business partners, Barclay Farenga or Gerard Papa, had gotten into trouble and was bargaining his way out by revealing such interesting news as murder victims buried under factory floors. Savino also assumed that either man had probably told the FBI about the windows scheme, which further meant he was about one step away from a prison cell. Savino gave in and told the men with shovels where to dig, carefully noting for the record his "cooperation." They shortly found two graves that included discarded chicken bones—just as Farenga said they would.

Attention now focused on Savino, who wasted no time: he wanted to make a deal. He had some high cards to play, for he was at the very center of the ongoing windows operation, sufficient leverage to open discussions about the possibility of lenient treatment for the charges of narcotics trafficking and accessory to murder that he was confronting. But as Rose made clear, his revelations alone would not be enough to clinch the deal, certainly not enough for an ambitious plan he was formulating. Essentially, Rose wanted to put together a second Commission case, and, like the first—which used the concrete industry ripoff as the central criminal conspiracy—it would use a similar scheme, this time window installation, as a means of taking down the new hierarchy of the four Mafia families. But the problem was that the Commission case was built around tapes, especially the Jaguar bug, which in effect recorded the conspiracy as it unfolded. As Rose and every other federal prosecutor knew, juries in RICO cases tended to acquit without solid evidence of the conspiracies alleged, almost invariably meaning tape evidence. Several prosecutors had learned, to their chagrin, that relying on the testimony of criminal coconspirators alone was not enough; juries, aware that such witnesses might be simply making it all up to win leniency (a possibility defense lawyers consistently raised), in effect wanted to hear the accused convict themselves out of their own mouths.

To solve that problem in the windows case, a simple yet dangerous plan was devised: Savino would wear a wire. As the key figure in the scheme, the man who routinely dealt with all four Mafia families involved (the Bonanno Family was excluded because it had not yet been restored to Commission membership), Savino would be in a perfect spot to get the kind of incriminating conversations a RICO case would need.

Eager to win at least some absolution for his legal troubles, Savino consented to the idea.

The chief targets of the Savino wire were to be the various family bosses involved, for they would be the crux of the new Commission case, centered on one specific, Mafiawide criminal enterprise. The Mafia, still not recovered from the 1985 disaster, might be crippled forever by a new prosecution. But, as Rose was aware, he could only achieve that goal if he could keep the case out of the clutches of his most ruthless enemies. Not the Mafia, but his fellow prosecutors on the other side of the East River in the Southern District of New York.

From his first day on the job in 1972, Rose learned that the federal law enforcement establishment in New York was split among three high-profile and fiercely competitive entities: the Southern District, the Eastern District, and the Eastern District Organized Crime Strike Force (this latter organization, although it operated in the Eastern District's jurisdiction, reported exclusively to the Justice Department). The three entities, which operated in the highest concentration of media in the United States, often competed for high-profile cases. Usually, the entity that had the most aggressive U.S. Attorney—or one with the best political connections in the Justice Department—would prevail. Some of the nastiest battles for turf took place over organized crime cases, which seldom fit neatly into the geographic jurisdictions of the two U.S. attorney offices.

What would become known as ''the windows case'' was a perfect demonstration of the problem. It involved men from all four Mafia families, ripping off publicly funded contracts that covered buildings in all five boroughs of New York City. So which set of federal prosecutors would handle the case, the Southern District (whose purview included Manhattan, the Bronx, Staten Island, and Westchester), or the Eastern District (Brooklyn, Queens, and Long Island)? By custom, the answer lay in the district in which the crime had first occurred or was investigated. In practice, however, a U.S. attorney could take any case through sheer aggressiveness, as proven by the career of Rudolph Giuliani.

For most of the six years he was the U.S. attorney in the

Southern District, Giuliani was a jurisdictional black hole, swallowing every case he wanted (usually because they were high profile). Thanks to his previous service as a Justice Department official, he had a wide range of key contacts there, incalculable help in his relentless drive to corral all big cases. Routinely, he took over promising Eastern District cases, running roughshod over his weaker counterparts in Brooklyn. Rose had lost a number of cases to Giuliani's poaching, including the so-called "pizza connection" narcotics case that began when Rose recruited a defector from the Sicilian Mafia. Things didn't change until 1986, when Andrew Maloney was appointed the new U.S. attorney for the Eastern District.

A former West Point boxer and later narcotics prosecutor in the Southern District, Maloney was a curious mix of absent-minded professor and aggressive prosecutor. He was notorious for his forgetfulness, often forgetting the names of people he had known for years (in which case he would address them as "your honor" or "doctor"). On other occasions, he would mangle the names of people he was introducing during public ceremonies. This Magoo-like habit stood in sharp contrast with another marked trait, an iron-hard determination to destroy the Mafia. And that destruction, Maloney decided, would take place in the Eastern District. He went head to head with Giuliani in several jurisdictional wrestling matches, finally winning a victory of sorts when Giuliani decided to leave law enforcement to enter politics.

Subsequently, Maloney was able to achieve the Eastern District's greatest success, the exclusive right to prosecute John Gotti. But before that, Maloney announced that he would keep control of the windows case, the first step in what he told Rose was a larger goal: "We are going to take the Lucchese Family apart, piece by piece."

First, however, Rose had to make sure he could keep the case away from the Southern District, where, he discovered, old habits die hard. To his fury, Rose learned that his Southern District counterparts, having learned that Farenga wanted to cooperate, saw a fine opportunity to construct any number of major cases built around his revelations. They had Farenga brought in for a discussion of how his life would improve in their hands. In the course of the conversation, they told Farenga that Rose was a "scumbag."

It had little effect on Farenga. A street-shrewd student of how good guys and bad guys operate, he reported to Rose, whom he had grown to respect, about the tenor of the conversation. "I ain't going with them, Mr. Rose," Farenga said. "See, I figure if they were saying such bad things about you behind your back, just imagine what they say about me behind *my* back." Hardly mollified, an angered Rose stalked into the Southern District headquarters and delivered a loud complaint to one of its leading prosecutors, Louis Freeh. Later named director of the FBI, Freeh professed to be horrified, then abjectly apologized for the behavior of his fellow prosecutors.

Territorial imperatives established, Rose returned his attention to windows. Savino's body mike began to accumulate interesting tapes as he made his rounds of the conspiracy. But just as the case entered its most promising phase, with especially incriminating conversations among bosses and Mafia mid-level executives, something went wrong. FBI taps on several phones used by mafiosi revealed the alarming news that they were onto Savino, somehow.*

"He's a fucking rat!" shouted one mobster over a tapped line to Vincent Gigante, demanding that he order Savino's execution. "He's gotta be hit!"

Gigante refused to order the hit, a refusal detected in another tap that recorded Vic Amuso telling Sammy the Bull Gravano, "Ah, the Chin loves him." Whatever Gigante's reasoning, the essential fact was that Savino was now exposed. Further confirmation came when his new tapes revealed that the mobsters had suddenly become very cautious in talking to him. An urgent meeting between Rose, Jules Bonavolonta, now head of organized crime investigations for the FBI, and other agents and detectives involved in the case resulted in a consensus: although the investigation was not yet finished and Savino had

---

*Several years later, an FBI bug planted in John Gotti's operations center at the Ravenite Social Club in lower Manhattan revealed that Gotti had been tipped off by a girlfriend, a detective working in the police department's Intelligence Division. Gotti warned the rest of the Mafia.

not yet recorded the most juicily incriminating conversations, it was time to end the operation. Savino's tape recorder was shut off and a wave of indictments began.

Among the more vulnerable in the process were Vic Amuso and Gas Pipe Casso. News that the case was built around tapes made by Peter Savino made them instantly aware they were in big trouble, for they knew their many conversations with him were largely criminal. They convened an urgent strategy session: how could they beat the case? Savino, a protected federal witness, was out of reach, but John Morrissey, the union leader, was not. In their deadly calculation, they stood at least a chance of defeating the Savino tapes, but that slim chance disappeared if Morrissey were to become a prosecution witness. Both Casso and Amuso, afflicted with strong streaks of paranoia, came to convince themselves that Morrissey was the gravest danger they faced. He had been indicted in the case, and, while out on bail, he proclaimed himself a ''standup guy'' with no intention of trying to cut a deal. But Amuso and Casso were now certain he would do precisely that under the threat of a heavy prison stay.

Unfortunately for Morrissey, this conclusion sealed his fate. Amuso ordered Peter Chiodo to arrange for Morrissey's murder, with firm instructions that the body must disappear, so as to create the impression that he had fled to avoid prosecution. Chiodo lured his victim to a friendly lunch at a good restaurant, after which he took Morrissey for a walk. Amuso and Casso were proud of him, Chiodo told him, and didn't have a second's worth of doubt that he was standup guy. In fact, they were so proud of him, they wanted to meet him the next day, a Sunday, at a safe house in New Jersey. The following morning, still not suspicious, Morrissey, dressed in his best suit, showed up for his rendezvous with Chiodo. Chiodo drove him over the George Washington Bridge and into the New Jersey countryside, all the while chatting with his prey as though the only pressing business of the day was a friendly Sunday jaunt. They arrived at a housing development under construction.

His suspicions still not aroused, not even by the odd sight of the notorious hitman Michael DeSantis at the controls of a backhoe, busily digging a large trench in the back of a model home, Morrissey was ushered inside the house. There, he encountered Richard Pagliarulo and Tommy Carew. He felt the first glint of suspicion at their unannounced presence, confirmed when he saw Pagliarulo reach into a wastepaper basket and pull out a pistol with a silencer.

"I'm no rat," Morrissey said simply as Pagliarulo pumped several shots into him. He fell on the floor, twisting in pain. "Oh, Christ, it hurts. Finish me," he begged. Pagliarulo tried to fire another shot into him, but the gun jammed. Carew pulled out a .38-caliber and fired four shots into Morrissey, who continued to moan. Pagliarulo unjammed his gun and fired a shot into Morrissey's head. Finally, he lay still. Chiodo and Morrissey's two executioners wrapped the body in a rug and carried it outside, dumping it into the trench DeSantis had dug.

Morrissey had disappeared from the face of the earth, but as Amuso and Casso discovered, it made no difference in terms of the case they confronted. As defense attorneys began to get the required copies of the evidence arrayed against their clients, the two Lucchese leaders realized they had no hope of getting an acquittal; they simply had been too expansive when discussing the scheme with Savino. Even without Morrissey, the case against them was looking stronger each passing day as teams of cops and FBI agents gathered further evidence to back up the Savino tapes.

As they considered their bleak prospects, trying to think of what other drastic action they might take to change the odds, equally bleak news arrived from other arms of their criminal empire. Indeed, it seemed like everything was going sour all at once.

The first bad news arose in the Lucchese Family's most lucrative and reliable source of cash, the Kennedy Airport operation. The trouble that would eventually loosen the family's grip on the airport had begun several years before, when an FBI agent named William Cardin, who worked at a small Bureau substation there (mainly to handle hijackings and other terrorist acts), noticed that a striking number of mafiosi had jobs in Teamsters locals 295 and 851. Curious, Cardin dug deeper and began to divine the dim outlines of the great clock-

work of crime that was at once vast and virtually invisible—
Mafia control of the union locals that in turn controlled a cartel
of shipping and trucking companies, loan-sharking and gambling operations among airport workers, and an organized system of thefts from air freight.

Cardin's first reports led to an elaborate FBI operation code-
named Kenrac, run by the Eastern District Organized Crime
Strike Force. Its chief, Edward McDonald, announced his intention to cleanse the airport of the Mafia, and to that end
unleashed a full-court press against the bedrock of the mob's
control at Kennedy, the two Teamsters locals. An FBI bug
planted in the home of Frank Manzo, the Lucchese capo who
ran Local 295, turned out to be the key that unlocked the
secrets of the network his organization had constructed.

Manzo, a voluble, boastful mobster, filled some five hundred reels of tape with what amounted to a running commen-
tary on how the Mafia ran things at JFK. "I own the airport;
the field is mine," he bragged one day, accurately. The bug
also detected his frustration in trying to instruct his two dumb
and lazy sons in the arts of airport racketeering. At one point,
their furious father screamed at them that he had been embarrassed because they had not bothered to even show up for two
executive jobs paying six-figure incomes he had extorted for
them at an air freight company. Manzo was further enraged
when they told him they'd rather party, and besides, such jobs
were their "right" because their father ruled the airport. "You
dumb fucks!" Manzo berated his two sons. "*I* rob the money,
not you!"

Of consuming interest to the FBI were more incriminating
statements, such as when Manzo told Frank Calise, his chief
henchman at Local 295, "God forbid somebody gets the
book." To anybody with even a passing acquaintance of Mafia
jargon, that meant there was a loan shark book around somewhere, a detailed list of loan shark customers and a record of
their loans and payments. Prosecutors like to call such evidence "slam dunk," meaning rock-solid evidence impossible
to refute, especially if the loan shark has maintained the accounts in his own handwriting. FBI agents went looking for
the book mentioned in the Manzo-Calise conversation, and
found something even better.

After fluttering a search warrant in Calise's face, an FBI search team went to work in his office, finally discovering a black journal hidden in the ceiling (along with a loaded gun). The journal, marked "cash" on the front cover, turned out to be not a loan shark book, but a detailed record of every payoff he and Manzo had received from air freight companies. A more incriminating volume could not be imagined, and it proved very costly later in court. Of the ten mafiosi indicted in the case, nine, including Manzo and Calise, immediately pleaded guilty, and the tenth went on trial, a waste of taxpayers' money that cost him twelve years in prison. All told, Edward McDonald's assault put thirty mafiosi away, in the process wrecking what had been the Lucchese Family's most lucrative cash cow. (Among the casualties was Paul Vario, the once mighty Lucchese capo whose criminal career, already in decline, was finally ended. Sentenced to a fifteen-year prison term, he died after serving only two years.)

None of those convicted wanted to take the dangerous step of easing their legal problem by providing information or testimony against Vic Amuso and Gas Pipe Casso, the ultimate beneficiaries of their crimes. But the damage was severe enough. The flow of money from the airport had suddenly declined to a trickle, a disaster made all the worse because another tributary of cash, the Bypass Gang, had come to grief.

The gang's downfall began when police in Nassau County on Long Island concluded that the break-in at a jewelry exchange, in which some $3 million in cash and uncut gems had been taken, was no ordinary burglary. A careful review of all known burglars and break-in artists in their jurisdiction failed to turn up any capable of carrying out the sophisticated operation the break-in revealed: the thieves had first cut a hole in the roof, then disabled a state-of-the-art security system before peeling open several high-quality safes as though they were tin cans.

In the new era of local-federal law enforcement cooperation, the cops compared notes with the FBI, and discovered the break-in matched a pattern. Throughout the New York metropolitan area, a wave of break-ins of banks and other high-value targets since 1981 had the common denominators of holes in the roofs, security systems professionally disabled, and, in the case of targets with safes or vaults, a professional penetration.

The New York FBI's resident expert on robberies, Steve Carbone, agreed with the conclusion, and added one of his own: whatever gang was committing the robberies was part of organized crime. Consider the criminals' requirements for these big jobs, Carbone noted: what ordinary gang of burglars could afford the expensive equipment necessary to balk highly sophisticated security systems, the advanced industrial torches to cut through office safes, the diamond drills to penetrate almost two feet of the finest carbon steel vaults? And no run of the mill burglars, he added, would risk such an investment to an interruption by police, so they would need the best scanners and walkie-talkies for security. Only the Mafia had the working capital to provide those tools, not to mention disposal of the take (for example, ordinary street burglars had no hope of disposing of millions of dollars in uncut gems by themselves—an action virtually guaranteed to bring police to their door).

Carbone did not know which Mafia organization was behind the robberies, but the answer would come soon enough, when Carbone's agents decided on an innovative attack. They reasoned that while there were plenty of burglars and electronics experts out there who might have been recruited for the robbery gang, recruitment of a safecracker capable of carrying out the quality of the work seen in some of the robberies could dip only into a small pool of such talent. Agents targeted the elite safecrackers, finally emerging with a likely suspect: Dominick Costa.

When he wasn't cracking open safes that didn't belong to him, Costa ran a locksmith business. Actually, he was one of the better locksmiths around, but safecracking remained his passion. Every morning of his life, he carefully sandpapered the tips of his fingers to keep them sensitive enough to detect the combination of a vault's time lock from the mere feel of the vibrations of the tumblers clicking inside.

"You know, I actually come when I bust open a safe full of money," Costa liked to tell friends, part of a general tendency to discuss his criminal life, even with people he didn't know well. That habit soon caused detectives and FBI agents to zero in on him, and before long, they were convinced that Costa was the master safecracker who had starred in many jobs carried out by the Bypass Gang. As the screws were tightened, Costa remained defiant. He didn't make much of an effort to deny his involvement, but challenged his adversaries to prove it (which they couldn't yet), and further noted that even if they could, he would never give up anybody else involved.

He had in mind Amuso's on-site supervisors for the Bypass Gang, Salvatore Fusco and Michael (Smurf) Bloome, two street hoods noted for emulating their criminal hero, John Gotti, by adopting his distinctive swagger, expensive suits, and hair style. Costa also knew that the overall supervisor for the gang was a dim bulb of a street hood named Vincent Zappola, a protégé of Gas Pipe Casso, who was the boss of the entire operation.

What Costa did not know was that the FBI already was aware of their involvement because one of the low-ranking members of the Bypass Gang, a talented burglar named Angelo Soto, had been arrested in another case. Attempting to bargain his way out of a stiff prison sentence, Soto revealed that he was a member of the Bypass Gang and offered to testify against other gang members. One morning, the FBI's Carbone laid out an array of two hundred mug shots on a table and asked Soto to pick out anybody he knew. Unerringly, Soto selected the mug shots of Dominick Costa, Smurf Bloome, Salvatore Fusco, and ten other foot soldiers in the gang, then confirmed what the FBI and the cops had already figured out: it was a Lucchese Family operation.

Casso, increasingly worried as he watched the developing law enforcement offensive against the Bypass Gang, sought to stop the hemorrhage before total collapse—and the probable indictment of himself and Amuso. He ordered Vincent Zappola to do something, but Zappola didn't have even a glimmer of an idea of how to stop what seemed to be an entire brigade of FBI agents and police detectives from rolling up the entire operation. As things went from bad to worse, Zappola was summoned for a face-to-face meeting with Casso to discuss his failure to do anything about it.

Zappola found Casso, an obsessive record-keeper, riffling

through a card file he kept on all members and associates of the Lucchese organization, categorized by criminal specialty. As Casso searched through his cards—presumably looking for a miracle worker who would somehow solve the Bypass Gang problem (or, it suddenly occurred to Zappola, a hit man to dispose of him)—the nervous supervisor sought to ease the tension in the room.

"Anthony, what you got me under?" Zappola asked.

"U," Casso replied, without bothering to look at him.

"U? My name ain't with a U."

"It is to me—useless."

"What do you mean saying 'useless'?" asked Zappola with some alarm, concerned that his boss's notorious hair-trigger temper might be about to erupt in murderous rage.

"You're fucking useless," Casso snarled, now glaring at him. "I go to rob a bank with you. I don't get nothing. I call you up to meet me. You don't show up. I call you up to check a [license] plate for me. You can't do it. Useless! That's what I got you under."

Zappola was relieved when Casso's fire then shifted to another target, the "fucking rats" who were going to put everybody in jail. Angelo Soto, obviously, was beyond reach, having been shepherded into the protection of the Witness Protection Program. But, Casso noted, there was one certain prosecution witness still unprotected: Dominick Costa. Zappola blanched; Costa was in fact defying his pursuers to do their worst, and was proud to say that not even the threat of a twenty-year prison sentence would compel him to give up a single name. As Zappola knew, killing Costa wouldn't achieve anything, but decided to keep mum in the face of Casso's foul mood. He quietly endured another tirade from Casso about his failures, then agreed to help a hit man Gas Pipe would recruit to dispose of Costa. Casso wanted someone other than a Lucchese killer who might be recognized by Costa, and thus would be unable to get close enough to carry out the hit. He turned out to be a notorious shooter named Carmine Sessa, borrowed from the Colombo Family.

A few days later, with Zappola acting as fingerman, Sessa got close enough to Costa to put five bullets in his head. Incredibly, however, Costa survived. While he was recuperating in his hospital bed, he was visited by Steve Carbone of the FBI, who concentrated Costa's damaged mind on a salient fact: his unswerving loyalty to the Lucchese organization had now been betrayed. It was time to exact his own vengeance and purge himself of his criminal past by becoming a prosecution witness. Even with five bullet holes in his head, Costa was reluctant to switch sides. Finally, Carbone was able to bring him around, in the process managing to deflect Costa's unusual demands for special treatment—such as having the FBI bring a top-grade safe to his hospital room, where he could keep himself in practice. (Later, in the Witness Protection Program, authorities made the mistake of relocating him in a rural Minnesota town in a small apartment directly across the street from a bank. Unable to resist the temptation, Costa broke into the bank and solved the vault combination using just his sandpapered fingers, emerging with $40,000. As usual, though, he bragged about his feat, was caught, and went off to jail. He remained unrepentant, telling the cops, "I had the greatest orgasm of my life opening that vault.")

With Costa and Soto as main prosecution witnesses, the Bypass Gang had no hope: Zappola, Salvatore Fusco, and Smurf Bloome each got twenty years in prison, and the lesser lights of the gang got ten years. But neither Amuso nor Casso were among those caught in the net. Having decided they had no real chance of beating either the windows case or the Bypass Gang prosecution—or anything else in the assault that now seemed to come from every direction—they hit upon a curious strategy: go on the lam, run the family by long distance via intermediaries, and, more ominously, arrange for the murder of all actual and potential witnesses against them. Even more ominously, a purge would be conducted of the entire family organization, with all "weak links" to be killed.

This bloody blueprint was conveyed to Little Al D'Arco when he was summoned to a late-night rendezvous near the Verrazano Narrows Bridge and informed he would function as the on-site boss of the family while Amuso and Casso were in hiding. D'Arco did not regard this plan as especially intelligent, but was not about to argue the point with either man, considering their homicidal mood. Almost immediately, however, he got a preview of just what Amuso and Casso had in mind.

Coincident with the hurried flight of the Lucchese Family boss and underboss, Tumac Accetturo, head of the New Jersey faction, made his final decision about the new family leadership's demand for a larger slice of his profits. Undoubtedly emboldened by news of the troubles afflicting Amuso and Casso, his message to Amuso was to the point: "Go fuck yourself."

The decision did not sit well with either Amuso or Casso, and the former passed his first order from exile: Anthony Accetturo and the entire New Jersey faction—all thirty of them—were to be murdered. The order was perfectly insane, but Peter Chiodo and Richard Pagliarulo, the family's chief killers, dutifully set to work to carry it out. The first target was Accetturo, but Tumac, apparently aware of how Amuso and Casso would react to his rejection of their demands, had holed up in Florida under tight security. There were several unsuccessful attempts to penetrate his shield, and finally the killers gave up.

Angered at the failure, Amuso and Casso ordered a new attempt, this time using a plan both men had devised: Joseph LaMorte, a close aide of Accetturo, would be kidnaped, then tortured to reveal where Accetturo was hiding. Chiodo and Pagliarulo, joined by fellow mobster George (Georgie Neck) Zappola and two other street hoods, went back to Florida. The new plan worked no better than the first. They still couldn't find Accetturo, and LaMorte proved to be no help, since the hit team decided, for some odd reason, to shoot him without torturing him first. Convinced that LaMorte could not have survived the six bullets in his body, they returned to New York to encounter personally the growing fury of Amuso and Casso. Casso had left his hideout for a secret meeting in Brooklyn, during which he conveyed his displeasure. When Chiodo said they had at least killed LaMorte, the first step in the eventual slaughter of the entire New Jersey group, Casso glared at him and said, "Yeah, well, the only problem is that guy in Florida [LaMorte] ain't dead."

A third plan now unfolded: Thomas Ricciardi, another top Accetturo aide living and operating in New Jersey, would be murdered. But Ricciardi, who owned a horse farm, had bar-

ricaded himself in his house and never seemed to venture far
from a knot of bodyguards. The hit team tried to spin a web
around him, including the purchase of an estate adjoining the
Ricciardi property, but that didn't help; Ricciardi still remained unseen. Finally, fulminating against the "assholes" in
his own organization who had managed to waste a lot of time
and several hundred thousand dollars to no effect, Casso
passed the word that the murder of Acceturo would be handled
by a "professional," a Cuban Mafia hit man from Florida.
Casso sent him a $10,000 down payment on the hit contract
wrapped in Christmas paper and sent through ordinary mail.
But the planned hit on Acceturo never took place; the Cuban
hit man, it turned out, had more pressing concerns on his mind
(an indictment for drug smuggling), so he used the money for
legal expenses.

On that note of low comedy, the grandiose plan to wipe out
the New Jersey faction ended, at least for the moment. But
there was nothing funny about the next Amuso-Casso hit plan,
for this one cost the lives of two men who did not deserve to
die.

The moment that Robert Kubecka had fought so hard to
achieve came one summer morning in 1989 when he strode
to the witness stand in a state court on Long Island and recited
the long, sad story of the Mafia's grip on the garbage collection business. He was the star witness in a state case brought
against Salvatore Avellino and twenty-five other defendants,
including six public officials accused of taking bribes to approve fixed bids for waste removal. Shortly after Kubecka began testifying, Avellino considered the impact of the star
witness' testimony on the jury, along with the pile of other
evidence, including the Jaguar bug, and realized the odds were
strongly against him. He changed his plea to guilty, a gamble
that paid off better than he dared hope when the judge,
astoundingly enough, sentenced him to a slap on the wrist: a
hundred hours of community service. That service was to be
accomplished by Avellino arranging for one of the carting
companies he controlled to pick up garbage from a number of
charitable organizations without charge. A more lenient community service could not be imagined. For a man like Avel-

lino, it was hardly a punishment and even less of a deterrent
to further criminal behavior.

Depressed by this unbelievable result of all his efforts, Kubecka talked of abandoning his father's garbage hauling business and taking up a whole new career—perhaps something
connected with his passion for gardening and gourmet cooking. Donald Barstow, his brother-in-law and business partner,
was equally discouraged; he began to talk about becoming a
carpenter to take advantage of his love of building things. But
they finally decided to carry on, hoping against hope that their
long fight against the Mafia would at some point finally
achieve victory.

That prospect did not seem likely. To Kubecka's further
discouragement, he learned that many of his fellow haulers
were furious at him for testifying in the state trial and jeopardizing a rigged system that guaranteed them profits. He was
approached by one angry hauler, who told him, "What do I
have to do, break every bone in your body? Don't you guys
ever learn?" Another took a swing at him. More dangerously,
Kubecka was at a construction site one day trying to drum up
some business when he spotted a man operating a forklift suddenly veer toward him. Kubecka just managed to duck out of
the way. Meanwhile, the old pattern of harassment continued:
Kubecka found some of his dumpsters welded shut; others
were dumped into a river.

Kubecka's spirits did not improve until U.S. Attorney Andrew Maloney, appalled over the events in state court, announced that if the State of New York was not prepared to
end the Mafia garbage cartel on Long Island, he was. He filed
a civil RICO suit against 112 haulers, mobsters, and Mafia
associates whom Kubecka had identified (and taped) as involved in the garbage racket, along with the Mafia-tainted officials from Local 813 of the Teamsters Union. Asked to give
his deposition in the case, Kubecka happily provided it. As a
result, he immediately experienced a new round of threatening
phone calls. As they increased in number and severity of
threat, state cops urged Kubecka to enter the Witness Protection Program. But, reluctant to uproot his family and determined to finish the fight that had gone on for over eight years,
Kubecka declined.

The late-night phone calls got even uglier, and Kubecka approached local police for some sort of protection. They did not share his growing alarm; after all, they argued, Kubecka had already testified in open court and had given a deposition in the government's RICO suit, so there was little likelihood of the Mafia attempting to kill a witness who had already done the damage. Under standard Mafia working procedure, there was no sense in killing such a witness; the idea was to kill witness *before* they could testify, not after.

This calculation failed to reckon with the kind of homicidal minds now ruling the Lucchese Family. Salvatore Avellino, determined to wreak vengeance on Kubecka for testifying against him, approached the family's figurehead boss, Al D'Arco, and announced his intention of having Kubecka murdered. D'Arco didn't think much of the idea, citing the same line of logic that the police on Long Island had already followed: Kubecka had already testified, so what would be the point of killing him? Besides, Kubecka presented no threat; he had his little, lonely crusade that nobody was following. Let him keep tilting at windmills.

But Avellino was insistent, and the final decision was bucked up to Gas Pipe Casso. To D'Arco's surprise, Casso readily agreed that Kubecka (and Barstow as well) had to go: "We can't let these guys walk around. They testify against us, and we let them get away with it? No, get rid of them." With that sanction, Avellino recruited two shooters from the Bronx faction of the family, Frank Federico and Rocco Vitulli, and ordered them to kill Robert Kubecka and Donald Barstow. (Avellino's idea was that using men from the Bronx faction would help deflect suspicion that he was involved in the hit.)

One morning a few weeks later, police on Long Island received a phone call. The voice, barely able to speak, identified himself as Robert Kubecka. "I've just been shot, please hurry," he said as the cops heard the phone clatter to the floor. At Kubecka's office, police found Donald Barstow dead in a heap near the front door. In the office, Kubecka was slumped over his desk, barely alive, bleeding from multiple wounds. Rushed to the hospital, he was dead on arrival.

Homicide detectives who swarmed over the office deduced that Robert Kubecka had fought the last great fight of his life there. The place was in a shambles, with bullet holes in the blood-spattered walls. Kubecka had apparently fought savagely with his attackers, who left behind a duffle bag and the two guns used in the killings. But investigators found no useable fingerprints, the duffle bag was an ordinary mass-produced model, and the guns were "clean" (standard Mafia weapons, probably stolen from a gun store, with the serial numbers filed off). Clearly, it was a Mafia hit. And although no one said it openly, everyone involved knew the record in such cases was bleak: the murders of Robert Kubecka and Donald Barstow probably would never be solved.

On a bright, sunny summer's day, Robert Kubecka was buried in a small cemetery not far from the municipal organic garden that once had been his pride. A number of the organic gardeners attended the graveside service out of respect, still trying to understand how the gentle man they knew had led another life as a stubborn, courageous crusader willing to take on the Mafia.

An ailing and distraught Jerry Kubecka hobbled to the graveside clutching two yellow roses, his son's favorite flower. "I wish," he said, "I was half the man he was."

A clergyman intoned the Lord's Prayer and the Twenty-sixth Psalm, with emphasis on the lines, "I have hated the congregation of evildoers; and will not sit with the wicked," and, "Gather not my soul with sinners, nor my life with bloody men: In whose hands is mischief, and their right hand is full of bribes."

That night, Jerry Kubecka, sitting in mourning in his darkened home, heard the telephone ring. When he picked it up, he heard a voice on the other end: "Two down, one to go."

The news of the murders of Kubecka and Barstow struck the offices of the U.S. attorney for the Eastern District of New York like a thunderclap. There were plenty of recriminations—why hadn't the New York State Organized Crime Task Force taken better care of its witness? why wasn't there a twenty-four-hour police guard around the two men? why hadn't the local police responded more urgently when the two men were clearly in danger?—but for Charles Rose, the larger meaning was that the killings served as a stark reminder to potential jurors of the real nature of the people he was about to prosecute. The murders also put him in a foul mood, and *United States of America v. Venero Mangano* et al. was about to begin with an extremely angry prosecutor.

His coprosecutor shared that anger. Gregory O'Connell, who some time before the windows case had become a partner of Rose in prosecuting narcotics cases, had the reputation as a very serious prosecutor ("I think I saw him smile a few months ago," Rose liked to joke), known for his doggedness and a booming basso profundo voice that could rattle a jury box. Like Rose, exposure to the realities of the Mafia narcotics business and the further depredations of organized crime had bred in O'Connell a visceral hatred for mafiosi, especially those of the Lucchese variety.

In the windows case, Rose and O'Connell had ensnared four particularly loathsome examples of that variety—Vittorio Amuso and Anthony Casso, two violent psychopaths; Joseph (Joe Cakes) Marion, a fat, nasty Lucchese associate who ran a window installation company; and Peter Chiodo, a massive strongarm thug. Amuso and Casso had fled before trial, and Chiodo, to the surprise of the prosecutors, was offering a guilty plea. (Chiodo's plea would prove to have dramatic consequences later, but for the moment it appeared to be simply a calculated decision by a defendant who saw no point in spending a lot of money on lawyers for a case which he had no hope of beating.)

That left Marion as the lone remaining Lucchese-affiliated defendant. He was among eight defendants to actually make it to trial. Five others, including Amuso and Casso, were otherwise occupied: Chiodo had pleaded guilty, Vincent Gigante, predictably, had checked himself in to a psychiatric hospital, claiming he was crazy and unfit for trial; and another defendant had suffered a heart attack and was severed from trial. With the absences of Amuso, Casso, and Gigante, the trial had lost its highest-profile defendants. Of the remainder, the most interesting were Venero (Benny Eggs) Mangano, Gigante's second in command; Peter Gotti, brother of John Gotti, who had given his sibling the Gambino Family's role in the windows scheme as a means of providing him with his own criminal enterprise; and Benedetto (Benny) Aloi, a Colombo

Family capo, who oversaw his family's interests in the scheme.

From the first moment of the trial, there was tension in the air. Rose and O'Connell were clearly on edge, and relations with defense attorneys were flinty. The presiding judge at the trial, Raymond Dearie (the former U.S. attorney whose patient, deliberative style made him an ideal candidate for the bench), sought to dampen any possible early fireworks by warning both sides that he would not tolerate any nastiness. He suspected, rightly, that the defense lawyers would attempt to divert the jury's attention by shifting the trial's focus to how the government and Peter Savino contrived to entrap their clients, a strategy certain to light the prosecutors' short fuses. Dearie summoned the lawyers to a sidebar. "Now listen," he warned, "I don't want to hear a lot of crap in the opening. I want to hear facts and only facts. I want this jury to hear facts, not a lot of half-baked theories."

The words were no sooner out of his mouth than one of the defense lawyers, Jeffrey C. Hoffman, started telling the jury about "the Savino-FBI laws of evidence." Rose nearly rocketed out of his seat, and Dearie struggled to referee what was rapidly becoming a street brawl. Dearie already suspected he might become involved in trench warfare, given the cast of characters: two angry prosecutors, several highly aggressive defense lawyer superstars, and every judge's nightmare, Peter Gotti's bombastic advocate, Bruce Cutler, notorious for his high-decibel theatrics.

A sample of Cutler's style could be divined from his opening statement to the jury, when he announced in a voice as loud as a football stadium cheering section, "Savino is a ruthless, degenerate, low-life bum!" He went on to describe Savino further as "subhuman" and the case "a cancerous offspring of the marriage between Savino and the government." Cutler had won national notoriety for defending the man he described as "my role model," John Gotti, and there were knowing smiles all over the courtroom as it became clear that his real function was to prevent the jury from wondering about the actual role of the Gambino Family boss. Further, aware that Gotti was about to face a gathering federal RICO case, Cutler did not want potential jurors for that case to hear anything linking him to a Mafia conspiracy.

"Where would you ever deal with John Gotti, a bum like you!" Cutler shouted at Peter Savino when the chief prosecution witness took the stand. Savino simply shrugged off the attack, and proved just as resilient when he locked horns with other defense lawyers. When one lawyer pressed him on his failure to record an allegedly criminal meeting, Savino explained that his tape machine had malfunctioned during that period.

"Just that day, right?" the lawyer asked, with deliberate sarcasm.

"Thank your lucky stars," Savino snapped back, and Dearie finally managed to calm the storm from the resulting eruption of outraged objections and exchanges of invective. The jurors often had difficulty hiding smiles at this noisy tableau unfolding before them, which was quickly becoming the best spectator sport in town. They seemed to derive further amusement as Savino and the defense lawyers continued their hand-to-hand combat. At one point, when Savino was being questioned about a tape that had been played previously, he asked to hear it again.

"I'm getting married at Christmas," the defense lawyer said, "and I don't have enough time."

"Are you getting married in December?" Savino replied, with a smile. "Don't do it." Jurors, aware from previous cross-examination that Savino had recently remarried for the third time (a marriage that had since ended in estrangement), erupted in laughter.

They might have been even more amused if they had been able to listen in on some of the exchanges out of their hearing. There was, for example, the bizarre exchange between Peter Gotti and Rose during one recess that began when Cutler said to the prosecutor, "Charlie, my client wants to talk to you." Such exchanges between defendants and prosecutors during criminal trials are extremely rare, but Rose, curious, decided to listen to what Gotti had to say.

It turned out to be further evidence of why Peter Gotti, noted for a level of stupidity that even his famous brother found breathtaking, was known as "retard" within the Gambino Family. "Listen, Charlie," Gotti said, "what the fuck am I doing here? I didn't make a fucking quarter out of this thing." Rose was silent a moment, hardly able to believe Gotti actually would ask so stupid a question.

"Let me explain it this way, Peter," Rose began, as though he were talking to a child. "Suppose you go into a bank with a gun and announce a stickup. You discover there's no money in the bank. No matter: you get charged with bank robbery. It's not how much money you get, but the act. Do you follow me?"

"No," a genuinely puzzled Gotti replied.

Later, Rose asked Cutler if there was any hope Gotti would understand if his own lawyer explained the legal facts of life to him. "No," Cutler replied, with a sigh.

Then there was the incident in Dearie's chambers when the judge convened a meeting on a request by defense lawyers to introduce their own chart for the edification of the jury. Dearie had already approved Rose's request to use several FBI-prepared charts, showing the structure of the various Mafia families involved in the windows scheme, along with a business-type flow chart showing how the money was extorted and later divided. Now he was confronted by a large chart brandished by Jeffrey Hoffman, one of the defense lawyers.

"What, precisely, is the point of this?" Dearie asked, staring with some disbelief at an elaborate FBI-style organization chart that showed a Mafia family's structure, complete with boxes for a boss, an underboss, a consigliere, capos, and soldati. It was headlined, THE SAVINO-FBI ORGANIZED CRIME FAMILY. All the names contained in the various boxes were prosecutors and FBI agents, including Rose, who nearly bounced off the ceiling when he noticed he was listed as "boss" in the "law enforcement criminal enterprise."

Dearie waved him back to his seat, then turned to Hoffman. "You've got to be kidding," he said. "No, this will not come in."

"Well, your honor," Hoffman said, "I didn't think we'd get it in, to tell the truth. But it was fun to try, just to see the look on Charlie Rose's face."

When he calmed down, even Rose found this moderately funny, but he was distinctly less amused when word reached him of still another attempt by Amuso and Casso to derail justice. One morning during the trial, Savino's third wife, clearly terrified, called the FBI and opened the conversation with an unsettling question: "How come there's a bomb on my front seat?" She went on to relate that she had received a phone call earlier. An anonymous voice called her estranged husband a "rat," then went on to say that she and her six-year-old son would be killed. She immediately gathered up her boy and ran outside, intending to drive to safety. But as she opened the door of her car, she spotted what appeared to be a bomb resting on the front seat.

Police and FBI agents rushed to her house, where a bomb squad found what they determined to be a gasoline bomb in the car. Apparently, it was designed to ignite just when Mrs. Savino answered the phone, the idea being that a car erupting into flames would terrorize her into pressuring Peter Savino to end his career as prosecution witness.

If that was indeed the intention, it was not an especially bright way of achieving the goal, for Savino was not about to stop testifying because his wife had been threatened. Moreover, because he was estranged from the woman, he was hardly in a mood to be influenced by anything she might have to say. And Savino well knew he was invulnerable from even the most determined Mafia assassination attempt: ensconced in a safe house, he lived in a tight cocoon of protection by U.S. marshals and FBI security details.

Savino was unruffled by the episode, but Judge Dearie was not. Angered, he ordered defense lawyers into his chambers, where he read them the riot act. There would be "severe consequences," he warned, in the event of any further attempts to intimidate government witnesses. After extracting elaborate assurances that none of their clients would ever stoop to such base acts, Dearie sent them back into the courtroom.

They returned to renew battle with the two prosecutors now fairly seething with rage. Rose and O'Connell suspected, correctly, that the fugitives Amuso and Casso were behind the gasoline bomb episode. They were even more angered when Joe Cakes Marion, the remaining Lucchese-connected defendant, openly began challenging them. "Why don't you stick those papers up your ass?" he hissed at O'Connell at one point as the prosecutor sought to introduce some documents into evidence. Noticing the back of O'Connell's neck turn a bright red, Rose thought he would have to physically restrain his partner from punching out Marion right there, in front of the jury.

Meanwhile, an astonishingly calm Savino continued to testify and play his tapes. Standing to ease the pain in his lower back from bone cancer, he was clearly proud of his central role in the investigation, undoubtedly the only act of good citizenship he had ever performed in his life. Occasionally, to the discomfort of Rose (who worried about the effect on the jury), Savino would smirk as one of his tapes played, the painter stepping back to admire an especially brilliant brushstroke on the canvas. However admiring of his own handiwork, Savino had trouble convincing the jury that all his tapes were as incriminating as he hoped. Some were, but many were not; there were too many that contained references like this: "So Tony Nose has to go to Louie Dap." The prosecution was now paying the price for an investigation that a corrupt police source had aborted before it reached full fruition.

Nevertheless, there was enough for the jury to convict three of the defendants, including Benny Aloi and, to O'Connell's immense personal satisfaction, Joe Cakes Marion. The hardest hit was Benny Eggs Mangano, who took it all philosophically. At seventy-four, the veteran mafioso knew the twenty-year jail term he would receive represented a death sentence. "Ah, the hell with it," he told a knot of relatives after the verdict. "In my line of work, you know, you got to expect the possibility of dying in the can. It's better than the street, believe me."

The verdict left Rose and O'Connell less than satisfied, for their main focus of concern had been the two defendants who weren't there, VicAmuso and Gas Pipe Casso. "Don't worry, we'll get them," Rose was assured by Lucian Gandolfi, head of the FBI squad targeted against the Lucchese Family. "Like we say, Charles, you can run, but you can't hide."

Perhaps, but Gandolfi added a warning: Amuso and Casso were homicidal maniacs who were demonstrating signs of worsening mental instability. Their killing of one defendant in the windows case merely on the presumption that he might become a prosecution witness and the attempt to intimidate the chief witness during the *U.S.* v. *Mangano* trial were unmistakable indications that the two fugitives were prepared to kill *anyone* who they thought might be a threat.

"These guys," Gandolfi warned, "will make Tony Ducks Corallo look like a saint." Subsequent events would prove him right—more violently than he could have imagined.

• NINE •

Night of the Locust

Mother is the best bet and don't let Satan draw you too fast.

LAST WORDS OF DUTCH SCHULTZ

Corrado (Dino) Marino could not have been more clear: the meeting was *important*, so don't be late. Gas doesn't like people who are late to important meetings. Frank Arnold hastened to reassure the emissary from Gas Pipe Casso that he understood the message. He'd be there, right on time.

On the appointed day, Arnold stood outside his home at the precise moment and was picked up by Marino and driven to the meeting site, an unused warehouse on Staten Island. He was nervous, for any meeting with a man of Casso's reputation was not an appointment to be regarded lightly. But he felt no fear. For one thing, he trusted Marino, an old friend. More important, Marino had not used the word "sitdown," which would have signified some kind of problem that had to be ironed out. And, as far as Arnold knew, there was no problem. As the new Lucchese man in the Painters Union, succeeding the murdered James Bishop, Arnold had things running smoothly. The money from the labor extortion operation was flowing regularly upward to Casso, the organization's chief executive in charge of the racket. To be sure, the union's international was breathing down his neck, and federal investigators were sniffing around, but so far they apparently hadn't found anything of consequence.

Perhaps, Arnold speculated, Casso had bigger and better things in mind for him. Or perhaps he simply wanted to establish face-to-face contact with his man in the union. Whatever the reason, Arnold felt honored that the new underboss of the Lucchese Family would take the risk of emerging from his hideout to meet with him.

But Casso was nowhere to be seen in the warehouse. Instead, Arnold encountered Peter Chiodo and Richard Pagliarulo, the Lucchese Family's most infamous enforcers.

"What's the problem?" Arnold asked, feeling the sickening tremors of fear. He looked at Marino, who simply stared at him impassively.

"*This* is your fucking problem," said Pagliarulo, jamming a sawed-off shotgun into Arnold's throat.

"Gas is sure you're gonna flip, Frank, so that's the way it is," Chiodo said, almost apologetically.

"Are you fucking crazy?" said Arnold, his knees shaking uncontrollably. "What the fuck am I gonna flip about? I'm not in any trouble; I got no indictments. Gas knows I love him."

"Gas had a dream," Chiodo explained. "In the dream, you ratted him out."

"*A dream? A fucking dream?*" Arnold was shrieking in wild fear as he fell to his knees.

His bowels gave way.

Chiodo wrinkled his nose. "I hate when they do that," he said. He signaled to Pagliarulo, and they both began walking away in disgust.

"Get the fuck out of here," Chiodo commanded over his shoulder to Arnold, who gathered his soiled self and on rubbery legs somehow managed to run for his life.

The wings of death had whispered very close to Frank Arnold, and were it not for the squeamishness of his executioners, what remained of him would have become a pile of ashes or dismembered parts scattered in garbage cans all over New York City. But he would be one of the few lucky ones in a bloody slaughter that had begun, among the bloodiest in the history of organized crime. It was also among the more senseless.

The slaughter was ordered by Vic Amuso and Gas Pipe Casso from exile. Seized by a murderous rage over the events that had forced them to flee to their rat holes, the two mobsters saw killing as the solution to all their legal problems and the essential object lesson for anyone in their organization who might be wavering. With a praetorian guard of killers, led by Pagliarulo and Chiodo, the Lucchese Family's boss and underboss set about to eliminate all threats—defined as anyone who had even the potential to cause problems. Like Hitler and his diehard band of Nazis in their Berlin bunker, they constructed for themselves a mad world in which paranoia became reality and the vaguest suspicion was sufficient for a death sentence.

In the process, they would destroy their world.

Bruno Facciola was among the first to discover that, in the new regime, even thirty years of unswerving loyalty to the organization was no immunity against death. From the days when he served as an apprentice to Paul Vario in Brooklyn crap games, through his years as an enforcer and his later career as one of the Lucchese Family's best fences, Facciola was a model mafioso who prided himself on his reputation as a standup guy, the kind of mobster who actually spat into the faces of cops who tried to get him to talk. He had served several prison terms uncomplainingly, and in 1990, he was facing his latest legal trouble, an indictment for fencing stolen jewels. Out on bail while awaiting trial, he got a call one night to attend a "very important meeting" with Gas Pipe Casso. After dressing in his Sunday best suit, he drove off. Six days later, residents of a Queens neighborhood some distance from Facciola's home called police to complain of a foul odor coming from a parked car. In the trunk, cops found the broken body of Facciola, shot and stabbed so many times that the medical examiner found it difficult to arrive at a precise number of fatal wounds.

The style and method of Facciola's disposal instantly suggested a Mafia rubout, the savagery traditionally used to signify that the victim was a traitor. But since Facciola wasn't an informant, police were puzzled. They were equally puzzled by the subsequent murder of Michael Salerno, a leading Lucchese Family loan shark active in the Garment Center. Salerno was not facing any legal trouble and had the reputation of a loyal family soldier with a consistent record: whenever approached by a police detective or FBI agent, he invariably opened the conversation by saying, ''Go fuck yourself.'' Yet when the medical examiner investigated his body, also retrieved from a car trunk, he discovered that Salerno's throat had been slashed from ear to ear, the traditional Mafia signal that the victim had been executed because he was talking to authorities.

As far as the police were concerned, the only consistent pattern established thus far was that two solidly loyal Lucchese Family mobsters had been murdered. It could be safely inferred that the murders had been ordered by the family's leadership, but why murder two men whose loyalty was unquestioned? The same enigma arose in the case of a third murder, that of Patrick Testa, a premier auto thief who worked in the Lucchese Family's Brooklyn faction. Testa was not only fanatically loyal, but he was also known to be slavishly devoted to Gas Pipe Casso (he stole the black jeep Cherokee that his superior used to flee New York). He had served a prison sentence for auto theft, refusing to utter even a word to cops. But somebody one morning walked into the Brooklyn chop shop where Testa hung out and pumped nine bullets into him.

Two more murders were also mysterious. Larry Taylor and Al Visconti were low-level Lucchese street hoods who liked to consider themselves classic Mafia tough guys openly defiant of cops. They were both found shot to death. The only discernible connection with the previous murders lay in the fact that they were both very close friends of Bruno Facciola, a previous victim, and had openly vowed vengeance against whoever had carried out his slaying (although, like the police, they hadn't been able to figure out any reason for it, much less any suspects).

Peter Chiodo, the Amuso-Casso regime's chief executioner, knew why these murders were occurring. He knew that Michael Salerno had died because Casso had a *feeling* he might try to take over the organization while his boss was in exile.

Additionally, Casso said, he was *probably* going to become an informant. Facciola died because Amuso and Casso had a *hunch* he would become an informant. Testa died because Casso deduced he knew too much about his flight into hiding and *maybe* would consider becoming an informant. And Taylor and Visconti died because, Casso decreed, their search to avenge their friend's slaying *might* eventually result in their learning of Casso's execution order, creating possible witnesses.

Like a tiny candle lighted in a dark room, these flimsy justifications for murder lit the first flickering rays of doubt in the mind of Chiodo. No one prided himself more on unquestioning loyalty to the organization, but even Chiodo began to wonder if Amuso and Casso were in the grips of some insane paranoia. As the veteran of several dozen murders, Chiodo had no qualms about killing witnesses, informants, and Mafia miscreants who stole money from the organization or defied the orders of family leadership. But this was different; men were being killed on what seemed to be the faintest whispers of suspicion.

This first crisis of faith, however faint, also made Chiodo begin to consider his own place in the scheme of things. As he was among the first to realize, if his bosses ordered men killed on merely the vaguest of suspicion, what about himself? Would they order his death if they woke up one morning and decided that their unquestionably loyal hit man might become an informant some day? Or that he knew too much?

Sooner than he could have anticipated, Chiodo was forced to consider the matter further when he committed an error— the kind of error his bosses had come to not forgive.

Of all the men for whom Amuso and Casso felt a deadly animus, Joseph Martinelli may have been one of the few who deserved it. A contractor who had functioned as a Lucchese Family associate for several years, Martinelli paid $100,000 a year to the family for the privilege of participating in the construction rackets. But coincident with the fall of Tony Ducks Corallo and his three chief executives, Martinelli stopped paying. The new Lucchese generation, in the person of Christopher Funari, Jr., son of the imprisoned Lucchese mobster, demanded that Martinelli resume paying. When Martinelli stalled, Funari consulted his father on what he should do. Beat him up, the elder Funari advised. Martinelli subsequently received a severe battering.

But that still wasn't enough to get the money flowing again, and the problem was brought to Casso for resolution. "Kill this cocksucker," he ordered Chiodo, who detailed two dim-witted street hoods to do the deed. They botched two attempts before any shots were fired (Martinelli was unaware of them), and an exasperated Chiodo decided to take matters into his own hands.

"Fuck it, I'll do it myself," Chiodo announced, then set about to lure Martinelli into his grasp. He approached Marti-nelli and, under the guise of peacemaker attempting to resolve a problem, told him that he had arranged a sitdown between him and Casso. Martinelli, eager to avoid another beating, agreed to the meeting, which he was told would take place at a deserted shorefront area on Staten Island.

The next day, Chiodo picked up Martinelli and drove him to the meeting site while Pagliarulo trailed at some distance behind in a car as backup. As they reached a swampy area, Chiodo pulled out a .45-caliber pistol, pointed it at Martinelli's head, and pulled the trigger. Nothing happened. As the color drained from Martinelli's face, Chiodo pulled the trigger again.

And again, nothing happened.

"Look how real they make these toy guns nowadays," Chiodo said, laughing. "Scared you, huh?"

It sure did, and while Martinelli shook in fear, Chiodo pulled up to a roadside pay phone, telling him he was calling to "double-check security arrangements." He returned a few minutes later to announce that the meeting was off; Casso had detected law enforcement surveillance in the area. Chiodo drove Martinelli home. His intended victim seemed to have trouble breathing.

Later, Chiodo met with Pagliarulo to check out the gun. To his chagrin, Chiodo discovered he had failed to properly seat the clip. "Listen," he pleaded with Pagliarulo, "whatever you do, don't tell Gas about this. You know the way he is."

Telling Gas is precisely what the ambitious Pagliarulo did.

As he probably calculated, the news sent Casso into a towering rage while igniting his paranoia. In the process, Chiodo became in Casso's mind the very personification of treason, the kind of rotten apple that had to be destroyed before he infected the entire barrel. In Casso's calculation, the sequence of events involving Chiodo assumed very sinister connotations. Chiodo had allowed Frank Arnold to live, and although Arnold's later indictment and imprisonment made the question of his execution academic, the fact was that Chiodo had violated a direct order. Following that, he had begun to openly question the decision to murder other people. Then came the Martinelli incident; was it possible he had deliberately fouled up that assignment? Perhaps that botch should be judged in the context of another Chiodo action that disturbed Casso, his guilty plea in the windows case. Could it be that Chiodo had made a secret deal with the authorities and was deliberately messing up murder assignments?

In a mind like Casso's, the conclusion was inevitable. So was Chiodo's fate: Casso ordered Pagliarulo to arrange for the execution of Peter Chiodo. Shortly afterward, Chiodo one morning pulled his Cadillac into a Staten Island gas station to check why the car's engine seemed to be knocking. He had opened the hood and was peering inside when a car with three men screeched to a halt near him. Two men jumped out and began firing, one shot chipping a piece of cement near Chiodo's foot.

Pulling out his gun, Chiodo fired back as he scurried into the mechanic bays. While the gun battle raged on, he was hit by seven bullets. Finally, weak from loss of blood, Chiodo collapsed. As his consciousness ebbed away, he heard the sound of an approaching police siren and one of the shooters say, "Let's get the fuck out of here; we've been here too long. He's dead, anyway."

But Chiodo wasn't dead. Astounded doctors later found that of the seven bullets that struck him—five of which passed clean through his body—none struck a vital organ. Chiodo's 547 pounds of blubber somehow had absorbed the kind of firepower that would have killed any other man.

While Chiodo recuperated in a hospital, Richard Pagliarulo was practically beside himself with rage. Now confronted with the difficult task of telling Casso that his important murder assignment failed, he vented his frustration to Dino Marino. "Jesus H. Christ," Pagliarulo fumed, "I told them to aim for the head. They must've seen a western."

He would have loved to get a second crack at Chiodo, but his target was out of reach. Under twenty-four-hour guard by federal marshals, Chiodo was recuperating behind an impenetrable security screen. His brief periods of consciousness were occupied by a steady parade of police detectives and FBI agents, who assumed that Chiodo was now ready to talk about events in the Lucchese Family. But ever the Mafia loyalist, Chiodo made it clear even seven bullets in his body were not sufficient to make him violate his oath of *omerta*. He was willing to talk only to the extent of anything he might know about the rat holes in which Amuso and Casso were located, but nothing else. His interrogators finally gave up, telling prosecutor Charles Rose there was no point in trying to convert a man that even an attempted assassination had failed to move.

Rose was not willing to give up yet, for Chiodo was a glittering prize—if he could be convinced to switch sides. A few nights later, Rose appeared at Chiodo's hospital room carrying a king-size pizza. He began a deceptively casual conversation and the two men chatted awhile about various inconsequential matters. Chiodo, occasionally wincing in pain from his wounds as he lay virtually immobile in a posture that enabled him to move only his head, began warming to the prosecutor. When Rose felt he had established a rapport, he got around to the more interesting subject of Chiodo's shooting.

"You know, Mr. Rose," Chiodo said through a thicket of intravenous tubes, "it's really strange when somebody tries to kill you. You can feel the breeze a bullet makes when it goes past your ear."

"I've never had the experience, thank God," Rose said. "Which raises the question, Peter: do you have any idea why somebody would want to kill you? Just thinking aloud, I wonder if Gas Pipe Casso perhaps may have felt angry at you for some reason and dispatched a few of his friends to kill you. You wouldn't have any idea of why Mr. Casso was so ticked off, do you?"

"I don't know anything about that kind of shit," Chiodo

said grimly, but Rose noticed that his attention had begun to focus on the large box resting in the prosecutor's lap. Rose slowly opened it, letting the aroma of the warm pizza waft around the room.

"I hope you don't mind," Rose said, detaching a slice. "I haven't had any supper, and I'm hungry as hell."

"No problem, Mr. Rose," Chiodo said. Rose saw that Chiodo had become nearly bug-eyed as the smells of the pizza penetrated the breathing apparatus in his nostrils; he was actually drooling while he watched Rose start to devour a slice. Apparently, the seven bullets had failed to put a dent in his gargantuan appetite.

"Jeez, I could go for a slice," said Chiodo, unable to resist any longer.

"Oh, I don't think the doctors would like that," Rose said, taking another bite from his slice. "How could I justify it? Federal prosecutor feeds forbidden food to gravely wounded mafioso! My God, I'd be in terrible trouble."

"Listen," said Chiodo, almost whining like a dog for its dinner, "what the fucking doctors don't know won't hurt them. So we'll eat a little pizza, and, you know, talk."

The process began. Drawing a chair close to Chiodo's bedside, Rose detached a slice and slowly moved it toward his mouth. All the while, he conducted a dialogue with him; how fast the pizza slice was advanced depended on the extent and quality of Chiodo's end of the conversation. Occasionally, Rose would withdraw a slice when Chiodo appeared not to be fully cooperative.

Finally, Chiodo had devoured most of the pizza in the box. In the process, he became a witness for the federal government. His transformation came about in large part when he was persuaded by Rose's argument: since his superiors had tried to kill him without sufficient cause, Chiodo was no longer bound by his oath of *omerta*. It was a simple matter of contract law, Rose told him, a case where one side had broken a solemn contract. As Rose argued, the Mafia initiation ceremony was in effect an unwritten contract sealed by blood oath; while Chiodo had vowed to adhere to certain rules, the other side, among other things, guaranteed that he would not be executed without the Mafia version of due process. Where was the due process in his case? Was there a sitdown to discuss any grievances Amuso and Casso might have held against him? Was Chiodo permitted to present his side of events?

The result was a deal: Chiodo would plead guilty to one count of racketeering in the windows case in satisfaction of all charges (including the murders which he had either carried out personally or was involved in some way), and receive a sentence of twenty years in prison. In return, Chiodo would provide Rose and the FBI with everything he knew about the Lucchese Family. Given his role in that organization, Chiodo's revelations promised to be nothing short of sensational.

Something along the line of that very thought occurred to Amuso and Casso. Assuming that a wounded (and understandably angry) Chiodo might decide to defect to the other side, they tried to devise some way that would deflect him from that course. The method they chose, however, succeeded only in convincing their former hit man that he was doing the right thing in joining "Mr. Rose's team," as he liked to call the new organization to which he now pledged allegiance.

First, Casso dispatched two hoods to the office of Chiodo's lawyer, who was given a message for his client: "Tell him his wife is next." Then Mrs. Chiodo arrived to visit her husband in the hospital and told him she had begun receiving threatening phone calls. She was whisked into the Witness Protection Program.

That left Amuso and Casso with little leverage, and they then decided on an act that was to rock the Mafia to its foundations: Richard Pagliarulo was instructed to murder Chiodo's sister as a means of terrorizing him into silence. Pagliarulo assigned the job to three submorons from the most recent class of Lucchese Family recruits, Dino Basciano and the brothers Michael and Robert Spinelli. They stalked Mrs. Patricia Cappozalo for a month, and ambushed her early one morning outside her house as she returned home after dropping off her children at school. She was severely wounded, but survived.

No single act would so discredit the American Mafia as the shooting of a Brooklyn homemaker. For many years of its existence, the Mafia had an ironclad rule barring the involvement of "civilians" (ordinary citizens) in any of its organizational disputes. There was, of course, a sound political reason for this dictum: involving citizens in shooting wars was an almost certain way of arousing public wrath against organized crime. A subsidiary rule mandated that the non-Mafia relatives of mafiosi be kept out of any disputes on the sensible grounds that involving them would only set off dynastic struggles in which entire families might be consumed.

Casso's decision to begin killing innocent relatives of Chiodo—his sister had no connection whatsoever with organized crime and knew nothing of her brother's criminal life—set off a public outcry against the Mafia. It got even louder when Casso made his next move, ordering the murder of Chiodo's uncle, Frank Signorino. The body of Signorino was found stuffed into plastic bags in a car trunk. He had died simply because he was the only Chiodo relative available; he had refused to join the exodus of other relatives into the Witness Protection Program.

Among the more alarmed at this turn of events was the Lucchese Family's on-site boss, Little Al D'Arco. A veteran mobster who had spent most of his sixty-five years in the organization, D'Arco was perfectly aware that killing Chiodo's relatives was a colossally stupid act. It not only threatened to harden Chiodo's resolve to destroy the organization (which it did), but it also represented a public relations disaster of the first order. The rest of the Mafia began to regard the Lucchese organization as outcasts, and the newspapers were filled every day with accounts of the Mafia "animals" loose on the streets.

D'Arco became further unsettled when, in secret meetings with Amuso and Casso, he heard even more elaborate plans for wholesale murder. In one meeting with Casso, he was shown a list of forty-nine people Gas Pipe had picked to be murdered. With a start, D'Arco realized that half the names on the list were members of the Lucchese Family. Asked why so many people were targeted for elimination, Casso replied that they were "creeps." In another meeting, Casso insisted that the government would never be able to prove his and Amuso's guilt in the windows case. At some point, he said, the government would be forced to drop the case against them, and then they would return to New York. "When I come home," Casso vowed, "I'm going to have a party and invite all the creeps I want to kill. Then I'll kill them all." At still another meeting, this time with Amuso, D'Arco was ordered to contact the Philadelphia Mafia to recruit bombing experts for the purpose of another attempt to kill John Gotti. When D'Arco raised the possibility of retaliation by the Gambino Family after Gotti's murder, Amuso replied, "Don't worry about it; the robe knows about it."

"The robe" was Amuso's nickname for Vincent Gigante, boss of the Genovese Family, which suggested that Amuso and Gigante were still intent on killing Gotti, for reasons which seemed unclear. D'Arco took his sweet time contacting the Philadelphia Mafia, by which point the murder plot was academic: Gotti was ensnared in a RICO case that ultimately would send him to prison for life without parole. In any event, D'Arco had made up his mind that he would derail the plan to kill Gotti, somehow. The idea struck him as particularly stupid; considering the disrupted state of the Mafia at that point, the last thing the organization needed was another high-level murder—just the thing to stir up some real chaos.

For the first time in Al D'Arco's criminal career, thanks to his promotion as stand-in boss of the Lucchese Family for such purposes as dealing with the heads of other families and attending Commission meetings, he had a panoramic view of the Mafia's upper level. He was not impressed by what he saw. In a general atmosphere of disintegration, the high command was as unruly as an unsupervised kindergarten class, with hardly a real criminal brain in evidence. D'Arco's own Mafia family was a mess, but it was a paragon of stability compared to what was going on in the other families. The Gambino Family, disrupted by Gotti's legal troubles, was degenerating into warring factions, a chaos largely caused by Gotti's insistence that his arrogant and stupid son, John Gotti, Jr., take command of the family. Widely despised throughout the family as an untalented punk with insufficient experience in running a criminal enterprise, the younger Gotti informed anyone questioning his leadership abilities that he would tell his father, who would arrange for their murder. The Bonanno Family, still barred from Commission membership, was preoccupied with dominating the heroin trade, while the Genovese Family was attempting to conduct business via a shaky communications line to a boss in a psychiatric hospital. As for the Colombo Family, it was busily self-destructing in a bitter internal struggle between rival factions that had already consumed a dozen lives.

In such an atmosphere, business negotiations at the upper level tended to be tense. One scheduled sitdown between the Gambino and Lucchese organizations on the subject of division of spoils from a Bronx construction racket assumed the dimensions of a meeting between rival colonels of a South American military junta. D'Arco, the representative of the Lucchese Family, was concerned that the representative of the Gambino Family, Sammy the Bull Gravano, intended to use the sitdown as an excuse to gun down D'Arco and any other Lucchese man he could get his hands on. Not an unreasonable suspicion, considering Gravano's well-deserved reputation for disposing of business rivals (he would eventually murder nineteen of them). D'Arco armed seven Lucchese hoods with Uzi submachine guns and spotted them around the meeting site, unaware that an equally suspicious Gravano—believing that D'Arco would use the site to dispose of *him*—had spotted his own gunmen around the area.

D'Arco tried his best to keep things on an even keel while collecting enough money to keep Amuso and Casso satisfied during their regular rendezvous, when the chief topic of conversation was how much cash he had brought with him. The amounts usually ranged in the hundreds of thousands of dollars, but, as D'Arco perceived, both Amuso and Casso were beginning to regard him with suspicion. D'Arco had tried to keep track of all the various sources of cash payments by writing notes on little pieces of paper, but the sheer volume and complexity soon confused him, and he was having difficulty getting a firm grasp of exactly how much was coming in.

"You sure this is what we're supposed to get?" Amuso or Casso would ask with increasing frequency. D'Arco sensed the question meant he was in deepening political trouble, confirmed when he was summoned to a meeting and told he was being demoted. From now on, on-site operations of the family would be run by a four-man committee consisting of himself, Salvatore Avellino, the boss of the Long Island garbage racket;

Frank Lastorino, the notorious hit man; and Anthony (Bowat) Barratta, a capo in the family's Bronx section.

D'Arco suspected that his demotion was merely a prelude to more drastic action Amuso and Casso had in store for him. He was on a heightened state of alert when, shortly afterward, he attended a meeting with four fellow Lucchese mobsters at a midtown Manhattan hotel. He noticed that one of the men had a suspicious bulge under his shirt that had disappeared when he returned from a trip to the bathroom. Immediately, another mobster said he had to go to the bathroom, a scenario that suggested to D'Arco a classic Mafia hit operation—one man planting a gun in the bathroom, to be retrieved by a second man who would do the actual shooting.

Whether this was in fact the plan has never been determined. The important fact is that D'Arco thought it was. He excused himself to step outside the room for a moment, and, before anyone quite realized what was happening, he raced down the stairs. On the street, he jumped into his car and headed for his apartment in Greenwich Village. "We'll go—now!" he announced to his wife of thirty-eight years. Leaving a meal she was about to put on the table, they drove around for a while, finally ending up in the small city of New Rochelle, a few miles north of New York City. D'Arco walked into the FBI field office and announced his intention to defect. Agents, hardly able to believe what had dropped into their laps, immediately took him up on the offer. Within an hour, D'Arco and his entire family had been enrolled in the Witness Protection Program.

After agreeing to a plea deal in exchange for his cooperation, D'Arco got right down to work. In his first debriefing, he concentrated on two topics of immediate interest: his knowledge of anyone marked for murder in the ongoing Amuso-Casso murder spree, and any clues he might have to where the two Mafia leaders could be found.

In terms of imminent murder victims, D'Arco rang an alarm bell: he remembered Casso telling him just a short while before that the priority target was Aniello Migliore. At one time Tony Ducks Corallo's second in command, Migliore had been convicted in a 1987 racketeering case, but the conviction was overturned on appeal. While the government was considering whether to retry the case, Migliore was freed. Migliore had no intention of returning to the Mafia's upper echelons; sickened by the insanity that seemed to have gripped the organization, he passed the word that he intended to retire from organized crime and concentrate on his highly profitable tile business.

But Amuso and Casso didn't believe a word of it. As D'Arco learned, they regarded Migliore as a major threat, the man who undoubtedly would rally the diehard forces loyal to Tony Ducks Corallo, eliminate Casso and Amuso, then take over the organization as the boss. D'Arco carefully asked Casso what proof they had of this scenario, and was alarmed to hear Casso tell him they didn't have any proof, just a "feeling." It was enough to set in motion a plan by Amuso and Casso to eliminate what they considered a looming threat.

D'Arco's revelation brought three FBI agents to Migliore's door. "Mr. Migliore," one of the agents said formally, "we are morally bound to tell you we have incontrovertible evidence that Anthony Casso and Vittorio Amuso have planned your death."

Migliore demonstrated no reaction, although he became agitated when the agents decided to use the opportunity to mention the possibility that he consider the wisdom of seeking federal government protection—in exchange for his cooperation. "I wasn't raised that way," Migliore replied stiffly. "I've lived all my life with dignity and honor, and I'll die that way, too."

The agents rolled their eyes at this recitation of Mafiaspeak, shrugged, and left. A few nights later, Migliore was sitting in the glassed atrium of a Long Island restaurant when two shotgun blasts from a passing car shattered the atrium in a shower of glass. Migliore was hit by glass and pellets in the head, neck, and chest, but the wounds were slight. It was a close call that moved Migliore to play an interesting gambit to convey to Amuso and Casso that he was serious about his retirement plans. He gave an unprecedented interview to *Newsday*, the Long Island daily, in which he revealed the FBI visit to his home and his refusal to even consider cooperating.

"They must think I was born yesterday," he was quoted as saying, "coming to the house in the middle of the night, telling me they want to save my life, and all I have to do is tell 'em everything I know. C'mon!'' Having established the point he would remain impervious to all blandishments from the other side, Migliore then addressed the question of any ambitions he might harbor to take over the Lucchese Family. He laughed that off, and when asked about rumors that Salvatore Avellino would become the boss of the family, replied, ''He's welcome to the title—and the forty years [in jail] that goes with it.'' Amuso and Casso gradually became aware of the Migliore interview, and, while they weren't entirely convinced, it was sufficient to induce at least a temporary delay in their plan to eliminate him. (Like Chiodo and D'Arco, Migliore's devotion to Mafia protocol precluded an obvious solution: kill Amuso and Casso.)

There was a larger meaning to Migliore's gambit. Aside from the fact that Mafia leaders do not give newspaper interviews, his comments underscored a new fatalism that was beginning to infect the Mafia's upper echelon. Migliore was not the only senior mafioso who had come to believe that any leadership position was a certain guarantee of jail, an extraordinary transformation from only a few years before when a position in the hierarchy was a virtual guarantee of untouchability. The fact that Migliore, a figure of immense prestige and respect within the Mafia, had decided he wanted no part of it spoke volumes about the effect that relentless law enforcement pressure had exacted on la Cosa Nostra.

On a more prosaic level, the attempted murder of Migliore proved D'Arco right, and his debriefers now sought from him anything he might know about where they could find Amuso and Casso. D'Arco was more than willing to help, because he shared the general alarm about these two psychopaths. FBI and police teams, amounting to more than a hundred agents and police detectives, were busy looking into every corner of the underworld, thus far without success. D'Arco now pointed them in the right direction.

While on the lam, D'Arco related, Amuso and Casso maintained contact with their organization by means of a highly secure communication system. D'Arco and others were summoned to meetings via prearranged calls on pay phones, during which the meeting site was announced, usually the parking lots of various shopping malls or deserted areas. The same meeting site was never used twice. To coordinate this system, D'Arco said, Amuso and Casso would need a "callbox," one trusted member of the organization they would notify to set the meeting system in motion. There were a number of possibilities for that job, although D'Arco suspected that it was Frank Lastorino, the hit man who was very close to Casso.

The FBI and police hunters began to concentrate their attention on Lastorino, but before they could establish a link between him and the fugitives, quite unexpectedly Vic Amuso fell into their hands. It began with an anonymous phone call one afternoon to the FBI: Amuso could be found the next day around noon in a small suburban shopping mall in Scranton, Pennsylvania. The call electrified no one; two weeks before, the Amuso and Casso flight had been dramatized on the "America's Most Wanted" television show. While the FBI was pleased that two of its most wanted were displayed for the show's several million viewers, any one of whom might have some information, the flip side was that it inspired many fruitless calls that had to be checked out.

At the time the anonymous call arrived at the FBI, the Bureau had already run down hundreds of false tips phoned in by viewers, so the call was regarded as probably another dead end. Two of the most junior agents in the Bureau's Scranton field office—one had been on the job less than a year, the other less than six months—were dispatched to the shopping center to check it out. Accompanied by a posse of local police, they staked out the area and waited. Some forty minutes went by with no sight of Amuso, and the agents were about to give up when they noticed a man strolling into a store. They double-checked the photos of Amuso they had been given: there was no doubt. The man was suddenly surrounded by gun-wielding cops and the two FBI agents.

"Vittorio Amuso?" one agent asked, and when the stunned man didn't reply, added, "FBI. You're under arrest for unlawful flight to avoid prosecution."

Amuso made no attempt to deny who he was. "Fuck," he said as he was handcuffed.

There was a small celebration in Charles Rose's office on the news of Amuso's capture. When it ended, Rose and his partner Gregory O'Connell immediately set to work preparing a case against him. The still-pending charges that had led to Amuso's flight—his involvement in the windows scheme—were now embellished with an entire law library's worth of felonies as D'Arco and Chiodo piled on their recollections. Peter Savino, the chief prosecution witness in the original windows trial, was also enlisted to add whatever he knew firsthand of Amuso's involvement.

Within weeks, the two prosecutors had a fifty-four-count RICO indictment alleging crimes from racketeering to murder. A grand jury unhesitatingly approved it, setting the stage for the first skirmish in the spring of 1992 with Amuso's lawyer, Gerald L. Shargel, a highly regarded defense attorney with a long roster of prominent Mafia clients. At a bail hearing, Shargel fought vigorously to get his client released on million-dollar bail, but Rose had a strong counterargument: since Amuso was demonstrably a flight risk, he should be remanded to jail without bail.

Shargel lost that argument, as he probably expected he would; it is almost unheard of for a federal judge to grant bail to any defendant who is a flight risk, as Amuso incontestably was. But Shargel didn't give up, and was back in court that December, arguing that Amuso should be released temporarily on what he called a "Christmas furlough." To buttress his argument, he packed the courtroom with Amuso's relatives, some of whom occasionally dabbed their eyes in sorrow at the thought that their beloved relative would be behind bars on Christmas. These relatives, Shargel told Judge Raymond Dearie (the original windows case judge now assigned the Amuso case) were pledging a total of $4 million in bond to guarantee Amuso's return to prison.

Rose found this move fascinating. A conversation with his new star witness, Little Al D'Arco, had provided some insight into what was really going on. The anonymous phone call that had led to Amuso's capture, D'Arco noted, was very interesting. Consider, he said, the circumstances: only someone with intimate knowledge of Amuso's movements could have made that call. The likely suspect was Casso, who had apparently decided to become boss by betraying his close friend and business partner. There already existed some evidence for this thesis: as Rose was aware, Amuso was increasingly suspicious that Casso had given him up. From his prison cell, he sent a note to Casso referring to ''black Sunday'' and demanding that he find the culprit who had dropped a dime on him. Casso had replied cooly, saying he would try. Casso's distinctly unenthusiastic answer hardened Amuso's suspicion about his underboss. The Amuso request for a Christmas furlough was in fact a bid to obtain the time necessary to kill Casso, along with anybody else he thought might be too closely allied with his underboss.

Rose argued that the request for furlough was a subterfuge for Amuso to kill his enemies—even assuming he would return. Amuso had no concern about jeopardizing the homes and businesses his relatives put up for his bond. ''The only reason why Mr. Amuso is even in this court in the first place,'' Rose said, ''is because an FBI manhunt tracked him down. There is absolutely zero prospect that Mr. Amuso will return to this courtroom in the event that his motion for furlough is granted.''

''I quite agree,'' Dearie said. ''Motion denied. The defendant remains remanded.''

Amuso shot Rose a malevolent look as he was led back to jail, and little imagination was required to understand what was going through that homicidal mind. Rose would come to expect that look as the pretrial process ground on during the next several months, a look he hoped the jury would see during the actual trial. In his years of dealing with some of the more deadly mafiosi on the planet, Rose had never seen anyone who could project quite the sense of evil that Amuso could.

Rose was convinced that he had a sufficiently strong case to put Amuso away for good, but O'Connell worried it might not be strong enough. ''We need more tape,'' he fretted. True, Rose conceded; ideally, they would have liked the kind of tapes that had destroyed John Gotti—clear, unequivocal recordings of the defendant's own voice incriminating himself. They had a few tapes, mainly from the windows case and several culled from other cases, but nothing like the dramatic recordings of Gotti boasting of ordering murders.

Rose sought to reassure his fellow prosecutor. ''We've got a secret weapon in this case,'' he said. ''You know what the name of that secret weapon is? Alphonse D'Arco.''

O'Connell was skeptical, for an objective look at the battlefield and how the opposing forces were arrayed revealed that the prosecution had several handicaps. Shargel was well aware of them, as the smugly confident look on his face demonstrated when the trial finally opened in the spring of 1992— no slam-dunk tapes, and a roster of criminals turned prosecution witnesses, all of them vulnerable to cross-examination, when their odious pasts would be dragged before the jury.

Shargel's early confidence was rattled when Rose pulled a surprise move: his opening remarks took the form of a Mafia initiation rite, complete with the burning of a picture of a saint. Shargel noted the jury's rapt attention, which meant that Rose had won the first round—jurors had been swept into the world of the Mafia, precisely where the defense did not want them to be. Shargel attempted to minimize the damage as the case went on and was more than holding his own when Rose brought out what he insisted to O'Connell was the prosecution's secret weapon, Little Al D'Arco.

Unlike Chiodo and Savino, who testified with the unmistakable air of well-rehearsed prosecution witnesses playing out their required roles to win at least partial leniency for their crimes, D'Arco approached his inaugural appearance as government witness as the opportunity to conduct a seminar on organized crime. Relaxed and expansive, he came across as every family's black-sheep uncle, the skeleton in the closet now trying to reenter the good graces of his blood relations. D'Arco was taken through his criminal career—street hood, heroin trafficker, racketeer, acting family boss—by the booming voice of O'Connell. In conversational tones, D'Arco elaborated on his criminal career, along the way educating jurors in the real world of the Mafia. More significantly, he discussed at great length his first hand knowledge of Amuso's own criminal career, including every act alleged in the indictment.

The climactic moment came when O'Connell summarized D'Arco's life in crime and asked him, ''Mr. D'Arco, was it all worth it?''

''No,'' D'Arco replied without hesitation, then launched into an extraordinary soliloquy about life in the Mafia. It was a cry from the heart, the anguished words of a man who was now confronting a nightmare: his life had been a total waste. "I'm sixty-five years old," he concluded. "What has it gotten me? Nothing, absolutely nothing. Yes, I have my wife and I have my son. But I was the one who got my son into the Mafia. And what did I accomplish by doing that? My son is a drug dealer! No, I've got nothing to show for it. What a waste of my life."

O'Connell was about to go on, but he felt Rose tugging his sleeve. "Stop now," Rose whispered. "You can't do any better." O'Connell glanced toward the jury; deeply affected by D'Arco's heart-wrenching testimony, the jurors were sitting there in rapt silence. The courtroom had become hushed.

"I told you," a smiling Rose whispered to O'Connell, who nodded in understanding. D'Arco had reached the jury on an intensely personal level, which meant they found him credible. And that in turn meant that they were prepared to convict Vic Amuso.

Aware of the danger, Shargel went after D'Arco, but the witness proved surprisingly nimble, parrying the defense lawyer's best shots. To Shargel's distress, he noticed several jurors actually smiling at the witness as D'Arco established eye contact with them, chatting away as though he were at a family dinner, discussing the vagaries of his profession. Frustrated, Shargel began to get disoriented and finally made the mistake of asking, "Do you consider yourself a rat?"

Like a home run hitter given a fast ball right down the middle of the plate, D'Arco pounced. Pointing a finger at Amuso, he adopted an outraged tone: "I'll tell you what a rat is. There's nothing worse than trying to kill someone because they think he's a rat when they're really not!" Rose and O'Connell smiled contentedly as they noticed fascinated jurors staring openmouthed at the exchange.

Although Rose was confident the prosecution had won, a worried O'Connell paced as the jury retired for its verdict. Only seven hours later, word came that a verdict had been reached. "Trust me, Greg," Rose told him. "Only seven hours for fifty-four counts? You can bet the house they found the son of a bitch guilty."

Rose was right: the jury convicted on all fifty-four counts. Amuso, chewing on a mint, showed no emotion, but he gave

Rose a long, lingering look of pure hate as he was led away. Four months later, during a sentencing hearing, he gave Rose another malevolent stare as Dearie threw the book at him: life in prison without parole. As he left the courtroom and into a crowd of reporters gathered outside, Rose was confronted by an angry Barbara Amuso, the convicted boss's wife.

"There's been an injustice done!" she screamed as reporters scribbled in their notebooks. "You should hide your head in shame! You intimidate women and children!"

"The only women and children I think about," Rose snapped back at her, "are the wives and children of the men your husband had killed."

"Pretty good," O'Connell said as he watched accounts of Rose's confrontation with Mrs. Amuso on the evening TV news that night.

"Well, it was a genuine reaction," Rose said. Shoes off, feet up on his desk, he was celebrating the courtroom victory with O'Connell by sipping a soda.

"Well, one animal to go," O'Connell said.

"Ah yes, the animal," Rose sighed, instantly understanding that "animal" could only mean Gas Pipe Casso, who had now achieved his dream of becoming boss of the Lucchese Family. "I wonder if our friends in the constabulary are any closer to locating America's leading psychopath."

As if on cue, a grim-looking delegation from the FBI visited Rose the next day. But instead of the happy news Rose hoped they would bring, they had a distinctly disturbing piece of information. Casso had decided to kill the one man whose elimination, he was convinced, would end all his troubles. That man's name was Charles Rose.

"Was it something I said?" Rose joked, but nobody laughed. Rose was told that Casso's decision to murder the federal prosecutor was not idle Mafia gossip; the FBI had solid evidence that not only had Casso ordered Rose's assassination, but planning for it was already well under way.

The key piece of evidence was a fairly high-ranking member of the Lucchese Family—to be called Mr. X here—who had approached the FBI and offered to provide information about a Casso plan he considered so insane that the only way to stop it was to let the FBI know. Mr. X's reasoning process came into sharper focus when he agreed to a meeting with Rose.

"What, is he fucking crazy?" Mr. X asked, somewhat rhetorically, referring to Casso. "Forget about it. The FBI will shoot us down in the streets like dogs. Forget about arrests; they'll just hunt us down and you know what happens to us next."

"Not quite," Rose said. "Suppose you tell me."

X fixed him with a stare that suggested he wasn't quite sure if Rose was putting him on. "Oh, c'mon, don't tell me you don't know about the death squad," he said.

Rose decided to play the return volley cautiously. "Tell me how you learned about this squad."

Mr. X snorted. "What, are you putting me on? You fucking well know the FBI has a secret assassination squad. Anybody shoots one of their guys or a federal prosecutor, they get whacked. Clean. The bodies disappear. Nobody's the wiser. That's it. Fucking Casso, he gets a federal prosecutor whacked, and what'll happen? Right: the FBI assassination squad gets busy, and they whack every fucking wiseguy they find. End of me. End of la Cosa Nostra."

"Very interesting," Rose said noncommitally, aware now that Mr. X was concerned not about the murder of a federal prosecutor named Charles Rose, but about the presumed consequences to him and his fellow mafiosi.

"So, obviously, you don't want that to happen, correct?" Rose asked.

"Fucking right I don't," X replied. "You think I want the squad to blow me away some night just because Gas has a hard-on for you?"

Rose did nothing to disabuse Mr. X of his strange notion about a secret FBI assassination squad, all the better to keep him at work providing a pipeline into the murder plot. As X subsequently reported, Casso had become obsessed with the notion that Rose was the source of all the damage the Lucchese organization had undergone. As usual, homicide was the solution: killing Rose would bring an end to the relentless assault against his organization. And, Casso concluded, the murder of so well-known a federal prosecutor would also serve to terrorize the entire federal law enforcement establishment and cause it to withdraw its talons from the Mafia.

Besides, Casso told X, Rose deserved to die for other reasons. For one thing, Rose was a "traitor to his people," by which Casso meant he had betrayed the Italian people by his pursuit of criminals predominantly of Italian descent. Puzzled, Mr. X asked Casso how Rose possibly could be guilty of that charge, in view of the fact he wasn't Italian. Actually, Casso replied, Rose was Italian and had Anglicized his name from his real one, "Rosetti." Casso did not explain how he had come by this interesting conclusion, except to say that Rose spoke Italian. (In fact, Rose was his real name; he was the son of a Welsh father and an Italian mother; he picked up the language from her.)

As Mr. X learned, Casso had delegated the task of murdering Rose to one of his protégés, George (Georgie Neck) Zappola, a somewhat dimwitted street soldier. But, however deficient mentally, Zappola had enough sense to realize that killing a federal prosecutor would be an insane act. He decided to stall Casso by insisting that a detailed reconnaissance would have to be carried out before the murder could take place. For weeks on end, while Casso pressed him to carry out the killing, Zappola, aided by several other mobsters, conducted an extensive espionage mission to determine where Rose worked and lived, along with his daily patterns.

FBI taps on several pay phones in the Manhattan neighborhood where Rose lived detected mobsters delivering cryptic reports on the location of his apartment, the layout of the lobby in his apartment building, and traffic patterns on the street. Combined with what the FBI was learning from Mr. X, the taps provided conclusive proof: Charles Rose was being stalked in preparation for his murder.

"Well, just even the score, that's all I ask," Rose said in an uncharacteristic descent into fatalism when an FBI delegation arrived in his office to deliver the news of Zappola's operation.

"*Nobody,* least of all Gas Pipe Casso," one of the agents assured him, "is going to shoot you." The agents threw a twenty-four-hour security blanket around Rose, who liked to joke he now felt like a Mafia boss with a bodyguard. But the heightened security was also inconvenient: it cramped Rose's busy bachelor lifestyle (mainly involving his weakness for tall blond models) and crowded his apartment, already populated by two cats, a retired bomb-sniffing dog that Customs agents had begged him to adopt, and an abandoned pet rabbit Rose had found shivering and hungry in Central Park one day.

Within the Eastern District offices, there was an air of disbelief at the sight of its most noted prosecutor walking around inside a phalanx of FBI bodyguards. After all, Rose had been in much more dangerous situations—nose to nose with mobsters during the pursuit of Gus Farace, transported by armored car to the heart of Sicilian Mafia territory while investigating heroin trafficking, and prowling around the narcotics underworlds in Burma and Thailand. Indeed, Rose had a reputation for fearlessness to the point of recklessness. Why, then, was the FBI now so concerned over the threat from one Mafia nutcase?

Because Gas Pipe Casso was different. He was the worst example of an ominous new trend in American organized crime, the rise of violent, unpredictable men who killed with an insane disregard for consequences. No one could have imagined a time in the history of the Mafia when it would actually take on the entire law enforcement establishment by attempting to kill a federal prosecutor simply because he was doing his job. A far cry from the day in 1960 when Gaetano Lucchese and three of his street hoods, sitting in a restaurant, were interrupted by a raiding party of several detectives investigating a shooting case that appeared to be Mafia-related.

"Good evening, Mr. Lucchese," one detective said. "Sorry to bother you, but I need to ask you—"

"Hey, fuck you, flatfoot," one of the hoods at the table interrupted. "Why don't you go outside and see if anybody's putting slugs in the parking meters?" Lucchese immediately slapped him in the face.

"*Respetto,*" Lucchese said. "Never show disrespect to police who are only doing their job. He does his job, we do ours; it isn't personal. Now apologize, and it better be sincere." The terrified mobster obsequiously apologized.

Of all the prosecutors Casso might have targeted, the threat against Rose was most certain to arouse the anger of the federal law enforcement establishment, where Rose was among its most popular and highly regarded members. A jovial man whose wit concealed a strong sense of moralism, he was renowned among federal law enforcement agencies for his handling of major narcotics and organized crime cases. He was also the subject of any number of "Rose stories," as the one in which he offered a plea bargain of ten years to the chief defendant in a counterfeiting case. "I spit on your offer," the counterfeiter said, then went to trial and beat the case. Years later, arrested in a heroin case, the counterfeiter was looking at a fifty-year sentence, at which point he was approached by Rose, who told him, "You should've taken the ten years."

Determined to smother Casso's murder plot, the FBI-police task force redoubled its surveillance of known minions of Casso, with particular emphasis on Frank Lastorino, D'Arco's candidate as the most likely callbox. A tap on Lastorino's phone detected no contact with Casso, but the connection was revealed one night when Lastorino made a traffic mistake.

Trailed by two police detectives in an unmarked car, Lastorino was driving near his home when he pulled up at a stop light. But as the light turned green, Lastorino sat there, not moving. The cops beeped twice, but Lastorino still didn't move. They flashed their red dome light at him, and Lastorino suddenly took off at high speed, careening around a corner.

It was sufficient cause for the cops to pull him over. "What the fuck do you assholes want?" Lastorino said. He continued to mouth off as the two detectives laboriously examined his driver's license and registration, using the time to take a look at the interior of the car. They spotted a canvas bag with the butt of a pistol protruding.

"You got a license for that gun?" one cop asked.

"That ain't my gun," Lastorino said. "What do you think, I'm crazy? Shit, I got like seven surveillance cars following me. I wouldn't have a gun in the car."

"But you do," the cop said. "You're under arrest for illegal possession of an unregistered firearm. We call it the Sullivan Law, in case you never heard of it. That's a year in jail, by the way." Frisked and handcuffed, Lastorino's legal situation continued to worsen as a folded dollar bill fell out of his pocket. It contained several grams of cocaine.

Although Lastorino's prospects appeared bleak, they suddenly brightened when a local criminal court judge, in one of those decisions that have made New York's judicial establishment notorious for bias in favor of criminal defendants, threw out the charges. Lastorino, he ruled, would not be stupid enough to keep a loaded gun in plain sight in his car, nor would he have cocaine in his pocket. Therefore, the police planted both items of evidence. Lastorino walked out of court smirking at the two enraged cops, unaware that the Lucchese task force wasn't finished with him yet.

Among the things the cops had noticed in his car was a cellular telephone, an item that intrigued a strategy session of the task force. Taken together, the cellular phone and the gun suggested the strong possibility that Lastorino had replaced D'Arco as the contact between Casso and the supply of money: the phone was for communication, and the gun was to protect the large amounts of cash Lastorino would be carrying. To prove it, cops and FBI agents began the laborious task of checking every single number Lastorino had called on his cellular phone for the previous year. Most of them turned out to be various phone booths scattered throughout the New York metropolitan area, but there were several calls to a number in the suburban community of Mount Olive, New Jersey. Further checking revealed that Lastorino had no family or friends in that area, and certainly none who lived in a $300,000 house on a quiet street there.

A surveillance net descended around that house, whose owner turned out to be a young woman from Brooklyn. For a woman with no visible means of support, it seemed odd she could afford so expensive a house. But there was something even more interesting about her: she was the high school sweetheart of a married man named Anthony Casso. One night, a tap on the home's telephone heard a male voice order three dozen roses to be sent to his mother for her birthday. He dictated the accompanying card: "Happy birthday, mom. From your son Anthony."

The next morning, on January 19, 1993, a twelve-man FBI SWAT team burst into the house and encountered Anthony Casso emerging from the shower. He was wearing only a towel.

"FBI, Gas Pipe!" one of the raiders yelled. "You're under arrest!"

"I don't like being called Gas Pipe," Casso said as he put up his hands.

Some hours later, following his arraignment, Casso decided to use his one legally mandated phone call to contact his wife. Already aware from television news bulletins that her husband had been caught living in a girlfriend's house, she screamed "Drop dead!" and hung up the moment she heard his voice.

"I refuse to believe this," Charles Rose said as the FBI agents began laying material on the table. "Can our friend be that stupid?"

Apparently so, judging by the haul from Casso's hideout. Agents had found $340,000 in cash concealed in various hiding places around the house (along with his 10.5-carat diamond ring), plus another $200,000 in the safe deposit box rented in the maiden name of Casso's wife at a nearby bank. More incriminating, the agents found the card file Casso maintained on members of the Lucchese Family, each one filed under a nickname to denote a criminal specialty (for example, "Patty Cars" for an auto thief, and "Tony Air" for an airport racketeer). They also found a trove of documents relating to the family's various operations, each one specifying an individual operation (filed under such easily decoded cryptonyms as "garb" for garbage and "garctr" for the Garment Center), plus the names of those involved, which union officials were corrupt, and the names of anyone receiving payoffs. (For good measure, a raid on the home of Frank Lastorino, now in renewed legal trouble, turned up an account book that Casso demanded he maintain, which detailed all the Casso regime's outlays, including lawyers and narcotics wholesalers.)

While Rose considered this astounding pile of evidence, Casso was busy in his prison cell, planning how to thwart the latest attempt to put him away. His solutions were characteristic. First, he planned to be sprung from jail during one of his trips to court by means of an ambush of the U.S. marshal's van in which he would be transported—to be carried out by Lucchese gunmen armed with submachine guns and orders to slaughter everybody but their boss. When he concluded that the logistical requirements for this plan would be too complicated, he turned to his next plan: to assassinate federal Judge Eugene H. Nickerson, the jurist scheduled to preside at whatever RICO case Rose would present against Casso. In Casso's calculation, killing Nickerson would so terrorize the federal law enforcement establishment that it would decline to prosecute him. And, if that didn't work, Casso planned to spend whatever was necessary to learn the identities of all prospective jurors who might be assigned to his case; each would be offered $100,000 to vote not guilty.

Stupidly enough, however, the fellow inmate whom Casso was using as a go-between with his hoods on the outside was a Mafia turncoat who saw the opportunity to score further points with prosecutors. Consequently, Casso was thrown into solitary confinement, there to be confronted with a demand for exemplars of his handwriting (which the FBI hoped to match with the handwriting on the treasure trove of documents found in his hideout).

"Fuck you," Casso said. "I ain't giving you nothing."

He was taken before Nickerson, who was not in a good mood, having been informed by the FBI of Casso's plans to kill him. When Casso repeated his refusal to give handwriting samples, an angry Nickerson threatened to fine him $5,000 for each day he continued his refusal, to a maximum of $1.2 million. Casso gave in, and dutifully provided the samples—which handwriting experts had no trouble matching with the handwriting on the documents found in his New Jersey hideout.

Casso's resistance to providing handwriting samples struck Rose as odd, given the mountain of evidence he was confronting. By this point, Casso was aware that both Chiodo and D'Arco had defected to the government. Either one of them could provide devastating testimony against Casso; taken together—along with the documentary evidence—he had absolutely no hope of beating the case Rose was formulating.

"Oh, he knows very well he can't beat the case," D'Arco advised. "He's just looking for weak spots. When he can't find any, I'll tell you exactly what he's gonna do. He's gonna flip."

When Rose expressed skepticism that a man of Casso's temperament would actually roll over to his enemies, some of whom he planned to kill, D'Arco laughed. "Don't you understand?" he asked. "Why do you think Gas has been keeping such detailed records all this time? Why do you think he used to demand from me every detail of what we were involved in, no matter how small? Because he was putting this stuff in the bank. He was preparing for the day when he might get caught, and he always planned to have some bargaining chips. He knows how many people he can put away, and he's sure you gonna want to deal."

The FBI was equally skeptical, but several agents visited Casso in prison to determine whether he was actually prepared to become the first Mafia boss in the history of American organized crime to become a government witness. Initially, it didn't seem as though he was interested, but he was actually waiting for his visitors to show their high cards. At last, the agents played one: they silently shoved a document across the table to Casso. Casso scanned the affidavit of Peter Chiodo attesting to his personal knowledge of felonies committed by the man he consistently referred to as "Gas."

Casso slowly slid the document back across the table. "Let's talk deal," he said.

TEN

The Big Heat

God is a fucking fag.
JOHN GOTTI

"Welcome to my new home," said Anthony Casso, with a slight bow to his visitor. The very picture of the gracious host, he motioned Charles Rose to a chair.

"Nice place you got here," Rose said wryly, glancing around the prison cell. Since it was in the so-called "Valachi wing" of the federal prison in Otisville, New York, a section set aside for Mafia turncoats and other government witnesses, the cell was larger than the conventional model. As a measure of the government's eagerness to keep its canaries happily comfortable, it had a few amenities not ordinarily seen in prison cells, including a set of weights for Casso to keep his bantamweight physique in trim. But unlike most cells, it was spotless, and everything was arranged with military-style neatness. The blankets and sheet on the bunk, Rose noticed, had been made up with a tight precision that would have passed the most rigorous Marine Corps inspection.

"There are a few things we need to discuss, Anthony," Rose said, placing the paper cup of coffee he had brought into the cell on a table. He withdrew some papers from his briefcase and picked up the coffee cup. Casso instantly rushed over and, withdrawing a handkerchief from his pocket, carefully

294

wiped up the dim ring of moisture the cup had left. Rose stared at him a moment, then put the cup down on another area of the table. When he lifted it, Casso again sprang to wipe away the moisture.

To Rose's fascination, this routine continued as the two men talked. The slightest deviation in the order of things, the smallest drop of moisture, the most subtle disarrangement, the tiniest speck of dust, were all attacked by Casso with the lunatic avidity of a man in charge of a biological warfare laboratory.

All the while, apparently unaware of his obsessive habit, Casso chatted with his visitor. Rose kept the opening phases of the conversation deliberately casual, restricted to such non-sensitive topics as how Casso was adjusting to life in the isolation of Otisville, the weather, and a few tidbits of Mafia gossip. The prosecutor occasionally got up to stroll around the cell, taking the effort to move some of the items on the shelves a millimeter or so. Each time he moved something, Casso was behind him to restore the precise placement. As Rose asked Casso about his weightlifting, he lifted one of the weights, then put it down. Casso rushed to realign the weights, carefully stacking them in mathematically precise order of size. Rose began to deliberately spill a drop or two of his coffee just to watch Casso's routine.

My God, Rose thought, I'm in a prison cell with Lady Macbeth.

The visit to Casso's current address was to determine if the government's highly publicized new witness could actually fulfill the promise his sensational defection suggested—the first Mafia godfather willing to testify against the organization. Given his cooperation and the position he once occupied, what he knew had the potential of destroying the Mafia once and for all. At the very least, he could wreck the Lucchese Family organization (his meticulously maintained card files alone could put dozens of men in jail), and his firsthand knowledge of the rest of la Cosa Nostra could keep the federal courts busy for years.

But as Rose was aware, questions of veracity and credibility had arisen in Casso's early debriefings. Rose's partner Gregory O'Connell, among others, had concluded that Casso was a psychopathic liar who would never be converted into a credible witness. Rose suspected O'Connell was probably right, but decided to subject Casso to one final test.

Rose's standard technique in such cases was to adopt the role of defense lawyer, probing the areas certain to arise in cross-examination when the witness would be under furious attack, his personality, background, criminal record, and odiousness exposed to a jury. And if a defense lawyer could succeed in portraying the witness as the lowest form of human life, so disreputable a creature that his word on any given topic could not be trusted, there went the witness' credibility. Essentially, Rose was conducting a dry run of this process; how well a potential witness handled it determined in his mind whether a turncoat witness could survive the certain legal firestorm to come.

In the matter of Gas Pipe Casso, Rose was not overly optimistic, for he had already learned enough to wonder if any jury would accept a single word his star turncoat might say.

At the moment Casso decided to defect, Rose and O'Connell were in delicate negotiations with his lawyer, Michael Rosen, on the possibilities of some kind of plea deal. Since Casso was facing a potentially lengthy indictment involving murder and racketeering, these negotiations were complex. The furthest thought from Rosen's mind was that his client—who had always played the standard Mafia *omerta* routine—would obviate all his negotiating efforts by rolling over when the FBI showed him just one piece of paper. Unaware of that event, Rosen was still busy earning his fee on the morning of March 1, 1994, when a curious series of events took place at the federal prison in lower Manhattan.

On the prison's seventh floor "Mafia manor," Anthony Casso was being led from his cell by two guards. The prison telegraph was instantly alert: where was he going? Unless it was a routine court appearance, transferring a prisoner out of the general population meant that he was being moved to an isolation unit—the certain indicator he had defected to the other side.

Aware of how this intelligence system operated, the FBI devised a plan to keep word of Casso's defection secret for as long as possible. They especially wanted to keep the news from two of Casso's fellow inmates, Richard Pagliarulo and Frank Lastorino, who had been arrested as the result of D'Arco's conversations with Charles Rose. If killers like Pagliarulo and Lastorino were to learn that Casso was "flipping," as their world called it, that knowledge could have serious consequences for other potential witnesses whom the killers might want to get rid of to minimize any damage Casso would cause.

"Can you believe these cocksuckers?" Casso said in a loud voice as he was being escorted from his cell. "I gotta give handwriting samples today."

"You're kidding," Lastorino said.

"I ain't kidding. Didn't you read it? The judge was gonna fine me five Gs a day, and double it each day, up to $1.2 million."

"Yeah, I saw that in the paper," Lastorino said, shaking his head. "Fucking lice cocksucker judges. Well, if you gotta give him the fucking sample, give him the fucking sample, Gas. Then tell him to go fuck himself." (Lastorino had indeed read the news accounts of Judge Nickerson's order that Casso produce exemplars, but not closely enough: in fact, that issue had been resolved. Casso already had produced the samples.)

"Yeah, I'm gonna give him some writing, and then I'll shove the paper up his ass," Casso vowed on his way out of the cellblock, pure Gas Pipe that caused Lastorino to smile. He quickly spread the word that everything was okay; Gas was being taken away to give a handwriting sample. He'll be back at some point.

But to the growing unease of Lastorino and the other mafiosi on the seventh floor, by that night, Casso had not reappeared. Guards, on FBI instructions, passed the word that a "problem" had arisen during Casso's court appearance, and he was being held temporarily in another prison. Actually, Casso had been taken before Nickerson in a closed court hearing, where he entered a guilty plea to several murder and racketeering charges, with a potential sentence of life. How much he would be able to reduce that sentence would depend on the extent and quality of what he had to say during his next destination, an isolated FBI safe house in Pennsylvania, where his debriefing began.

While that was going on, a shocked Michael Rosen received a phone call from Gregory O'Connell informing him that his client was pleading guilty to multiple counts of violations of the RICO Act, and had agreed to accept a sentence of life in prison. When Rosen began to furiously protest that his client had not been permitted legal representation, O'Connell cut him off: "Mr. Casso no longer needs your services. He's on Team America now." Within the hour, a messenger arrived at Rosen's office with a letter, signed by Casso, dispensing with his services and announcing that he would henceforth be represented by two new lawyers named Charles Rose and Gregory O'Connell.

Having disposed of that matter, the two prosecutors rushed to the Pennsylvania safe house to hear whatever revelations Casso was prepared to offer. What they experienced was what Rose later was to call "a descent into the heart of evil."

For the FBI agents and prosecutors, who thought their many combined years dealing with the violent world of the Mafia had inured them to anything they might hear, Gas Pipe Casso offered an entirely new dimension. They had never experienced the kind of pure malevolence Casso projected, an evil that hung in the air like a toxic cloud as he sat at a table and discussed the men he had either murdered or arranged to have murdered with all the concern of a man discussing how he mowed his lawn.

Within a week of his debriefing sessions, Casso admitted to thirty-six murders—and those were just the ones he apparently thought his interrogators knew something about. (How many people he had actually killed would remain an open question.) Discussions of these murders had a depressing similarity. Casso would be asked if, as rumored, he had a dispute with so and so. Casso would admit it, then go on to explain how this dispute escalated. And then what happened? he would be asked.

"I killed him, of course," Casso would reply, genuinely puzzled why his interrogators did not consider the result in the natural order of things.

A true psychopath, Casso felt no twinges of conscience about murdering even his closest friends. Casually, he mentioned his plan to invite twelve leading members of the Lucchese Family (including five close personal friends) to a dinner, at which time he would murder them all. He did not carry out the plan, he added, only because he could not figure out a way of disposing of so many dead bodies. And why would he want to murder these twelve people?

"Because they're all fucking creeps," he replied, without any further explanation.

There was not a single victim in his bloody history whose death seemed to cause even a spark of emotion in Casso—except, to the surprise of his questioners, when he uncharacteristically seemed to express anger about one particular murder. The victim was the leader of a large drug smuggling ring in Florida who had entered into partnership with Casso to move an entire boatload of narcotics to New York, where the Lucchese Family would distribute it. But the boat was intercepted by the Coast Guard, and Casso, infuriated by the loss of a million dollars of his investment, decided to kill every single member of the Florida organization. When Peter Chiodo, among others, pointed out the difficulty of killing, and then disposing of, more than a dozen men in another state, Casso relented: only the leader of the Florida gang would be murdered.

Casso decided to handle this murder personally. The Florida dealer was lured to a meeting in a deserted area near Miami, at which time Casso fired several bullets into his head. Casso conceded that the dealer was not really responsible for the loss of the boatload of drugs; in narcotics, such losses were considered ordinary business hazards. So, Casso was asked, why was he so angry at a man who was not responsible for the loss?

"Because the guy really pissed me off," Casso replied. "When I shot him in the head, his blood spurted all over my car. I had just washed that goddamn car!" Rose and O'Connell looked at each other: they could just imagine the reaction of a jury hearing this story.

There were a few useful nuggets in what Casso had to say during the next few weeks (including the identities of several cops he had corrupted), and, combined with the revelations from Chiodo and D'Arco, a wave of arrests of Lucchese mobsters began. But the higher purpose that Rose hoped Casso would serve—as star witness in a series of trials against the Mafia's new command structure—began to fade as the FBI caught him in a number of evasions, half-truths, and outright lies.

The first serious credibility problem arose when Casso claimed that Daniel Marino, a capo in the Gambino Family, had plotted with him and Vincent Gigante, boss of the Genovese Family, in the bomb plot against John Gotti in 1986 that mistakenly killed Gotti's underboss. Additionally, Casso claimed, Marino had recruited the actual bombers from the Irish organized crime gang known as the Westies. Marino, serving a prison term for murder conspiracy at the time of Casso's revelation, was immediately taken from the general prison population and moved to an isolation section of a federal prison in Colorado to protect him from possible retaliation by other Gambino mobsters. But a puzzled Marino had no idea of what the FBI was talking about. Further checking revealed that what Casso had claimed wasn't true. The probable motive for the untruth was that Marino happened to be a relative of James Hydell, the mobster who tried to kill Casso some years before; apparently, Casso wanted further revenge against Hydell and his blood relations, notwithstanding the fact that he had already murdered Hydell.

Then there was the matter of the shooting of Peter Chiodo's sister, the shooting that had so blackened the Mafia's reputation. Casso, in the face of all evidence, flatly denied any involvement. "He's full of shit," D'Arco said when he heard of the denial, and he was right: there was no way some low-ranking street hoods would carry out such a hit unless ordered to do so by their boss. The motive for Casso's refusal to admit ordering the woman's murder was not difficult to understand: that act caused an evaporation of respect for him throughout the Mafia. In Casso's universe, lack of respect from an organization that was his very life was intolerable.

Casso persisted in his denial even after confronted with testimony from other Lucchese mobsters—most notably, Little Al D'Arco—that he had in fact ordered the death of Chiodo's sister. As the FBI and prosecutors were trying to understand

teen times. And according to the same document, he was shot in the knees, in the groin, in the abdomen, and in the head. Does that refresh your recollection in any way?''

''Not really,'' Casso replied cautiously. ''I just remember shooting that cocksucker in the head.''

''Oh, I see. So you shot him in the head *first,* to put him out of the misery? Well, that leaves the problem of the other fifteen bullet holes in him. And the pattern of those wounds is very suggestive. I think we can safely speculate that you first shot Mr. Hydell in the knees. Pretty painful a wound, which I gather was the point. Then there were the shots into his intestines; now he's in agonizing pain, and he's probably begging you to kill him. Then a few more shots just to make your point. And then, finally, when you've had your fun, a shot in the head to end it. That's about the way it happened, isn't it, Anthony?''

''I don't remember.''

Rose gave him a small, tight smile. ''Okay, let's determine how your memory functions in connection with another matter. You'll recall when you were first imprisoned in the MCC [Metropolitan Corrections Center, the federal prison in lower Manhattan]. You'll further recall that among your first actions there was to plan a breakout in the form of your people ambushing the van taking you to court.''

''Oh, yeah, I remember that. Listen, Charlie, nobody was gonna get hurt.''

Rose regarded him with a long, lingering stare. ''Nobody was going to get hurt, you say. That's very interesting. You would have had some guys with submachine guns out there. And I suppose they would have approached the marshals escorting you and said, 'Oh please, gentlemen, release Mr. Casso to us; he'd like to go home now.' And if the marshals had said no, then what?''

Casso said nothing as Rose began putting the papers back in his briefcase. ''Well, it's been a fascinating dialogue, Anthony, but I must run.''

''That's it, Charlie?''

''Yes, that's it,'' Rose said, not bothering to tell Casso he had just flunked the dry run test: three questions certain to arise in any trial where Gas Pipe would be a prosecution witness, and he had blown each of them.

"We're gonna talk again, right, Charlie?" Casso asked, hopefully.

"That remains to be seen," Rose replied. On his way out, he deliberately spilled what remained of his coffee and heard an anguished cry as Casso frantically began mopping it up.

Whatever slender reed of hope existed that Casso still might win the favor of Rose and O'Connell disappeared in the next forty-eight hours when Casso, apparently not content with the relatively benign treatment he was receiving in the "snitch wing," sought to improve his prison existence even further. He bribed a secretary who worked in the prison's Witness Protection Program unit and began receiving drugs, gourmet food, cigars, cellular telephones, and other contraband.

Casso decided to let three fellow inmates in on the bounty, one of whom was Salvatore (Big Sal) Miciotta, a monster street soldier of the Colombo Family who stood nearly six feet, eight inches tall and weighed 350 pounds. Casso somehow overlooked the fact that Miciotta at the moment was desperately trying to get back into the government's good graces. He had originally cut a deal to testify against his fellow Colombo mobsters, but when the FBI discovered he had committed perjury on the witness stand, an unforgiving trial judge ordered him thrown into prison for the next fourteen years.

Now, Casso had presented him with an opportunity for redemption. After devouring some of the gourmet goodies and puffing on one of the after-dinner cigars Casso had provided, he contacted the FBI. Casso was in trouble after guards rousted his cell and turned up further supplies of contraband. Things went from bad to worse for Casso: after learning that Miciotta had blown the whistle on him, he attacked a man who was a foot taller and outweighed him by nearly 180 pounds. Miciotta beat him to a pulp.

While Miciotta got his reward—a reduction in sentence to five years—and Casso was transferred to another cell with considerably reduced amenities, Rose and O'Connell considered what to do with their star witness who clearly was not going to be a star witness. For O'Connell, the incident confirmed what he had been saying all along: "Lucifer," as he had come to call Casso, was an animal so evil that there never existed even a shred of a hope that anybody, even Rose and his considerable talents, could transform him into a credible witness. "As far as I'm concerned," O'Connell said, "he can start with life [in prison] and work his way down, and I wouldn't even give him that." In other words, when a future sentencing hearing was held for Casso, the government was not about to recommend any consideration for his "cooperation."

Neither Rose nor O'Connell felt much regret over the loss of Casso as witness, because they had found an even better one, Little Al D'Arco.

"You know how the Mafia got started in this country?" D'Arco asked Rose one day. He went on to recount a dramatic story about sheepherders in the Wild West, locked in a deadly struggle with cattlemen, importing some Sicilian mafiosi who murdered the gunslingers hired by the cattle barons. After the sheepherders triumphed, the mafiosi scattered to the cities and founded the American Mafia.

"Didn't I see this in a movie?" Rose wondered.

D'Arco missed the joke. "Jesus, they made a movie about it? I gotta see that movie. What's the name of it?"

"*Shane,*" Rose replied. "It's a spaghetti western."

Admittedly, D'Arco was a little weak on history, but on the subject of the modern American Mafia, he was proving sensational. With the abandonment of Casso as a possible witness, that left Chiodo and D'Arco as the prosecution's main weapons. Of the two, D'Arco was the most valuable; blessed with a photographic memory, he was continuing to fill pages of FBI reports with a virtual encyclopedia on the Lucchese Family and whatever he knew about the rest of the Mafia. The most detailed double-checking by police detectives and FBI agents failed to find even the slightest error in D'Arco's accounts.

Like an earthquake sending tremors in all directions, D'Arco's defection caused an entire row of dominoes to totter. One of the more important tremors rattled Corrado (Dino) Marino, the Sicilian immigrant barber whose consuming ambition to become a mafioso had gotten him involved in Casso's murder sprees. (Marino had lured his friend, the crooked Garment Center businessman Frank Arnold, into the murder trap Arnold miraculously escaped when his bowels gave way.) When he heard that Chiodo had defected, Marino fled to Europe to avoid what he assumed would be Chiodo's inevitable revelation of his own role. But the FBI was on his trail—and so was Richard Pagliarulo, who got to him first.

In one of his last acts as a free man before being arrested, Pagliarulo decided to forestall any possibility that Marino would join Chiodo as a government witness. He traveled to Greece, where Marino was hiding out, and announced that Marino, in tribute to his loyalty to the Lucchese organization, would shortly receive "made" status. Pagliarulo, insisting that Marino return to Brooklyn for the ceremony, then described how it would take place: "You're going to be put in the back of a car between two people, be driven around a few streets to make sure the cops aren't following, and then you're going to be taken to a place where you're going to be sworn in."

This scenario struck Marino as one for an execution, not an induction ceremony. Convinced that he had been marked for death by the organization, he fled to Belgium, but the FBI caught up to him. Thrown into a Belgian prison cell while Rose prepared extradition papers, Marino had plenty of time to consider his position. It wasn't good: on one hand, he faced death from an organization that believed he knew too much for his own good, while on the other he faced serious charges of abetting murder, with Chiodo as the probable chief prosecution witness. Marino weighed his options, a process hastened by his living conditions—his cell was a dank dungeon alive with rats and roaches. A few weeks in that cell were sufficient to hasten his final decision. Dino Marino would become a government witness.

Marino's defection caused the fall of the next domino, Thomas (Tommy Irish) Carew. Without any hope of defeating murder charges for for his involvement in the killing of John Morrissey, the corrupt union leader, Carew too announced his switching of sides within minutes of an FBI posse at his door. The same posse swept up the notorious hit man Michael DeSantis. He joined Lastorino, Pagliarulo, Carew, and Marino in prison. Pagliarulo and Lastorino thus far were refusing to cooperate, but Rose assumed that event was only a matter of time once they considered the evidence against them. (To Rose's disappointment, another member of the Lucchese murder crew, George Zappola, who had been assigned the task of killing the prosecutor, was not among those swept into the net. He went on the lam, remaining just one step ahead of FBI and police fugitive-recovery teams.)

Rose's intention was to take the Lucchese Family's most dangerous members, Casso's crew of killers, off the streets. With that priority mission accomplished, Rose now turned his attention to some of the larger targets in the Lucchese Family. At the top of his list was a capo whom Rose had suspected for some time was the man behind the killings that the prosecutor found especially infuriating, the murders of Robert Kubecka and his brother-in-law, Donald Barstow. Salvatore Avellino was a man Rose was determined to put behind bars.

His golden source, Little Al D'Arco, provided the required leverage. Since Avellino had first approached him for approval to kill Kubecka and Barstow, D'Arco had firsthand knowledge of the murder plot, as well as the identities of the actual shooters. Within twenty-four hours of D'Arco laying out the murder plot, a police-FBI team was at the door of Avellino's Long Island home one morning. He and his wife were about to enter a stretch limousine.

"Hey, Sal, where's your Jaguar?" one cop asked as Avellino was frisked and handcuffed.

"I sold it," Avellino answered sourly. "It was a fucking lemon."

Not too far away, another posse was arresting Avellino's brother Carmine on charges of helping to arrange the Kubecka-Barstow murders, while one of the actual shooters, Rocco Vitulli, was picked up. The other shooter, Frank Federico, was not available; he had disappeared, and has not been seen since (he is presumed to have been murdered on Avellino's orders to remove a potential witness).

Also arrested was another capo, Anthony (Bowat) Baratta, already in prison on an extortion charge. Baratta, an up-and-comer in the Lucchese organization and regarded as a possible replacement for Casso as family boss, ran its branch in East

Harlem. He was a living symbol of the family's roots: the last living alumnus of the 107th Street Gang, he was one of the handful of Italians who still lived in the old immigrant neighborhood, now almost exclusively Hispanic. He was also a survivor of another important taproot of the Lucchese Family's history, the Pleasant Avenue Connection narcotics supermarket. Although the organization's center of gravity had long since shifted outward to other areas, Baratta had made his name by managing to find sufficient profit in narcotics, illegal gambling, and a few low-scale construction ripoffs.

Baratta had another source of profit, a hook into topless bars on Long Island. He had placed one of his street hoods, Joseph (Joey Bang) Massaro, in charge of that operation, an executive appointment he would come to regret. Massaro made several serious mistakes. The first was to get into a shoving match with Bonanno Family mobsters over his demands for exclusive control over the network of topless bars, demands that set off tensions that threatened to involve both families in a shooting war. His second mistake was to murder a low-level hood named Joseph Fiorito for the crime of stealing a Rolex watch from a friend. The third mistake was to fire a bullet into the already-prostrate body of Fiorito as it lay in the trunk of Massaro's car, preparatory to final disposal.

Baratta and Massaro were among the topics discussed by Little Al D'Arco when he began talking to the FBI, and the immediate result was a sweep that netted both men and four other Lucchese mobsters on RICO charges involving three murders, arson, loan-sharking, and extortion. As soon as they learned that D'Arco would be the chief prosecution witness, five of them opted for a plea bargain under which they got ten years in prison. But Massaro held out for a five-year term, informing Rose he would not agree to any more time "unless I get a sign from God." Apparently, no divine signal arrived. Massaro went on trial and discovered that divine intervention cuts both ways.

Although the prosecution had a fairly substantial case against Massaro, one of the key counts in the indictment—the murder of Joseph Fiorito—lacked an essential piece of evidence: a bullet to match the murder gun. Aware from informants that the boastful Massaro bragged to friends of pumping

The Big Heat • 309

a bullet into the already dead body of Fiorito, a team of police detectives went looking for his car. It turned out that Massaro had sold the car quite some time before. The cops finally tracked down the car and laboriously took it apart, piece by piece. Finally, only three days before Massaro's trial was to begin, they found a bullet buried in the bodywork. It was a perfect match for Massaro's gun.

From that moment, what little hope Massaro had of beating the case disappeared. His trial, which featured a celebrity witness—FBI Agent Joseph Pistone, the undercover agent "Donnie Brasco"—ended in a guilty verdict on all counts, followed by a life sentence.

Massaro thus became another in the lengthening list of casualties caused by Rose's small band of turncoats, chiefly D'Arco. Within eighteen months of the first defection, that of Peter Chiodo, entire sections of the Lucchese Family were being dismantled—East Harlem was gone, Brooklyn was in a shambles, Long Island was falling apart, and the Bronx was teetering because the family's underboss, Steven Crea, who ran that branch, was in jail. Even the profitable arrangement with the Greek Mafia in Queens had come to grief: with Chiodo and D'Arco providing the main firepower, Spyredon Velentzas, the so-called "Greek Godfather," and nine others in his organization were convicted of racketeering.

That left one major branch office still functioning: New Jersey. But that enterprise was also collapsing. The proximate cause wasn't D'Arco (although he would apply the final coup de grace), but because the organization committed an elementary mistake.

The mistake was named George Fresolone, a lowlife Philadelphia Mafia associate who worked gambling operations with several organizations, including the Lucchese New Jersey branch. As Fresolone was among the first to realize, the organization was making a huge amount of money—which is why he was so angered when it failed to advance even a dime to his family when he went off to jail for a brief stretch, a gross violation of Mafia working rules. After his release, the organization compounded the mistake by dismissively waving aside his complaint, further angering him. Seeking revenge, he approached the New Jersey State Police, which wired him for sound.

The result was six hundred hours of highly incriminating tapes recorded over a period of two years, including Fresolone's own Mafia induction ceremony, taped by means of a device planted behind his testicles. The tapes were the foundations for RICO indictments against thirteen members of the New Jersey organization's upper echelon, including the boss, Anthony (Tumac) Acceturo. But Acceturo and his codefendants laughed off the indictments; after all, they had easily beaten another RICO case filed against them in 1987 in New Jersey. That case featured a raucous trial in which one defendant called the judge a "yellow motherfucker," another challenged the prosecutor to a wrestling match in the courtroom, and a defense attorney opened his final summation by singing the theme song from the movie La Bamba. The jury acquitted, largely because the few tapes introduced by the prosecution were poor-quality recordings of discussions about gambling operations, one important prosecution witness was an ex-drug addict, and most of the alleged crimes concerned gambling, hardly the kind of crime to impress a jury from a state with a state lottery and gambling casinos in Atlantic City.

The government learned from its mistakes, and the new RICO case six years later included not only Fresolone's tapes, but the result of an FBI bug planted in the New Jersey organization's main headquarters in a Newark social club. Moreover, among the counts in the indictments were fourteen murders, including one startling taped recollection of a mobster boasting how a murder victim was beaten to death with golf clubs ("Those number four drivers work the best when you gotta bust open the guy's skull"). The prosecution witnesses included Little Al D'Arco, who told the jury details about his business meetings with Acceturo during his days as acting boss of the Lucchese Family.

Acceturo's organization, after learning that Fresolone's tapes constituted the crux of the RICO case, centered their fury on the man who had betrayed them. He was safely out of their grasp under police protection, so to make their feelings known, they arranged for the making of a large plaque that was mounted on the wall of their Newark headquarters:

GEORGE FRESOLONE
THE BIGGEST MOTHER-FUCKING RAT IN NEW JERSEY HISTORY
AND THE OTHER 49 STATES

Acceturo and his codefendants would need more than that to beat a very strong case, which was precisely what they didn't have. Predictably, without anything to offer in the way of an effective defense, Acceturo and his twelve codefendants were convicted on all counts. To complete the humiliation, Acceturo and his second in command, Thomas Ricciardi, facing life in prison, defected to the government in hope of lighter sentences. The price was information and testimony that enabled the FBI and local police to roll up what remained of Acceturo's organization. Within less than eight months, what had been among the most powerful and wealthy organized crime entities in the United States had virtually disappeared.

Having served his role in the destruction of Acceturo, Little Al D'Arco returned to New York, ready for his next assignment. Rose planned to use him as the main prosecution witness against the last remaining old-time Mafia boss still free, Vincent Gigante. The Chin had been severed from the original windows trial, and since then had been fighting Rose with an apparently interminable series of delaying actions centering, on his alleged mental incapacity. An entire medical school's worth of government psychiatrists unanimously concluded that Gigante was faking mental illness, but just when it seemed he would go on trial at last, Gigante would check into still another psychiatric facility and convince at least one psychiatrist that he was insane. Then the process would start all over again.

While that process dragged on, Rose considered the possibility of using D'Arco against lesser targets, including the three Lucchese hoods arrested for shooting Peter Chiodo's sister. But Dino Basciano took a plea deal, agreeing to testify against two others involved, the brothers Michael and Robert Spinelli. Robert was in jail on a narcotics conviction, while his brother, aware he had no chance in court against the potential testimony of his coconspirator and D'Arco, agreed to plead guilty in exchange for twenty-two years in prison.

In terms of pending prosecutions, that left only Richard Pagliarulo, who, to Rose's surprise, decided he wanted a trial. His decision represented legal insanity, for he confronted a mountain of evidence without anything to refute it. Rose was prepared to offer the same plea deal given to Chiodo—twenty years in prison in exchange for a guilty plea to a single RICO count, and his "cooperation"—but Pagliarulo rejected it out of hand.

The motive for Pagliarulo's decision to undergo trial on murder and racketeering charges that carried a potential sentence of life without parole was unknown. "I want a trial," he told Judge Eugene Nickerson during a pretrial hearing. "I'm innocent."

But there was a lot of evidence to prove that he was not. "You realize, I hope, Mr. Pagliarulo," Nickerson gently reminded him, "that a trial may not necessarily be in your best interests." Nickerson meant the insurmountable pile of evidence a grand jury had already heard and seen: testimony from Gas Pipe Casso, the man who ordered Pagliarulo to carry out most of the forty-nine murders he was known to have committed; testimony from three of his chief confederates in murder, Peter Chiodo, Thomas Carew, and Dino Marino; testimony from Little Al D'Arco on how murder contracts were passed to Pagliarulo; and, most startling of all, a trail of American Express receipts from the defendant proving conclusively he had been in Florida on the dates when the prosecution charged he had participated in the shooting of Joseph LaMorte and the attempt to murder Tumac Accetturo.

"My client insists on a trial," Pagliarulo's lawyer told Nickerson in a tone meant to suggest that he had already advised his client that he was about to commit the biggest mistake of his criminal career.

"Very well, then," Nickerson said. "That is his right. We will have a trial."

Rose was distinctly displeased by Pagliarulo's decision, for he regarded the trial as a waste of his time, the equivalent of using an elephant gun to kill a mosquito. "I suspect," he told

O'Connell, "that he's doing all this simply to break our chops."

"Perhaps not," speculated O'Connell, the Eastern District's resident criminal psychiatrist. "The more likely motive is that he wants to play Mafia bigshot, another John Gotti who's never going to give in, et cetera, et cetera."

There was some evidence for O'Connell's theory. As Chiodo had related to the two prosecutors, Pagliarulo's mind was dominated by an ambition to become a big-time Mafia leader. "They're treating me like shit," he had complained to Chiodo when he felt that Vic Amuso and Gas Pipe Casso rewarded him insufficiently for such tasks as the killing of John Morrissey. He regarded their conferring "made" status on him as ingratitude for all the killings he had carried out. He was mollified later when Amuso and Casso gave him a lucrative loan-sharking operation and elevated him to capo, a promotion he marked by playing Mafia supremo—he ordered Dino Marino to come to his home to perform regular maintenance on his hair (and his ill-fitting toupee), and began conducting business from a table in a Brooklyn restaurant, where he surrounded himself with a bodyguard of local street hoods and demanded signs of respect from anyone who approached him. The only thing missing was an insistence that supplicants kiss his hand.

Pagliarulo's new status did not, as he hoped, inspire any respect within the Mafia; as everyone was aware, he had the brains of a flea and had risen in rank only because he killed a lot of people. He inspired even less respect among his adversaries, who regarded him as a moron without an ounce of criminal talent. FBI agents shook their heads in wonderment at a criminal who used his American Express card to travel to a murder operation in Florida, an unbelievable lapse that they learned stemmed from Pagliarulo's desire to accumulate frequent flier miles.

In Rose's view, no better evidence existed for the low state to which the Lucchese Family had fallen than the fact that a man like Pagliarulo had been promoted to capo. Further evidence, if needed, came just as Pagliarulo's trial was about to open, when Frank Lastorino, the notorious Lucchese hit man and partner with Pagliarulo in murder, finally decided to accept a plea deal. That meant Rose had virtually the entire Lucchese Family prepared to testify against Pagliarulo, which further meant that the possibility of his conviction had now been raised from likely to certain. Rose, busy with a growing docket of cases and eager to avoid wasting time in a pointless trial, renewed his offer of a plea bargain to Pagliarulo. "Fuck you," Pagliarulo responded. "I want a trial."

The result was nearly surreal. While Pagliarulo sat there glaring at them, Peter Chiodo, Dino Marino, and Thomas Carew paraded to the witness stand and recounted events of mayhem and murder that alternately fascinated and repelled the jury. Their accounts were so compelling, Rose felt it unnecessary to bring up his heavy artillery, Little Al D'Arco and other witnesses. He also made a tactical decision not to use Casso as a witness. First, he had no real need for Casso's testimony, and second, the odiousness of Casso's background exceeded even the defendant's, raising the possibility that a jury might actually regard Pagliarulo sympathetically in their repulsion at being in the same room as Casso.

Pagliarulo offered no alternative to the drumroll of slaughter that rumbled out from the witness stand, except to claim that all the prosecution witnesses were lying. He presented only one defense witness: himself. Against his lawyer's advice, Richard Pagliarulo decided to take the stand in his own defense, apparently believing he could singlehandedly refute all the documentary evidence and the witness testimony. If that was his intention, he failed miserably. Rose tore him to pieces on cross-examination, a merciless dismemberment that had a number of highlights, including a series of questions relating to his trips to Florida during the efforts to kill Tumac Acceturo. Unable to deny the trips because of the American Express receipts Rose carefully laid before the jury, Pagliarulo tried to explain those sojourns by claiming he went to Florida only to visit his mother. Rose noticed the eyebrows of two male jurors suddenly shoot up, and he could almost read the questions that had crossed their minds, questions he asked Pagliarulo: if a man takes a long a journey to visit his mother, why would he stay in a hotel so far from her home? Wouldn't he stay in his mother's home? And if for some reason that wasn't feasible, why would he stay in three different hotels during his visit, as the credit card receipts showed?

The jurors clearly were not impressed with Pagliarulo's answer: "Well, I couldn't stay with my mother because I was cheating on my wife."

It was all downhill from there, and it took the jury only a few hours to find Pagliarulo guilty on all counts. Several weeks later, during a sentencing hearing, Judge Nickerson began reading through a roster of all the crimes Pagliarulo had committed. At one point, he mentioned forty-eight murders.

"It was forty-nine, your honor," Pagliarulo interrupted, almost pridefully.

"Thank you, Mr. Pagliarulo," Nickerson said, entering a correction on his documents. Then he sentenced him to life in prison without parole.

As Pagliarulo went off to prison, what remained of the once mighty Lucchese Family continued to fall apart. Not only had all its leading figures—and several dozen of the organization's street soldiers—been jailed, but, even more important, the enterprises that represented the bedrock of its power were shattered. The destruction of the enterprises had a much more devastating effect than personnel casualties, for the loss of the millions of dollars earned from the organization's hooks into the construction, airport, and garbage hauling industries was irreplaceable.

The first enterprise to fall was the construction industry. The Lucchese Family's most profitable segment of that racket, its control of the Painters Union, was ended by a two-year police investigation, including a video camera planted in the Painter's Union main headquarters, that led to twelve indictments (including Vic Amuso and Gas Pipe Casso). Significantly, the investigation began when a contractor openly defied the Mafia by filing a complaint with the Manhattan District Attorney's Office—a rare occurrence in an industry that traditionally tolerated Mafia control in exchange for labor peace and guaranteed profits.

A similar complaint, this time filed by union dissidents, finally brought an end to Lucchese influence in another construction union, Local 66 of the Laborers Union. The organization's stooge as head of the union, Michael (Big Mike) LaBarbara, was convicted of labor racketeering and went off to prison for nine years, ending a reign during which he had extorted $3.8 million from contractors (most of which found its way to the Lucchese Family). LaBarbara's conviction left unfinished his greatest monument, the personal golf course he was building on the grounds of union headquarters.

The most striking success in the offensive against Lucchese enterprises came at Kennedy Airport, where the combined efforts of the FBI and a half-dozen other law enforcement organizations finally brought to an end the organization's forty-year-long rule. The key, it turned out, was ending the cycle of mobsters replacing other mobsters who went off to jail, a process best illustrated by what happened after Frank Manzo, the Lucchese capo who headed Local 295 of the Teamsters, was convicted of racketeering.

The prison doors had no sooner clanged shut behind Manzo than he was replaced by another violent thug, Patrick Dellorusso, who had murdered one henchman who dared to argue with him, and beat a union shop steward nearly to death for not following his orders quickly enough. The Lucchese Family control continued, as though nothing had happened.

But although a racketeering case could not be proven against Dellorusso, he was removed from Local 295 anyway. This was accomplished by use of civil RICO, an adjunct of the criminal statute, which allowed the government to take over unions it could prove to a court had been under the sway of organized crime. Under the law, the government could then appoint an overseer and weed out mafiosi and Mafia associates on a standard of proof somewhat less stringent than that required by a criminal court. The effect was devastating to the Lucchese Family: six mobsters were removed from union positions in Local 295 and its adjunct, Local 851, along with a dozen other mobsters seeded among shop stewards and foremen.

Civil RICO also proved the key to removing the Lucchese organization's most pervasive influence, in the garbage hauling industry. For more than thirty years, the industry had been the subject of one investigation after another. Dozens of mobsters had been jailed, but it had no effect on the enterprise, which simply replaced them with other mobsters.

The Eastern District's civil RICO suit finally changed everything, because it attacked the linchpin of the enterprise, the Lucchese Family partnership with Local 813 of the Teamsters. Once accurately called "*our* fucking union" by Salvatore Avellino, the Lucchese capo in charge of the garbage racket, the local waged a long court fight against the government's RICO suit, finally giving in and agreeing to a court-appointed monitor. The monitor promptly removed mobsters from the local's payroll while Bernard Adelstein, the union's longtime partner of organized crime, went off to prison for labor racketeering. Deprived of its critical control lever of labor, the Lucchese grip on the garbage industry began to wither. The process accelerated when a federal judge, responding to a government motion as part of its civil RICO assault, barred Avellino for life from any involvement in the garbage hauling industry, ordered him to repay any "illegal monies" earned in the racket, and further ordered him to divest himself of any hauling companies he either owned or in which he had an interest. (The order ended the criminal career of Avellino, who had been sentenced to ten years in prison and twenty years of supervised probation for his role in the murders of Robert Kubecka and Donald Barstow.)

The removal of the Lucchese Family influence cleared the way for two developments that are still revolutionizing the garbage hauling industry. One was the restoration of competition: individual haulers went back to prevailing market conditions, and prices have been falling ever since. The second was the entry of huge waste management companies into the business. Once shut out of such lucrative markets as New York City and Long Island because the Mafia had the market sewed up tight, they began to move aggressively into these markets as the Mafia's control loosened. Since these companies did not add a Mafia tax in their calculation of charges, they were able to lure business away from haulers who for many years had been padding the bills. In New York City, for example, the WorldTrade Center, which had been paying $1.2 million annually to a Mafia-controlled garbage service, pleasantly discovered that its bill dropped to $150,000 when it signed up with a non-Mafia hauler.

Alarmed at the entry of large waste management companies into the business, the Mafia fought a brief rearguard action. When Browning-Ferris Industries, a huge Texas-based waste management company, decided to enter the New York market in 1992, coincident with the loosening of the Mafia's control, a Browning-Ferris executive based in New York one morning woke up and went out to the front porch of his suburban home to retrieve the newspaper. Instead of the paper, he found the severed head of a dog with a handwritten note clenched in its teeth: WELCOME TO NEW YORK. On Long Island, trucks for a Browning-Ferris operation were vandalized and shot at, requiring wire mesh screens to protect windshields and armed guards to protect the drivers.

It is a mark of how much things had changed that Browning-Ferris simply ignored the threats, and they gradually stopped. Given the Mafia's control over garbage hauling, a stranglehold that went back for decades, there were any number of experts who predicted it was so ingrained that no amount of effort would root it out. Yet, within a few short years, it was shattered forever.

A similar cynicism was popular in an even more timeworn Mafia enterprise, the Garment Center, where businesses had come to accept the 7.5-cent tax they had to pay to the Mafia trucking companies for each garment shipped as simply a necessary cost, like the lighting bill. At least a dozen investigations over several decades had put some mafiosi in jail, but they were replaced, and things went on as before.

All that changed one cold night in 1989 when FBI surveillance teams watching the Ravenite Social Club in the Little Italy neighborhood of lower Manhattan noticed something interesting. Thomas Gambino, the owner of several Garment Center trucking companies, was seen strolling the street outside the club deep in conversation with the Gambino Family boss, John Gotti. The scene was suggestive. Gambino, the son of the crime family's progenitor, had no criminal record, yet there he was, in what seemed to be a significant discussion with America's most infamous criminal. Even more suggestive was their choice of meeting site: outside in the bitter cold, walking up and down the street in a prescribed pattern that indicated that here were two men who did not want to talk indoors, where they might be overheard. Further surveillance detected a consistent pattern of regular weekly Gambino-Gotti talks on the street that took place in even the nastiest weather. Other surveillances where Gambino did business in the Garment Center detected encounters between him and Lucchese mobsters. It was time to take a look at the trucking companies.

That look ultimately led to an elaborate undercover operation involving the creation of a phony sweatshop that attracted hulking visitors, who informed the owners—actually police detectives—that they were required to use only certain trucking firms to ship their goods. At the same time, a New York State Organized Crime Task Force team of bugging experts, fresh from their triumph with the famed Jaguar bug, picked thirteen locks guarding Thomas Gambino's office, bypassed an elaborate security system (including laser motion detectors), hollowed out a ceiling tile, and installed an electronic bug. Conversations in that office over the next several months revealed why the office had so much security. Put simply, all trucking in the Garment Center was handled by a half-dozen firms that were jointly controlled by the Gambino and Lucchese families. The Teamsters Union local that represented the truck drivers was totally Mafia-controlled, which in turn allowed the two Mafia organizations to fix shipping costs and extort payments for labor peace.

When the bugging warrant expired and the operation ended, the OCTF team returned to Gambino's office, where Joseph Gambino, Thomas's brother and business partner, stared ashen-faced as the cops took out the bug. "Please forgive the intrusion, Mr. Gambino," one of the cops said pleasantly, "but the law requires us to take out our bugs when the warrant for them expires. I hope we're not unduly disturbing your daily routine. We'll be out of your way in a minute."

Gambino, already in foul mood upon discovering that the business conversations (most of them incriminating) of himself and his brother had been recorded, now received a final insult. Answering his phone, he heard a fundraiser's pitch for an ad in the journal for a police charity dinner. Gambino almost went into orbit, and the caller got quite an earful: "What balls! What shocking motherfuckers! I got every cop in New York here! You want a donation? To the death of every cop in New

York I wanna put. Love, Joe Gambino. You wanna put that in the ad? All you go fuck yourselves. Love and kisses, the Mafia.'' He hung up with such violence that the phone was out of service for the next twenty-four hours.

Gambino's mood did not improve when he learned soon enough that tapes of the Gambino brothers' conversations were the basis of an indictment for racketeering. Also unhappy was Sidney Lieberman, the Lucchese associate who oversaw the family's interest in the trucking racket. He was lucky to avoid jail under a complex agreement that required the Gambinos to pay $10 million in restitution and Lieberman to stay away from the trucking business the rest of his life. (Thomas Gambino went to prison for five years in a separate racketeering case.) The Teamsters local was put into federal receivership.

In one blow, the bedrock of the Lucchese Family's (and the Mafia's) power in the Garment Center was removed. Within weeks, independent trucking firms, long frozen out of the Garment Center, began actively competing for business. The customers found it hard to believe that there were actually trucking companies now selling their services on the basis of *lower* prices, the same kind of astonishment they experienced when they learned that they no longer were in servitude to a specific garbage hauler.

Unlike in past years, there was no Mafia counteroffensive to retake the high ground, for the simple reason that there was nobody capable of doing it. The Mafia's catastrophic personnel losses had not only decimated the ranks, they had also removed any criminal talent. What remained tried to burrow deep underground, witness events in the Genovese Family, whose boss, Vincent Gigante, put up an old World War II-era poster in his social club showing an evil Nazi listening to several chattering sailors under the headline THE ENEMY IS LISTENING. Gigante decreed that his men sell their expensive cars, avoid nightclubs and fancy restaurants, and stop wearing the standard Mafia uniform of Armani jackets, black turtlenecks, and gold chains. (One Genovese capo, Liborio (Barney) Bellomo, took the clothing edict a little too literally, showing up for a wedding dressed in a T-shirt and jeans.) Already elaborate security arrangements were tightened even further, with participants in family business meetings driven to secret sites while concealed under blankets in the back seat.

But even the most stringent security precautions were not enough to balk an implacable enemy that seemed to be everywhere. Worse, the racketeering enterprises that had once brought so much wealth were gone. Mafiosi now found they had to work hard for every dollar. There was still money to be made in the old standbys like loan-sharking and gambling, but they earned nowhere near the kind of profits that had once ranked the Mafia among the world's wealthiest corporate entities.

There was no real solution to the worsening personnel crisis, for the talent pool that once provided an endless supply of recruits from whom the Mafia could select the best and brightest was now almost entirely dried up. Consequently, the families began enrolling street punks in wholesale lots (the Genovese organization took in forty of them) without any regard to whether these new recruits had any criminal talent. In the main, they didn't; Generation X of the criminal world represented the most untalented and self-destructive group of miscreants that world had ever seen. Almost all of them were drug users in various degrees of addiction, and had an even worse habit: they liked to sell the stuff.

In an era of "heroin chic," when a burgeoning market of two hundred thousand addicts was willing to pay sky-high prices, the new recruits found the drug irresistibly easy as a route to instant wealth. A typical street small-timer would buy one ounce for $3,000 from a wholesaler, and in three or four days could sell it retail for a profit of $7,000. For more ambitious dealers, a kilo of heroin would return $1 million profit, and a steady worker could earn $30 million in a year. Unlike the old days, however, the new mobsters didn't use their profits to invest in legitimate businesses or create "street money" (working investment capital for loan-sharking and gambling). Instead, they spent the money as fast as they earned it in an orgy of conspicuous consumption that only made it easier for the authorities to track them. And very few of the new generation of criminals could resist dipping into their own supplies to support drug habits that in some cases ran to thousands of dollars a day.

As the fading older generation of mafiosi realized, the new Mafia generation's obsession with drugs represented an organizational disaster of the first magnitude. To begin with, narcotics was impossible to control by means of the Mafia's traditional central command structure and its rigid divisions of authority; every mobster who sold drugs was in effect his own Mafia family. For another, narcotics undermined all discipline procedures and dismantled organizational cohesion because the heavy sentences for drug trafficking represented strong temptations for those arrested to cut deals with prosecutors. And, worst of all, narcotics undercut community tolerance for organized crime; there were plenty of communities that overlooked such things as illegal gambling parlors, numbers operations, and labor racketeering because they threatened no one's health and safety in those neighborhoods. But heroin and crack cocaine were quite something else—they were poisons that no community wanted to infect their children.

The new generation of mobsters, oblivious to such factors and unconcerned about the future, continued to deal in drugs. The consequences of such heedlessness were best demonstrated by events in the Lucchese Family.

As the Lucchese organization began to fall apart, it fractured into a number of uncoordinated street gangs composed of young street punks who had hurriedly been recruited to fill the family's decimated ranks. Their propensity for violence, drug use, and narcotics trafficking soon caused problems. In Bensonhurst, the longtime stronghold of the family's powerful Brooklyn faction, the community for many years had been tolerant of its homegrown mafiosi (Paul Vario, Vic Amuso, and Gas Pipe Casso, among others) in a time when the Mafia was careful not to involve the neighborhood in shooting wars and kept narcotics outside its borders.

All that changed when a local street punk, James (Jimmy Frogs) Galione, and a band of his equally delinquent punks were enlisted to fill the Brooklyn faction's depleted ranks. Galione had started out stealing cars, but soon became heavily involved in drugs as a shortcut to big money. Violent and a heavy cocaine user himself, Galione had won Gas Pipe Casso's eternal gratitude by killing Gus Farace, the Mafia dope dealer who had murdered Everett Hatcher, a DEA agent. Galione, however, ignored Casso's sound advice about keeping drugs out of Bensonhurst: he set up a large-scale crack cocaine operation that sold in neighborhoods throughout Brooklyn, including, unforgivably enough, his own. Dazzling local kids by brandishing a huge wad of one-hundred-dollar bills, he enlisted them as runners and couriers for thousands of dollars a week. Soon, an alarmed community noticed a number of their seventeen-year-old boys driving Lexus sedans and Toyota "rice rockets" while other kids could be seen nodding off from the effects of a crack high.

To the surprise of police, whose experiences in Bensonhurst taught them that its residents had never been notably cooperative in investigations involving organized crime, those same people now complained to the cops. They wanted these criminals off the streets. To the further surprise of police, when they later arrested Galione and forty of his confederates, residents of Bensonhurst gathered in the streets to cheer. And still later, there were murmurs of satisfaction throughout the community when newspapers reported that Galione not only faced narcotics charges, but he was also being charged in the murder of Gus Farace. (Galione pleaded guilty to the murder and was sentenced to twenty-two years in prison.)

The same scenario was enacted in areas of the Bronx that were once tolerant of Lucchese mobsters. The new breed, a wild bunch of doped-up street hoods who liked to call themselves the "Tanglewood Boys," lost the Italian community's respect because they dealt narcotics in the neighborhood, burglarized local stores, killed several local young men during violent disputes over drug territories, and murdered a man in a bar in front of thirty witnesses for the crime of "dissing" one young mobster. As still another measure of how things had changed, the eyewitnesses ignored death threats from the new mobsters to volunteer their testimony to police, who put a dozen of the "boys" away.

What had happened represented a form of reverse natural selection. As the previous Mafia generation passed into jail cells or cemeteries, the succeeding generation that evolved in its place produced not stronger and smarter animals, but much dumber ones. ''Thank God they're stupid,'' cops and FBI agents involved in organized crime investigations liked to say. They were often astonished at how the stupidity of their adversaries made their professional lives easier, shaking heads in wonder at a man like John Gotti insisting that all his capos gather for a meeting with him once each week at the same place, day and time (thus making surveillance almost blissfully simple). Or Gotti's son and successor, under investigation for extortion, stashing $350,000 in cash for the cops to find in a social club he ran (and then insisting that the money had been a gift for his wedding, an event that had taken place nine years before). Or Daniel (Danny Squires) Latella, a Generation X Lucchese mobster, getting caught in a police sweep of ''johns'' (customers of prostitutes), and then explaining the gun and vials of crack cocaine found in his pockets as the result of putting on the wrong pair of pants that day.

Meanwhile, the older Lucchese generation was passing on, sometimes ignominiously. John (Johnny Blue) Ferreri, a sixty-one-year-old veteran Lucchese mobster, along with his friends and fellow Lucchese mafiosi—Albert Puco, seventy-three, and John (Johnny Echoes) Campopiano, sixty-three—were caught trying to set up a partnership with some Chinese gangsters to sell heroin. Ferreri asked the judge at his arraignment for a Legal Aid lawyer, since his income for the past several years had consisted only of a modest pension. Campopiano asked for the government to pay for his heart medicine, while Puco, in the first stages of Alzheimer's disease, seemed to barely understand what was happening. Although all three men accepted the reality that the twenty-year sentences they would shortly receive meant they would die in prison, they seemed most bothered by the shame of failed careers that had led them into the desperate step of selling heroin.

And in a Brooklyn barber shop, Angelo (Sonny Bamboo) McConnach, a sixty-eight-year-old veteran Lucchese associate and once a major loan shark, mournfully contemplated the FBI posse that had just arrested him. He stood beside another veteran Lucchese associate, Frank (Frank the Barber) Pellicane, who used his barber shop as cover for receiving McConnach's loan shark payments.

"Tony Ducks never got arrested with no fucking barber," McConnach lamented. "That's how low we are now—we get arrested with fucking barbers."

Requiem

Crime doesn't pay—well, not like it used to.

JOE E. LEWIS

On a frigid winter day in January 1995, George (Georgie Neck) Zappola stamped his feet and blew on his hands as he stood beside an outdoor phone booth on a Greenwich Village street. The icy temperature did not improve his mood.

"Put the fucking fear of God into him," advised the man beside him, George Conte, christened "Georgie Goggles" by Gas Pipe Casso some years before to distinguish him from his similarly named friend and fellow Lucchese Family soldier.

Entering the phone booth, Zappola dialed a number. Normally, he would not have taken such a chance; a federal fugitive for the past three years, Zappola had been careful to stay out of sight and avoided using telephones. But the cupboard was bare. He and Conte, also a fugitive, were running out of money, and nobody in the once rich organization seemed to have any. Now, they were desperately trying to raise some cash by pressuring a loan shark debtor whose interest payment of $500 was late. In the old days, $500 was pocket change, the kind of money guys like Zappola would have spent during a good dinner. Now, however, that relatively small sum represented at least temporary survival.

To get it, Zappola swung into his best hood routine when his target answered the phone. "Listen, you cocksucker, I was supposed to see that 500 [dollars] day before yesterday, and

326

you didn't show up! What, are you fucking suicidal? You want your fucking arms ripped off and shoved up your ass? Here's what's gonna happen: me and Goggles are coming over to your place and that 500 better be laying on the table when we get there! Otherwise, you're out the fucking window!'' He slammed down the receiver.

The terrified debtor would get a reprieve because as Zappola stepped out of the phone booth, six men with guns suddenly materialized, seemingly out of nowhere. ''FBI,'' one of them announced. ''You're under arrest.''

Another agent shook his head in amazement. ''Jesus, you guys have sunk pretty low, Georgie. Trying to muscle some guy for a crummy five hundred bucks?''

''Listen,'' Zappola replied, ''the way things are going, five hundred bucks looks pretty fucking good, believe me.''

Rose would not be Zappola's prosecutor. He and his partner Gregory O'Connell had decided it was time to leave the U.S. Attorney's Office. Their boss, Andrew Maloney, had left; as a Republican, his departure had been mandated by the election of the Democrat Bill Clinton (U.S. attorney appointments are strictly political). With his departure went the office's strong commitment to fighting organized crime. Maloney's replacement, a Clintonite named Zachary Carter, immediately made it clear organized crime would henceforth rank lower in the office's priorities, considerably below such matters as civil rights.

To a large extent, however, the changing of the guard was academic because Rose had already decided to go. The end of the Lucchese empire, a task to which he had devoted much of his career as a government prosecutor, meant that his central mission was now concluded, forcing him to think of his future. For years, he had been relentlessly recruited by some of the biggest criminal law firms. Taken to elaborate dinners, a subtle hint of the kind of lifestyle he could enjoy in the private sector, Rose listened patiently to recruiting pitches, then said no. Intent on finishing the job he had set for himself, he put aside the issue of his eventual entry into the private world of criminal law.

Rose and O'Connell joined two other lawyers to set up shop

as a Fifth Avenue law firm devoted mainly to white-collar criminal cases. But thanks to a wide network of friends among prosecutors, FBI agents, police detectives, and DEA agents, Rose was never far from current events in the Mafia world. The chief event concerned one of the unfinished cases from his time in the Eastern District: Vincent Gigante, the last remaining Mafia godfather from the organization's glory days.

Gigante was still fighting the Eastern District on the question of his sanity. His ninety-four-year-old mother was his biggest booster, occasionally sallying forth from her apartment to tell reporters that her sixty-eight-year-old "Cinzino" was mentally ill and no more a Mafia boss than she was. "Boss?" she would ask in her thick immigrant accent. "No boss. He's boss of the toilet. My son is sick. Boss of shit."

Judge Eugene Nickerson was not very impressed with this claim, and even less with the arguments of Gigante's who inundated him with reams of reports from their psychiatrists to the effect that Chin was undeniably insane. Government psychiatrists continued to insist he was faking. Nickerson finally came to conclude that Gigante was a very sane mafioso and ordered him to stand trial. His decision rested not on psychiatric evidence, but on two irrefutable facts of Gigante's world.

As Nickerson noted, Mafia history was instructive in Gigante's case, for it was clear the organization did not tolerate truly crazy people in the ranks, much less the senior leadership positions, because crazy people not only were bad for business, they also had the tendency to say things aloud that might be incriminating. Whenever the Mafia was confronted with the problem of any of its members who became crazy, they were invariably murdered. (The most prominent example was William (Willie Moore) Moretti, a New Jersey capo in the Genovese Family, best known for arranging the revocation of the contract that held a young singer named Frank Sinatra in virtual bondage—a release Moretti negotiated by sticking a revolver into the mouth of Tommy Dorsey and *threatening* to pull the trigger unless Dorsey agreed to let Sinatra out of the contract. But by 1954, Moretti, his mind deranged by syphilis, was blabbing uncontrollably in public. The Commission decreed he was a danger, and he was duly shot to death, a murder described as a *"mercy killing."*)

Nickerson's second line of reasoning was even more devastating to Gigante: the grand jury minutes of testimony by Little Al D'Arco, former acting boss of the Lucchese Family, and Sammy the Bull Gravano, former underboss of the Gambino Family, attesting to the many business meetings they had held with Gigante, during which he certainly didn't appear to be insane. Obviously, Nickerson said, no senior Mafia leader would conduct business with a crazy man, nor would any insane boss be permitted to hold a seat on the Commission.

Gigante finally faced justice in the summer of 1997, when he was wheeled into a courtroom to face a number of RICO charges, including Rose's old windows case. Apparently believing that his crazy act might yet save the day, Gigante sat at the defense table constantly mumbling to himself. He demonstrated no reaction to the parade of prosecution witnesses, all Mafia turncoats, who testified about their business dealings with the accused, a man they said always demonstrated business acumen when discussing such matters as division of spoils. The most striking of these witnesses was Peter Savino, testifying via videotape recorded in his hospital room, where he was in the final throes of his battle with terminal cancer (he would die several months later). A now gaunt figure barely able to speak through waves of horrible pain, Savino told the story of the windows racket, including his discussions with Gigante on how the scheme worked and how much money Gigante's organization would earn from it. No impeachment of Savino was possible; given the fact that he was literally at death's door, the jury would not believe that a man perhaps only days from death had any motive to lie.

Although he didn't intend to, Rose became peripherally involved in the trial when he received an urgent request from the U.S. marshals guarding one of the trial witnesses, Peter Chiodo. The problem was that Chiodo, feeling that he had been treated with disrespect by the trial judge who allowed the defense to give him a fearsome pounding far beyond the normal scope, was refusing to testify any further. "I'm not saying another word until you let me see Charlie," Chiodo said.

Rose arrived to find a highly agitated Chiodo, whose state of mind was worsened by the severe discomfort he was still experiencing as the result of his seven-year-old wounds. Rose finally got him calmed down and ready to testify further. He stayed to watch the rest of Chiodo's testimony, then took in the trial's highlight, the appearance of Little Al D'Arco. As the defense lawyers were aware, D'Arco, the man who had held direct negotiations with Gigante during his days as acting boss of the Lucchese Family, was potentially the most damaging witness. Accordingly, they had reserved their heaviest artillery for him.

D'Arco indeed proved a very damaging witness. In the kind of chatty, anecdote-filled testimony that had so impressed other juries, he held the Gigante jury spellbound with tales of life in the Mafia—including, incriminatingly enough, the saga of the plot by Gigante and Vic Amuso to murder John Gotti. To mitigate the damage, Gigante's lawyers opened a furious assault on him, all to no effect. The jury did not seem taken with the fact that the government had spent $1.5 million to date to keep its star witness alive, nor were they impressed to hear a lengthy recitation of D'Arco's criminal record. (D'Arco had already made it clear that he had spent almost his entire life as a criminal.) Hoping for a big finish, the lawyers concentrated on D'Arco's deal with Charles Rose, emphasizing the relative absolution Rose had given him for a long list of felonies, including a dozen murders. And, they noted, for a criminal, he was living quite well these days in the government's comfortable embrace.

But D'Arco shattered the assault with one sentence. Staring straight at the jury, he let out a profound sigh and said, "I'd trade it all for an apartment on Spring Street."

The jury needed only a few hours to arrive at a guilty verdict against Gigante, who did not seem to comprehend. Whether he understood what had happened was to a large extent academic, for he was no longer relevant. Even before his trial, the once powerful organization over which he so oddly presided had been vaporized in a furious assault by a team of FBI agents and police detectives. Despite Gigante's elaborate security screen, it was penetrated by some new wonders of FBI surveillance technology, including the laser listening device that shot invisible beams at a building's windows to read the vibrations on the windows. The technology enabled cops and FBI agents to learn such interesting details as the $1.5 million the organization had skimmed from the annual San Gennaro Festival and the $16.5 million it had made from gambling and loan-sharking. As a result, nineteen of the Genovese Family's top leaders—its entire upper echelon—wound up in prison. The organization then fragmented into a few street gangs busily hustling after nickels and dimes.

By the time Gigante was finally brought to trial, the Mafia itself lay in tatters. Of twenty American cities once listed by the U.S. Justice Department as having "pervasive organized crime influence," only six remained, and the Mafia organizations in those cities were falling apart. Formerly powerful Mafia organizations in Chicago, Philadelphia, Boston, Detroit, Cleveland, and Buffalo had disappeared altogether. In New York, once the Mafia's center of power, la Cosa Nostra was considered still "active," but all five families were on life support. They were now in fact ordinary street gangs—ironically enough, a return to their very roots.

Gigante's conviction brought to an end the reign of the godfathers. Simply put, there weren't any more of them because nobody wanted the job, which seemed to guarantee only a jail sentence. "I don't know if I want it," fretted Nicholas Corozzo, a veteran capo in the Gambino Family, when the depleted ranks of street soldiers and capos begged him to take command in place of the disgraced John Gotti, Jr. Corozzo's concern turned out to be justified: he had no sooner taken the reins of what remained of his shattered organization than he was nailed for racketeering (he pleaded guilty in return for a ten-year prison sentence).

As for the Lucchese Family, no one wanted to run the risk of taking command. Not that there was much to command; reduced to less than half its peak strength, the organization was an organized crime enterprise in name only. Its last godfather, Gas Pipe Casso, was still trying to stir up trouble, spending his days preparing angry legal briefs demanding that the government lighten his life sentence for his "cooperation" in bringing his organization to its current lowly state. The government argued that it was men like Charles Rose and Gregory

O'Connell who were responsible for that achievement, accomplished in spite of Casso, not because of him.

The people who did the heavy lifting in a decade-long effort to destroy what had been the greatest criminal organization in history—the prosecutors, FBI agents, and police detectives—were refocusing on new targets, new breeds of organized crime moving into the vacuum left by the Mafia. But as they were the first to admit, the Russian Mafia, the Colombian drug cartels, the Chinese triads, the Jamaican Posses, and a dozen other new ethnic criminal groups were not (and probably never would be) of the same caliber as la Cosa Nostra. As Charles Rose once told a class of new street agents at the FBI Academy in a lecture on organized crime, "By the time you hit the streets, the Mafia you heard so much about and saw in the movies, the mysterious organization of myth and legend, will be gone. The new organized criminals you'll encounter will speak with new accents. And you better hope you never have to deal with a Russian or a Chinese Gaetano Lucchese. One Lucchese every 100 years is enough."

There exists no monument to the crusade that destroyed the Lucchese Family and the rest of the American Mafia—except one. It stands in a municipal organic garden on Long Island, where a collection of small vegetable plots, flower beds, and compost pits one spring morning was renamed in honor of the man who had brought it to life, Robert Kubecka.

Those attending the renaming ceremony were struck by the remarkable profusion of plants and flowers that had burst into life from the earth in the unseasonably mild spring weather. It was, they all agreed, the signal of a beautiful spring to come, the eternal symbol of hope.

The Best in Biographies from Avon Books